# THE BOOK SYDNEY SUBURBS

—— COMPILED AND EDITED BY FRANCES POLLON ——

Original manuscript by Gerald Healy

To Dad,
Happy Xmas, 1993,
Hope this will be fun
to dip into & enhance
your memories of Sydney.
Love from Sarah, Mark
& Holly. XXX

ANGUS
& ROBERTSON

An imprint of HarperCollins*Publishers*

AN ANGUS & ROBERTSON BOOK
An imprint of HarperCollinsPublishers

First published in Australia in 1988 by Angus & Robertson Publishers
Reprinted by CollinsAngus&Robertson Publishers Australia in 1990
This revised edition published in 1991 by
CollinsAngus&Robertson Publishers Pty Limited (ACN 009 913 517)
A division of HarperCollinsPublishers (Australia) Pty Limited
4 Eden Park, 31 Waterloo Road, North Ryde, NSW 2113, Australia

HarperCollinsPublishers (New Zealand) Limited
31 View Road, Glenfield, Auckland 10, New Zealand

HarperCollinsPublishers Limited
77-85 Fulham Palace Road, London W6 8JB, United Kingdom

National Library of Australia
Cataloguing-in-Publication data:

The Book of Sydney suburbs.

  ISBN 0 207 14495 8.

  1. Sydney Suburban Area (N.S.W.) — History.
  2. Suburbs — New South Wales — Sydney — History.
  I. Pollon, Frances. 1923-   . II. Healy, Gerald.

994.4'1

Preliminary picture research by Sheena Coupe
Additional research selection and captions by Tracy Tucker
Cover illustrations by Elizabeth Seymour
Typeset in Bembo
Printed in Singapore

 7   6   5   4   3
95  94  93  92  91

# CONTENTS

# ACKNOWLEDGEMENTS

Staff of the Mitchell Library

Mr Frank Dunn, Royal Australian Historical Society (RAHS) Library

Staff members of the Geographical Names Board

The Heritage Council

Members of the local historical societies affiliated with the RAHS

Local council library historians, especially Pam Garland (Sutherland), Lesley Johnson-Friend (Liverpool) and Joan Warton (Campbelltown)

Local History Sections at Gladesville Municipal Library, Rockdale Municipal Library and Leichhardt Municipal Library

Mr Kenneth More and Mr B. Powyer, for detailed information quickly and painstakingly given

Mr Keith M. Murray, Institute of Marine Engineers, Aust/NZ division

Associate Professor Brian Fletcher, MA, PhD, Dip.Ed

Miss Nell Mackie for reading the manuscript and offering valuable comments

Thanks also to Frances Pollon's historically knowledgeable colleagues and many friends who answered her insistent questions about the suburbs in which they live or have lived.

Thanks to Frances Pollon who wrote the additional manuscript for the suburbs and cities founded since 1980.

# INTRODUCTION

This collection of short histories is intended to take you on a journey through many of the suburbs of Sydney. The historical significance of your district, indeed of the very street in which you live, may well become more interesting because of what this book tells you.

The choosing and naming of most places was not done without thought. We find proof of this is an extract from the orders of Surveyor-General Sir Thomas Mitchell to his staff. He directed them to "be particular in noting the native names of as many places as you can on your map".

Some early settlers, starting their new life, had little liking for strange-sounding Aboriginal names. We find therefore many English place names also on our New South Wales map, some remembering home towns left far behind; some, bestowed by the Colony's governors, honouring officials who they admired or under whom they served. Sometimes they honoured themselves in this way.

All these names tell us something about the area or the people who went to live there. Almost all can be translated into simple meanings, so we begin, through our history, to try and think as those early people thought; to imagine, with more understanding, the details of their existence. After you read the stories of the settling of the suburbs, you will come to appreciate the immense task of survival faced by those early people, and gradually the meaning of the word "history" will have a greater significance.

People from all walks of life have lived in Sydney's suburbs. The reasons for opening up new districts were varied. Some of the main motivations were land grants, soldier settlements and extensions to railway lines.

Social history, which covers the way a population lives and reacts to the laws of the land, has been made by the subjects of every story on these pages. Because some areas are still developing and have not had time to achieve a true historical identity, their story in this book will be short. Others cannot yet be written because their foundings are so recent.

In a book of this nature we need to consider paths of development, in some cases from settlement to suburb to city as happened with Parramatta, Liverpool, Blacktown, Campbelltown, Bankstown, Fairfield and Penrith. As these former towns acquired the population figure to give them city status, they embraced suburban areas on their peripheries. Such suburbs developed their own individual identities, whilst still remaining under the administrative umbrella of the city which created them.

As you read the following pages, let the facts remind you that the development of today's new suburbs is making history. Suburbs which have their roots in the past and are already well established may show a changing pattern. The future of all suburbs lies with you, its residents.

FRANCES POLLON,
*Sydney, 1988*

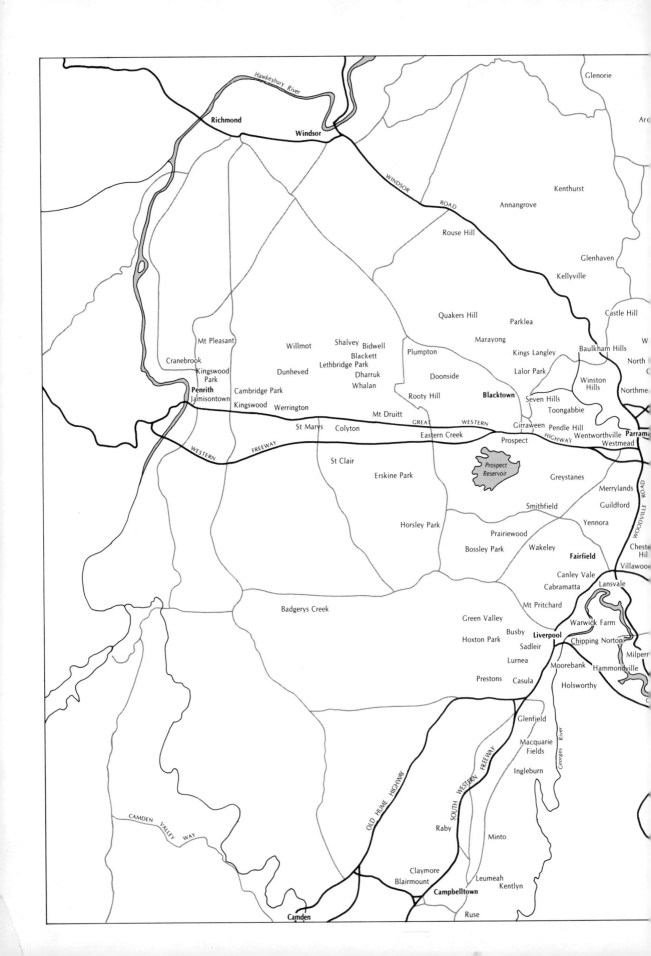

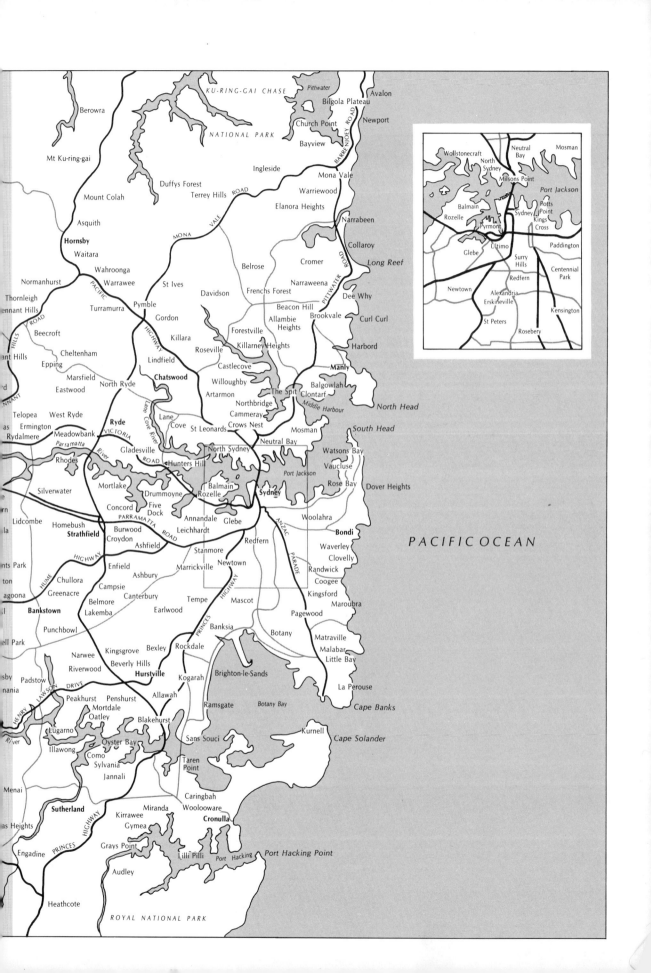

Imperial measures have usually been retained for the areas of colonial land grants and estates, the distances between early settlements and the dimensions of colonial buildings.

| Acres | Hectares | • | Miles | Kilometres | • | Feet | Metres |
|-------|----------|---|-------|------------|---|------|--------|
| 1 | 0.405 | | 1 | 1.6 | | 1 | 0.3 |
| 10 | 4.05 | | 2 | 3.2 | | 10 | 3.05 |
| 20 | 8.09 | | 3 | 4.8 | | 20 | 6.09 |
| 30 | 12.14 | | 4 | 6.4 | | 30 | 9.14 |
| 40 | 16.19 | | 5 | 8.1 | | 40 | 12.19 |
| 50 | 20.02 | | 6 | 9.6 | | 50 | 15.24 |
| 60 | 24.28 | | 7 | 11.3 | | 60 | 18.28 |
| 70 | 28.83 | | 8 | 12.9 | | 70 | 21.33 |
| 80 | 32.37 | | 9 | 14.5 | | 80 | 24.38 |
| 90 | 36.42 | | 10 | 16.0 | | 90 | 27.43 |

# ABBOTSFORD

*Municipality of Drummoyne*
Location: 10 kilometres west of
Sydney bordered by Hen and
Chicken Bay and the Parramatta
River

The name of this suburb has a
literary flavour. It was named after
the village of Abbotsford where Sir
Walter Scott, the famous
nineteenth century English poet
and novelist, lived. The village is
near Melrose Abbey on the River
Tweed, and Scott immortalised the
abbey by moonlight in one of his
poems. Scott was a prolific writer
who worked at his craft to pay off
personal debts. He was known in
his home village as the Laird of
Abbotsford.

Abbotsford was first known by
the Aboriginal name Bigi Bigi.
The suburb was part of Five Dock
Farm, and, on subdivision in 1837,
was called Feltham. When Sir
Arthur Renwick, a doctor,
philanthropist and cabinet
minister, built his home there in
1890, he called it Abbotsford in
honour of Scott's home, and later
the district took this name.

Arthur Renwick

Renwick sold the property in 1903,
and it was later acquired by Nestlé,
the chocolate manufacturers, for a
factory site. The house became
their administrative offices. In 1987
Jennings Industries Limited was
granted approval to develop the
site for prestige office blocks.
Abbotsford House is to be
refurbished and the waterfrontage
will remain a park.

Another event of significance in
the suburb was the death of the
Australian poet Henry Lawson
(1867–1922) in Abbotsford House
on 9 September 1922, when
Lawson was 55. He is
commemorated by Henry Lawson
Park and Henry Lawson Avenue,
Abbotsford.

The Great North Road marked
out by Major Thomas Mitchell in
1828, continuing north from Five
Dock, reached the Parramatta
River at Abbotsford. From 1831,
from that point, a punt, known as
Bedlam Ferry, conveyed
passengers across the river to
Gladesville. Until 1884 the punt
remained the only way to cross
from the Five Dock Peninsula to
the northern bank of the
Parramatta River. The first
Gladesville Bridge, begun in 1878,
changed this. The second
Gladesville Bridge, built in 1964,
carries hundreds of cars and trucks
daily across the river into
Abbotsford and beyond. It is a
superb piece of bridge design.

Abbotsford's boundaries are
Chiswick to the east, Hen and
Chicken Bay to the west, and Five
Dock to the south.

View of Abbotsford from the Nestlé factory
site. Production began at Nestlé in 1918 and
continued till 1976 when the factory was
demolished

# AIRDS
*City of Campbelltown*
Location: 50 kilometres
south-west of Sydney on the lower
Georges River

One of the oldest suburbs of
Campbelltown is Airds, chosen in
1810 by Governor Macquarie as a
site suitable for small farm grants
to free settlers. The land was south
of Liverpool, between Bunburry
Curran Creek and Georges River.
He named it Airds in honour of his
wife Elizabeth's family estate and
the first land grants were made
between January 1810 and October
1811 (see Campbelltown).

Airds was an excellent area for
cattle and sheep raising, and so
Macquarie's original idea of small
settlement farms was eventually
lost and by 1816 most of the
holdings in Airds were large.

The best-known early settler
was William Redfern (see
Campbelltown). Another famous
name connected with Airds is that
of Thomas Rose (1749?−1833). In
1818 Rose, a well-known
innkeeper at the Rose and Crown
in Sydney, came to the district,
where he purchased 400 acres from
Reuben Uther. Rose added to his
original holding and beautified his
property with artificial lakes and a
splendid windmill, still
remembered as Mount Gilead
Windmill.

Today Airds is a suburb with
many attractive homes in streets
named to commemorate early
history and local fauna and flora.
Modern schools standing in semi-
bushland settings cater for
hundreds of local children. The
first school in this district was
conducted by the Methodist
Church, where a Mr Reddall gave
"a regular classical education".

# ALEXANDRIA
*City of Sydney*
Location: 4 kilometres south of
Sydney off Botany Road

This inner city suburb was
originally residential. It was named
after Princess Alexandra, who
married Edward, Prince of Wales
(later King Edward VII), in 1863.

With passing time, however,
Alexandria became the site of
many factories and extensive
brickworks, until by the 1930s it
was regarded as an industrial
suburb. This pattern has not
changed, and the noise and odours
of the various manufacturing
works have added to its industrial
reputation.

The suburb separated from
Waterloo in 1868 and incorported
as the Borough of Alexandria.
Eighty years later it was made part
of the City of Sydney.

Trams were its principal means
of transport, and the old Rosebery
Racecourse its only claim to
sporting fame. It is now one of the
suburbs through which one drives
to the Kingsford Smith Airport,
and one wonders what is the first
impression of overseas visitors and
official dignitaries as they travel its
roads into Sydney.

# ALLAMBIE HEIGHTS
*Shire of Warringah*
Location: 17 kilometres north of
Sydney between the Wakehurst
Parkway and Allambie Road

The name of this suburb means "a
peaceful place". It came into being
when an estate of that name was
subdivided and sold by auction in
1918. It is one of the newer
suburbs that developed after the
Second World War, when
convenient land areas were sought
by returned soldiers, anxious to
settle down to a normal life, to
acquire land and build a home. It is
west of North Manly and, as its
name indicates, is one of the
highest points in the area, with
splendid views over the ocean to
the east.

The association with the Second
World War is reflected in many of
the suburb's street names. Palermo
Place, Cassino Close, Dunkirk
Street, and Normandy Road bring
back memories to those who saw
action in those areas, or who had
family members serving there.
Moresby Place, Owen Stanley
Road, Burma Place and Kokoda
Crescent all recall the campaigns
in New Guinea and the Far East.

A famous soldier of the First
World War, General Allenby, is
honoured in the suburb by Allenby
Park. The Australian poet and war
correspondent A. B. Paterson is
said to have met Allenby during
that war; he described him as "a
strict disciplinarian, at least six feet
tall, and as broad and strong as a
London policeman". Allenby in
Egypt presented a lonely figure,
whose opportunities for friendship
were limited by his greatness.

One valuable institution
established in Allambie Heights is
the New South Wales Spastic
Centre, which is well known for
its splendid work for adults and
children with cerebral palsy. The
Miss Australia Quest has become
identified with the development of
the centre and provides funds
invaluable to its progress. This
institution also works with the
nearby Sunnyfield Centre for the
mentally handicapped.

# ALLAWAH
*Municipality of Kogarah*
Location: 16 kilometres
south-west of Sydney between
King Georges Road and the
Princes Highway, on the Illawarra
Line

The name of a tribe of Aborigines
who lived around Botany Bay,
Allawah means "make your abode
here". The comfortable homes in
garden settings to be seen in this
suburb suggest that its residents
have accepted that invitation.
Originally this suburb was part of
a land grant made to Captain John
Townson (1760–1835) in 1808 (see
Hurstville).
   The suburb lies between Carlton
and Hurstville on the Illawarra
railway line. Allawah station was
opened officially on 23 October
1925. The coming of the railway
linked this area to Sydney and
stimulated a house-building boom.
Estate agents gave the subdivisions
enticing names, a clever ploy, to
encourage people to associate their
future lives with the promise of the
names chosen. The first post office
was ready for business in May
1933. Today this suburb and its
neighbour, Carlton, are busy
residential areas, benefiting from
their proximity to Hurstville's
modern shopping facilities and
excellent library.

# AMBARVALE
*City of Campbelltown*
Location: 54 kilometres south-
west of Sydney between Appin
Road and Menangle Road

In the early months of 1984 a
community debate was held in the
Campbelltown area about the
naming of a new railway station.
The name Macarthur was

favoured, but the name Ambarvale
was equally popular. The
Macarthurites considered that the
name Ambarvale had little claim to
history, but after some searching
among historic records, a colourful
story surrounding the name was
unearthed.
   In 1816 an artist named Samuel
Larken acquired land on the Appin
Road, and he named his property
Ambarvale. He was a convict,
bright of hazel eye, with light
brown hair, who had been
transported for stealing a watch
and some silver spoons. Sentenced
to life in 1800, he received an
absolute pardon within a short
time of his arrival. Perhaps the fact
that he was a well-educated man
had much to do with his release.
He became a clerk to Governor
King, and later Governor Bligh.
When Governor Macquarie took
up the governmental reins, he
made Sam Larken an extra clerk in
the commisseriat, at £50 a year, no
small sum in those far off days.
   Sam Larken married Elizabeth,
the daughter of John Wild, whose
property adjoined Ambarvale.
These two properties were later to
become the site of a new suburb,
named St Helen's Park. Later the
family, which by then included
four children, moved to
Parramatta, where they opened a
store, which flourished owing to
their hard and enthusiastic work.
   Sam Larken, himself convicted
for robbery, was a victim of the
same crime when in 1814 he was
robbed by three men. Later the
same felons held up a coach on the
highway, were apprehended, and
hanged for their crimes. In 1818,
his shop suffered a break-in, and
several containers of tobacco (a
valuable commodity in the colony)
were taken. Sam was able to offer
a reward of £20, but history does
not record if he had reason to pay
out the money.

Today Ambarvale is a busy
suburban area, developing its
individual identity.

# ANNANDALE
*Municipality of Leichhardt*
Location: 5 kilometres south-west
of Sydney at the junction of
Parramatta Road and Pyrmont
Bridge Road

The name of Major George
Johnston (1764–1823) features
largely in the beginnings of
Annandale. On 7 February 1793 he
was granted 100 acres of land in
what is now known as South
Annandale and Stanmore. The area
was first known as Johnston's
Bush, but later the major renamed
it Annandale after his birthplace,
Annan, in Dumfriesshire,
Scotland. In 1799 he began building
a fine residence on his grant, which
he called Annandale House.
Constructed from bricks made on
the estate, it stood well back from
Parramatta Road, at the end of an
avenue of Norfolk pines. Johnston
had been lieutenant-governor of
Norfolk Island in 1796, and it is
easy to understand how he
developed a love for these noble
trees, and so brought some back to
plant in the grounds of his new
home. The house was demolished
in 1905, although the gatehouse
still stands in Johnston Street,
Annandale.
   There are stories that Johnston,
as a First Fleet marine officer,
jumped ashore when the fleet
landed at Sydney Cove and became
the first white man to set foot on
the land. Others of his actions,
however, are more certain. In
1804, he led a military force that
broke up the rebellion of Irish
convicts at Castle Hill, attacking a
group of several hundred armed

3

Johnston Street, Annandale, c. 1880

and desperate men with a small force. He was also responsible for arresting Governor Bligh at Government House during the famous Rum Rebellion in January 1808.

Johnston asked to be sent back to England so that he could relate the details of events in the Rum Rebellion and his part in it. He was tried for mutiny but was given a very light punishment, as a matter of form, and he returned to the colony as a private citizen.

Johnston set up home in Annandale House with Esther Julian, and had seven children by her. They married in 1814 at St John's, Parramatta, and one of their sons, Robert, became the first Australian-born man to serve in the navy. When he died at Annandale in 1823, Johnston was buried on his estate, but later his remains were removed to Waverley cemetery.

Johnston's name is remembered in Johnston Street, a main thoroughfare running down to the harbour where Annandale Wharf

Annandale House shortly before it was demolished

was built, and by Johnston's Creek and Johnston's Bay. His son Robert Johnston named Nelson and Trafalgar Streets.

On his father's death, Robert inherited the estate, but in 1877 he sold it to John Young, who was a businessman, architect and mayor of Sydney. He set to work to turn the Johnston estate into an attractive suburb and built a group of four houses, two of which featured the picturesque "witch's cap" style of roof common to that period of local architecture.

One of those houses was Kenilworth, where Sir Henry Parkes died. Some time before his death, Parkes (1815−96) had become ill and poor, an unbelievable state for a former brilliant premier of New South Wales. The value of his money had diminished because of the 1890s Depression, and John Young, seeing the value of a well-known name as a resident of his beloved Annandale, offered Parkes Kenilworth at a very low rent. So the Father of Annandale (Young) and the Father of Federation (Parkes) each contributed to a suburb that retains the elegance of those early days, even though it is now a bustling mixture of flat dwellers, students and elderly people of an earlier generation.

The municipality of Annandale was incorporated on 2 January 1894, but the suburb now forms part of Leichhardt municipality.

## ANNANGROVE
*Shire of Baulkham Hills*
Location: 42 kilometres north-west of Sydney between Pitt Town Road and Annangrove Road

This suburb in the Hills District is between Kenthurst and Kellyville. It was named after Annangrove House, which was the home of Edward Charles Johnston, a grandson of George Johnston, who had received a large grant in present Annandale. He named his house Annandale after his birthplace in Scotland, Annan, and his grandson likewise recalled this place when he named his home Annangrove.

The first European activity in the area was timber-getting, and land was being taken up by the 1880s, mainly for orchards. Edward Johnston had bought land here in 1893 from Bennett William Johns, who had made a conditional purchase of crown land in 1886. The post office in 1895 took the name of Johnston's house, as did the school in 1896. By 1915–16 the name Annangrove was in general use for the suburb.

The racing circuit known as Amaroo Park is in this district, which also has a dog-training centre and native plant nurseries. Cattai Creek flows through Annangrove, which retains its natural bushland setting, with homes built among existing trees.

## ARCADIA
*Shire of Hornsby*
Location: 42 kilometres north-west of Sydney off Arcadia Road north of Galston

The romantic name of this suburb, reminiscent of Greek mythology, means "a pastoral retreat". Arcadia lies north-west of Hornsby, in an elevated area dotted with rocky sandstone outcrops. The suburb came into being around 1817, when timber-cutters pressing south from the Hawkesbury River formed several small settlements in the Dural area, which were known as Upper Dural, Middle Dural and Lower or North Dural. Later parts of these areas were renamed Arcadia, Galston and Glenorie.

As the area developed with additions of orchards and farms, and their accompanying farm animals, cattle duffers became common and their tracks remained well into the present century, until improved roads for buses and coaches obliterated evidence of those early days.

The first public school, conducted by Mr J. Aubrey, was opened in 1894 for two days each week. The name Arcadia was given to the public school in 1895 and later adopted for the locality. Today, the public school continues to teach local children in a bushland setting in Arcadia Road.

Because of its peaceful nature, Arcadia has been favoured as a church retreat area. The Benedictine monks have a monastery there, and the Central Methodist Mission (now the Wesley Central Mission of the Uniting Church) built a complex known as Vision Valley on one of the suburb's hills. The peaceful atmosphere is perfect for the purpose of these two churches. Holiday facilities have been included in Vision Valley, and a swimming lake, tennis courts and facilities for horse-riding and bush walking offer physical relaxation between hours spent in spiritual meditation.

Although future progress may encroach on the tranquillity of the area, for the present it is a natural retreat, filled with fresh breezes and the calls of dozens of bush birds. A visit to Arcadia Park, a reserve between Bay Road and Calabash Creek, will introduce many of these Australian songsters to the visitor.

## ARNCLIFFE
*Municipality of Rockdale*
Location: 11 kilometres south-west of Sydney at the junction of Forest Road and the Princes Highway, on the Illawarra Line

Reuben Hannam, a brickmaker in Governor Macquarie's time and an overseer of the government brickmakers, was an early grantee in this area. He was rewarded in 1825 by a grant of 100 acres of land along the banks of Wolli Creek in the St George area. Governor Macquarie had earlier recommended that Reuben Hannam's wife and children be allowed to join him, and this is how his son David came to the colony. In 1833 David obtained a 60 acre grant just south of Cooks River and directly behind the Tempe estate, on which Alexander Brodie Spark (1792–1856) built a delightful home, Tempe House, in 1828. The house, probably designed by John Verge, became a showplace of the colony. (It is now St Magdalene's Good Samaritan Training College.) The estate gave its name to the suburb of Tempe on the opposite side of river.

At that time, Arncliffe Hill was known as Cobblers Hill, and the area became the vegetable garden of Sydney. When the Hannam land was subdivided and the railway line came through the area in 1884, many new small holdings became farms, spreading towards Black Creek or Muddy Creek, which assured them of a year-round water supply.

Athelstane, owned by W. G. Judd, was another notable home in the district. This large house gave its name to the street in which it was built. It later became the site of Athelstane Public School. One

of the main streets, Barden Street, is named for Frederick Barden, whose house, Highbery Heights, stood nearby in early days. The name of the district engineer for railways, T. R. Firth, is commemorated by Firth Street, which runs parallel to the railway line.

Hannam's land grant had no specific name, and it was William Meadows Brownrigg, who handled the subdivision of the area, who suggested the name Arncliffe for the area. It has ancient and interesting historic origins, appearing in England's Domesday Book of 1086, where it is written as Arneclif, meaning Eagle Cliff.

## ARTARMON
*Municipality of Willoughby*
Location: 9 kilometres north-west of Sydney near the junction of Mowbray Road and the Pacific Highway, on the North Shore Line

This suburb, in Sydney's lower North Shore, began its life as a farming area. In 1794 and 1796 land grants west of the railway were made to soldiers and emancipists to encourage farming. The most important farm in the area was that owned by William Gore (1765–1845), the provost-marshal under Governor Bligh. Gore received a grant of 150 acres in 1810 and settled there,

Athelstane, Arncliffe, in its heyday

"ATHELSTANE" ARNCLIFFE

calling it Artarmon after his family estates in Ireland. The grant covered an area extending from the present Artarmon Station, along Mowbray Road, to Willoughby Road, and Gore added to this by purchase. In 1818, Gore's property was auctioned to pay off a mortgage. It then passed to several owners, including Richard Hayes Harnett, who built Artarmon House, and George Robert Riley, who renamed the house Valetta.

William Gore had a difficult life in the colony. In 1808 he was sent to work at the Coal River mines at Newcastle by the Rum Rebellion officers who had deposed Bligh. Freed by Governor Macquarie in 1810 and reinstated in his official position, he was again removed from office in 1814, this time the victim of a legal dispute. The year

Artarmon Station, c. 1908. The building in this photo was originally at Glenbrook Station in the Blue Mountains, but became inadequate and was relocated to quieter Artarmon

1820 saw him committed to a debtors prison, and four years later he was tried for shooting and wounding one Private Andrew Beattie, who worked as a military grass-cutter on the Gore property. In spite of his supposed notoriety, or perhaps because of it, William Gore is remembered in the names Gore Street, in Greenwich, Gore Cove and Gore Hill.

With the coming of the North Shore railway line, Artarmon station opened on 6 July 1898, and the area was opened up for subdivision and residential settlement. Many of the bungalow homes built at this time are still standing.

On 1 December 1909 the suburb's post office began operations. A new railway station site was chosen on 7 October 1910, the same year as the opening of the local school. From that time Artarmon lost completely all signs of its early farming origins.

## ASHBURY
*Municipalities of Canterbury and Ashfield*
Location: 9 kilometres south-west of Sydney between Old Canterbury Road, Georges River Road and the Hume Highway

This suburb lies between Ashfield and Canterbury, and, like Lidcombe, which derived its name from two different words, Ashbury borrowed the 'Ash' from Ashfield and the "bury" from Canterbury for its name. Not very original, perhaps, but a neat solution to suburban naming at the time of its settlement. Previously the suburb had been known as Goodlet's Bush, after an early settler, John Hay Goodlet. Goodlet Street also commemorates this pioneer and marks the area of his property. In 1878 he had purchased Canterbury House, which had been built by Arthur Jeffreys. The house was demolished in 1926,

after Goodlet's widow died.

The first land grant in the area was made in 1793, when 100 acres were given to the Reverend Richard Johnson (1753–1827), the colony's first chaplain. The land, which extended over the area of Ashbury, was called Canterbury Vale. By 1800, when it was sold to Lieutenant William Cox, the property covered 600 acres. In 1803, when it covered 900 acres, it was sold to Robert Campbell the elder, (1769–1846), who then bought up most of the land north to Liverpool Road. The estate then passed to his son-in-law Arthur Jeffreys and was gradually broken up.

The Ashbury post office is located in King Street, and a public school is nearby in Trevenar Street. Ashbury is a typical suburban area, and it is close to Canterbury Park Racecourse.

## ASHCROFT
*City of Liverpool*
Location: 35 kilometres south-west of Sydney near Liverpool

This suburb, between Sadleir and Mount Pritchard, was formed by the housing development of Green Valley, north-west of Liverpool. Ashcroft lies in a small valley surrounded by natural gum trees. Although the area was cleared of trees, residents have planted poplars and pines, which along with the area's cultivated gardens have softened the stark outlook of hundreds of tiled roofs.

The suburb's name was chosen by the housing commission to commemorate the fact that the Ashcroft family gave the land for the site of the development. This family, one of the pioneers in the

district, was active in establishing the meat industry's wholesaling and retailing activities at the Homebush Abattoir. One member of the family, E. J. Ashcroft, was a carcass butcher at Liverpool in the 1890s, and another member became mayor of Liverpool.

Ashcroft has a public school in Sheriff Street and a secondary school in Maxwells Avenue, both busy places because of the numerous young families in the area. Although Ashcroft received its title earlier, its name was officially gazetted on 7 April 1972.

## ASHFIELD
*Municipality of Ashfield*
Location: 9 kilometres south-west of Sydney on the Hume Highway, on the Main Suburban Line

Ashfield was occupied at an early date in the colony's history. The first colonist to live in the area was Augustus Alt (1731–1815), Governor Phillip's surveyor-general, who in 1794 received a land grant of 100 acres in the Croydon area. In 1801 he acquired another 250 acres, which covered most of Ashfield. Another early grant in the area was made in 1793

to Lieutenant John Townson (1760–1835). He called his 100 acre grant Marsh Gate Farm (see Five Dock). Townson later sold his land to Samuel Terry, who in turn sold it, in 1813, to Robert Campbell (1789–1851), nephew of the Sydney merchant of the same name. He bought several other farms in the area, including Alt's 250 acres, to make an estate of 480 acres. His father, William Campbell, was laird of Ashfield in Scotland and Robert was described on his tombstone as "the last of the lairds of Ashfield in Argyllshire". Campbell may have named the area Ashfield after his Scottish home. The name would also have appealed to the later owner, Joseph Underwood, who came from the parish of Ashfield in Suffolk.

In 1815 Campbell sold to John Laurie, who in turn sold the Ashfield land in 1817 to Joseph Underwood (1779–1833). Underwood added more land to the property, including Hermitage Farm in 1818, to make a total of over 605 acres. In the 1820s he built his house, Ashfield Park, on the land he had purchased. He lived there until his death in 1833, and his widow continued to occupy the house until her death.

*Ashfield Park* by S. T. Gill, c. 1850

View of Ashfield from the Town Hall,
c. 1921

One of Underwood's foibles was to hoist a flag to show when he was at home.

Elizabeth Underwood gave the 5 acres of land on which St John's Church of England in Alt Street, Ashfield, was built. The foundation stone of the famous old church was laid by Bishop Broughton, the colony's first bishop, on 9 September 1840. The Underwood home was later purchased by the Roman Catholic Church, and became a convent of the order of Our Lady of the Snows.

The area of the present Ashfield Park is part of 175 acres granted to and bought by Henry Kable between 1794 and 1804. In 1822 it was sold to James Underwood, brother of Joseph, and leased out until 1879, when it was acquired as public parkland.

Several street names in Ashfield commemorate famous people: Queen Street, Charlotte Street and George Street are named after King George IV and his wife, Princess Charlotte. Alt Street recalls Baron Augustus Alt; the orchard of his home, Hermitage Farm, was on the land now occupied by Croydon station. The surgeon Dr William Bland (1789–1868) bought 35 acres of land in Alt Street from Elizabeth Underwood when she sold parts of her estate in 1838–39. Both have streets in Ashfield named after them. Milton Street recalls Milton House, originally part of Robert Campbell, the elder's, land at Canterbury Vale (see Ashbury).

On 24 March 1838, an advertisement in the newspaper the *Colonist* advised that "The allotments for the village to bear the name of Ashfield have been laid out near the junction of Liverpool and Parramatta Roads". These two roads were the first in the colony: Parramatta Road was built in 1810–11, and the Great South Road to Liverpool was opened in 1814 by Governor Macquarie.

The first post office in Ashfield opened on 1 January 1856 and the first school opened in January 1862. By 1866 the suburb's industrial life had progressed to include one steam mill, Boylson's bakery, Tancred's soap and candle manufacturers, and a bone-dust mill. In 1871 Ashfield was incorporated as a municipality.

For a long time the area between Ashfield and Burwood was known as Underwood's Bush, and when the railway line came through from Redfern to Granville, some extremely thick scrub had to be cleared. Ashfield was one of the six original stations ready when the line opened in 1855, although the first station was merely a wooden platform with a small brick house adjoining it. Population at that time was small, but the area developed quickly after the coming of the railway. Underwood's land was the first big holding to be offered for sale in Ashfield after the opening of the railway and Elizabeth Underwood's death. Mr Richardson, who founded the firm Richardson and Wrench, handled the auction in February 1859.

The suburb then became an area of gardens and orchards. At that time, a pleasant creek ran through Underwood's Bush. In fact it was a series of small ponds, with several good waterholes, and was a popular place with the local lads and for family picnics. This area was about 300 metres from Parramatta Road, not exactly the place for a day's fun today.

Today this once small village is a large and thriving suburb. The first town clerk of Ashfield was Frederick Underwood, Joseph Underwood's son. Several early council members are commemorated in local names. Herbert Pratten, Ashfield's mayor during 1909–11, gave his name to the well-known and much-used Pratten Park, and Clissold Street is named after an alderman in Ashfield's first council, Frederick Clissold.

Road-widening in Miller Street, Ashfield, 1949, looking north

# ASQUITH
*Shire of Hornsby*
Location: 26 kilometres north-west of Sydney on the Pacific Highway, on the Main Northern Line

Like many of the northern district suburbs, Asquith developed as a result of the coming of the railway line. This area to the north of Hornsby had been subdivided at the time of the First World War by Halloran and Company, Estate Agents. When their request for a railway station was refused, the firm offered to pay for it, knowing it would greatly enhance the land sales in their subdivision. The railways department agreed, and in 1915 the station was opened and named in honour of the British prime minister of the time Henry Herbert Asquith, First Earl of Oxford and Asquith (1852–1928), and the new suburb began its life.

At this time some local shops

had been erected between the Pacific Highway and the railway and the names of the Amor family and of Wal Beattie were well known in Asquith households. When the road was widened, the shops were moved to the western side of the highway. A non-official post office operated from April 1924; the official post office opened in 1933. A public school opened in March 1930.

From a quiet beginning as an orchard area, Asquith's momentum was increased in the 1950s and 1960s when a big residential building program took place in the area. Young families were settled there, necessitating the erection of three new schools: a Catholic primary school and two state high schools, a boys high school and a girls high school, in Jersey Street and Stokes Avenue respectively. A pleasant park and oval, bounded by Mills Avenue, Wall Avenue and Rotherwood

Avenue, were also laid out.

In the 1980s young people in the area were greatly affected by unemployment, despite the development of nearby Hornsby as a regional shopping centre and the growth of light industrial areas.

## AUBURN
*Municipality of Auburn*
Location: 19 kilometres west of Sydney off the Great Western Highway, on both the Main Southern and Main Western Lines

Interestingly enough, the explorers who discovered the Auburn area were Arthur Phillip, the first governor of the colony, and John Hunter, who was to succeed him. On 5 February 1788, they followed the course of the Parramatta River until they arrived at today's Homebush Bay, where they camped for the night. The following day they explored a tributary, the Duck River, which now forms the western boundary of Auburn.

The land south of Parramatta Road in the suburb of Auburn was not settled until 1806, but by 1823 the whole area had been divided among a number of people. The grantees were a mixture of free settlers and convicts whose terms of imprisonment had expired. Little is known of the suburb's history at that time, but familiar names are Samuel Haslam, whose name is given to Haslam's Creek, on the east side of which stood his grant, and Thomas Bates, who in 1806 acquired 50 acres near the present Auburn Park.

Auburn developed slowly until the coming of the railway — a station was built in 1877 — and the first road, Macquarie Road, linked the station with Parramatta Road. Subdivision and land sales followed in 1878. The grants of two time-expired convicts, Thomas Bates and another named Turner, had been acquired in the 1860s by two speculators, Messrs Mills and Pile. On the day of the big land auction, 1 June 1878, they chartered a special train to bring prospective buyers to the area. In 1876 these two agents had suggested the name of Burford for the station and estate, but this was rejected because of its similarity to Burwood. Then Mr Mills proposed that the area should be known as Auburn, a name immortalised in Oliver Goldsmith's poem "The Deserted Village", which describes Auburn in England as the "loveliest village of the plain". The suggestion was accepted, and Auburn moved slowly forward.

The first post office opened on 16 June 1880. In 1884 Miles and

A far cry from today—Parramatta Road, Auburn, at Newtown Street, c. 1920

Pile made another big subdivision, and in 1886 the first public school was opened. The railway station on a new site was opened on 8 December 1909.

Like Granville and Clyde, Auburn was an early industrial centre. Ritchie Brothers had carriage works there from 1878 and in the same year the engineers H. Vale & Sons moved into the suburb.

Auburn was incorporated as a municipality in 1892, after years of agitation. (It was amalgamated with Lidcombe municipality in 1948.) The first mayor was George Wright, and the first council clerk was J. W. Lees. At that time, the number of people living in the area was estimated at just over 2,000. The population in the municipality today is over 46,000.

## AUDLEY
*Shire of Sutherland*
Location: 31 kilometres south of Sydney in the Royal National Park, on the Hacking River

This small suburb in the Royal National Park was named after Lord George Edward Audley, who made the first survey of the Hacking River in 1864. He was married to Emily, second daughter of Sir Thomas Mitchell, surveyor-general and explorer. Because Mitchell insisted on drawing up his own will and allowed Audley, a beneficiary, to witness it, the young blue blood was disinherited, and his two unmarried daughters lived and died in genteel poverty.

Kangaroo Creek joins the Hacking River at Audley. The river is crossed by a causeway, and Lady Carrington Drive runs along its eastern bank from the picnic area to the south boundary of the park. The surrounding area of almost 15,000 hectares is the Royal National Park. In 1879, 18,000 acres had been reserved for the park, and a further 18,300 acres were added in 1880. Deer, originally a gift to the park, can often be seen. In 1954 they assumed pest proportions and were invading Bundeena, an idyllic picnic spot on the southern shore of Port Hacking.

Audley was popular in the 1900s as a venue for boating, and rowing boats could be hired at a reasonable cost. Holiday-makers and honeymooners often stayed at the peaceful old Allambie House guesthouse. Audley is still a peaceful and popular place for a day's outing, although its popularity as a holiday resort has declined. Today it is the administrative headquarters for the Royal National Park.

View of Audley, as popular a picnic spot in the 1900s as it is today

# AVALON

*Shire of Warringah*

Location: 35 kilometres north of Sydney on the Barrenjoey Peninsula facing the Pacific Ocean

The first land grant in the Avalon area was of 60 acres given to John Farrell in 1827. But it was two other men, entirely different in character and profession, who had the greatest influence on the northern beach suburb of Avalon. This delightful area, with its village shopping centre, was part of a 1,400 acre grant made in 1833 to an early Irish Catholic chaplain, Father John Joseph Therry (pronounced Terry). Therry (1790–1864) arrived in Sydney in 1820 and, perhaps more than any other early priest, fought hard for recognition of the Catholic Church in the colony. His name appears many times in the history of those early days, as he worked tirelessly as far afield as Parramatta.

Therry could not agree with Governor Darling, and was removed from his position as chaplain. It was not until Richard Bourke became governor in 1831 that a change of attitude in religious tolerance was evident. In fact, it was Bourke who gave Therry the grant he had been promised by Governor Darling shortly after his arrival in the colony. The next grant he received extended from what is now Whale Beach to Newport, on the Palm Beach peninsula. Therry built a little wooden church in the Avalon area and planned that a settlement would eventually be built around it. The idea failed, but as late as the 1920s the ground near the Avalon Public School was known as Priest's Flat.

During Therry's time, only a few farms and fishermen's cottages were built in the area, but the suburb really came to life when

Father John Joseph Therry

Arthur J. Small handled a big subdivision of land in 1921. Small was interested not only in making money, but also in preserving the peaceful beauty of the area. He stipulated that blocks were to have frontages of no less than 66 feet where possible, and their depth was to be 200 feet. He also put a covenant on the subdivision to prevent unnecessary destruction of trees. A suitable name for the area seemed to elude this "live wire", but he eventually chose Avalon — in Celtic mythology, an earthly paradise and the final resting place of the legendary King Arthur.

At first Avalon developed as an ideal weekend and holiday retreat. It gradually acquired permanent residents and in 1933 the first post office was opened in a well-known store run by Stanley Wickham, a former 1890s Rugby Union player. Wickham's Store was situated on the south-west corner of The Boulevarde, and it eventually became McDonalds. The story goes that Bill McDonald, an old Avalon identity, first rode into Avalon as a boy, atop a cart load of goods that his uncle was bringing to stock a small store. Another well-known sportsman, boxer Jimmy Carruthers, became a

storekeeper in Avalon in the 1960s.

Like its neighbours on the peninsula, Avalon developed after the Second World War, when roads and bus services were improved. At the same time, family car ownership also increased, making Sydney more accessible and making living permanently in Avalon a desirable possibility. By 1946 there was a village shopping centre in Avalon Parade; weekend movies were shown in a marquee on the site of the present Avalon Picture Theatre; and a good home could be bought for £3,000. By 1950 a public school had opened, with T. E. Maguire as headmaster.

Father Therry would probably be delighted with Avalon's growth and development. He was a great believer in progress, and he even sank a shaft to explore for coal on what is now the south-east corner of Avalon Golf Links. The project failed, but when we regard present-day Avalon with its natural beauty, and family atmosphere, we can feel very glad it did.

# BADGERYS CREEK

*Cities of Liverpool and Penrith*

Location: 49 kilometres west of Sydney off Elizabeth Drive

Badgerys Creek is a rural area south of St Marys. It was named after James Badgery, a free settler who was given 100 acres on the Nepean River in 1803. He was offered a further 640 acres on what is now known as Badgerys Creek, and he called this land Exeter Farm. Badgery died in 1827 and was buried in St Luke's Cemetery, Liverpool. His descendants still live in Sydney.

The district became a centre of

controversy in the mid-1980s when it was proposed as the site for a new airport to relieve pressure on Mascot's Kingsford Smith Airport.

## BALGOWLAH
*Municipality of Manly*
Location: 12 kilometres north of Sydney just west of Manly

Situated on rising ground west of Manly, Balgowlah has a pleasant aspect with sea breezes and water views. It was one of the first of ten villages established in the County of Cumberland; the name Balgowlah (or Bulgowlah) is an Aboriginal word meaning "north harbour". In its early days, many people referred to the area as Little Manly but today it has an identity of its own.

An early writer described Balgowlah as "a township which affords large opportunities to picnic parties, being fairly accessible. A quarter of an hour's walk by way of the Sydney road leads to the surveyed streets, where a turn-off may be made, and water, firewood and shade found in a hundred convenient spots. The North Harbour Reserve is immediately below. Wildflowers are abundant here, and delightful harbour views obtainable."

Long before this description was written William Romaine Govett carried out the survey of the Pittwater area. The earlier hamlet named Balgowlah was mentioned in the description of the road he used in the *New South Wales Calendar* in 1834. There were already several farms in the area, considered as important to the colony, so the way to reach them was carefully outlined in the directory. Like many other early government villages, the first

Balgowlah is now only a mark on a map, and the present Balgowlah, built on higher land, has adopted the name.

Balgowlah's shopping centre runs along each side of Sydney Road. The main road turns into Condamine Street, which runs north to Pittwater Road. The street is reportedly named after Lieutenant de la Condamine, a member of a regiment in the colony during Governor Ralph Darling's time (1825–31).

Balmoral, the first village named Balgowlah, is cut off from the city by Middle Harbour, so residents depended on sailing boats for transport. In 1850, Peter Ellery started running his hand punt from The Spit, giving easier access to the north side. Later, trams ran from North Sydney to The Spit on Middle Harbour, where the passengers alighted and crossed the narrow neck of water by punt. By 1911 they could board another tram on the north side to continue their journey to Balgowlah, Manly, and, by 1913, north to Narrabeen. In those days the excursion was often undertaken for pleasure, but regular commuters must have heaved a sigh of relief when a bridge was built at The Spit in 1924, and, like its neighbours, Balgowlah became a suburb with easy access to the city, affording an opportunity for city-workers to settle in this pleasant suburb.

## BALMAIN
*Municipality of Leichhardt*
Location: 5 kilometres west of Sydney east of Victoria Road on the southern side of the Parramatta River

This historically interesting suburb was incorporated in February 1860 and has never been still since. Its earlier history and development are full of interest, beginning with a grant made in 1800 to William Balmain (1762–1803), who was appointed in 1786 as an assistant surgeon at Botany Bay (at a salary of £91 5s a year). Balmain sold his grant of 500 acres, which covered nearly the whole of the present suburb, in 1801 to John Gilchrist for 5 shillings, probably as part of a business deal. In auctions in 1836 and 1882 the area was sold in lots.

William Balmain was born in Perthshire in 1762 and enlisted with the Royal Navy as a surgeon's mate, which meant he did not need to be fully qualified. He is reported to have operated on Governor Phillip's shoulder to remove a spear thrown by an Aborigine. In 1796 he became the principal surgeon of New South Wales, and one of his official duties was to treat members of the Royal Navy who became ill in port at Sydney. He was entitled to claim 13s 6d for every cure he achieved, but the fee could only be collected in England! And if his patients died, he received nothing. However, William Balmain did make some sure money in another venture. He traded in liquor and other goods, and at one time he had accumulated over 1,300 gallons of spirits.

The area was a favourite fishing spot for Aborigines and cockles and mussels covered the rocky shoreline, which was backed by a thick tea-tree forest.

Morts Dock, 1874, Australia's first large-scale dry dock, grew to become the biggest industrial establishment in the country covering ten hectares and employing over 1,000 men. The dock was closed in 1959

Edmund Blacket

The early settlement of Balmain was slow until the 1830s. Few people lived there because of the difficulty in transport, although people living in the Iron Cove Creek area were able to get to Sydney via Parramatta Road. Ferries did not operate as they do now, and anyone wishing to use the harbour as a means of transport had to row to Sydney — a long, hard pull to the main part of the city. In the 1840s, a ferry began running between Balmain and Millers Point, and the suburb gradually became a fashionable residential area.

Thomas Sutcliffe Mort (1816–78) had an important influence on Balmain in the 1850s. In 1854 he established a dry-dock in Waterview Street, Balmain. Mort added coal sheds,

engineering shops and ship building yards to his dockyard, and the suburb's character began to change with the introduction of industry. By 1892, the population had changed to include ship builders, engineers, boilermakers, and carpenters, mainly because of the location of Mort's dry dock and the shipbuilding yards at Waterview Street.

The winding main road was widened and lengthened from Parramatta Road to Darling Street Wharf and named Darling Street to honour Governor Darling. Edmund Blacket (1817–83), the architect who designed several important Sydney buildings, including St Andrew's Cathedral and the Great Hall of the University of Sydney, lived in Darling Street for about five years.

Fred Spofforth, the "demon bowler", who once took fourteen wickets in a test cricket match, was born here.

During the 1970s, when industry began to move away from the inner city areas, Balmain became popular with professional and business people who wanted to live close to the city. Workers' cottages and terraces, as well as the larger stone houses of colonial times, have been renovated and now command high prices.

# BALMORAL
*Municipality of Mosman*
Location: 8 kilometres north of Sydney on Middle Harbour

This delightful suburb was named after the private residence at Balmoral, in Braemar, Aberdeenshire, purchased for Queen Victoria in 1848 by her consort, Prince Albert. It still belongs to the royal family, who spend each Christmas there.

Australia's Balmoral has safe, sandy harbour beaches, Edwards Beach to the north and Balmoral Beach to the south, broken in the middle by a jutting piece of land, known as Rocky Point. Steps over this rocky mass lead to its summit, which looks across Hunter's Bay to Grotto Point, Dobroyd Head and Manly Point. Just when the suburb received its name is not known, although the beach front

had been taken up by four land grants in 1830.

In 1924 a religious group known as the Theosophical Society came to the area. The members believed they had direct contact with divine forces and could forecast the exact date of the coming of a second Messiah. One of the leading lights was Annie Besant, a friend of the Irish playwright George Bernard Shaw. They built a large structure, known as the Star Amphitheatre, which stood at the end of Edwards Beach, looking out towards the magnificent views of the Heads. People began to book seats for the event — and subscribers could lease their seats for twenty-five years! At weekends devotees were

Balmoral tram terminus, 1920. Sydney had the second largest tramway network in the world; starting in 1861 with a two-kilometre horse-drawn system along Pitt Street, the network grew through steam, cable and electric eras until in 1923 there was a street mileage of 290 kilometres

A day at the beach! Balmoral, 1911

busy at Balmoral with their collecting boxes, seeking donations to further their cause.

The amphitheatre was designed in classical style, with tiered seats and fluted columns. On 28 July 1923 Charles Webster Leadbeater, a leading theosophist and patron of the Order of the Star of the East, performed the opening ceremony. The spirit of the second Messiah was supposed to manifest itself in the person of Jiddu Krishnamurti, a young Brahmin, but things fell apart when this young religious dissociated himself from the movement in 1929. For a time the amphitheatre was used for concerts and entertainments, but gradually it was abandoned, fell into decay, and ultimately disappeared.

The houses on the steep hill behind Balmoral Beach are set in attractive grounds, although many of the larger blocks have been subdivided. Balmoral Beach and its vicinity have been classified by the National Trust as an urban conservation area. The naval depot and military reserve adjoin Balmoral Park, extending over Middle Head to the harbour side and south to include George's Heights. Because of its sheltered aspect, Balmoral has been popular with generations of Sydneysiders for picnics and swimming. Ask a visitor or resident why, and the answer is pretty predictable — "Fine beach, pretty views and swimming baths, what else does one need?" What else, indeed?

## BANKSIA

*Municipality of Rockdale*
Location: 12 kilometres south-west of Sydney off the Princes Highway, on the Illawarra Line

This suburb was part of property acquired by Simeon Pearce (1821–86) and his brother James in the 1850s, which extended from Rockdale to Brighton-le-Sands. Until the late nineteenth century, like many of the neighbouring settlements, the area was heavily timbered, the scene of tree-felling and timber-getting. Soon after the railway line was extended from Sydney to the Illawarra, a railway league was formed to agitate for a local station. This seems to have

17

View of Rocky Point Road, Banksia, c. 1900 by photographer Charles Kerry

continued for about fifteen years, until a station was finally opened on 21 October 1906. Many names for the station were put forward, but the final choice was the suggestion of David Stead, father of the novelist Christina Stead. He suggested the name Banksia, to recognise the eminent naturalist Sir Joseph Banks. After this time the area developed rapidly.

By August 1924, Banksia had its own official post office. Young couples were building in the new streets of the suburb, and a pleasing variety of individually styled homes appeared. Today, Banksia is a pleasant suburban area, with no evidence of the early quarrels to establish its identity.

## BANKSMEADOW
*Municipality of Botany*
Location: 11 kilometres south of Sydney off Botany Road

This suburb of Sydney, not far from Botany, is named after Sir Joseph Banks. Captain James Cook described the area in 1770 as "as fine a meadow as ever was seen". Cook arrived in Botany Bay when the swampland surrounding the bay would have been covered with a deceptive crop of rushes. As he did not make a closer inspection, its true nature was not discovered until Governor Phillip had cause to reject it as unsuitable for a settlement eighteen years later when the First Fleet arrived and dropped anchor. He saw it as swampy, lacking a fresh water supply and unsheltered.

What later became the suburb Banksmeadow was originally part of the Church and School Estate, land set aside for eventual sale to pay clergy and teachers. It later reverted to the crown. In 1830 Robert Hoddle was instructed to mark out a road (later Bunnerong Road) and allotments for the New South Wales Veterans Corps, as well as an area for the village reserve, which became the village of Banks Meadow.

Today Banksmeadow has a park leading into Botany Municipal Golf Links and the adjacent Sir Joseph Banks Park provides the suburb with a great leisure attraction with the main thoroughfare, Botany Road, running alongside. A public school in Brighton Street, Botany, serves the children resident in Banksmeadow.

# BANKSTOWN

*City of Bankstown*
Location: 20 kilometres
south-west of Sydney between
Canterbury Road and the Hume
Highway, on the Bankstown Line

This area 20 kilometres south-west
of Sydney, was selected for
settlement by Governor Hunter,
who named it Banks Town, in
honour of the eminent botanist, Sir
Joseph Banks. In 1795 George Bass
(1771–1803) and Matthew Flinders
(1774–1814) had explored the
Georges River, named after King
George III, the reigning monarch.
They sailed along what would later
be the southern boundary of the
Bankstown municipality. The two
explorers reported their findings
along this waterway and received
land grants in the Georges Hall
area. Bass received the first grant
in the area in 1798. His 100 acres
lay in the vicinity of the present
Hazel and Flinders Streets. He did
not farm it, and it eventually
reverted to the crown. Matthew
Flinders' grant was alongside
Bass's. He bought more land, until
he held 300 acres, but did not farm
it. Lieutenant Shortland and
Surveyor James Meehan also
received grants. By 1799, 1,200
acres on both banks of the river
had been granted to marines and
ex-convicts.

The area developed slowly, as it
was isolated from both Sydney and
Parramatta. After the Liverpool
Road was constructed in 1814 it
began to develop rapidly, and
settlements grew up along the road.

Bushrangers were a problem
along the road, and in
Bankstown's early days, two
bushrangers, Patrick Sullivan and
James Moran, were taken to a set
of makeshift gallows on the site of
the present Bankstown watertower
and hanged. A few days later three

Sir Joseph Banks

of their companions met the same
fate. The intention was to
discourage any convict from
becoming a highway robber; the
hangings had the required effect.
There is no record of where the
victims were buried; they were
probably interred in nearby
unconsecrated ground. In 1831,
Michael Ryan was granted 100
acres in Bankstown, which
included the site of the hangings,
and for many years the place was
called Ryan's paddock.

The Church of England school
established here in 1862 became the
first public school in 1868, but was
moved to North Bankstown in
1813. The first post office opened
in 1863, but closed in 1918.
Bankstown now has two post
offices, one in Restwell Street and
one in Bankstown Square.

Greenacre Park Estate was one
of the first subdivisions in the
Bankstown area. Subdivision
began in about 1909 when the total
population of Bankstown was less
than 2,000. It was handled by
famous estate agent and land
developer Sir Arthur Rickard, who
invented the scheme of £1 deposit
down and the balance paid at 10
shillings a week, which gave many
young couples the chance to own
their home. One hundred and
seventy-four blocks were sold by

this method. Rickard built a statue
at the entrance to the estate, calling
it the Statue of Liberty — very
appropriate when we consider his
brilliant idea of time payment that
gave so many people the freedom
of property ownership.

When Bankstown railway
station opened in 1909, when the
railway line was extended from
Belmore to Bankstown, it was
known as Chapel Road. In 1926
the electrification of the railway
took place and Bankstown became
an easily accessible residential area.
After the coming of the railway, a
new business centre grew up
around the station and gradually
services and business moved down
to the new centre from Liverpool
Road. In 1963 the first stage of
Bankstown Civic Centre was
opened. Three years later the
Bankstown Shopping Square was
completed, and the Bankstown
town hall opened in 1973.

An old home in Bankstown,
lovingly restored to its first
elegance, is The Pah, now known
as Archway House. It has been
named by the National Trust as
worth preserving. The house was
built in 1894 by Samuel J. Hale,
whose furnishing emporium was
on the corner of Market and
Clarence Streets, Sydney. Today
the beautiful gardens surrounding
the house have been replaced by
modern cottages, but apart from
slate tiles giving way to modern
ones, the house is very little
changed.

Bankstown Aerodrome, used by
light aircraft, lies about 7
kilometres from Bankstown
railway station. During the Second
World War it was used by the
RAAF and was the first aerodrome
to accommodate the United States
Air Force during the later part of
the war. As a result of their
presence in the suburb, it soon
became known as Yankstown.

This once almost rural area is now alive with families, and many migrants have made their homes here. Bankstown became a municipality in 1895, and was proclaimed a city in May 1980. How different to the report in the *New South Wales Gazetteer* of 1866, which advertised "Banks Town is an isolated town, where only one coach per day runs to Sydney, starting out at 7.30 a.m. in the morning and returning at 7.45 p.m. at night."

Today, standing in its main shopping street, it is hard to imagine Governor Hunter classifying Bankstown as good for farming, its suburban character is so strong. Civic pride runs high here. The annual Bankstown Show and an Eisteddfod are both well patronised by local residents, as is the Civic Centre's theatre restaurant and the huge Bankstown Square shopping complex.

Bankstown from the watertank, 1922. The same view today would look over the Hume Highway

## BANTRY BAY
*Shire of Warringah*
Location: A locality 15 kilometres north of Sydney on the north side of Middle Harbour

Bantry Bay was used as an outlet for timber-cutters from the time of James French (see Frenchs Forest). In 1907 the area was surveyed for a public explosives magazine. This was built in 1915 and the complex of thirteen buildings still stands. In 1974 the area was transferred to Davidson State Recreation Area, and is a popular weekend anchorage for Sydney's boating fraternity.

## BARDWELL PARK
*Municipality of Rockdale*
Location: 12 kilometres south of Sydney between Bexley and Earlwood, on the East Hills Line

This suburb south of Cooks River was originally a farming area. It was named after an early resident who acquired land in the area, Thomas Bardwell. His name is also recalled in the names Bardwell Road, Bardwell Creek, Bardwell Crescent and Bardwell Valley Golf Club. His grant was bounded by Wolli Creek, Dowling Street, Forest Road and Wollongong Road, and like the rest of the area, was originally heavily timbered.

In 1881 the land was auctioned and 1,600 acres were subdivided and sold. The coming of the East Hills railway line made a great difference to the area, by opening residential home sites for buyers interested in living in a new suburb within reasonable distance of the city. When the station opened on 21 September 1931, Bardwell Park

was the name chosen for it.

The first school opened in September 1943, and the official post office followed in May 1946.

The homes in Bardwell Park are of individual design, set in well-cared-for gardens, and with an air of the stability of a prosperous family life-style.

## BASS HILL
*City of Bankstown*
Location: 23 kilometres south-west of Sydney off the Hume Highway

This suburb developed and expanded after the Second World War when returned soldiers and newly arrived migrants were looking for land on which to build homes in a pleasant and reasonably priced area. It is named after George Bass (1771–1803), a surgeon who came to the colony on HMS *Reliance* in 1795. He became friendly with Matthew Flinders (1774–1814), a midshipman on board, and on arrival they decided to explore parts of the colony. In a small boat owned by Bass and called *Tom Thumb*, and accompanied by a young lad named Martin, they sailed around Botany Bay and up the Georges River, 20 miles beyond previous exploration. For this and other exploration Bass and Flinders were rewarded in 1798 with grants of 100 acres each in the Bankstown area.

Bass Hill was originally called Irish Town, because of the Irish settlements in the area. It later became Upper Bankstown, but the name changed again when the enlarging area of Bankstown was reclassified, and this portion was renamed Bass Hill in 1924.

George Bass is also remembered by Bass Hill High School, and at least seven other Sydney suburbs have a Bass Street.

The story of George Bass has a sad ending. In 1803 he set sail for Chile, but was never heard of again. The district named after him, however, has become a busy suburb with children and young people very evident in its population.

## BAULKHAM HILLS
*Shire of Baulkham Hills*
Location: 31 kilometres north-west of Sydney off Windsor Road

There are several versions of how this high area between Castle Hill and Parramatta was named. The most likely is its resemblance to the pastoral border county of Roxburgh, between Scotland and England, which bears a similar name, Buckholm Hills, the home of one of the area's early settlers. Andrew McDougall, who arrived in Sydney in 1798 from Roxburgh, was one of several settlers to receive grants in the area in 1799. He called his 150 acre grant Roxburgh Hall. The estate remained in the family until 1876 and Roxburgh Hall was built in 1860. McDougall was one of the trustees appointed when 3,000 acres were set aside as Baulkham Hills Common in 1804. Whatever its origin, the name has been officially recognised since 1802.

One of the earliest land grants in the area was of 30 acres given to George Best in 1796. He gradually acquired more land until he had 185 acres. Best's land was acquired by the Masonic Lodge, which began building homes and a school, known as the William Thompson Masonic School, in

1922. It is now owned by Baulkham Hills Shire Council.

The oldest farm-house in the area is Joyce Farmhouse in Valerie Crescent, near Seven Hills. It was built in 1804 by William Joyce, destroyed by fire and rebuilt in 1806, and used as an inn between 1811 and 1826. Joyce had received his 30 acre grant in about 1794.

One of the oldest pioneer families in Parramatta came into this area when George Suttor received a grant of 186 acres in 1802 and settled on the property, which he called Chelsea Farm, after his birthplace in London. Here he planted the first orange trees in the district and became a prominent orchardist. He later received another grant, in Bathurst, and the Suttor family moved to the plains beyond the Blue Mountains, but Suttor continued to hold Chelsea Farm until his death in 1859. The main house, Chelsea Farm, was built in 1873 by one of his grandsons.

In 1856, an official post office was opened in the area, followed by a school in 1868.

Parramatta's increasing population affected Baulkham Hills, as more settlers spread into

George Suttor

the district to plant orchards in the area's ideal conditions. By 1890 residents were clamouring for better means of transport. As a result of many official discussions, a steam tramline was opened in 1902 to carry passengers from Parramatta Station to Baulkham Hills. The route was along Church Street, over the Lennox Bridge and along Windsor Road to its destination 5 miles away. The tramline was changed to a railway connected to Westmead on 28 January 1923, but the line was closed in February 1932.

Pye's Crossing, over Toongabbie Creek, is named after John Pye senior, well-known in Baulkham Hills' early development, and Mullane Avenue remembers Mr B. Mullane, once president of the Baulkham Hills Shire Council. A walk through St John's Cemetery at Parramatta will reveal the names of many other pioneers of this formerly quiet rural area.

Present-day Baulkham Hills is a busy place, and many home-builders have secured pleasantly placed sites in this healthy area.

# BAYVIEW
*Shire of Warringah*
Location: 31 kilometres north of Sydney, facing Pittwater

The name of this suburb is descriptive of the environment, with its beautiful view across Pittwater. Governor Phillip came into the area in March 1788 while on a short journey of exploration from Manly, and Captain John Hunter prepared a map in 1792 showing the outlines of bays and inlets. Phillip was very impressed with the whole area. Writing of it in his journal he said, "immediately around the headland is the finest piece of water I ever saw and which I honoured with the name Pitt Water", after William Pitt, then prime minister of England.

The settlement of the district began in the 1820s. One of the first settlers was Peter Patullo, who built a house in 1821 on the site of the present Bayview Golf Links, in Pittwater and Cabbage Tree Roads. The early settlers were mostly farmers and orchardists. Robert McIntosh, who was granted 200 acres in 1832, began cultivation there, but the Shaw and Oliver families were more prominent. They were involved in the timber trade and built ships to carry shingles to Sydney. Joseph and Susan Shaw came to the suburb from Yorkshire in 1834 as shell-diggers and shoemakers. Their son James married Ann, daughter of William Oliver, and one of the children of this union

". . . the finest piece of water I ever saw", said Governor Phillip of Pittwater. This photograph from Bayview was taken in the early 1900s

was a well-known identity, James Shaw (1881–1963), who taught himself the trade of blacksmith and wheelwright.

The name Bayview was officially recognised on 21 August 1882, when a post office was opened at the residence of Mrs Collins and her daughter, Katherine Mary Collins, who was appointed postmistress. The post office was situated on the Collins' 80 acre farm; the office was officially name Bayview and the suburb adopted the name. Bayview estate had been part of Robert McIntosh's grant.

In 1893, Bayview received the added honour of being created a telephone office, and Katherine Collins, by then married to a Mr Roche, became the telephone attendant. The family continued farming and Mr J. Roche also took part in running the post office. The family were renowned for their preserves and jams, made from their orchard produce.

The wooden church of St John the Baptist, erected in Newport Road in 1871, was moved and re-erected in Bayview Road in 1888. It remained a place of worship until 1906, by which time it was in need of considerable repair. A new stone church was built in Mona Vale to replace it. Around 1900 a brickworks operated in Bayview, and in 1901 the Bayview Wharf was built.

Today Bayview is largely unspoiled by progress, although modern conveniences of roads and transport are evident. Pittwater High School is also in Bayview, adjacent to the golf links.

# BEACON HILL
*Shire of Warringah*
Location: 18 kilometres north of Sydney off Warringah Road

This suburb stands on high ground between Frenchs Forest and Dee Why. Claims have been made that a fire was lit here by a First Fleet exploring party as a signal to others at Manly, and that this beacon led to the district's name. However, there is no record of the name until 1877, when it appeared on the county maps. The area was given the title Beacon Hill when the department of lands built a trigonometric beacon there in 1881. The hill is situated on the projection of the southern boundary of the Australian Agricultural Company's Warrah grant.

Less than three months after the arrival of the First Fleet, Governor Phillip explored this area. Records tell us how the party walked through thick forest (today's Frenchs Forest) and climbed a hill from which a fine view was obtained. This is now Governor Phillip Lookout, 148 metres above sea level. It was named in 1929 and a cairn was erected by the Manly-Warringah Historical Society. The cairn was demolished in 1942. The lookout is on the site of the trigonometric beacon. It is interesting to reflect on these early local explorations. How intimidating the Australian bushland must have appeared to British eyes used to softer colours and English woods. Some of the First Fleet diarists give vivid descriptions.

George Caley (1770–1829), a botanist protégé of Sir Joseph Banks, explored the adjoining area in 1805, setting out from Pennant Hills and tramping as far as the Narrabeen Lagoon, known by him as Cabbage Tree Lagoon. Caley

returned by way of Beacon Hill, travelling along the ridges of Middle Harbour and the Lane Cove River. The country was thick with trees and later became a favourite haunt of bushrangers, who were protected from detection by the heavy bush and the lack of roads.

In 1857 Daniel Egan purchased two 40 acre blocks in the area now known as Beacon Hill. In 1909 there was brickmaking on the eastern side of the hill, a venture that led to the formation of the Manly Beacon Brick Company.

The area around Beacon Hill remained almost untouched even after 1913 when a tram service was extended from Manly to Narrabeen, which encouraged day trippers and holiday-makers. In the 1930s some riding schools were set up in the area, and this tendency has continued, the surrounding area offering peaceful trails for riding and bush walking.

Today the suburb retains its bushland charm. Homes in the area blend with natural contours and foliage. Good roads wind through the district and, the views from its highest points are still as spectacular, in spite of progress, as those seen by the first white men.

# BEACONSFIELD
*City of Sydney*
Location: 6 kilometres south of Sydney off Botany Road

A small area once part of Alexandria is now known as Beaconsfield. It lies between Bourke Street and Botany Road, and is adjacent to the large industrial firm Austral Bronze adjoining the suburb of Rosebery. It was named after Benjamin Disraeli, Lord Beaconsfield, a great British prime minister during

Queen Victoria's reign, who was responsible for purchasing shares in the Suez Canal on behalf of Great Britain. The name was officially gazetted on 10 June 1977. Street names in the suburb relate to royalty, including Queen Street, Victoria Street, and William Street.

Like other suburbs in the area, Beaconsfield is primarily a manufacturing suburb. Early factories were soap and candlemakers, and brickworks, but today mechanical and engineering works predominate. Some of the office blocks adjoining these are modern and, as is the trend today, have attractive garden settings.

In the 1920s Rosebery Park Race Course, the venue for pony races, was nearby but the sport died out in Sydney, and time and progress have overrun that early racecourse.

Beaconsfield has a limited residential area, with two small parks and the larger McConville Reserve like islands in a sea of industrial activity.

# BEAUTY POINT
*Municipality of Mosman*
Location: 11 kilometres north of Sydney on Middle Harbour

This is the name given to the headland between Long Bay and Pearl Bay west of The Spit and facing Middle Harbour. It is a small residential area, and its name derives from the natural scenic beauty that surrounds it on all sides. It has magnificent views of Middle Harbour and of The Spit, the narrow neck of sandy land stretching to the north that enabled a bridge to be built spanning the water and linking Seaforth with Mosman.

As early as 1834 a ferry,

operated by Barney Kearns, ran across the narrow stretch of water. A heavier punt, operated by Peter Ellery, replaced this in the 1850s. The charge to cross was sixpence each way for passengers, and 1s 6d for horse-drawn vehicles. If the horses were swum, there was a reduction of sixpence. In 1889 it was replaced by a government steam punt. After electric tram lines were extended to The Spit, a wooden bridge was built, opening in 1924. It was replaced by a new bridge in 1959, to cope with increasingly heavy traffic between the northern beach suburbs and the city.

# BEECROFT
*Shire of Hornsby*
Location: 22 kilometres north-west of Sydney at the junction of Beecroft Road and Pennant Hills Road, on the Main Northern Line

Although land grants in the area were made as early as 1799, Beecroft, like many suburbs, owes its origin to the coming of the railway line, in this case from Strathfield to Hornsby. On 17 September 1886 the section of the line passing through this area was declared open. Sir Henry Copeland, the minister of lands who had a survey done of the area for residential purposes in 1886, decided to name the new suburb Beecroft, the maiden name of his wives, Hannah and Mary (two sisters whom he married in succession). Their Christian names were also given to two streets running parallel to the main road.

Coincidentally a Mr W. Abra, of the Italian Bee Company, which imported bees, came from Parramatta to Beecroft in 1889,

and established a bee farm. He eventually built the first house in Malton Road. Legend has it that the suburb was named Beecroft because of this farm, but this is incorrect.

In the 1890s part of the area was subdivided and some splendid homes with gardens, and sometimes an orchard, were built. One notable sale was to Judge Fitzhardinge, who purchased five blocks and erected a residence at Red Hill. The cost for the total purchase was £451.

Beecroft's development was slow and gentle, and many of the families who went there intermarried. It was not unusual for their descendants to also settle in the suburb. A local joker once said it wasn't wise to talk about anyone on the local bus, because one of their relations would always be sitting in the seat behind!

The first Church of England service was held in 1889 in the home of Mrs Hull, on the corner of Beecroft Road and Kirkham Street. Frederick Mason offered his home for the first Methodist services in 1893, and the early Presbyterian services were held in the School of Arts.

A non-official post office opened on 20 August 1895, and the public school followed in April 1897. It was a real bush school in its bushland setting, alive with many varieties of birds. The general store opposite the school was built with hitching posts for riders and buggy drivers coming in for their supplies. The small building at the rear of the store, later used for grain storage, had at one time been consecrated for conducting church services. The original School of Arts, founded in 1904, was the scene of many early local activities, and it is still standing.

The names of many early settlers include L. J. "Squire" Nathan, who initiated a boys club in 1915; George Sargent, of meat-pie fame; the Seale family; Andrew Fuller, the public school's first teacher; and two familiar local identities, Robert Dunn and his horse Peggy, who kept the streets swept and immaculate.

Today Beecroft retains its residential character, although modern shopping arcades and boutiques have been built.

## BELFIELD
*Municipalities of Canterbury and Strathfield*
Location: 15 kilometres south-west of Sydney off Punchbowl Road

Until the early 1900s, Belfield was a rural area belonging to an Arthur Langley, who ran horses and had a piggery and a boiling-down works. After the First World War, the land was subdivided and sold as home sites, some for war service homes. Three of the streets in the area are named after troop ships of the period.

The suburb lies south of Strathfield, adjoining Belmore and Enfield, from which its name, gazetted in June 1977, was derived.

Today, Belfield is a closely built up residential area, serviced by buses. Rudd Park is in the vicinity, and Cooks River Canal forms its northern boundary.

## BELLEVUE HILL
*Municipality of Woollahra*
Location: 5 kilometres east of Sydney betwen Old South Head Road and New South Head Road

This suburb is set high on a hilly area of the Eastern Suburbs. Its highest vantage point is 100 metres above sea level. During the governorship of Lachlan Macquarie (1810–21), some Irish migrants referred to it as Vinegar Hill, after an historic battleground in Ireland, but Macquarie took great exception to this and officially named the suburb Bellevue Hill, the "belle vue" meaning "beautiful view". In 1820 Macquarie ordered a large signpost to be erected on top of the hill so that no one would have any doubt about the area's correct designation and it became one of the governor's favourite vantage points.

A natural beauty spot in the suburb, which slopes northwards towards Double Bay, is known as Cooper Park. The parkland, leading into a gully, was given to Woollahra council by Sir William Cooper and is named after him. The suburb is renowned for its beautiful residential areas and well-kept gardens. One charming old home is Leura, which has a magnificent vista of Sydney and its harbour. It was valued at $1 million in 1983. Built in 1890 for Mr T. F. Know, the big

The grand mansions of Bellevue Hill, captured in an aerial picture taken around 1910

three-storeyed house has had only four owners in its lifetime. It stands in 1 acre of grounds. A feature of the beautiful mansion is the galleried staircase, which is cantilevered from the wall. Leura represents perfectly the type of home and life-style of the suburb in the last century.

Bellevue Hill's history would not be complete without a mention of the well-known school for boys — Cranbrook. The house Cranbrook was built in 1848 for Sir Robert Tooth, the brewery magnate. He named the mansion after his home town in Kent, England. Later, the house passed to the merchant Robert Towns, who founded the city of Townsville in Queensland, and then to James White, a Hunter Valley pastoralist. Between 1901 and 1917 this grand old home was the residence of the New South Wales governors. It was occupied by three successive governors — Sir Harry Rawson, Lord Chelmsford and Sir Gerald Strickland — and this period is marked by the crown on the front gate and the vice-regal coat of arms on the stairs.

A group of men of the Parish of St Mark, including Mr Justice Harvey, Mr Bertram Clamp, the Reverend Cannon Lee, Sir Samuel Hordern and Dr Stacey, decided the Eastern Suburbs needed a Church of England boys school similar to Shore across the harbour. Sir Samuel Hordern bought Cranbrook on their behalf, and on the opening day in 1918, forty-six boys were enrolled. Harvey House, a school for junior boys, opened in 1927.

# BELMORE

*Municipality of Canterbury*
Location: 15 kilometres south-west of Sydney between Canterbury Road and Punchbowl Road, on the Bankstown Line

Situated between Campsie and Lakemba, Belmore was named after a popular governor of New South Wales, Sir Somerset Richard Lowry-Corry, Earl of Belmore, who held office between 1868 and 1872.

Early land grants in the area include 100 acres to Richard Robinson, east of Sharp Street and Kingsgrove Road, and 60 acres to Thomas Mansfield, to the west, both in 1810. In 1823 Francis Wild and John Sullivan were each granted 30 acres. The area was one of market gardens and small orchards until the coming of the railway, when subdivision began. The Towers in Forsyth Street is one of the few mansions still standing in the area. It was built in 1870 by David Jones.

The railway station, known as Burwood Road during its construction, was opened on 1 February 1895. The first school opened in 1903. First known as Belmore North, its name was changed to Belmore in 1907, then back again to Belmore North in April 1918. The post office opened in 1907. The 1920s saw the development of the shopping centre and further home-building.

A 1923 directory spoke well of this suburb: "the land here lies eighty-five feet above sea level, the atmosphere is most invigorating, and all around this centre bids fair in time to become one of Sydney's most popular suburban retreats. Land for so long locked up in this neighbourhood is now being subivided in all directions and is eagerly sought after."

Belmore lived up to that

prediction and has become a busy residential suburb, completely contradicting a name given to it in its earlier days, when it was referred to as Darkwater.

# BELROSE

*Shire of Warringah*
Location: 19 kilometres north of Sydney off Forest Way

This attractive suburb, in a semi-bushland setting, lies about 10 kilometres west of Long Reef. It is bounded on the west by Middle Harbour Creek and on the south by the suburbs of Davidson and Frenchs Forest. It was developed and named after the Second World War, although parts of it remained semi-rural until the housing boom of the 1960s and 1970s. It is thought that George Caley (1770–1829), the botanist who worked for Sir Joseph Banks and sent quantities of Australian flora back to him in England, may have crossed this area in 1805. Native plants and flowers were thick around Belrose, and the suburb's name is derived from two flowers, the Christmas bell and the native rose.

The houses in this suburb have been built to blend in with the natural surroundings, and home gardens mix cultivated and native plants with pleasing effect. The main road, known as Forest Way, connects Belrose to Frenchs Forest in the south and Terrey Hills in the north.

# BERALA
*Municipality of Auburn*
Location: 21 kilometres west of
Sydney just south of Auburn, on
the Bankstown Line and the local
line joining the Main Southern
Line

When the railway line was being
extended from Lidcombe to
Regents Park, the construction
names of the intervening station
included Bareela, Sidmouth and
Torrington. The area surrounding
the new station was swampy, and
wild birds abounded, including
large flocks of native ducks, so the
Aboriginal name for musk-duck,
*bareela*, was chosen for the suburb.

The station was officially opened
on 11 November 1912. A public
school was built in the district in
1922 and the first post office
opened in 1927.

This district is near an area once
known as Liberty Plains. The
name reflects the fact that many
who received land grants in the
area had come to the colony of
their own free will rather than
arriving as convicts, or members
of the New South Wales Corps or
the marines. Liberty lass became a
title for the women free settlers,
and a favourite name for several
inns in those days.

Today Berala is a busy
residential suburb, with some
industries located in the district. It
is also close to Carnarvon Golf
Club.

# BEROWRA
*Shire of Hornsby*
Location: 38 kilometres north of
Sydney at the junction of Berowra
Waters Road and the Pacific
Highway, on the Main Northern
Line

This name, Aboriginal in origin
and meaning "place of many
winds", was first given to the
parish and thence to the settlement.
It is also the name of a nearby
creek.

Captain John Hunter showed the
area on his map of the
Hawkesbury in 1789. The source
of Berowra Creek was traced to
the Castle Hill area by the
government surveyor, William
Romaine Govett, who, as a
member of Sir Thomas Mitchell's
surveying team, also found
Govett's Leap, with its beautiful
Bridal Veil Fall, near the Blue
Mountains township of
Blackheath. One of the early
grantees in the Berowra area was
John Crumpton in 1867. George
Collingridge, who selected 88 acres
in 1880, played a part in having the
Northern railway line extended
some years later, and a station was
opened on 7 April 1887.
Collingridge had demanded a
railway station for the small
settlement. He also supported two
other essential facilities: a road to
the water's edge (approved in 1888
and completed in 1902), and a local
post office. The first land grant in
the town area was made to Mrs
Mary Wall in 1887, which she
subdivided in 1909. The village of
Berowra was proclaimed in 1890.
In November 1894, a public school
opened in Berowra, and an official
post office followed in August
1900.

Berowra has become an outer
suburb of Sydney, and many
comfortable homes have been built
in the area. When we see this
progress it is hard to believe that
this suburb began its life with four
houses and fifteen inhabitants
located near a small waterway
known as Mother Marr's Creek.
Today's residents enjoy the peace
of a bushland suburb, and visitors
have the same privilege. The first
motor-boats available for hire in
Australia were leased from
Berowra Waters by Rex Jones in
1927.

# BEVERLY HILLS
*Municipalities of Canterbury and
Hurstville*
Location: 17 kilometres
south-west of Sydney off King
Georges road, on the East Hills
Line

This suburb, situated between
Riverwood and Hurstville, began
its life as a farming property
named Dumbleton, established in
the 1830s on what is now the
corner of King Georges Road and
Stoney Creek Road.

The area south of the present
railway was part of John
Townson's 250 acre grant of 1810
(see Hurstville). The area was once
thickly forested, and many of the
early settlers were timber-cutters
and carters. Forest Road and
Stoney Creek Road tell their own
story of the time when this suburb
was first called Dumbleton.

The area retained a rural
atmosphere for many years. Older
folk often retired here from
outback properties, attracted by its
rural feeling, while conveniently
close to Sydney. One such was
Henry Augustus Swan, who had
been a pioneer in the Gulgong area
during the gold rush of the 1870s.
He had later moved to Wellington,
New South Wales, and built some
of the first shops in the main street,

including a bakery where he made all the bread and cakes. He remained in Dumbleton until his death in 1918, a victim of the flu epidemic that swept through Sydney.

In the 1930s a large residential development led to different types of people settling in the suburb, and agitation began for a change of name. The name Dumbleton, which had identified the railway station since the East Hills line opened in 1931, was thought to be not "smart" enough, and in 1940 the suburb was renamed Beverly Hills, possibly after the Californian district in the United States, home of many famous film stars.

Beverly Hills now has a public school and a girls high school in King Georges Road, where there is also a major post office.

## BEXLEY

*Municipalities of Rockdale and Canterbury*
Location: 14 kilometres south-west of Sydney on Forest Road, on the East Hills Line (Bexley North)

In 1820 a young Englishman, James Chandler, migrated from Kent to the colony as a free settler. In 1822 he bought an existing farm known as Sylvester's Farm, which had been granted to Thomas Sylvester about ten years before. Chandler was also granted in 1822 1,200 acres of high land, in its virgin state, which stretched from what is now Bexley North almost to Brighton-le-Sands and overlooked Botany Bay. To this sprawling estate Chandler gave the name of Bexley, after Bexley Heath in his native England.

The area granted would today include modern Bexley, most of

Rockdale, and large areas of Bexley North and Kogarah. The estate was heavily timbered, and Chandler paid an annual quit rent of sixpence per hundred acres — today he would be a millionaire. A track used by timber-getters, today called Forest Road, ran through the centre of his huge estate. Queen Victoria Street, Gladstone Street and Beaconsfield Street commemorate the British queen and two of her prime ministers.

Chandler became a respected citizen and was known locally as the Squire of Bexley, but his property was not without its problems. Bushrangers, escaped convicts and other odd types roamed its acres. Chandler was not very happy with such an ill-assortment of neighbours and in 1836 he sold the land to Charles Tompson. Later it was bought by Charles Tindell, who by 1856 began to subdivide the land and sell it for home-sites.

A gracious mansion, known as Lydham Hall, stands on part of the original Bexley land grant made to James Chandler in 1822. Joseph Davis settled in this historic home, the oldest surviving residence in the area, well over a century ago. Herbert Street and Frederick Street were named after his two sons. Other early settlers were Henry Kinsela who lived in Kinsel Grove and George Preddy who occupied Besborough. Bexley Park now occupies part of the grounds that surrounded the latter.

Bexley responded to the opening of the railway from Redfern to Hurstville in 1884 with a tremendous upsurge in its development. Some of the largest estates in the area were purchased by wealthy merchants and subdivided, and many beautiful houses were built. A two-storey waggonette and a hansom cab conveyed train travellers to their

respective homes, and in 1909 a steam tram ran through Bexley as far as Arncliffe station.

Many inns gave local colour to the suburb: the Man of Kent, the Robin Hood Inn and the Highbury Barn, once the scene of merry gatherings, are now only vague memories. Indeed we wonder how Bexley's original owner, James Chandler, would find his way around this vastly changed suburb, if he were able to return today.

## BIDWILL

*City of Blacktown*
Location: 49 kilometres north-west of Sydney, north of Mount Druitt

This suburb of Blacktown is named in honour of John Carne Bidwill (1815–53), who was an early director of Sydney's Botanic Gardens and a government botanist. While Bidwell is the registered geographical name, the name used for this suburb is Bidwill, which is the correct spelling of his name.

Bidwill had gathered plant specimens in New Zealand and taken them to Kew Gardens in London in 1841. He was sent to Tahiti in 1845 and in 1847 he was appointed Botanic Gardens director by Governor Fitzroy, but he was superseded by Charles Moore, who was appointed by the colonial office in England.

Shane Park and Marsden Park are close to this area, and two schools are located there: a public school in Daniels Road, and Bidwill High School in the same street.

# BILGOLA PLATEAU
*Shire of Warringah*
Location: 33 kilometres north of Sydney on the Barrenjoey Peninsula

The Aboriginal name of Bilgola was noted on Surveyor James Meehan's records of 6 May 1814 as Belgoula, which is reputed to mean "a pretty beach with steep slopes in the background studded with cabbage palms". Robert Henderson, who had received his land grant by 1822, gave his 100 acres another version of this name, Belgoola. After Henderson moved to Brisbane Water, a quarrel arose over ownership of his grant. His neighbour, John Farrell, petitioned Governor Darling in 1826 for a transfer of the grant to his property, as he needed it for extra grazing land (see Newport). The problem apparently resolved itself, and the district eventually adopted the simplified spelling of Bilgola.

From Bilgola Beach, which is backed by a deep gully with a remnant of subtropical rainforest thick with cabbage palms, the suburb stretches westward across a high plateau to Refuge Cove on Pittwater. Father Therry (1790–1864), the fiery Catholic priest, was granted land at Avalon in the 1830s, and the area behind Bilgola Head, just north of the beach, was first known as Mad Mick's Hollow, perhaps after Therry.

On Father Therry's grant two natural curiosities were found. They were the Hole-in-the-Wall and St Michael's Cave. The hole in the wall was a natural arch. It was 22 feet across and 40 feet high, and its soft underlying sandstone floor had been washed away. The surface had not been eroded, but during a violent gale in 1866 the arch fell, and it became known as St Michael's Cave. Father Therry had planned to build a church on the headland above the cave, and had a great heap of stones marking the site for many years. He also cultivated the ground above the cave, employing men to plant wheat, maize and onion crops there.

William Bede Dalley, famous lawyer, orator and politician after whom Dalley Street, Sydney, is named, once lived at Bilgola. Dalley, a convict's son, was influential in calling together the New South Wales contingent that went to the Sudan War in 1887. In 1887 he became the first Australian Privy Councillor.

His property was bought by Oswald Watt, who was drowned in the surf at Bilgola Beach. When Mrs Maclurcan bought the cottage, she had it demolished and replaced with a charming weekend home.

This area has never lost its natural beauty although the whole plateau has been subdivided and hundreds of houses have been built there. Some streets in the area are named after famous ships — Mariposa Road, Monterey Road and Kanimbla Crescent — while others, such as Grand View Parade, The Outlook, and Hillslope Road, reflect the nature of the terrain and the views it commands.

William Bede Dalley

# BIRCHGROVE
*Municipality of Leichhardt*
Location: 5 kilometres west of Sydney facing Iron Cove on the Parramatta River

When surgeon William Balmain was granted a large slice of present-day Balmain in 1800, a small area was not included. This is now the suburb of Birchgrove. The 30 acre area had been granted to George Whitfield, a private in the New South Wales Corps, in 1796. It passed through several hands before being acquired by John Birch, paymaster of the 73rd Regiment, in 1810. He built Birch Grove House, from which the suburb derived its name. The house was demolished in 1967.

The small suburb extends from Snails Bay, so named in 1810, to Long Nose Point. When this point was named, a rocky protuberance, like a pointed nose, jutted into the Harbour. This rock has since been eroded away.

Part of this area was originally a swamp, but the land was reclaimed and transformed into Birchgrove Oval. Birchgrove School, the third primary school built in the Balmain area, was opened in 1885.

The suburb is justly proud of Dawn Fraser, who has had the swimming pool in Elkington Park named in her honour. Dawn Fraser, who was born in Balmain, won gold medals for the same event swimming at three successive Olympic Games, an outstanding record when we consider that the games are held every four years.

# BIRRONG
*City of Bankstown*
Location: 22 kilometres
south-west of Sydney north of the
Hume Highway, on the
Bankstown Line

This suburb, between Bankstown and Regents Park, developed with the opening of the railway line in the area in 1928. Its nearest neighbour is Yagoona, and both stations are on the City–Bankstown–Lidcombe line.

In 1835, Joseph Hyde Potts received a large grant of 625 acres in the area, which became known as Pott's Hill. Potts was a foundation employee of the Bank of New South Wales, which opened in 1817. He was also the security man who slept in the bank. His first opportunity to marry was dampened by the bank officers' refusal to allow him to bring a bride into the premises, for fear it would lessen his concentration on his duties.

The Water Board has two large water storages on Potts Hill, the water being piped from Pipe Head in Guildford. Birrong is also self-sufficient in schooling, having a primary school and two secondary schools. The official post office opened in 1955. Birrong Park, subject to flooding until it was drained as relief work during the 1929–34 depression, is now a pleasant district park catering for the residents of this small but busy area. The suburb's name, said to be Aboriginal for "star", was given in about 1927.

# BLACKETT
*City of Blacktown*
Location: 48 kilometres
north-west of Sydney, north of
Mount Druitt

A fairly new suburb, dating from the 1970s, Blackett is situated in the Mount Druitt housing development area near Blacktown. It was named in honour of George Blackett, superintendent of the government cattle station at Rooty Hill in the period of Macquarie's governorship. During that period (1810–21), a small settlement was also established in this area, where it is believed that Blackett occupied a two-storeyed family home.

Many of the suburb's streets are named after Australian writers and poets: Literature Place, Keesing Crescent, Idriess Crescent, Franklin Crescent, Niland Crescent, Brennan Place, Slessor Place, Hardy Street and Boldrewood Road. The people living in this suburb are of necessity hard-working, and there are many single parent families with young children.

A modern public school is situated in Boldrewood Road.

# BLACKTOWN
*City of Blacktown*
Location: 34 kilometres west of
Sydney between Richmond Road
and the Great Western Highway, a
junction station for the Main
Western and Richmond Lines

Governor Macquarie had what is probably the most understanding attitude to the Aborigines of any of the colony's governors, and he made several attempts to raise their standard of living. One of his ideas was to grant them land of their own. This was Blacks' Town, established in 1821 in the area of present Plumpton. The name was moved south-west when a village grew up in the area around the later railway station. The Native Institution, a school for Aboriginal children, established near Parramatta in 1814, was moved to the same area by Governor Brisbane in 1823. The Native Institution had been established by William Shelley, a missionary who had come from Tahiti, and Mrs Macquarie is said to have taken a great interest in the scheme, teaching the women and girls sewing and singing. However, the idea gradually failed owing to staff shortages and the institution closed in 1825. By 1848 Blacks' Town was a deserted village.

Today's Blacktown stands on the site of two large grants: 1,200 acres, north of the present station, given to Frederick Garling in 1819, and 2,000 acres given to Robert Lethbridge in 1823. These two properties were subdivided into lots of 6 to 98 acres in the 1850s and 1860s. After 1860, when the railway line came, the suburb showed signs of revival. The station was called Blacktown Road and a small village grew up around it. In the late 1860s Mrs Chisholm's school was established, and it received government aid in 1871. A post office was opened in July 1862, the year when the name of the suburb was officially changed to Blacktown. In 1871 the increasing population necessitated the opening of a public school.

The area remained semi-rural until after the Second World War. The population explosion of the 1960s turned it into a thriving area, a shopping mecca for nearby suburbs. Blacktown has a number of fine educational institutions, a large hospital and the second largest recreation club in New South Wales. Blacktown is also the

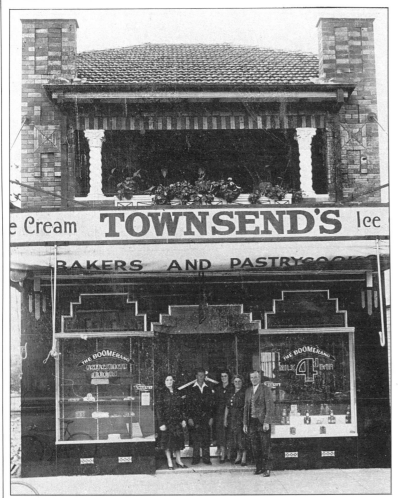

The proud owners outside "The Boomerang Refreshment Rooms", Main Street, Blacktown, c. 1930

railway junction of the Richmond line, which was opened in 1864. Blacktown Shire Council was established in 1906 and the first council chambers were opened in 1912.

The full and interesting story of the Blacktown Aborigines has never been written, because of lack of information about the traditions and culture of the tribes that lived there. The area is rich in red sandstone, and some stone tools have been located over the years. The style of the artefacts already found belongs to the past thousand or more years.

## BLAIRMOUNT
*City of Campbelltown*
Location: 50 kilometres south-west of Sydney west of the Hume Highway

This suburb of Campbelltown was an area of vineyards and wine culture in the nineteenth century. By 1912, there were many dairy farms, and one of note was owned by a family named Dean. Between 1920 and 1940 Blairmount's character changed once more: a Mr Young was breeding Clydesdale horses and some sheep in the area. Young was a manager of the Commonwealth Wool Company.

In 1986 Blairmount was a designated area only, and its

boundaries could be subject to rationalisation when final detailed planning proposals are accepted by the council.

## BLAKEHURST
*Municipality of Kogarah*
Location: 18 kilometres south of Sydney on the Georges River

William Blake, a road assessor who was appointed postmaster for the Cooks River in 1863, gave his name to this pleasant suburb on the western shore of Kogarah Bay on Georges River. Blake's father ran a small farm in this area, which was part of the grant of 75 acres made to Robert Townson in 1808. The Aborigines called the whole district Coggery, which means "a place where rushes grow". Later this became Kogarah, now a suburb north of the head of the bay.

Blakehurst has a comfortable residential air; its homes are individual in design, and there is a pleasing lack of high-rise. The land is hilly and the bushland setting has been retained as far as possible. Many homes have wide vistas to Kogarah Bay.

Blakehurst is serviced by buses, and its nearest railway station and major shopping centre is Hurstville, which has a convenient train service to the city and eastern suburbs. Carss Bush Park, a nature spot with many native birds, an olympic pool and swimming baths, has a long frontage to Kogarah Bay.

Tom Ugly's Point is the southernmost part of this suburb, a long strip of land where the Georges River Bridge crosses from Sylvania. The point is said to have been named after a local resident called Tom Huxley, whose name was transformed by

The Sea Breeze Hotel on the Princes Highway at Tom Ugly's Point was a popular pit stop for river crossers, 1927

mispronunciation by the local Aborigines.

When the punt service was established at Tom Ugly's Point in 1864, Thomas Holt (see Sutherland) promised to donate £30 annually to help keep the service operating, seeing it as a vital link in establishing the road from Sydney south to the Wollongong area. In 1883 a government punt was introduced, to be replaced later by vehicular ferries and in 1929 by the Georges River Bridge.

## BLUES POINT

*Municipality of North Sydney*
Location: A locality 5 kilometres north of Sydney extending into Port Jackson

A curving finger of land jutting out into Sydney Harbour between Berry Bay and Lavender Bay, Blues Point has a strong identity of its own.

In 1817, Billy Blue, a West Indian immigrant, was granted 80 acres, called Northampton Farm, on the north side of the harbour. Billy Blue, popularly known as the Old Commodore, ran a ferry from a point he called Blue's Point across to Millers Point, the eastern head of Darling Harbour. He also had the task of preventing smuggling from the south side to the north, but in 1818 he was convicted of smuggling rum ashore and was dismissed from his positions as constable and watchman.

Governor Macquarie had a great regard for Billy Blue, and helped

him to increase his fleet of small boats. His grant would be worth millions on today's real estate market, so choice is its position. Billy Blue lived to be a hale and hearty 97-year-old. He died in 1834. The point named after him is now a park, with magnificent views of Port Jackson.

Billy Blue, from a lithograph published in Sydney in the early 1830s

# BONDI
*Municipalities of Waverley and Woollahra*

Location: 7 kilometres east of Sydney at the junction of Old South Head Road and Bondi Road reaching down to the Pacific Ocean, on the Eastern Suburbs Line (Bondi Junction)

At various times, spelled Boondi, Bundi, Bundye, and Boondye, until 1827, when the present spelling was accepted, Bondi is an Aboriginal word with the appropriate meaning of "sound of the waves breaking on the beach" or "noise of water breaking over rocks".

Almost the whole of Bondi Beach and the adjacent land was included in a 200 acre grant to the early road-builder, William Roberts, on 22 December 1809. This land was sold to Edward Smith Hall, fiery editor of the Sydney *Monitor*, as trustee for his daughter and son-in-law, in 1851 for £200. In 1856 the government acquired the beach and foreshore for £4,500, and the rest of the land was subdivided and sold between 1879 and 1935. A residential area sprang up, with both permanent residents and holiday-makers coming to the suburb.

At the northern end of the beach, another grant of 30 acres, made in 1809 to John Hurd and in 1831 regranted to Rich and Hurd, was known as Ben Buckler, the rocky headland which affords magnificent views. Legend has it that Ben Buckler was named after a convict who inhabited a cave in the cliffs and died after a fall from one of the ledges. Another version says it was originally named Benbecula by Governor Macquarie, because of its resemblance to a place in the Hebrides.

Bondi Junction was earlier known as Tea Gardens after the Waverley Tea Gardens Hotel. The licence for this hotel was granted to Alexander Gray in 1854, and the original building was set out in a large garden, where one could enjoy a cup of tea or a soft drink. The refreshments were served in delightful summerhouses surrounded by flowers and trees, and games lawns where quoits were played.

The name was changed to Bondi Junction when the first trams began the trip from Darlinghurst to the Bondi area in 1881. The building of a crossing loop line commenced in 1882, and the tramway junction off the Waverley line to Bondi (then Durham street, now Fletcher Street) opened on 24 May 1884. Bondi Junction is now a major shopping centre, at the end of the Eastern Suburbs Railway line, which opened in 1979. It is estimated that the line carries 16 million passengers a year.

An official post office was handling mail as early as 1858, and the first school opened in January 1879.

Ever-popular Bondi Beach in 1931, complete with canopied deck chairs for comfort-seekers and the sun-cautious

Another first for Bondi was more unusual. In February 1890, two sisters interested in hot-air balloon travel devised a daring act of ascending to 5,000 feet and then parachuting to earth! In 1890, when young ladies were expected to be content with embroidery and the vapours, the idea was almost scandalous. After trying their act in Maitland and Newcastle, the Van Tassell sisters set their sights on Bondi. At that time Bondi boasted a large enclosure known as the Bondi Aquarium, which was a kind of mini Luna Park, where people could enjoy roller skating, donkey and pony rides, and all the fun of the fair. The Aquarium was even lit by electric light, a distinct novelty in those days. When the manager of this fun area, Alfred Wyburn, heard of the exploits of the Van Tassells he lost no time in approaching "the only lady aeronaut in the Southern Hemisphere", as the act was billed. Daredevil Miss Van Tassell's proposed jump became quite a talking point, and on the appointed day several thousand people turned up to watch, many having paid fourpence for the tram ride to Bondi, and 1 shilling for admission to the Aquarium, where the lady proposed to land.

The ascent was publicised for 4 o'clock, but when the hour arrived, the wind was blowing in an unfavourable direction and it was too dangerous to make the attempt. Mr Frost, the stunt organiser, worked hard to placate the murmuring crowd, who stayed on in breathless anticipation. Then the wind changed. The signal was given to inflate the balloon. The bored crowd shivered with excitement, which increased as Miss Val Van Tassell appeared and, smiling happily, mounted the trapeze attached beneath the balloon. Then away she went, rising with great ease, and, to the delight of the watching thousands, executing a number of daring trapeze acts as the balloon rose higher and higher. Letting go of the trapeze, she jiggled her parachute cords with great expertise and landed, to the players' great astonishment, in the middle of a game of cricket on an oval in Coogee. Gentlemen always, the cricketers folded up the parachute and found a horse cab to take the lady back to her waiting fans at the Bondi Aquarium.

Today the residents of Bondi are mostly permanent, but since the 1920s blocks of flats and units have replaced many of the large old homes. Bondi Beach remains one of the most magnificent surfing beaches in the world, although in high summer it is hard to see the sand for people.

Bondi Aquarium, c. 1890

# BORONIA PARK
*Municipality of Hunters Hill*
Location: 11 kilometres north of Sydney between Gladesville and Hunters Hill on the Lane Cove River

Not a well-known suburb, Boronia Park is bounded to the east by the Lane Cove River. It is named after the Australian native boronia, a sweetly scented shrub still abundant in the surrounding bushland.

The suburb is residential with attractive homes in flower-filled gardens. Well known in the area is the Sir Moses Montefiore Home, "a home for the shelter and support of aged, infirm and distressed people of the Jewish faith". The original home was in Dowling Street, Sydney, in 1889, and was instituted by the Sydney Hebrew Philanthropic and Orphan Society, which was founded in 1883. It was moved to Bellevue Hill in 1923, and to its present site in 1939, where it was incorporated with the Isabella Lazarus Home for Jewish Children. Its original 40 beds, have been increased to 324 units. Sir Moses Montefiore and his family took an active part in community life in Sydney, and the name is still known in the field of philanthropy.

A splendid reserve, Boronia Park, overlooks the peaceful beauty of the Lane Cove River and is connected by a narrow strip of bushland along the river's edge to the Field of Mars Wildlife Reserve to the north-west. The Field of Mars park and cemetery form the surviving remnant of the former Field of Mars area.

# BOSSLEY PARK
*City of Fairfield*
Location: 39 kilometres west of Sydney off The Horsley Drive

In the 1850s pioneers John Brown Bossley (1810–72) and his wife, Louisa, of Edenson Park (1806–73), settled on the open plains west of Sydney. They owned one of the first stores at Cabramata.

In the late 1890s their estate was subdivided and sold. People with a liking for the open spaces bought home-sites here, and the district began to develop. Attractive golf links are situated at Bossley Bush Recreation Reserve, adjacent to the Fairfield showground and trotting track. Orphan School Creek, which runs through the reserve, received its name because nearby was land set aside for an asylum for orphans in the time of the Reverend Samuel Marsden, the first Protestant chaplain to live at Parramatta.

Cowpasture Road, running through the western part of Bossley Park, was the first road from Sydney to Camden. The Cowpastures was the first name given to the Camden area, as cattle that had strayed there from the early Sydney herd had multiplied in this area rich in lush grass. Appropriately a hill in the vicinity was named Taurus Hill on a map drawn by First Fleet diarist David Collins.

Bossley Park is adjacent to Prairiewood and to Fairfield West, with access to high schools and shopping facilities in Fairfield. The suburb is developing rapidly, a far cry from those first quiet days when John Brown Bossley settled in the area that now bears his name.

# BOTANY
*Municipality of Botany*
Location: 10 kilometres south of Sydney on the northern shore of Botany Bay

On 29 April 1770 Captain James Cook made his first landfall in Australia at Botany Bay. The *Endeavour*'s botanist, Joseph Banks, and his Swedish assistant, Daniel Solander, spent several days ashore collecting vast numbers of previously unknown plants. Cook was in two minds about a suitable name for the bay — his journal first refers to it as Sting Rays' Harbour, then as Botanist Bay, then both were crossed out and the present Botany Bay inserted, no doubt because of Banks and Solander's work. Since its name comes from the bay on which it stands, Botany can well claim to have the oldest place name in Australia.

Cook's recommendation and Banks's enthusiasm were largely responsible for the British government's decision to found a penal settlement at Botany Bay. When Governor Phillip arrived in mid-summer eighteen years after Cook, however, he found the harbour shallow and exposed, and the shore swampy and lacking sources of fresh water. As a result, the First Fleet sailed on to Port Jackson, finding a more suitable site for settlement at Sydney Cove.

Botany was first planned as an agricultural district, and the principal industry was to be market gardening. Instead it became an industrial area, boasting a fellmonger's yard and a slaughter works. As early as 1809, Mr E. Redmond came to settle in the district, but the first important developer was Simeon Lord (1771–1840), who built a fulling mill in 1815 on the site that later became that of the old

Ultimately subdivided into flats, the Sir Joseph Banks Hotel, in Anniversary Road, Botany, was once part of a unique private zoological garden. This picture was taken around 1933

waterworks. In 1823 he received a grant of 600 acres, followed by further grants. Part of the estate was subdivided in 1859, to become Booralee Township, and the rest was subdivided by 1887. Lord, "the merchant prince of Botany Bay", manufactured fine wool cloth, and he was also one of the merchants instrumental in the founding of Sydney Hospital. He gave land for the sites of two early churches in Botany, and Lord Street is named after him. Banksia Street, Sir Joseph Banks Park and Booralee Park all commemorate those early days.

The Sydney Waterworks were established in Botany in 1858 and were fed by the many springs in the area. In 1886, the last year of full pumping, 1,864 million gallons of water were supplied to Sydney from these waterworks. Although the scheme was Sydney's major source of water for thirty years, it did not supply water to the Botany area, and local residents depended

on natural sources and tanks.

Another first in Botany was the private zoo at the Sir Joseph Banks Hotel. Here birds of all varieties, an elephant and a Bengal tiger were inspected by guests who came to enjoy a ten-course meal at the hotel. When the zoo owner died, and the council did not wish to maintain the zoo, the former owner's widow poisoned the lot!

Botany was also prominent in encouraging early sportsmen who showed talent as runners. Frank Smith, who bought the Sir Joseph Banks Hotel in 1884, promoted the race known as the St Patrick's Day Handicap. Cinder tracks were laid down at the hotel, and the sport increased in popularity. From these beginnings the famous Botany Harriers made their appearance. These enthusiastic long distance runners were a regular sight from 1907, when the Botany Harriers Club was formed.

Botany Cemetery, established in 1886, is located in the neighbouring municipality of Randwick, but it is important for its associations with many of the men and women who pioneered

the district's development. In 1888 Botany was proclaimed a municipality. In 1934 Botany Bay was declared a port, although its development as a port had begun in 1885 when a wharf was constructed. In 1961 redevelopment of the port began and in 1979 the Port Botany container terminal complex and Australian National Lines terminal came into operation.

## BRADBURY

*City of Campbelltown*
Location: 54 kilometres
south-west of Sydney off Appin
Road

A new residential suburb south of Campbelltown, bounded on the west by Appin Road, Bradbury nevertheless has a long history going back to the governorship of Lachlan Macquarie (1810–21).

An early farmer in Campbelltown South was William Bradbury. He was known to Governor Macquarie, who wrote in his diary on Monday, 14 January 1822: "On our arrival at Campbelltown we ordered breakfast at Bradbury's. Mr Bradbury is now building a very good two storey brick house on his own farm … as an inn for the accommodation of the public, and having asked me to give his farm a name, I have called it Bradbury Park."

The suburb took its name from Macquarie's choice for that early farm. A reserve at the junction of The Parkway and Appin Road, Bradbury Park and Bradbury Avenue also commemorate that early family. In 1822 Bradbury opened the inn Macquarie had mentioned, and by 1828 he owned between 6,000 and 7,000 acres nearby. He died in 1857.

Fisher's Ghost Creek, which runs through Bradbury Park, recalls an event that has become part of Sydney's folk history. In 1826 John Farley declared that he had seen a ghost at Campbelltown. He recognised it as Frederick Fisher, who had disappeared on 17 June 1826 and was reported as having left the district. Everyone thought Farley was dreaming or drunk. No one would listen. Farley, however, pleaded with the police to dig over the area near the creek. Fisher's body was found and George Worrall was tried for the crime, found guilty and executed.

Eventually the Bradbury estate was subdivided, houses were built and families began to settle in this suburb. The Convent of the Good Samaritan and St John's School are in St John's Road.

# BRADFIELD
*Municipality of Ku-ring-gai*
Location: A neighbourhood 14 kilometres north-west of Sydney, south of Killara

This small neighbourhood, south of Killara, was named in 1924 after Dr J. J. C. Bradfield, chief engineer during the construction of the Sydney Harbour Bridge. The approach to the bridge, the Bradfield Highway, is also named after him, and a federal parliamentary electorate bears his name.

Bradfield Park was an RAAF camp during the Second World War, and after the war it became a reception centre for migrants from Europe.

Famous people are remembered by some of the street names in the area. Lady Game Drive commemorates the wife of a governor of New South Wales (1930–35) and Fiddens Wharf Road is named after Joseph Fiddens, a Scottish convict who was a timber-getter in the area (see Killara). The wharf, at the foot of the road meeting the Lane Cove River, was used for loading timber.

Dr John J. C. Bradfield

# BRIGTON-LE-SANDS
*Municipality of Rockdale*
Location: 13 kilometres south of Sydney on the western shore of Botany Bay

In the 1880s a businessman and land-owner in this area, named Thomas Saywell, founded a new development on the western shore of Botany Bay. He called this suburb New Brighton, after the famous English seaside resort. His dream was to create a seaside holiday place for working-class people. He built a fine hotel, swimming baths and picnic facilities, and had a private steam tram connected to carry people from Rockdale station to the beach. The venture was a huge success, and its instigator made a fortune. To avoid confusion with the English Brighton, it became known as Brighton-le-Sands. Later the government took over the tram, and eventually it was replaced by buses. The beach front known as Seven Mile Beach was changed in 1874 to Lady Robinson's Beach, after the wife of the governor of New South Wales from 1872 to 1879, Sir Hercules Robinson.

But the history of this attractive suburb did not run as smoothly as Saywell had hoped. After a long run of popularity, he fell foul of the law and the hotel lost its liquor licence. The most imposing holiday hotel in Sydney suddenly went "dry", became less popular and began to look like a white elephant. However, Thomas Saywell, whose Huguenot ancestors had survived persecution in France by migrating to Britain, came up with a new idea: he offered the failing hotel to the Scots College and soon the following advertisement appeared in the Sydney press in 1893: "What has hitherto been known as the

The ocean baths at Brighton-le-Sands, 1931, from the Allen Family Album

New Brighton Hotel, Lady Robinson's Beach, is to be known as the Scots College, henceforth. The building is a large and commodious one, particularly well adapted to college purposes. Classrooms have been formed on the ground floor and the other large rooms have been utilised in a manner best suited to the requirements of a first-class educational institution. The dormitories are well lighted and well ventilated, and health as well as education has been carefully studied."

The project had been initiated in 1890, when the Presbyterian Assembly appointed a committee with instructions to take immediate action to establish a boys college in Sydney. The committee favoured the Botany coastline and saw in the failing hotel an ideal opportunity to establish the school immediately without the delay of building. When the school opened in January 1893, the ceremony was conducted by the state governor, the Earl of Jersey. He travelled on a vice-regal train to Rockdale, where the platform was decorated in honour of the event. The party then rode on Saywell's tram to the former hotel, where huge crowds waited to cheer and applaud at the opening ceremony.

You might think that all was peaceful once the school commenced its activities, but nothing was further from the truth. The boys were distracted by holiday-makers using Lady Robinson's Beach, and the beautiful seaside landscape was a constant temptation to skip classes. Another hazard was the proximity of the Brighton Racing Club, established in 1895. The course had been constructed immediately behind the building that housed Scots College, and masters found their pupils keeping books other than their lesson books and studying horse form along with their regular lessons. Eventually the school authorities decided to move away from this area of temptation, and Scots College was transferred to the more sedate suburb of Bellevue Hill.

Brighton-le-Sands continued to be a popular bathing resort. In today's more permissive society, the wording of the notice that appeared on the ladies' section of the swimming baths will raise a smile. It read "Gentlemen pass by: only blackguards peep in". Certainly a sign of the Victorian era!

# BRONTE

*Municipality of Waverley*
Location: 8 kilometres east of
Sydney facing the Pacific Ocean

Bronte is a beachside suburb
between Tamarama and Clovelly.
Its name is of Italian origin, and,
like many of Sydney's suburbs, it
was named after an early settler's
home.

In 1842 a free settler, Robert
Lowe (1811–92), who became
Viscount Sherbrooke, arrived in
the colony. A distant relative of
Governor Gipps, he was an
Oxford graduate, and had been
called to the Bar in the United
Kingdom. Once in the colony, he
purchased 42 acres of land from the
colonial architect Mortimer Lewis
(1796–1879), who had bought up
most of the beach frontage at
Bronte in the 1830s and had
already laid the foundations of a
house. Lowe had the house
finished and moved in 1845. He
called his new home Bronte House
in honour of Lord Nelson who
was Duke of Bronte, a place in
Sicily. The suburb later took its
name from Robert Lowe's house,
which faced Nelson Bay, also
named in honour of Lord Nelson,
hero of the Battle of Trafalgar.

Lowe became a member of the
New South Wales Legislative
Council and worked hard to pass
an act that abolished imprisonment
for debt. He was a courageous
fighter and took strong action
when a plan was put forward in
1849 to reintroduce convict
transportation. He stayed in New
South Wales for seven years and
then returned to London to
become a leader writer on *The
Times*. His opinion of Australians
in general was rather critical.
"Australians, it must be
confessed," he wrote, "take only a
languid interest in the brief annals
of their community."

Bronte House is still standing in
Bronte Road. It is in good
condition and remains a splendid
example of Mortimer Lewis's
colonial style of architecture.

Bronte Beach, 1912

## BROOKLYN
*Shire of Hornsby*
Location: 51 kilometres north of
Sydney on the Hawkesbury River,
on the Main Northern Line
(Hawkesbury River)

This small settlement, on the banks
of the Hawkesbury River, takes its
name from Brooklyn, New York,
but in a rather indirect way. The
first rail bridge over the
Hawkesbury was tendered for and
built by the Union Bridge
Company of America, which
received world acclaim for
building the Brooklyn Bridge in
New York. The name of the
suburb honours the company by
being named after the Brooklyn
Bridge. The Hawkesbury rail
bridge was completed in 1899; the
first piles remain beside the new
bridge, completed in 1946. In 1888
when the railway from Hornsby
was completed, the station was
called Brooklyn, but it was then
changed in 1890 to Hawkesbury,
and in 1906 to Hawkesbury River.

The area, which was discovered
by Governor Phillip in 1789, was
originally called Peat's Ferry. In
1840, 100 acres were purchased
there by two men called King
and Robinson and subdivided. The
half-time school established in the
district in 1875 was called Peat's
Ferry School. In 1884 it became a
full-time school, catering for the
childen of railway workers, and in
1888 the name was changed to
Brooklyn.

Brooklyn has the charm of both
an English village and a small
Australian country town. It is the
gateway to the Hawkesbury River,
a beautiful waterway considered to
be one of the most scenic rivers in
the world. English novelist
Anthony Trollope in the 1870s
described the river: "the
Hawkesbury has neither castles nor
islands, nor has it bright, clear
waters like the Rhine: but the
headlands are higher, the bluffs are
bolder, and the turns and
manoeuvres of the course which
the waters have made for
themselves are grander than those
of the European River".

What a splendid and apt
description of the river, which was
also the life-line for settlers up the
Hawkesbury. In the early 1900s
Brooklyn, with its little gaggle of
shops was an important source of
necessary food supplies, and indeed
a social centre for the area's
orchardists and boatbuilders. To
go down to Brooklyn was like a
trip to town for those early settlers.

## BROOKVALE
*Shire of Warringah*
Location: 16 kilometres north of
Sydney on Pittwater Road

The first man to acquire land in
this district west of Curl Curl on
the northern beaches was William
Frederick Parker. The date was
1836, and the area, then known as
Greendale, was a heavily timbered
valley between hills and the sea.
Parker was given convict labour to
help him clear his land, and he
continued to puchase until his
property covered 158 acres. He
built a house on his land, near
today's William Street, and named
it Brookvale. A village grew up
around it, but the present suburb
stands mostly on the 100 acre grant
held by a Mr Charlton.

In 1873 Sydney Alexander
Malcolm, bought land at
Greendale. Three brooks ran
through his property, and he
decided to call his residence
Brookvale House. This second
house named Brookvale stood near
the entrance to the present
Warringah Mall Shopping Centre.

In the 1880s, when Greendale was
still a struggling hamlet, confusion
began to arise with another
Greendale, near Bringelly
south-west of Sydney, so it was
decided to rename the northern
suburb Brookvale, after the two
houses of that name.

A succession of Malcolm
descendants inhabited Brookvale
House, which was finally sold and
demolished in the 1960s, to make
way for the shopping mall. The
Malcolm family had wide interests
in shipping freight from Sydney to
China, and Brookvale House, with
its 11 acres of gardens, was a
Sydney showpiece at the turn of
the century. The names Brookvale
Creek and Greendale Creek both
recall the early settlement of the
district.

In 1910 the steam tramline from
Manly was extended to Brookvale.
The tram was decorated with
flowers, and a ribbon-cutting
ceremony took place when Mr
Lee, the minister for works,
declared the new project ready for
regular passengers. The journey
from Manly to Brookvale in those
days took twenty-three minutes.

These days Brookvale is a busy
residential suburb, with light
industries on its boundaries. The
Brookvale Show is held annually at
Brookvale Oval, where some of
the most exciting and lively
football matches in the Sydney area
are also held each season.
Warringah Shire is based in
Brookvale.

# BURRANEER

*Shire of Sutherland*
Location: 26 kilometres south of
Sydney on the northern shore of
Port Hacking

This suburb was first named
Burrameer Bay, an Aboriginal
word meaning "point of the bay",
in 1827 when Surveyor Robert
Dixon used Aboriginal names to
identify many of the bays in this
area. In 1858 Mary and Andrew
Webster paid £108 15s, plus a
yearly quit rent of a peppercorn,
for their land. This term-of-rate
was not unusual in those days.
Land sales increased in the 1860s.
James Wilson purchased land there
in 1862, paying £252 for his block
of 252 acres. Four years later, in
1866, he sold to Thomas Holt, a
well-known land-owner in the
Sutherland area who added it to his
already huge 12,000 acre estate (see
Sutherland). In 1863, a Mr Webster
sold his land to Dominick Dolan.

Burraneer occupies the peninsula
separating Burraneer Bay from
Gunnamatta Bay, the headwaters
of which are about 100 metres
from the Cronulla railway station.
One small and beautiful inlet is
Dolans Bay, on the western side of
Burraneer Bay. Many attractive
homes are tucked among the
natural bushland.

# BURWOOD

*Municipality of Burwood*
Location: 12 kilometres west of
Sydney between Parramatta Road
and the Hume Highway, on the
Main Suburban Line

A grant of 260 acres was made to
Captain Thomas Rowley
(1748–1806) of the New South
Wales Corps in 1799. He called his
property Burwood Farm, probably
after Burwood in Cornwall,
England, where he had lived as a
young man. Part of that grant is
now Burwood Park. Later grants
increased his holding to 750 acres,
which extended from Parramatta
Road almost to Nicholson Street,
and from The Boulevarde to
Croydon station. Rowley's farm
gave the suburb its name.

On Rowley's death in 1806, his
will stipulated that the property
was not to be sold by the trustees.
After the original trustees left for
England, Governor Macquarie
nominated Thomas Moore as
trustee, and in 1812 the property
was sold to Alexander Riley for
£520. His son, W. E. Riley,
inherited it in 1833, but by that
time Rowley's children had come
of age and found that the property
had been disposed of contrary to
the will. They won the subsequent
court action and the estate was
divided among them. From 1834
the land was gradually subdivided
and sold.

The Bath Arms, established in
1834 on the corner of Parramatta

A humorous scene captured by Charles
Kerry at Burwood Superior Public School.
Those toward the back must certainly have
thought they were escaping the
schoolmaster's critical eye

and Burwood Roads, is the most famous of the inns established on Parramatta Road. It became a staging place between Sydney and Parramatta. It was built in 1930. Two other well-known inns in those days were the Red Lion and the Railway Hotel.

There were a few small dairy farms in early Burwood, and some settler families established market gardens. Cattle grazed in pastures which today are the streets and roads lined with Federation houses. Although the soil in the area is a yellowish clay suitable for brickmaking, and both sandstone and bluestone (basalt) were available, there was no manufacturing of any kind at first. Burwood Brickworks opened in 1913.

Burwood remained a roadside village until the coming of the railway line from Sydney to Parramatta in 1855, when it became one of the original stations on the line. From the late 1850s, city businessmen began to build large houses in the suburb. Humberstone, for instance, was built in 1869 by John Dawson; it is now St Anthony's Home. The Priory was built in the 1870s by Mowbray Forrest. Some of the beautiful homes in the second half of the nineteenth century serve the community today. E. T. Penfold's home, Woodstock, built in 1873, became the Woodstock Community Centre during the Second World War. It was built to the design of architect John Sulman (1849–1934) for Josiah Mullens. Elim in Shaftesbury Road, once the home of John A. Young, managing director of Lewis Berger's paint works at Rhodes, has become a wedding reception centre.

A public school opened in April 1858, and the post office followed in October 1861. St Paul's Church of England, still standing in Burwood Road, was designed by Edmund Blacket (1817–73) and erected in 1871. At about this time Burwood began to develop as a model suburb, a far cry from its first farming days. The Hoskins family were notable builders who subdivided a large estate, including the present Appian Way, and built some splendid Federation-style homes. About forty houses were constructed on the estate, which is thought to have been sold in 1904.

Burwood has become a popular residential suburb with fast, convenient train services to the city, and a good selection of school and shopping facilities. Westfield Shopping Town, opposite Burwood Park, has about ninety shops, and Burwood Plaza, near the railway station, has sixty shops. These two large complexes opened in 1967 and 1978 respectively. Burwood now has a huge population, with a big migrant influence.

# BUSBY
*City of Liverpool*
Location: 37 kilometres south-west of Sydney, west of Liverpool

A suburb in the neighbourhood of Green Valley, which was developed by the housing commission in the 1960s and 1970s, Busby was established in 1964. It was named after James Busby (1800–71), a pioneer viticulturalist who grew the first grapes in the area in the 1820s. He was the son of John Busby (1765–1857), the engineer who constructed the scheme to pipe water from Centennial Park to Hyde Park, saving the early colony from a serious shortage of clean

James Busby

water. This scheme, finished in 1837 and known as a miracle of engineering, is marked by a fountain in Hyde Park, Sydney.

In 1825 James Busby was appointed manager of the farm of the boys orphan school at Bulls Head, north of the present suburb of Busby; Orphan School Creek commemorates this institution. Busby taught vine-growing to the boys in return for one-third of the produce of the farm. However, the farm closed, and the vine-growing venture failed. Busby wrote two books on viticulture in the colony: *A Treatise on the Culture of the Vine and the Art of Making Wine* (1825) and *A Manual of Plain Directions for Planting and Cultivating Vineyards and for Making Wine in New South Wales* (1830) both published in Sydney. In 1831 he visited the vineyards of Spain and France and collected seeds and cuttings for the Botanic Gardens in Sydney. Governor Darling employed Busby for a time as a collector of internal revenue. From 1832 to 1839 he was British resident in New Zealand, where he died in 1871. The district of Busby can feel proud of its clever and hard-working namesake.

The area today is residential, but its recent past as a dairying district is recalled by streets named after cattle breeds, such as Devon, Ayrshire, Guernsey, Hereford and Aberdeen. Whitlam Park, named after former prime minister Gough Whitlam, is a large reserve along Green Valley Creek in the north of the suburb.

## CABARITA
*Municipality of Concord*
Location: 16 kilometres west of Sydney on the Parramatta River

This suburb is known by an Aboriginal word meaning, appropriately, "by the water". Part of the suburb was originally granted in 1795 to David Anderson, a private soldier in the New South Wales Corps. The grant was described as being at "Caberita Point, at the upper part of the Harbour".

Cabarita Park, a pleasant picnic area on Cabarita Point, was known as Correy's Gardens in the 1880s. This part of the river was the venue for early regattas, including the GPS schools' Head of the River before these races were moved to the Nepean River. The park was dedicated for public use in 1880. The pavilion from which the Earl of Hopetoun, the governor-general, proclaimed the establishment of the Commonwealth of Australia in 1901 was later moved from Centennial Park to Cabarita Park.

Cabarita was once linked to Burwood station by tram, and the park was popular for family picnics. There was also a segregated swimming pool, with one half for men and boys, the other for women and girls. Husbands and wives, as well as lovers, would lean on the dividing fence for a chat as the water swirled around their legs.

France Bay, Exile Bay, and Canada Bay, adjacent to the park, commemorate a group of fifty-eight French-Canadian exiles. After an 1838 rebellion in Canada these prisoners were sent to New South Wales and held in the Longbottom Stockade in Concord, at which time the three bays received these appropriate names.

Factories have changed the character of the Concord area, but it still retains a strong residential element.

Poster advertising the "opening up" of Cabarita, 31 July 1907

## CABRAMATTA
*City of Fairfield*
Location: 30 kilometres south-west of Sydney off Cabramatta Road, on the Main Southern Line

The origin of this suburb's name is uncertain, but the Reverend John Dunmore Lang claimed that it came from an Aboriginal word for an edible fresh-water grub, the "cabra", joined to "matta", a point or jutting out piece of land.

The original site of settlement at Cabramatta was on South Creek, where the later road from Cabramatta to Woodville Road crossed the railway line, where the suburb of Rossmore now stands.

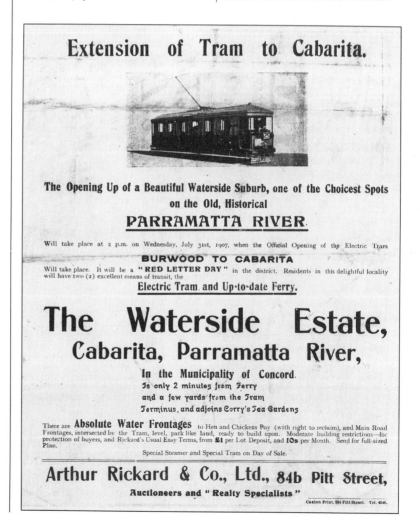

# Extension of Tram to Cabarita.

The Opening Up of a Beautiful Waterside Suburb, one of the Choicest Spots on the Old, Historical
## PARRAMATTA RIVER.

Will take place at 2 p.m. on Wednesday, July 31st, 1907, when the Official Opening of the Electric Tram

### BURWOOD TO CABARITA

Will take place. It will be a "RED LETTER DAY" in the district. Residents in this delightful locality will have two (2) excellent means of transit, the
**Electric Tram and Up-to-date Ferry.**

# The Waterside Estate,
## Cabarita, Parramatta River,

In the Municipality of Concord.
Is only 2 minutes from Ferry
and a few yards from the Tram
Terminus, and adjoins Corry's Tea Gardens

There are **Absolute Water Frontages** to Hen and Chickens Bay (with right to reclaim), and Main Road Frontages, intersected by the Tram, level, park like land, ready to build upon. Moderate building restrictions—for protection of buyers, and Rickard's Usual Easy Terms, from £1 per Lot Deposit, and 10s per Month. Send for full-sized Plan.

Special Steamer and Special Tram on Day of Sale.

## Arthur Rickard & Co., Ltd., 84b Pitt Street,
**Auctioneers and "Realty Specialists"**

Caxton Print, 234 Pitt Street. Tel. 4546.

In about 1795, an early settler named Hatfield called the area Moonshine Run, because it was so heavily timbered that in parts moonlight could not penetrate. Cabramatta's first settlers were Irish political prisoners, one of whom, Joseph Hole, received a 100 acre grant on the creek. This property later became the home of the Bull Family, who called their property Cabramatta Park. When the small village formed around there in about 1814, it took the name of this early estate. In 1803, 12,300 acres were granted for the benefit of the Orphan Institution to Samuel Marsden, John Palmer and John Harris. Michael Murphy acquired the land in about 1833 and called it Longfield Estate. It was subdivided between 1883 and 1914. An 1818 grant of 691 acres to Catherine Prout was eventually subdivided by Hardie and Gorman.

Cabramatta was known chiefly for agriculture, and its early settlers worked on freehold and leasehold farms and dairies. The area was very isolated and relied on its neighbour Liverpool for supplies and the maintenance of law and order.

By 1870 Cabramatta was becoming well established. In 1856 the railway came as far as Liverpool, but Cabramatta did not get a station until the early 1870s. The new railway station was operated by Mr J. Williams. A school opened in 1882, and a post office in 1886.

Today Cabramatta is a busy place, with a large multi-lingual population. Cabramatta Settlement Centre in Alick Street, behind Cabramatta High School, is a housing centre for many migrants in their early days in this state, and some settle in the district.

Cabramatta Sports Ground, between Cabramatta Creek and Jasmine Crescent, and Warwick Farm Racecourse and Motor Racing Circuit are within easy driving distance. Adding to Cabramatta's fame is the fact it was once the home of Australia's controversial prime minister, Gough Whitlam. The municipality of Cabramatta and Canley Vale broke away from Liverpool in 1892 and in 1948 became part of Fairfield.

# CAMBRIDGE PARK

*City of Penrith*
Location: 53 kilometres west of Sydney, north of Penrith

Cambridge Park borders the eastern side of Richmond Road leading north from Penrith. Phillip Parker King, son of Governor King, was one of the first settlers here. He received a grant of 1,500 acres in 1831 and he named his property Cambridge Park after a family friend, the Duke of Cambridge.

In the early 1880s King's estate was subdivided and sold as lots suitable for orchards and vineyards. The new neighbourhood took the name Cambridge Park, after King's early grant.

# CAMELLIA

*City of Parramatta*
Location: 23 kilometres west of Sydney on the Parramatta River, on the Carlingford Line

Camellia is an industrial suburb on the south bank of the Parramatta River, adjoining Rosehill. The railway station, which was opened in 1885, was originally known as Subiaco, but this caused confusion as Subiaco was also the name of the mansion originally known as the Vineyard built by Hannibal Macarthur (John Macarthur's nephew) on the opposite side of the river at Rydalmere. The station's name was altered to Camellia in 1901, after the nearby garden, Camellia Grove Nursery, belonging to Silas Sheather, who specialised in growing camellias. The land leased in 1852 to Silas Sheather was part of the Macarthur consolidated estate (Elizabeth Farm) of 850 acres.

The wife of convict Christopher McGee, who occupied land in the area, is buried in this suburb with her baby daughter. Elinor McGee, the worse for drink, and her child were drowned in the Parramatta River in 1793 while on their way home by boat from Sydney. Their grave, one of the oldest in New South Wales, is on the river bank at Camellia, near the James Hardie & Company factory. The company was established at Camellia in 1916 to manufacture asbestos-cement sheets.

Camellia is the site of one of the state's largest oil-seed crushing plants, Meggitt Limited. This firm has been in the Parramatta area since 1908 and is able to crush up to 360 tonnes of seed a day, turning it into oil and meal for the stock-feed industry. The main seeds crushed are sunflower and soya bean.

Rosehill Racecourse forms the suburb's southern boundary.

# CAMMERAY

*Municipality of North Sydney*
Location: 5 kilometres north of
Sydney east of the Pacific Highway

A small suburb, with Crows Nest,
Naremburn and Cremorne as its
neighbours, Cammeray became a
popular residential district in the
second half of the nineteenth
century. It takes its name from an
Aboriginal tribe, the chief
inhabitants of the early St
Leonards–North Sydney area, the
Cammeraygal tribe, reputed to be
a group of fierce fighters.

Some early settlers established
dairy farms in Cammeray. One of
the largest was on Folly Point,
which overlooks Middle Harbour
and today is lined with neat rows
of homes and gardens. In 1828, Sir
Thomas Mitchell's plan of the
North Shore shows Alfred Thrupp
the holder of a land grant that
included Folly Point (not so named
at that time). The land was later
acquired by a man named Levy,
who built a house on the point.
But he mixed the mortar with salt
water, and the house collapsed.
Undaunted, he repeated the
process, and the same thing
happened again. The point became
known as Folly Point.

Buried in St Thomas's Church
of England cemetery, North
Sydney, is Australian poet,
Barcroft Boake (1866–92), who
died tragically by his own hand in
1892. A sensitive, talented young
man, whose work had been praised
by the critic J. F. Archibald, Boake
seemed obsessed with death and
tragedy, which revealed itself in
much of his verse. His ballads were
well-thought-of by Henry
Lawson, himself a tragic figure.
Boake spent much of his early life
working in the Australian outback,
and this influence can also be
detected in his poems. In 1891 his

Barcroft Boake

father's photographic business
failed. At about the same time
some close relatives died, and the
young poet became very
depressed. In 1892 he went
tramping in the Cammeray bush,
his favourite pastime, and was
found some hours later hanging by
a stockwhip from one of the large
trees near Folly Point.

# CAMPBELLTOWN

*City of Campbelltown*
Location: 51 kilometres
south-west of Sydney, on the Main
Southern Line

Like Parramatta and Liverpool,
Campbelltown began its life as an
isolated country village. By the
1961 census, however, it was
described as "a city with a
population of 16,374 people",
south-west of Macquarie Fields.

Development of the area began
in the time of Governor Macquarie
(1810–21). In November 1810
Macquarie made a tour of
inspection when he was planning
the sites of towns for new settlers,
and decided that the land between
Bunburry Curran Creek and the

Georges River should form a new
district, which he named Airds,
after his wife's family estate. The
first land grants were made
between January 1810 and October
1811, when William Redfern
received 800 acres; Henry Kable,
200 acres; Joseph Inch, 300 acres in
Guise Road; James Underwood,
200 acres; John Laurie, 50 acres;
and James Meehan, a combined
grant of 1,140 acres in Minto and
Airds.

William Redfern (1774?–1833)
called his estate Campbell Fields in
honour of the governor's wife,
who had been a Miss Campbell
before her marriage. Redfern
owned a great deal of land in other
areas, but the farm at Airds became
his favourite property. The soil
encouraged good crops, and the
pure air and feeling of freedom
created a sense of peace and
prosperity. Commissioner Bigge,
sent out by the British government
during Macquarie's governorship,
was most impressed with this
district. His report to the British
House of Commons on 19 June
1822 confirmed this: "Another
fertile district, that of Airds, has
been occupied principally by small
settlers of the class of emancipated
convicts, who are proceeding in
the same cause of rapid exhaustion
of their lands without regard to
their future means of support . . .
The farm of Mr Redfern, though
not consisting of good land, has
begun to exhibit the improved
system of English husbandry, and
reflects credit upon the intelligence
and spirit with which the
expensive operation of clearing the
land from trees has been
conducted."

In those early days Airds was
heavily wooded, and Bigge's poor
opinion of the soil as being "thin
and poor for cultivation" was
perhaps justified as the area proved
to be so suited for breeding and

Queen Street, Campbelltown, looking south, c. 1886

raising cattle and sheep that Macquarie's original idea of small settlement farms was lost. By 1816 most of the holdings in Airds were large.

By 1820 Airds had grown to the extent that the governor decided to found the last of what have been called the Macquarie Towns, and he named the new area Campbell Town in honour of his wife, Elizabeth. Surveyor Robert Hoddle measured the area in 1826 and described the allotments available "at a Quit Rent of 2 pence per square perch". By 1831 fifteen people had been given permission to take possession of the allotments.

Michael Byrne, a publican, was one of the original grantees. In 1842 he built Glenalvon, a two-storeyed colonial Georgian-style home situated in Lithgow Street, a splendid example of the type of house erected at that time. Byrne later mortgaged the property to his brother-in-law,

John Keighran, who lived at Glenalvon until his death in 1858. Between 1859 and 1878 the house was let, and it was then sold to the Fieldhouse brothers. One of the later tenants was Dr Mawson, brother of the Antarctic explorer, Sir Douglas Mawson.

Some of the old houses still standing in Campbelltown are colonial mansions, featuring smooth-cut stone and polished native-grown cedar. In Queen Street four of these gems form a harmonious group. They are all two-storeyed residences, probably erected in the 1840s, and bearing the mark of Georgian architecture. One is said to have been the staging post for the Cobb & Co. coaches passing through with passengers and mail. The wide coach entrance lends credibility to this claim.

Francis Lawless, a government overseer of bricklayers, built the main fabric of St Peter's Church of England, which was designed by Francis Greenway in Georgian colonial style. The church opened on 29 June 1823, but was dedicated

later. Legend has it that the first church service in the building was a Catholic mass, which was being held out-of-doors when a sudden downpour forced the congregation to take shelter in the unfinished St Peter's, where the service continued.

St John's Cemetery, which was built on the eastern slope of Campbelltown, is the resting place of James Ruse (1760–1837), the first ex-convict to seek a land grant. In April 1791 he received title to his land, at Parramatta, the first grant issued in New South Wales. He later farmed at Windsor, and finally in this area.

In 1825 Campbelltown's water supply was desperately low and a new site for the town was mooted. Nothing happened, however, and in 1832 the worried citizens appealed to the governor to have a reservoir built. Sir Thomas Mitchell, the then surveyor-general, had a site surveyed where two creeks met, but because of squabbles and delays work did not start until 1838. Two years later, the reservoir, and a cattle tank for stock water, were completed. The effect on Campbelltown was one of immediate jubilation. The town advanced rapidly, many new houses were built, and property values increased. A drought in 1867 caused the water level to fall, but street watercarts came to the rescue of the townsfolk. Part of the old reservoir is still visible, an historic reminder of the early days.

Fisher's ghost is another Campbelltown legend, although according to many people it is not without substance. The ghost made its appearance last century, near what is now the suburb of Bradbury, but some addicts of the supernatural still keep a vigil on 17 June, the date in 1826 when Frederick Fisher was said to have been murdered.

The need for land, accommodation and homes for Sydney's growing population has motivated the extension of Campbelltown, like Camden and Penrith, into new suburban divisions. The planning of its suburbs is being handled with care, and the new suburban names recall our early history.

As far back as 1973 a structure plan for the Campbelltown City was exhibited, and according to Campbelltown City Council, "since that date Council has been preparing Detailed Development Control Plans for the existing and new urban areas within the City". An exciting prospect lies ahead of this historic area. It seems certain that Governor Macquarie, who first declared its birthright, would be proud of its modern development.

The Macarthur Institute of Higher Education occupies a large site west of the city itself, on Narellan Road.

The newly planned suburbs have as yet only their past area history to give them an identity, and the council wants all new suburban names to have an historic base — what a splendid idea!

For separate entries on the suburbs of Campbelltown, see Airds, Ambarvale, Blairmount, Claymore, Kentlyn, Leumeah, Prestons, Raby, Rosemeadow, Ruse, St Andrews, St Helen's Park, and Woodbine.

# CAMPERDOWN
*Municipalities of Marrickville and Leichhardt, City of Sydney*
Location: 4 kilometres south-west of Sydney on Parramatta Road, near Sydney University

Now an inner-city suburb, Camperdown is named after the 240 acre estate granted to Governor Bligh in August 1806. Bligh called his land Camperdown in memory of a naval battle in which he took part in 1797. It was fought off the Dutch coast and near the town of Camperdown, 50 kilometres north of Amsterdam. The grant extended from the junction of the Orphan School Creek and Johnston's Creek in the north, and across the Parramatta Road to Cook's River Road. A model farm was established, but the idea failed, and in 1841 the estate was subdivided and became two hamlets: O'Connell Town on the Cook's River Road, owned by Sir Maurice O'Connell (Bligh's son-in-law), and Camperdown on the Parramatta Road.

In 1827 a racecourse was opened on O'Connell's land. The grandstand, if it could be dignified with that name, was on the side of Missenden Road where Royal Prince Alfred Hospital now stands. The course was in regular use until 1833, when the Randwick

Racecourse, popularly known then as the Old Sandy Track, was officially opened. The Governor Bourke Hotel in Camperdown was opened about this time; the licensee was a Mrs Thompson.

In 1850 the University of Sydney was incorporated, and during the fifties Edmund Blacket (1817–83) designed its first buildings. In 1859 Blacket's Great Hall at the university was opened. The northern area of the university was originally Grose Farm, which consisted of 30 acres leased to Lieutenant-Governor Francis Grose in 1792. By 1802 it was a government experimental farm and the name was applied to the whole block between Parramatta, City and Missenden Roads.

In 1868 a public meeting held in Sydney decided to erect a permanent memorial to commemorate the "providential escape of Her Majesty's son at Clontarf in March 1868". Prince Alfred, Duke of Edinburgh, had been wounded in a shooting incident on a picnic at Middle Harbour. An Irishman, Henry O'Farrell, shot the royal visitor. Fortunately the prince recovered, but O'Farrell was hanged at Darlinghurst Gaol. In 1873, 12 acres of the university paddock, intended for use as Wesleyan College, were chosen as the site for a memorial hospital. The hospital opened in 1882 and was named Prince Alfred Hospital.

Mallett Street, Camperdown, recalls an early mayor, C. S. Mallett, who was a strong supporter of ratepayers in this suburb. Carillon Avenue, on the Newtown side of the University, was originally named Bligh Street, but its name was changed when the university installed its war memorial carillon in 1928.

Today many of the terrace

houses in the suburb have been renovated by business and professional people wanting to live close to the city. Others are in demand by staff and students at the University of Sydney and Royal Prince Alfred Hospital, and as a result, Camperdown wears a bright face these days.

# CAMPSIE

*Municipality of Canterbury*
Location: 13 kilometres south-west of Sydney off Canterbury Road, on the Bankstown Line

This suburb is called after the hilly district of Campsie in Stirlingshire, Scotland, which is noted for the beauty of Campsie Glen and for the grandeur of a range of mountains known as the Campsie Fells.

Campsie began its life, like many other suburban districts, as a farming area. Subdivision of the area began before the railway line connected the area with Sydney in 1885. The line passed through the Campsie Park estate, which was owned by the Anglo-Australian Investment Company.

When the railway line was built, a large area of wooded land was cleared for construction of a station. This working site was known as Beamish Street, and a street of this name is well known today in Campsie. When the railway station opened on 1 February 1895, however, it was named Campsie. Five years later, in April 1900, the first post office began to serve the Campsie residents. The public school opened in August 1908.

South Campsie was part of the Laycock Estate (see Kingsgrove), and between South Campsie and Cooks River were the Redman

estates. John Redman had been granted 100 acres in 1812 and he added to this with the purchase of the area to the east, which had been a grant of 200 acres to Thomas Capon in 1817. Redman later acquired more land in the area.

The earliest model suburb in New South Wales was developed by William Phillips at Harcourt, between Burwood and Canterbury, in the years from 1889. The 200 acre area was originally scrub-covered and the home of wild birds. Up to 150 men were employed in clearing and levelling the land ready for road-building. The streets were called "avenues" on the model of New York City. Decorative trees were planted and a gardener and gangs of men were employed to tend the growing estate. Sales were slow, however, because of the

Beamish Street, Campsie, 1911

depressed conditions of the 1890s, and finally it was decided to sell the land outright, although £10,000 were set aside as a bonus to be distributed, after a number of years, to home-builders who adhered to certain laid-down conditions.

But Campsie did not really develop until 1925, when young couples began to build homes on the subdivisions, which were still quite heavily wooded.

A noted resident of Campsie was Herbert Thorncraft, MBE, who died in 1976, aged 81 years. Mr Thorncraft was an alderman on Canterbury council for thirteen years, and mayor for two years. He was on the board of Canterbury Hospital for thirty-four years, and Thorncraft House, one of the hospital buildings, honours him.

# CANLEY VALE
*City of Fairfield*
Location: 30 kilometres west of Sydney just north of Cabramatta, on the Main Southern Line

This suburb like its neighbour Cabramatta, was originally a woodland area, sloping gently down to a shallow valley. In 1803 Governor King assigned 12,300 acres to be rented out, and the funds thus accruing were to support the orphan schools in Sydney and Parramatta.

In 1856, the father of Federation, Sir Henry Parkes (1815–96), settled in the district in a house he called Canley Grange on the eastern side of the railway station. He named the railway station after his birthplace, Canley Moat House, at Stoneleigh in Warwickshire. Parkes is said to have built the first two houses in this district, which today is the busy junction of two railway lines,

one from Granville and the other from Regents Park.

An early road in this district, known as the Great Southern Road, was partly formed in 1806. It followed the bullock track to Sydney, and a Mr Potter conducted a camp for resting teams — the first camp on the way out of Sydney, and the last camp for the incoming teams. Hoy's Hill, on the boundary of Canley Vale and Cabramatta, was the site of a home built in the early 1830s by the first resident in the area, James Hoy. Hoys Road in Cabramatta is named after this family.

In 1899, the municipality of Cabramatta and Canley Vale, which had been established in 1872, was redivided, and the two separate wards were gazetted on 8

*Although no longer J. W. Thomas's general store, this building still stands on the corner of Railway Parade and Canley Vale Road opposite Canley Vale railway station*

January 1900. Today the suburb has a modern public school and Canley Vale High School. There is an excellent centre for shopping and entertainment, a place to relax at the squash and fitness centre, and a roller skating rink.

Canley Heights, once a tree-covered area, is now the site of many homes that look down towards the railway station and the green relief of Adams and Johnston Parks.

*Sir Henry Parkes with one of his eleven children*

## CANTERBURY
*Municipality of Canterbury*
Location: 11 kilometres south-west of Sydney west of Canterbury Road, on the Bankstown Line

The first land grant in this suburb in Sydney's south-west was given to "a very good, pious, inoffensive man", the Reverend Richard Johnson (1753–1827), in 1793. He called his grant Canterbury Vale, as a tribute to Canterbury in England, and the suburb took its name from the farm (see Ashbury).

The village of Canterbury was formed after 1841 subdivisions of this land, then owned by Robert Campbell. Sales of the land, in the area west of Canterbury Road and north of the railway, were successful, and several other sales followed in the 1840s and 1850s.

Although the soil in this area was rather poor, there was some farm cultivation, but the main work was wood-cutting and carting, and brickmaking. In 1840 the Australian Sugar Company bought 60 acres of Campbell's Canterbury estate beside Cooks River. A large factory was built and a steam engine installed, but after passing through the hands of several owners, the factory closed in 1856.

The first post office opened in April 1858, and the first official public school in March 1878, and the district slowly developed. The railway station, on the Bankstown Line, opened in 1895. Today, once quiet Canterbury has increased its population and its district facilities. A boys high school, a girls high school and an updated public school all proudly bear the name of Canterbury, as does the district hospital. A public school is attached to the hospital, to cater for its young patients' studies, and this facility was gazetted in 1976. Canterbury Racecourse, on the northern bank of Cooks River has been one of Sydney's major racetracks since 1871. The municipality was incorporated in 1879.

# CARINGBAH

*Shire of Sutherland*
Location: 23 kilometres south of Sydney off the Kingsway, on the Cronulla Line

The name of this suburb, which is on the strip of land separating Botany Bay from Port Hacking, is Aboriginal in origin and means "a pademelon wallaby". Earlier known as Highfield, history is silent as to whether this described its position or whether it was named after an early resident. The change of name was effected when the steam tramline from Sutherland to Cronulla opened in 1911. Areas around Caringbah and neighbouring Miranda developed slowly from the 1880s, and most were used for market gardening. One of the largest properties in the area was the Holt Estate, which was taken up in the 1860s (see Sutherland).

Until after the Second World War Caringbah remained a small centre for orchards and farming. Today the area is mainly residential, with attractive homes blending with natural trees and well tended gardens. Progress has provided an olympic swimming pool and a good shopping area; nature has provided fresh sea air and easy access to Cronulla Beach.

# CARLINGFORD

*Shires of Baulkham Hills and Hornsby, City of Parramatta*
Location: 22 kilometres north-west of Sydney off Pennant Hills Road, on the local Carlingford Line

The name Carlingford is Irish in origin. The suburb was named in honour of Lord Carlingford, under-secretary to the colonies from 1847 to 1860, whose title came to him from the town of Carlingford in County Louth, Leinster, Ireland. Originally it was part of the Pennant Hills area. Settlement began on farms in the area from the 1790s and later the area was known as Mobbs Hill, after William Mobbs, one of the area's most successful orchardists and farmers of the 1830s. A post office was opened on 1 July 1883, under that name, but on 16 July 1883, Mr A. H. McCulloch, MLA, on behalf of a large number of residents, requested that the name be changed to Carlingford, a name that remains to this day. The area at the junction of Marsden Road and Pennant Hills Road, however, is still known as Mobbs Hill.

The name Mobbs also brings to mind the legendary Mobbs Millions and reminds us of the belief many families hold that there is a vast fortune awaiting them held in chancery in England, if only they could prove their entitlement. This happened to the Australian Mobbses over fifty years ago. Their supposed fortune came to public notice during the nineteenth century, when a certain John Mobbs willed a sizeable area of suburban London to his family. When it seemed that an enormous amount of money was going begging, the Australian descendants of William Mobbs, the pioneer Carlingford orchardist, mobilised themselves into the Mobbs Millions Investigation Association. Nothing came of this golden dream. But it has always been said that London's pinstriped lawyers will make sure that any chancery claims will bring more profit to the legal profession than to the hopeful claimants.

An early Australian diary kept by Mrs Felton Mathew contains the following entry concerning William Mobbs: "Old Mobbs was among the first convicts who arrived in the country, and was for years employed in the Government garden, from whence he obtained a cutting from the first orange tree brought from Rio: this tree he showed with pride as being the parent of his whole orchard, either by cuttings, layers or seedlings ..."

The finer points of pruning may well have evaded one or two of the students in this picture, taken around 1905 at Carlingford Public School

he was the first possessor of Peaches."

St Paul's, Carlingford, is the oldest Anglican church in the area. On 4 February 1847 William Mobbs gave an acre of land for the site of a church. In January 1849, the foundation stone of a small chapel and schoolhouse was laid by Bishop Broughton, and later the small gem of a church was constructed.

Some of the best fruit in the colony in those early days came from Carlingford, and the names of Spurway and Neil became notable as fruitgrowers. But around the turn of the century, with the coming of the railway, a change came to Carlingford. In 1896 Carlingford station opened as part of a private railway, and it was then called Pennant Hills. In 1901 the railway became part of the New South Wales government system and the station took the district name of Carlingford. After the Second World War the housing commission undertook the development of the Dundas Valley and the new suburb of Telopea to the south. Roads were put through the new areas, and soon buses ran through the Carlingford district from Epping to Parramatta.

Today, Carlingford has a modern shopping square and a village centre, and its early orcharding days are largely forgotten.

In 1973 a body named the Carlingford—North Rocks Bushland Trust was formed to preserve the natural beauty of the remaining bushland. Part of the district has been declared a wildlife sanctuary, and 6,000 trees and shrubs have been planted, some grown from seed. Volunteers supervise fire and weed control, and two busy rangers, Ed Phillips and Bill Bruce, give time and talent to the trust.

# CARLTON
*Municipalities of Rockdale, Hurstville and Kogarah*
Location: 15 kilometres south-west of Sydney off Forest road, on the Illawarra Line

This suburb between Kogarah and Hurstville on the Illawarra line was named after a suburb of Nottingham in England. The name, which means "a village of free men", came from the subdivision of a large grant made in 1808 to Captain John Townson (see Hurstville).

The opening of the Illawarra railway altered the character of the suburb: large estates were subdivided and more residents were brought into the area. Carlton did not have a platform, however, until 1889. To finance its construction, a novel scheme was devised. Land-holders were given a block of land free, if they gave £400 towards the cost of building the platform and necessary station buildings. They were also guaranteed a first class ticket to Sydney for one year.

By the 1920s Carlton had become a comfortable residential area with attractive homes set in well-tended gardens. Forest Road reminds us that originally this place was heavily timbered. Townson, Gannon and Lord are all names of thoroughfares in adjacent areas, immortalising three early settlers — John Townson, Michael Gannon and Simeon Lord.

Shopfront Theatre for Kids, whose complex, which includes a house, a former shop and a theatre, is in Carlton Parade, was founded in 1976 by Errol Bray. A co-operative owned largely by the children, it has an international reputation and has made several overseas, as well as Australian, tours.

# CARRAMAR
*City of Fairfield*
Location: 29 kilometres west of Sydney off The Horsley Drive, on the Regents Park — Cabramatta Line

When the railway line from Sydney to Campbelltown came through this district in 1856, the area was already known as Carramar, an Aboriginal word meaning "shade of trees". From this we presume the place was originally forest land, although progress has turned it into a residential area. When the station opened for business in October 1924, however, it was known as South Fairfield, and it was not until 1926 that Carramar was adopted as the suburb's official title.

Prospect Creek flows through this suburb, and at the southern end of the Carrawood Park it is crossed by the historic Lansdowne Bridge. Named in honour of the Marquis of Lansdowne, it was built by David Lennox (1788–1873), a Scottish immigrant who arrived in Sydney in 1832. The bridge, opened in 1836, is one of his most elegant works, having a single masonry arch spanning 30 metres, and being 9 metres wide.

The first land was granted in this area on 12 August 1803, when Governor King declared that a total of 12,300 acres, covering several of the present suburbs, including Carramar, were to be rented out to prospective farmers. The money from the rents was to go to the support of the orphan schools of Sydney (see Cabramatta).

In 1806 and 1816 John Gowan was granted a total of 360 acres on Prospect Creek, extending over Carramar into Villawood. In 1840 the land was acquired by Dr William Bland, who built a homestead, which he called Mark Lodge. The land was auctioned off as small farms in 1885.

The first post office opened on 1 June 1927.

# CARSS PARK
*Municipality of Kogarah*
Location: 17 kilometres south of Sydney on the western side of Kogarah Bay

A neighbour of Blakehurst, the suburb of Carss Park is situated near Carss Point, on Kogarah Bay. Originally it was crown land, but it was sold to Jonathon Croft for £123 on 22 January 1854.

In 1831 William Carss, a cabinet-maker after whom the suburb is named, came to the colony as an emigrant mechanic under a scheme inaugurated by the Reverend Dr John Dunmore Lang. He had

worked his passage to the colony as a carpenter, and during his lifetime he made several trips back to England on the windjammers that were the long-distance ships of the time. Before acquiring the Carss property William lived at Ashfield, where his wife died in 1853. He had earlier lost two children, and when he became established in the Carss Bush property (as it was named in those days) he had his wife's body and those of the children exhumed and re-interred in a vault there. William Carss died in 1878 at the age of 78, and his remains were interred with those of his wife and children.

An historic and picturesque landmark in the suburb is Carss Park cottage, which was built on the point in the 1860s. It has stone outer walls 45 centimetres thick. There were originally two outbuildings, one of which was used for stables, but these have been demolished.

After William Carss died, members of the family continued to live in the house, including a daughter, Mary Carss. William Carss had always intended to leave the estate to the trustees of the Sailors Home in Sydney. When Mary died this clause in her father's will was honoured and the estate passed to the trustees in 1916.

The Carss Park and Kogarah areas were originally covered with a great variety of wildflowers and native trees, and there has always been a stream of fresh water running through the park. In 1921 the Blakehurst Progress Association made many attempts to secure Carss Bush for a public park, and in 1923 a newly elected council at Kogarah was able to

C. O. J. Munro, real estate agent, politician and prominent Sutherland Shire identity, points toward the enthusiastic advertising slogan for promoting land sales at Carss Bush Estate, 1923

acquire the area for the people. The park was dedicated on 26 January 1924, and on the same day the balance of the land was auctioned and 150 lots were sold in only 50 minutes. Many of the streets of the new estate were named after Aboriginal tribes.

Today this small suburb retains an air of natural beauty and its bushland setting harbours birds of many varieties, admired by residents and visitors alike.

# CARTWRIGHT
*City of Liverpool*
Location: 34 kilometres south-west of Sydney just west of Liverpool

The suburb of Cartwright is near Liverpool, lying between Cabramatta Creek and Prestons. It is named after the Reverend Robert Cartwright (1771–1856) of St Luke's, Liverpool. He was persuaded by the Reverend Samuel Marsden in 1808 to come to the colony as an assistant clergyman. Cartwright first worked in the Hawkesbury area, where he was an evangelical and popular minister, but in 1819 he was transferred to Liverpool. He received a grant of land and, like his mentor, Marsden, who had a profitable farm at South Creek (St Marys), Cartwright set up a small farm. In 1825 he was also made master of the Male Orphan School, which he greatly improved in his four years in office. When the housing commission established its Green Valley development scheme in the early 1960s, it named one of the new suburbs after this clergyman. The name of the suburb was officially gazetted in 1972.

Today all vestige of the early farmlands has disappeared. After twenty years of development, Cartwright is a busy, modern suburb, the home base for many young Australian and migrant families.

# CASTLE COVE
*Municipality of Willoughby*
Location: 11 kilometres north of Sydney on Middle Harbour

This small suburb between Roseville Chase and Castlecrag has a beautiful setting with views of Middle Harbour, natural parklands, and nearby the Castle Cove Golf Links. The houses are individual in design and the atmosphere is one of style and comfort.

It is believed that Castle Cove was named after a house built in 1905 by Henry Willis, a member of Parliament and later speaker of the Legislative Assembly. Using sandstone quarried on the site, which overlooked Sugarloaf Bay, the house, called Innisfallen Castle, was built in the late perpendicular Gothic style, sometimes called Tudor, and was set in 2 acres of beautiful gardens. It was completely private and for many years was accessible only by water or by a rough bush track reminiscent of the entrances to pioneer mansions on the Parramatta River. The original owner of this house is today remembered by Willis Road, which leads to Cherry Place, the site of this castle-like home.

A small weatherboard cottage on the water's edge was the family's home while the sixteen-room castle was being built. Innisfallen later passed to Henry Willis's son, Dr Hastings Willis, and his sisters. In 1966 Dr Willis decided to subdivide the surrounding bushland, and modern but beautifully styled homes were built.

Castle Cove gives its name to many facilities in its area, such as Castle Cove Park and Castle Cove Golf Links. The atmosphere in this small suburb is one of peace and beauty — but what else could one expect with a castle for a neighbour?

# CASTLECRAG
*Municipality of Willoughby*
Location: 8 kilometres north of Sydney off Eastern Valley Way reaching down to Middle Harbour

Few people realise that the American architect Walter Burley Griffin (1876–1937), who designed Canberra, also planned a Sydney suburb which created almost as much controversy as the national capital. The small northern suburb of Castlecrag was so named by Griffin became of a towering crag of rock known locally as Edinburgh Castle, which affords magnificent views of Middle Harbour.

When he arrived in Australia in 1913 to design the nation's capital, Walter Burley Griffin was aghast at the mediocre standard and style of most of Sydney's suburbs. In the 1920s the company of which he was managing director developed the subdivision now known as Castlecrag and created homes quite different from anything being built at the time. This was the first planned suburb to incorporate natural bushland in its design, although many have since followed the idea.

Griffin named the streets in the area, using such titles as Bulwark, Redoubt, Citadel, Parapet, Rampart, Bastion and Postern, all reminiscent of a mediaeval castle. At first, the houses in Castlecrag were most unpopular. Their design was too advanced for the period and when Griffin left for India in 1936, less than twenty had been constructed. Present-day trends, however, have caught up with his ideas and the suburb now has a reputation for elegance. Griffin also designed an outdoor theatre, the New Haven Scenic Theatre, which stands in a public reserve at the corner of The Scarp and The Barricade. A fountain has been erected as a memorial to this man of ideas.

Walter Burley Griffin and his wife Marion, also a trained architect and a highly regarded draughtsman, illustrator and designer of furnishings, outside their home at Castlecrag, 1930

# CASTLE HILL
*Shires of Baulkham Hills and Hornsby*
Location: 31 kilometres north-west of Sydney at the junction of Old Northern Road and Showground Road

Castle Hill is a picturesque suburb possibly named because of the fine views from the hilly areas in the district. It was first seen by Governor Phillip on one of his trips of exploration in 1791. Governor King wrote in 1802 that "Great progress has been made in clearing land at Castle Hill." In 1803 the convicts there were working "Sunrise till 8 a.m., 9 a.m. till 3 p.m. Saturdays, Sunrise till 8 a.m."

Two French prisoners of war were liberated from prison ships at Portsmouth and sent to Castle Hill in 1810 to start a wine industry, but the vines were diseased and the venture failed. A free settler followed, a Frenchman, Verincourt De Clambe, who received a 200 acre grant in 1802. He called his property The Hermitage, and here he planted vines and other crops. In a postscript to a letter accompanying a gift of some "very good carrottes seed", he wrote: "In this moment the thunder fall on my table did extinguish my light and broke my chimney piece. Thank God it is not my heade." He died six months later, in 1804, and was buried at Castle Hill in a bricked-in-grave.

Governor King established a government farm at Castle Hill in 1801. Over 300 convicts were employed there, and, by March 1804, 700 acres had been cleared and a number of stone buildings erected. The farm was closed by Governor Macquarie in 1811 because it was too expensive to maintain. The barn on the property was repaired and converted to an asylum for convict lunatics. In 1828 the land was transferred to the Church and Schools Estate.

The suburb gives its name to the Castle Hill Rebellion of 1804, an uprising of about 200, mostly Irish, convicts from the government farm who hoped to take control of the colony (another 100 convicts lost their way and did not join the main body). The revolt culminated in the Battle of Vinegar Hill (see Rouse Hill). It was doomed to fail, since the undisciplined rabble, most of whom were drunk and armed with only makeshift weapons, were no match for the regular troops of the New South Wales Corps. The rebels were arrested and disarmed,

A group of local residents at the Castle Hill Show, c. 1915

their ringleaders were hanged, and others of the group were given heavy sentences of flogging.

An official post office opened in the district in January 1869, and the public school took in its first pupils in July 1880. Today the suburb has a modern high school, in Castle Street, which caters for students in Castle Hill and nearby areas. Castle Hill is the headquarters of the Baulkham Hills Shire Council. One of Castle Hill's greatest assets is the modern showground and hall, on the south side of Showground Road and Gilbert Road. As well as being a popular place for community activities, it is the venue for many of the larger sections of the yearly Castle Hill Eisteddfod. The productions of the Castle Hill Players, an amateur drama group with professional ability, attract visitors from many other suburbs of Sydney as well as a good number of Castle Hill residents, who enjoy live theatre.

Many residents of Castle Hill own horses, and there are numbers of horse studs and riding schools in the area. The equine events at the

Castle Hill Show, which precedes Sydney's Royal Easter Show, give an indication of riding expertise and showmanship. The Castle Hill Shows began in 1886.

Mowll Memorial Village and the Nuffield Retirement Village are on the eastern outskirts of Castle Hill, providing a tranquil and happy retreat for older citizens.

## CASULA
*City of Liverpool*
Location: 34 kilometres south-west of Sydney off the Hume Highway, on the Main Southern Line

Situated between Liverpool and Glenfield, Casula is named for a land grant to Richard Guise, a member of an ancient French family well known for its merciless treatment of the Huguenots. He called his grant Casula after the place where he had lived in England. Guise was the first person buried in Liverpool Cemetery, final resting place of many of the district's pioneers.

The northern area of this suburb was part of Captain Eber Bunker's estate of 900 acres. He received two grants, one in 1804 and the other in 1810, and he called his property Collingwood, after a relative of his first wife, Margaret (née Thompson, d. 1808). It is believed that this was Cuthbert, Earl of Collingwood, a hero of the Battle of Trafalgar (1805) and admiral of the fleet after the death of Nelson.

Eber Bunker (1762–1836) first arrived in Sydney in 1701 as master of the *William and Ann*, carrying 188 convicts of the Third Fleet. He viewed the new colony with interest and on his next trip to New South Wales purchased 100 acres of land near Petersham Hill. He engaged in whaling on his first trip and later spent two winters whaling in Australian and New Zealand waters. During the second whaling voyage from England he discovered the Bunker Islands off the Queensland coast and accompanied new settlers to the Derwent in 1803. Bunker continued to act as a ship's captain and was whaling into the 1820s.

During the First World War the Casula camp riot had far-reaching effects on the law that regulated the trading hours of Sydney's hotels. On 14 February 1916, 5,000 troops at Casula camp were told that they were to accept a new training program which involved an extra one and a half hours a day. This meant that some men would be working twenty-seven hours on end, and the troops involved decided to strike. Unfortunately the leaders had already consumed a great deal of liquor, and they led a large body of men to storm the camp liquor stores. Taking every available bottle, they set out for the town, where they attacked the Golden Fleece Hotel, doing £700 worth of damage, and the

Commercial Hotel, causing damage worth nearly £2,000. Other hotels closed quickly and police mounted guard in the town, but by then the rioters had raided fruit and pie stalls near Liverpool Station and boarded trains to Sydney. During the journey they terrorised passengers and smashed windows, and on arrival they commandeered cars and waggons. One of these was a waggon load of Starkey's aerated waters, which they consumed, throwing the empties at the inoffensive crowd. When the military police arrived and cordoned off Central Station, the answer from the rioters was a pistol shot. The military police replied with fire from service rifles. Seven men were wounded, one of them a civilian from Queensland coming to book his ticket home, and a 19-year-old solider was shot dead.

Glenfield farmhouse, typical of the early colonial period, was built by Dr Charles Throsby on the 950 acre property granted to him in 1910. It has now been proclaimed an historic building

But the wild scenes continued, completely out of control. Shop windows were smashed, including those of Grace Brothers store in Broadway, a Greek restaurant, the German club, and the *Evening News* office. Terrified civilians sheltered in the grounds of St Andrew's Cathedral. Eventually the defence department issued a proclamation ordering all men to parade back at their camps by 11 o'clock the next day, those not returning to be posted AWL. The next day the rioting soldiers had sobered up, and shamefacedly reported at police stations and at the Central Police Court. Only about fifty went missing.

In the same week, the papers printed a government proclamation forcing hotels to stop trading at 6 pm. Six o'clock closing, and the resulting "six o'clock swill", remained in force until well after the Second World War.

Today, Casula is a busy residential suburb, with a public school and a high school bearing its name. This suburb, which is a railway station on the main southern line, extends south-west towards Cross Roads, the site of a well-known hotel. It is a healthy district, the air having the lighter quality of the Southern Highlands, with lower humidity than areas near to the coast.

## CENTENNIAL PARK
*City of Sydney, Municipality of Randwick*
Location: Locality 4 kilometres south-east of Sydney between Anzac Parade and Oxford Street

This small area, adjoining Moore Park, was itself named after a park. A famous and well-used "green lung", the park was named in 1888 to celebrate the one hundred years of settlement by Europeans in this country.

In 1886 the government had

decided on the plan for a celebratory park, and it only needed the passing of an Act of Parliament in the following year for work to begin. Grandiose ideas were put forward to erect an ornate building to be known as Phillip Hall, to be used for national assemblies and commemorative celebrations. Other proposals included a large museum, the Carrington Institute, where, documents, books, maps, Aboriginal relics and photographs showing the development of industries would be housed; an art gallery to hold sculptures and pictures of the governors and of notable men; and a mausoleum for the interment of governors and those worthy of a state funeral. And what happened? Only a miscellany of statues eventuated, and in recent years these have been badly vandalised. On the opening day, 26 January 1888, Lord Hopetoun, the governor-general of the time, dedicated the park "to

Federation celebrations at Centennial Park, 1901. The Federation Pavilion can be seen in the left background

the people of New South Wales forever". The pavilion built in the park at the place of proclamation by Earl Hopetoun was later moved from Centennial Park to Cabarita, and it was used for many years as a bandstand.

Centennial Park is a reserve of 662 acres, the largest public reserve in the Sydney area. It has a main drive, criss-crossed by a number of lesser drives, with avenues of palm trees. At one time the park was noted for its glorious rose trellises. It is favoured by horse riders, and bike riding has also become a popular family pleasure. The park is bounded by Oxford Street, York Road, Darley Road, Alison Road and Anzac Parade. The park contains many lakes, and it was the site of Lachlan Swamps, named in honour of Governor Lachlan Macquarie, which provided Sydney's first permanent water supply in 1837. The water was piped to Sydney along Busby's Bore, named after its designer, John Busby (1765–1857).

## CHATSWOOD
*Municipalities of Willoughby and Ryde*
Location: 10 kilometres north-west of Sydney on the Pacific Highway, on the North Shore Line

Not many suburbs are named after women, but Chatswood on the North Shore is one exception. This district commemorates Mrs Harnett, whose husband, Richard, was a notable figure on the North Shore, well known in Mosman, and an early mayor of Willoughby. In 1876 Richard Harnett subdivided an estate at Chatswood and named it after his wife. Her Christian name was Charlotte, but his pet name for her was Chattie or Chat and the family referred to the bushland areas of the estate as Chat's Wood. When the post office was established in 1879 the council suggested naming the area Chatswood after Harnett's successful estate, which was in the immediate vicinity.

The land on which the railway station is built was originally part

of a 200 acre grant made in 1805 by Governor King to Isaac Nichols (1770–1819). He called his property King's Plains and bought up other farms until, by 1808, he held 500 acres. In 1810 he received an additional 380 acre grant to the south-west. Eventually Nichols held 900 acres, and although he died in 1819, the estate was not subdivided until 1836. Although transported for theft in 1791, Nichols was the first postmaster appointed in the colony, as well as being principal superintendent of convicts from 1810 to 1814. He was described by Governor Macquarie as "a most zealous, active and useful man".

In the western part of the suburb, the first grant was made in 1807 to William Henry who took up 1,000 acres near the confluence of Blue Gum Creek and the Lane Cove River. He named the estate Millwood Farm, and the present Millwood Avenue was named after it. Later government authorities denied Henry's claim to the land and in 1850 he was evicted. After an inquiry he was reinstated ten years later. Lane Cove River State Recreation Area, a park with both natural bushland and cleared picnic areas, occupies both banks of the Lane Cove River from Fullers Bridge, at the western end of Millwood Avenue, northwest to West Pymble, and for some distance along Blue Gum Creek.

The first school in Chatswood opened in July 1883, and the first post office in August 1879. This closed in 1886, to reopen with improved facilities a year later.

When the railway came through the area in 1890, Chatswood began to develop rapidly, moving ahead of the older centre of Willoughby. By 1923 Chatswood was described as "a fashionable suburb and abounds with handsome villas. The township is growing and is

the centre of most of the business on the Milson's Point and Hornsby line."

In 1987 that description still applies. Chatswood has shopping facilities equal to those in the city, with the Chatswood Chase complex its crowning achievement. Many businesses have found modern office space in this convenient area, which nonetheless can still claim the charm of a suburb softened by natural bushland and cultivated gardens.

Above: Chatswood Ice Works as it stood in 1930. The site in Victoria Avenue now houses a BBC Hardware store

Below: Chatswood, c. 1910 from the railway overbridge looking toward Orchard Road. Although today's cabs are more mechanised, the taxi stand has remained at this location

# CHELTENHAM

*Shire of Hornsby*
Location: 21 kilometres
north-west of Sydney off Beecroft
Road, on the Main Northern Line

In 1890 a well-known Sydney
tailor and men's outfitter, William
Chorley, bought land between
Epping and Beecroft. He built a
house which he called Cheltenham,
after his birthplace in
Gloucestershire, England. Until
that time the area had been known
as Murray Farm Road. Chorley
began a long correspondence with
the government to build a railway
station near his home, and, when a
station was erected in 1898,
Chorley asked to name it, with the
result that Cheltenham was added
to the list of Sydney's suburbs.
Chorley Avenue recalls his name.

The area was part of Field of
Mars Common until 1874, when it
was resumed for residential land.
The suburb has not changed
greatly over the years. One
stipulation in its inauguration was
that no shops were to be built near
the station and that natural
bushland was not to be destroyed.
The result is a peaceful place with
an abundance of birds and pleasant
green surroundings. Cheltenham
in England is similarly peaceful. A
fashionable place from the time of
George III (1738–1820), it has
colonnaded tree-lined streets and
an air of elegant dignity. It is now
a half-way stop for coaches on
their way to Wales, but this has
not spoilt its natural charm. Birds
sing as sweetly there as in Sydney's
Cheltenham on the Northern line.

Cheltenham Girls High School,
situated in Beecroft Road, opened
in January 1958. Choirs from this
school have sung successfully in
overseas competitions and have
made a reputation for their school
and the district of which its
residents can be proud.

# CHESTER HILL

*City of Bankstown*
Location: 25 kilometres west of
Sydney near Villawood, on the
Regents Park — Cabramatta Line

There was quite a lot of discussion
about the naming of this suburb.
An early market garden and
orchard area north-west of
Bankstown, it developed into a
residential and light industrial area
after the Regents Park railway line
came through in 1924.

The construction site of the
station was known as Boroya, an
Aboriginal word of unknown
meaning, but when the station
opened on 8 October 1924, it
carried the name Chester Hill. It
had not, however, been chosen
without difficulty. A local resident,
Miss H. A. McMillan, suggested
that the new station should be
called Hillcrest, but so many
objections were raised that the
name was discarded. Miss
McMillan then suggested
Hillchester, after a pleasant town in
England, but this found no favour.
Nothing daunted, she turned the
name around to become Chester
Hill, and everyone was happy.

The area that became Chester
Hill was originally the southern
part of John Thomas Campbell's
Campbell Hill estate, which
covered 1,000 acres in 1815
between Parramatta, Liverpool and
Woodville Roads. East of
Campbell Hill Road was Charles
Fraser's 500 acre property, and
south of Waldron Road stood
T. L. Spencer's land (see Sefton).
Much of the land remained
undeveloped until the first
subdivision was made in the 1920s,
when the first shops were also
built.

The post office opened in July
1934, and the first public school in
January 1945. In the 1950s
Chester Hill developed and

expanded, and today it has all the
facilities of a busy residential area.
Thomas Mitchell's Road is named
after a New South Wales colonial
surveyor-general.

# CHIFLEY

*Municipality of Randwick*
Location: 13 kilometres south-east
of Sydney off Bunnerong Road

One of the newer south-eastern
suburbs, Chifley was named by
Randwick Council in 1964. It was
originally the southern part of
Matraville between Bunnerong
Road and Anzac Parade, taking in
Long Bay Prison. Chifley is
bounded by Malabar to the east
and Little Bay to the south. It is an
industrial area, with the container
and oil terminals of Port Botany
and the Pagewood Depot on the
site of the Bunnerong Power
Station (which was demolished in
1987) west of Bunnerong Road.

The suburb was named after
Australia's Labor prime minister at
the end of the Second World War,
Joseph Benedict Chifley
(1885–1951). Chifley was always
looked on as a man of the people.
He had been a railway locomotive
driver from Bathurst before
entering politics and he stayed
close to his friends even after his
election to parliament. Joseph
Chifley's engine, preserved in his
memory, stands outside Bathurst
Railway Station, and his simple
home in Bathurst is a tourist
attraction.

The first private dwelling in this
part of Sydney was Bunnerong
House, built by John Neathway
Brown in 1825.

The suburb's planners drew on
history when they chose the names
of many streets. Explorers were
especially favoured — Eyre,

Lasseter, Mawson, Wills and Dampier among them — and governors, including Macquarie and Brisbane, come a close second.

# CHIPPENDALE
*City of Sydney*
Location: 2 kilometres south of Sydney

William Chippendale was a free settler who arrived in the colony of New South Wales with a letter from Earl Bathurst, requesting Governor Macquarie to arrange a grant of land for the new immigrant. In 1819 Chippendale was given a grant of 95 acres, which included the present site of Redfern station. In time Chippendale sold the land to Solomon Levey (1794–1833), who was prominent in the commerical world. In 1838 part of the land was sold and subdivided and the suburb became partly residential and partly industrial. Today Chippendale is popular with people wishing to enjoy the convenience of inner-city living, and some excellent renovations have been carried out on the area's nineteenth-century terraces and cottages. Nearby are Victoria Park, with its bowling club and popular swimming pool; the University of Sydney; the Broadway shops; and Central Railway Station.

Chippendale, who gave his name to the suburb, is also remembered by two streets, Chippen Street and Dale Avenue. Levey Street honours Solomon Levey.

# CHIPPING NORTON
*City of Liverpool*
Location: 28 kilometres south-west of Sydney on the Georges River east of Liverpool

Situated near the Georges River, north of Moorebank, Chipping Norton was a farming area throughout the nineteenth century and into this century.

Chipping Norton was named after an old English village by William Alexander Long, who was born in Sydney in 1839, went to England to study law, and later lived in Chipping Norton in Oxfordshire. He bought up a number of former land grants in the area at the turn of the century and called his homestead Chipping Norton. The horse stud on part of his property produced many fine young horses. He died in 1915 and in 1919 the government bought his estate and subdivided it into farming blocks for soldiers returning from the First World War.

Today the suburb has a pleasant shopping centre and public school. On the other side of the river, which almost encircles the suburb, are Warwick Farm Racecourse, Liverpool Golf Course, Hollywood Picnic Grounds and Bankstown Aerodrome.

# CHISWICK
*Municipality of Drummoyne*
Location: 9 kilometres west of Sydney on the Parramatta River

This small suburb between Abbotsford and Drummoyne is surrounded on three sides by waters of the Parramatta River and Abbotsford and Five Dock Bays. Originally it was part of Five Dock Farm (see Five Dock), but in the 1850s a Dr Fortescue owned an estate in the area, which he had called after a village west of London on the River Thames. Chiswick takes its name from this property. At that time many fine homes were built, and the suburb took on the elegance of the Victorian era.

Some of the streets recall people associated with early Chiswick. Fortescue Street immortalises the doctor himself and Chiswick Street, his estate; Bortfield Drive honours Fred Bortfield, who was an alderman of the Drummoyne Council for eighteen years. Bortfield, a Drummoyne newsagent, served in both world wars. As a sniper in the Scots Guards in the First World War, he was awarded the Albert Cross, a Belgian decoration, for gallantry. He did not actually receive this award until sixty years after the action that merited it. In the Second World War he served as an officer in the RAAF.

The suburb still retains a delightful air of old world charm, even in an age of rush and bustle.

# CHULLORA
*City of Bankstown, Municipality of Strathfield*
Location: 18 kilometres south-west of Sydney between Rookwood Road and the Hume Highway

The name of this suburb is an Aboriginal word with the homely meaning of "flour", and history gives no reason for the choice of name, except that a nearby estate bore it.

The railway station opened in 1924 and the department of railways developed a large area in this suburb and erected the

Chullora Railway Workshops, which service and repair Sydney's suburban and inter-urban trains. Enfield Railway Marshalling Yards are on the eastern boundary, and a residential area is sandwiched in between the two railway properties. The Hume Highway comes through Chullora, and along the southern side of the highway are a series of commercial developments and a number of car sales yards stretching towards North Bankstown.

Chullora was originally part of the area known as Liberty Plains, which was land given to the first free settlers arriving in Sydney Cove on 6 January 1793, in the ship *Bellona*. They were offered land midway between Sydney and Parramatta, and their farms are now covered by the suburbs of Enfield, Chullora, Strathfield, Homebush and Flemington.

## CHURCH POINT
*Shire of Warringah*
Location: 32 kilometres north of Sydney facing Pittwater at the northernmost end of Pittwater Road

The first settler in this area, north-west of Bayview at the southern end of Pittwater, was Thomas Langford, who acquired 40 acres of land in 1852. The suburb was so named because the first church in Pittwater was built here. The first services in the area, however, were conducted under the trees on the site of the present Bayview post office. Originally the area had been called Chapel Point, because it was the site of a small Wesleyan Chapel built in 1872 on land given by William Oliver; Mrs Oliver was already conducting a Sunday school for the children of local

residents. The preacher came to services on a horse provided by another early settler, William Henry McKeown. The chapel was used by all denominations and became the pivot of social unity. It was demolished in 1932.

William Oliver was a dominant force in this small suburb in its early days. He seems to have had a variety of jobs before he settled for baking. He obtained 30 acres of land at Elvina Bay in 1842, where dense bush supplied him with just the right fuel for his baker's oven. Oliver used a bullock team for carting felled timber for his own use, and also to send to Sydney (see Terrey Hills).

The attractive home known as Melrose was built by Benjamin James, in 1888, who was its first resident. Some time later it was purchased by Major Phillip Charley, who made many improvements to the house. From 1900 it was run as a boarding house by several persons, including Mrs Friend, who named it Melrose in 1906. The site had been occupied by McKeown in 1882, when he had a camp and a few fruit trees there.

The fortunate people who now live at Church Point have the beauty of Pittwater on their doorstep. Governor Phillip considered Pittwater the finest stretch of water he had seen in the new colony. Because of its tranquillity, many writers and artists have made their homes at Church Point.

## CLAREVILLE
*Shire of Warringah*
Location: A locality 36 kilometres north of Sydney on the Barrenjoey Peninsula facing Pittwater

The origin of the name of this locality within the suburb of Avalon is not accurately recorded, although its combination of Clare and ville suggests it may have been called after an early home. The area benefits from the beauty of Pittwater and has been chosen by many people as the ideal place for retirement.

It was originally part of the land grant made to Father Therry (see Avalon). In 1840 the Stokes family were boatbuilders in this area of Pittwater, and Stokes Point recalls their name. The first Stokes was a pickpocket, who was transported for his crime, although he declared that he was innocent. Although he had been trained as a shoe-maker, he became a boatbuilder, obviously seeing the possibilities of that trade in the area. In those early days many farms of varying sizes were to be found in the surrounding district, and Pittwater was once a thriving port for farm produce.

Today, Long Beach at Clareville is a temptation to be idle sometimes and enjoy the surroundings. Clareville Beach, which joins Long Beach and is about 500 metres long, is on the eastern shore of Pittwater, and Woody Point and Taylor's Point are neighbours. The RAN has a torpedo testing range on Taylor's Point, and a wharf at the south end of Long Beach. Nearby is Clareville Beach Reserve, which runs along the shore off Delecta Avenue. Baths have now replaced the Clareville Wharf on Pittwater between Clareville Beach and Long Beach.

# CLAYMORE
*City of Campbelltown*
Location: 49 kilometres
south-west of Sydney off the
South Western Freeway

The name of this proposed suburb
of Campbelltown remembers a
farm sited in the area. The name
has been substituted for the
original suggestion, Badgally.

# CLEMTON PARK
*Municipality of Canterbury*
Location: 13 kilometres
south-west of Sydney just west of
Earlwood

This suburb was originally a
farming area and was part of the
Laycock estate in 1804. In 1820,
however, it could still be described
as a hunter's paradise. Its name is
associated with a wealthy resident
Frederick Moore Clements, whose
money was made by marketing
that family health restorer,
Clements Tonic. Later he owned
40 acres near William Street until
his death in 1920. Clementon Park
was an early suggestion for the
suburb's name, but the recorded
geographical name is Clemton
Park, which was used as early as
1925 in the name of the local
progress association.

Earlwood and Kingsgrove are
near neighbours to this busy
home-makers' suburb. A pleasant
reserve, Clemton Park, is situated
in Moorefields Road, Kingsgrove,
and Clemton Park Public School is
in Bexley Road, Earlwood.

# CLIFTON GARDENS
*Municipality of Mosman*
Location: 9 kilometres north-east
of Sydney on Port Jackson

This delightful spot on the north
side of Sydney Harbour was a
popular anchorage in colonial days
for American whalers refitting
their ships and taking on supplies
of fresh vegetables and fruit. An
early settler in the area was Captain
E. H. Cliffe, who owned the
whaler *Lady Wellington*. He
purchased a 15 acre property facing
across the bay in 1832, and called
his home Cliffeton. In 1871, D.
Butters built a hotel here called the
Clifton Arms. It was later bought
by David Thompson, who built
the Marine Hotel, which operated
from 1891 to 1967. Thompson
built a wharf and dancing pavilion
here, and it became a popular
picnic spot — hence the name
Clifton Gardens. Since the 1920s
Clifton Gardens has been a popular
place for families with children.
Clean and safe, it provides a rock
pool for bathing and sandy
harbour beaches.

A short walk from Clifton
Gardens is Bradley's Head, which
commands unsurpassable views of
the harbour and North and South
Heads. It was named after
Lieutenant William Bradley, who
accompanied Governor Phillip on
the flagship HMS *Sirius*, in the
First Fleet.

Clifton Gardens overlooks
Chowder Bay (once known as
Koree) and Chowder Head (its
Aboriginal name was Gurugal).
The derivation of this name is a
little doubtful, but it is believed to
refer to a food called chowder
much favoured by Americans,
made when "fish is boiled with
biscuit, and pork". As many of the
early whalers were from America
this seems possible. Ships often
remained at Clifton Gardens for
months at a time, while refitting
and taking on supplies, so there
would have been plenty of time for
cooking favourite foods.

Aerial view of Clifton Gardens, c. 1910. A
ferry guide proclaimed in 1913 that Clifton
Gardens was the most extensive pleasure
ground in Australia

# CLONTARF
*Municipality of Manly*
Location: 13 kilometres north-east
of Sydney on Middle Harbour

A picturesque residential suburb,
which overlooks Middle Harbour
from the north side, Clontarf may
well have been named by a
homesick Irishman. A suburb of
Dublin, Ireland's Clontarf was the
scene of a battle in 1014, when the
Irish hero Brian Boru succeeded in
driving back a Viking invasion
from Denmark.

Sydney's Clontarf became
popular in the 1800s as a picnic
ground and pleasure spot. This
reputation paled slightly when a
crazed Irishman, Henry James
O'Farrell, shot at Prince Alfred,
Duke of Edinburgh, the colony's
first royal visitor, on 12 March
1868. The prince recovered, and

Engraving of Clontarf, 1881

James O'Farrell

O'Farrell was captured and later
hanged at Darlinghurst Gaol.

On the opposite side of Middle
Harbour is The Spit, which was
originally known by its Aboriginal
name of Burra-Bra. Before the
construction of the Spit Bridge in
1924, passengers were ferried
across the water by punt, to join a
tram on the further side for the
journey to Manly and all points
north.

# CLOVELLY
*Municipality of Randwick*
Location: 8 kilometres south-east
of Sydney facing the Pacific Ocean

This pleasant seaside suburb was
known as Little Coogee, but in
1914 the name was changed to
Clovelly. When the change of
name was first mooted,
Eastbourne, the name of an
English seaside town, was
suggested, but F. H. Howe,
president of the local progress
association suggested instead
Clovelly, the name of a local estate
owned by Sir John Robertson.

In 1834 William C. Greville
bought 20 acres here, including the
whole bay frontage, for £40.
Present-day Clovelly is a
residential suburb. Clovelly Beach,
at the end of a long narrow bay, is
small and picturesque. Although it
is not a good surfing beach,
compared with its neighbours

Small and picturesque, Clovelly Beach, 1922

Bronte and Coogee, it provides safe swimming as the entrance to the bay is netted.

# CLYDE

*City of Parramatta*
Location: 21 kilometres west of Sydney off the Great Western Highway, a suburban junction station for the Carlingford and Sandown Lines and on the Main Southern and Main Western Lines

The name Clyde for the station and area between Auburn and Granville was chosen in 1883 by the then commissioner for railways, C. M. G. Eddy. Clyde was the junction for the Carlingford and Sandown lines, just west of the bridge across the Duck River.

In 1878 a subdivision of land in the area was called New Glasgow and included the area now known as Clyde. The railway station opened as Rosehill Junction in 1882. The name was changed again to Clyde Junction in 1901, but finally, in April 1904, reverted to Clyde, of which Commissioner Eddy said: "New Glasgow is close by, and as Old Glasgow is watered by the Clyde, to which Duck River may be likened, perhaps Clyde would not be unacceptable."

In the late nineteenth century, fruit growing was the popular means of livelihood in the district, but large-scale industrial development in nearby Granville gradually spread to Clyde. In 1882 Hudson Brothers established the Union Rolling Stock and Engineering Works in Clyde, which were sold in 1896 to W. M. Noakes and in 1899 to Clyde Engineering Company. The Clyde

Engineering Works manufactured trams for the electric tramways system and from 1906 heavy railway rolling stock, as well as a huge variety of fittings and parts to go with them. The works also manufactured enamelled bathroom and kitchen baths and basins, and agricultural machinery and implements, considered the best of their kind in Australia. Also at Clyde now is Commonwealth Engineering, which manufactures rolling stock for inter-urban electric trains.

Granville Technical College in South Street, Granville, had a great influence on the Clyde works. All apprentices were expected to attend the college. The classes for fitters, turners and toolmakers usually numbered from twenty to forty young men.

Factory hands at Clyde worked a full forty-eight-hour week, without morning or afternoon tea

The original Clyde Engineering works, c. 1927. In its lifetime the main building was used for manufacturing products ranging from car batteries to aircraft. The building to the right with the spire was the main office for the complex, but was demolished in 1941 as it was believed it would be a landmark for any aerial attack by the Japanese

breaks, and only a half-hour lunch break. Those days have now passed. It is easy to imagine what those early workers would think of the changed working conditions offered today.

Clyde is still a busy industrial area, with some residential areas, and a strong domestic shopping centre.

## COLLAROY
*Shire of Warringah*
Location: 22 kilometres north-east of Sydney on Pittwater Road facing the Pacific Ocean

Collaroy is an Aboriginal word meaning "long reeds". Originally the suburb was considered to be part of Narrabeen, but after the

coastal steamer *Collaroy* ran aground just north of Long Reef in 1881, the beach and the surrounding area became known as Collaroy. The grounded steamer created great excitement and attracted curious crowds, many of whom brought picnics and spent the day inspecting the victim. Later the steamer was refloated, and went back into service, only to be wrecked on the Californian coast in 1889.

The area was surveyed in 1816 by James Meehan (1774–1826), deputy surveyor of lands, when it was being used for grazing. The Jenkins family and later the Salvation Army owned land in the area (see Narrabeen).

Today Collaroy still attracts picnickers and surfers, although the beach is well known for its strong undertow and giant seas at certain times of the year. The residential area rises steeply west of the main road to Collaroy Plateau and Wheeler Heights. Happily much of the natural bushland here was preserved when houses were being built.

## COLYTON
*City of Penrith*
Location: 43 kilometres west of Sydney between the Great Western Highway and the Western Freeway

Almost midway between Mount Druitt and Penrith in the western suburbs, Colyton carries the name of a town in Devon, England. William Cox (1764–1837), an officer in the New South Wales Corps who became known as great road-builder, received a grant in

William Cox

this area in August 1819, and named it after his wife's home town. Cox subdivided the estate in 1842 into Colyton Village and some small farms. When the suburb was formed it took the name of Cox's grant. The area lies south of the Great Western Highway, and its eastern boundary, Rope's Creek, separates it from Mount Druitt.

Today the area is almost completely residential, part of the growing housing projects west of Blacktown. It is a busy family suburb, with most modern amenities, including a state primary school, opened in 1961, and high school.

## COMO

*Shire of Sutherland*

Location: 27 kilometres south-west of Sydney on the Woronora River where it joins the Georges River, on the Illawarra Line

This suburb on the south bank of the Georges River and bounded to the west by the Woronora River, was named after Lake Como at the foot of the Bernese Alps in Italy. The shoreline is deeply indented by several beautiful bays — Bonnet Bay on the Woronora River, and Scylla Bay and Carina Bay on the Georges River. It is easy to understand why early visitors regarded Como as a holiday or honeymoon destination.

James Murphy was an early land-holder in this suburb and is believed to have named it. He managed the affairs of Thomas Holt (see Sutherland). Murphy built Como House (which was

burnt down in 1969) and the extensive Como Pleasure Grounds. When Murphy died, the income from the estate provided scholarships to train young men in agricultural science, either at St John's College, Sydney, or at the Hawkesbury Agricultural College.

The first railway station was opened at the end of December 1885, and Como became a weekend resort. When the line was being built, the railway camp here was known as Woronora, and the first school was opened at the same time, namely 1881. The post office opened on 16 May 1883, but closed in 1886. A year later it reopened.

When a new railway bridge was opened in 1972, Como railway station was moved about a kilometre southwards, and some local residents found themselves much farther from a station.

Como railway bridge, c. 1895. The bridge still stands, but is no longer in use since the building of the new Como bridge in 1972

View of Como from the original train station, c. 1910

Some street names, such as Cremona, Genoa and Verona, are reminiscent of Italy, but others are pure Australian, with Aboriginal origins; among these are Taronga, Yamba, Burunda, Warraba and Woronora.

# CONCORD
*Municipality of Concord*
Location: 15 kilometres west of Sydney off Concord Road, on the Main Northern Line (Concord West)

A small suburb, which gave its name to the municipality incorporated in 1883, Concord is bounded by North Strathfield, Burwood, the Parramatta River and Hen and Chicken Bay.

The area was explored by men from the First Fleet in 1788 and was first settled in 1793, when the lieutenant-governor, Major Francis Grose, made ten land grants to six non-commissioned officers of the New South Wales Corps and four other settlers, in an area he named Concord. Some think it was so named to encourage a peaceful attitude between soldiers and settlers as relations between the two were often strained, but the name has an historical significance. During the American War of Independence (1775–78), the town of Concord was the site of the first battle. Among the British soldiers taking part as an advance guard against the colonists was 21-year-old Francis Grose. Seventeen years later he was in the penal settlement of New South Wales, and he named the newly opened grant area Concord in memory of the American town.

In 1791, at a place called Longbottom, in the area of the present St Luke's Park, a stockade was built on the Parramatta Road. The trip between Sydney and Parramatta was too long to be completed in one day, so the stockade was essential protection for overnight stays. It closed in 1842. A government farm was also established in the area, on 900 acres to the west of the stockade.

A number of well-known colonists were associated with Concord's early history. In 1797 a 50 acre grant was made to Isaac Nichols (1770–1819), who added further properties until he held 600 acres in the district. He called his estate Yaralla. The land was gradually sold off in the 1830s.

In 1798 we find the first stirrings by the women of Concord for liberation. They sought the right to vote in the election of a district constable. Needless to say, their plea was ignored.

William Lawson (1774–1850), the explorer who, with Blaxland and Wentworth, found a way across the Blue Mountains, arrived in the colony as an ensign in the New South Wales Corps. He was first posted to Norfolk Island, and on his return to Sydney in 1806 he began farming at Concord on 500 acres on the Parramatta Road between the later Burwood and Concord Roads, using his land for grazing sheep.

Governor Lachlan Macquarie visited Concord in 1810 and was not impressed with what he saw there: "The settlers are very poor, and live in mean, dirty, small habitations."

Thomas Walker (1804–86), who came from Scotland in about 1822 to work for his uncle, William Walker, a merchant, amassed a huge fortune and in the 1840s he bought Isaac Nichols's land at Concord. He gave the mansion he built on it in 1864 the name Yaralla, after the old property name. Walker had only one child, Eadith, and to give her companionship he adopted Anne Masefield, who later married the

Thomas Walker

The Thomas Walker Convalescent Hospital was built during the 1890s

noted architect John Sulman. Eadith became an untiring worker for charitable causes, and she was created a Dame of the British Empire in 1928. Thomas Walker's will had set aside £10,000 to establish and maintain what is now the Thomas Walker Convalescent Hospital at Concord. The rest of his fortune was left in trust to Eadith, and when she died aged 72 in 1937, half of the fund, by then worth £800,000, was left to charity. The Dame Eadith Walker Convalescent Home for Men was established in her old home, Yaralla. Concord Repatriation Hospital was also erected on some of the Walkers' land.

Noted men gave their names to streets in Concord. Henry Brewer, a midshipman on HMS *Sirius*, who was one of the first grantees in the area and became provost-marshal of Sydney Cove,

is remembered by Brewer Street; Correy's Avenue immortalises Mr Correy, an early alderman; Bray's Road commemorates the first mayor, Alfred L. Bray; and Majors Bay road probably refers to Major Francis Grose.

Concord West opened up when the northern railway line went through from Strathfield to Hornsby. Until then it had been part of Concord proper, and some settlers had small farms there. The construction site of the station was known as Brunswick Park, but when the station was opened on 1 September 1887 it was called Concord. As this part of Concord expanded, it was decided to change the name of the station to Concord West, and this was officially recognised in June 1909. Concord West Post Office opened in March 1915, and the first public school opened in 1929.

During the 1920s developers began to subdivide the paddocks formerly used for grazing dairy

cattle, and young families came to the area. Many of the attractive Federation-style houses built at this time survive in splendid condition.

## CONDELL PARK

*City of Bankstown*
Location: 22 kilometres south-west of Sydney between Milperra Road and the Hume Highway

Ouseley Condell, an engineer, arrived in Port Jackson on 8 May 1829. He had travelled on the barque *Swiftsure* with thirteen other settlers, via Hobart Town, then back across the rough waters of Bass Strait to Sydney. Here he applied for a position in the public service, and in 1830 he received a land grant. The grant, shown on the parish map of Bankstown, was called Condell Park. Bounded by today's Clarence, Augusta, Taylor

69

and Marion Streets, it was in four portions of 50 acres each.

Condell was well connected, being related on the distaff side to Sir Ralph Ouseley, a general in the English army, and Sir Gore Ouseley, an orientalist and ambassador-extraordinary at the Persian and Russian courts. These were men of high distinction and manners, but our Ouseley Condell seems to have had rather freer ways. He was gaoled overnight in 1841 for some misbehaviour, having already been in court in 1838 regarding a money loan. Condell married well, however, his bride being Mary-Ann Nicholson, a grand-daughter of Count de Visme. The marriage took place in St Phillip's, Church Hill, and a newspaper notice about the event reads, under the headline, "Marriage": "On Friday 2 March 1838 at St Phillip's by Rev. William Cowper, by special licence, Ouseley Condell, nephew of General Sir Ralph Ouseley, Bart., and cousin of Rt. Hon. Sir Gore Ouseley, Bart., to Mary Ann Nicholson, 2nd daughter of William Nicholson of Sydney, and grand-daughter of Count de Visme of the Coldstream Guards."

Ouseley Condell was known to have been in the office of Sydney merchants Aspinall, Browne and Company in 1835. Later he qualified as a voter in the 1842 city of Sydney elections, a privilege allowed only to property owners. Records after these dates do not show that he was active in the colony, so he may have returned to England.

Today Condell Park is a busy residential suburb. Its closest neighbour is Bankstown, and it enjoys all the modern shopping facilities of that area. Condell Park relies on a bus service for transport within the area and to stations.

## CONNELLS POINT
*Municipality of Kogarah*
Location: 20 kilometres south-west of Sydney on the Georges River

Connells Point, on the northern bank of Georges River, south-east of Hurstville, was named after John Connell, who acquired land in the area in the 1830s. Connell was a merchant who owned stores in Pitt Street, Sydney. The land he acquired was virgin forest and became known as Connell's Bush. It projected into the Georges River, and the name Connell's Bush gradually gave way to the present title, Connells Point. Nearby Connells Bay also takes its name from this early settler.

## COOGEE
*Municipality of Randwick*
Location: 8 kilometres south-east of Sydney at the easternmost end of Coogee Bay Road facing the Pacific Ocean

The original name for this seaside suburb south-east of Sydney is hardly complimentary. It was derived from an Aboriginal word, "koojah", which means "a stinking place", probably because of the intolerable smell of rotting seaweed washed up on the beach.

In 1835 William Charles Wentworth (1790–1872) bought 30 acres in the area bounded by the present Dolphin, Judge and Oswald Streets and Carrington Road. No further land was sold in the area until 1840, although the village of Coogee was gazetted in 1838. One of the first settlers was George Dodery, a retired soldier and a veteran of the Battle of Waterloo in 1815. He started a market garden, and the suburb gradually developed as an agricultural and horticultural area.

By 1866 Coogee had become popular for day trips and family picnics. The fine sandy beach, about a half kilometre long, was littered with shells, strangely shaped sponges and other interesting marine specimens, and "beach combing" became a favourite weekend pastime. The Coogee Aquarium, built in 1887, became a big tourist attraction, especially the seal tank. After about 1908 entertainments at the Aquarium declined, but the building still stands on the corner of Beach and Dolphin Streets, although it is in a poor state of repair.

In the 1880s bathing machines appeared on Coogee Beach. In the days before surfing these miniature sheds on wheels served as dressing rooms. The machines were wheeled a few yards into the sea and the bather frolicked within the confines of the enclosure attached to each machine. The idea had come from the English seaside resorts, but it did not survive long at Coogee.

Coogee, like Manly, was a popular and fashionable beach resort in the 1920s and 1930s. In 1928 an amusement pier became the main talking point in this suburb. It extended for 183 metres into the sea and had a number of structures built on it, including an auditorium and a dance floor. The plan to give Australians the fun offered by the English piers in Blackpool and Brighton, on which the Coogee construction was modelled, fell apart when rough seas pounded against sections of the structure and rendered it unsafe for use. In 1933 the superstructure was demolished and by 1945 Randwick Council had completed demolition of the pier. Far more successful in the suburb was the shark net at Coogee Beach, inaugurated in 1929.

Today Coogee is a residential suburb with mostly permanent residents. The suburb has a well laid-out playing area, Coogee Oval; a busy post office in Brook Street; and a primary school in Coogee Bay Road, where a large enrolment of pupils dream of the ocean only a short run away. The first school was started by a Mrs Birmingham in the 1850s. We may wonder what she would think of that happy, active, multicultural group learning in Coogee today.

True to the origin of its name, a rather seaweedy Coogee Bay beach, c. 1880. Note the movable bathing machines complete with changing sheds to the right

## COWAN
*Shire of Hornsby*
Location: 41 kilometres north of Sydney on the Pacific Highway and the Main Northern Line

The first people to inhabit Cowan were the Kuring-gais (meaning "the men"), who were members of the Aboriginal tribal group Eora, which disappeared within fifty years of Europeans coming to the area. The geological structure around Cowan made it an ideal home for Aboriginal people. Caves ran far back into the rugged cliffs, affording shelter and protection, and in many of these, drawings of fish and men can still be seen. Kangaroos and emus were numerous, and along the water's edge oysters were found in large quantities. So food was no problem, and the Aboriginal cooking places called middens have been identified from the accumulation of old shells and remnants of animal bones found

at many sites near Cowan.

Cowan is situated on top of the ridge that divides Berowra Creek and Cowan Creek. The origin of the suburb's name has not been clarified, although it was in use early in the nineteenth century.

Governor Phillip and his party saw the general area in 1789 when on their early explorations of the Hawkesbury. Botanist George Caley in 1805 walked from Pennant Hills to explore the gullies and the waters feeding Cowan Creek. The name Cowan Creek appeared in early settler William Bean's application for land dated November 1826, and in 1845 George Peat, who established Peat's Ferry across the Hawkesbury River, marked out a track from the water's edge up to the top of the ridge.

A rugged and thickly forested area, Cowan was an ideal place for bushrangers to escape from authority. It was also an excellent place for some illicit rum running. In 1842 Robert Henderson bought

rum and brandy from Sydney merchants Dunlop and Ross. Official papers declared the cargo bound for an overseas port, but instead it was landed on the banks of Cowan Creek and hidden in a nearby cave. Labels and brand marks were altered, at the same time as a notice was being posted up in Sydney regarding the smuggling of liquor. A man who had read the notice happened to be cutting timber in the area and found the hidden spirits. He rolled one of the barrels out of the cave and managed to get it as far as Middle Harbour. He then reported his find to the Sydney police. Henderson was apprehended, and we presume the timber-cutter received his reward.

Timber-cutting for coach-building was an early industry in this suburb, which developed slowly until the steam train linked Hornsby and Cowan, when Cowan became a popular holiday spot. In 1958 this section of the line was electrified, and the new service had a marked effect on local development. Cowan in 1937 was a tiny village, catered for by a small group of essential shops, and patronised by a population of holiday-makers and retired persons. In the late 1960s young couples began to settle there and today Cowan is another growing suburb in the metropolitan area.

In December 1894 Cowan and the surrounding area was declared a sanctuary for native flora and fauna. In 1895 lookouts were built and walking tracks were put through so that visitors could enjoy this attractive bushland. A causeway and jetty were opened in 1907.

Today Cowan offers its population and visitors the opportunity to live in natural bushland surroundings or visit and enjoy an area still unspoiled.

# CRANEBROOK
*City of Penrith*
Location: 58 kilometres west of Sydney near the Nepean River

An early farmer in the area named James McCarthy gave this suburb its name. He came to the area in about 1794 and farmed 30 acres of land there. In 1803 he received a 100 acre grant from Governor King, and built Cranebrook House on it. He grew grain and wine grapes on his property, which is believed to have been the home of many birds.

Today this suburb of the City of Penrith is a developing residential area.

# CREMORNE
*Municipalities of Mosman and North Sydney*
Location: 6 kilometres north of Sydney reaching north of Military Road to Middle Harbour and south to Port Jackson

It is hard to believe that the peaceful atmosphere of Cremorne Point, with its natural bushland and sharply projecting into the harbour on a finger-shaped piece of land, was once broken by the noise of an early pleasure park. The next-door neighbour to Mosman, this suburb, originally called Careening Point and later Robertson Point, was a grant made in 1829 to the father of parliamentarian Sir John Robertson (1816−91). In 1853 the grant was purchased by James Milson, after whom the main road to the point is named, and he in turn leased 22 acres in 1856 to Messrs Clark and Woolcott, promoters of a stylish pleasure ground, which they called Cremorne Gardens after a famous pleasure centre in London.

Steamers ran to Cremorne Gardens every half hour from Circular Quay and Woolloomooloo Bay, and the combined cost of the trip and entrance fee was 2 shillings. Among the entertainments offered were fireworks, dancing on a specially constructed stage, band music, archery, quoits, a shooting gallery, skittles and gymnastics. "Refreshments at Sydney prices" were also advertised. Later, masked balls were held there, the prices being 7s 6d for gentlemen, and 5 shillings for ladies. Bad lighting and poor catering caused problems, and the initially superior entertainment deteriorated. By 1862 the gardens had become a ruin. Later several efforts were made to revive the idea, the last in 1881 by Thomas L. Nicholson, but they failed, and in time the area became a residential and park area.

In 1895 coal was discovered near the corner of the present Hodgson Avenue and Cremorne Road. Shafts were sunk, but the government stopped the venture in response to popular protests.

In 1891 the foreshores and the reserve became the subject of a law suit. A syndicate had purchased part of the area when the land was subdivided in 1889, but two years later the attorney-general, Sir Julian Salomons, claimed that the land was government property. The syndicate had marked out the subdivision of the area for building sites, and they based their claim on continuous possession back to the original grantee, James Robertson. Fortunately for all lovers of Cremorne Point and its beautiful park, their claim was defeated, and this part of the harbour foreshore was reserved for public use for all time.

Many of the streets, including Murdoch, Boyle, Spofforth and Bannerman, leading from

View of Folly Point, Cremorne, c. 1880 by photographer John Paine

Cremorne Point to Cremorne Junction, were named in honour of Australian cricketers who succeeded in defeating England at a time when English cricket was paramount.

Cremorne Junction was born when a proposed tram link from Military Road to the Cremorne Point Wharf began regular services on 18 December 1911. Nowadays this is a busy modern shopping centre, but before the coming of the trams the area was notable for large homes surrounded by gardens and orchards. One of these was Ocean View, built on the Glover estate. Where the main Cremorne Centre stands was an open paddock, used by local lads as a cricket pitch and football field. A blacksmith and farrier conducted a lucrative business on the corner of Military and Belmont Roads, and the first bank in the area, the Australian Bank of Commerce, was built on Covey's Corner. In

those days the lamplighter did his rounds at dusk, lighting gas lamps to illuminate the streets.

Today the area to the north of Military Road is characterised by substantial homes, which continue to the shores of Middle Harbour, joining the boundary of Mosman at Spit Junction. The suburb is served by an excellent ferry and bus service.

## CROMER

*Shire of Warringah*
Location: 20 kilometres north of Sydney just north-east of Dee Why

Cromer and Cromer Heights, two small suburbs north of Narraweena, were once known as Dee Why West. The name Cromer honours a small town in East Anglia in England, which is noted for its abundance of wild birds and its golf club. The name was changed to Cromer when Dee

Why Golf Links Ltd, which had been formed in 1927, were taken over by the Cromer Country Club in 1940. The club applied to have the area's name changed to Cromer, and, permission given, a new suburb assumed its independence.

The land occupied by the golf links is on a grant of 100 acres, south of Narrabeen Lagoon, originally made in 1841 to Father John Joseph Therry (1790–1864, see Avalon). On his death, he left the land to the Society of Jesus, which sold it. By early this century the area was being used as a farm or a weekender by a succession of owners, one of whom probably named the property after the English town. The property was bought by Dee Why Golf Links Ltd in 1927.

Like its English namesake, birds of many varieties are found in this area, attracted by the Narrabeen Lakes to the north and the natural bushland stretching west to Wakehurst Parkway.

## CRONULLA

*Shire of Sutherland*

Location: 26 kilometres south of Sydney on the Pacific Ocean just north of the entrance to Port Hacking, on the Cronulla Line

In this area, at the south end of Bate Bay and north of the entrance to Port Hacking, John Connell was the first settler, receiving a 380 acre grant on 18 June 1835. The suburb's name is from the Aboriginal word "kurranulla" meaning "the place of pink seashells". Surveyor Robert Dixon was surveying here in 1827–28, and he named the beaches. In 1840 the beach was known as Kurranulla. In 1895 the area was

*Print from a "picture show" slide, c. 1920, used by the local council to lure bathers to Cronulla Baths*

subdivided and land was offered for sale at £10 per acre; in 1899 the government named the area Gunnamatta (meaning "sandy hills"), but on 26 February 1908, it was officially changed to Cronulla, and Gunnamatta became the name of the beautiful bay on the Port Hacking side of this suburb.

After the railway came to Sutherland in 1885, the area became popular for picnics — for which Cronulla has two assets: a fine ocean surfing beach, and on its southern side beautiful Gunnamatta Bay, an arm of port Hacking. Before Cronulla was linked to Sydney by rail in 1939, it was necessary to travel to Sutherland and transfer to a steam tram which chuffed its way through sandy, and sometimes bushland, areas to the beach.

Although today's train journey is undoubtedly fast, some of the excitement and anticipation of arrival was lost when the steam trams went. Time has also relaxed the rules that applied to Cronulla Beach and were enforced by vigilant beach inspectors: "no dogs allowed on the sand; no one allowed to leave the beach without a robe covering the swimming costume; no dangerous ball games allowed". Many regulars came to Cronulla each year, mostly to rent beach houses for school holidays. The Cecil Hotel was then alive with visitors, and the Ritz Cafe was booked out with hungry holiday-makers. Evening strolls along the Esplanade usually followed.

An official post office opened in January 1891, known as Cronulla Beach post office, as at that time most of the settlement was on the beach side. It was closed in 1893, reopened in 1907, and in 1929 its name was changed officially to Cronulla.

The first public school opened in January 1910. Today there are two public schools and a high school, as well as convent schools. Small ferries run regularly from a wharf near the railway station, taking passengers down Gunnamatta Bay and across the entrance of Port Hacking to Bundeena in the Royal National Park.

Salt Water Swimming Baths

Gunnamatta Bay CRONULLA.

Nearly ¾ of an acre salt water swimming pool.

ACCOMMODATE 240 BATHERS.

OPEN ON TUESDAYS, THURSDAYS, SATURDAYS and on PUBLIC HOLIDAYS from 7 to 10 P.M.

Continental Bathing. ......... Admission 3ᵈ

COSTUMES for HIRE.

OPENING NIGHT first SATURDAY in DECEMBER

J.W. Macfarlane ......... Shire Clerk.

*1292*

## CROWS NEST

*Municipalities of North Sydney and Willoughby*

Location: 5 kilometres north of Sydney on the Pacific Highway

The crow builds its nest on the highest place it can find, and "The Crow's Nest" was the name of a house built on 500 acres of land granted in 1825 to Edward

Crows Nest House, home of Alexander Berry (one of the richest men in Australia), was sadly demolished during the 1930s depression. All that remains are the great stone gates which front what is now the Pacific Highway

Wollstonecraft (1783–1832). The house stood on the estate's highest point, giving it a commanding view of Sydney Harbour and across land that is today crowded with high-rise buildings, to Botany Bay. Wollstonecraft farmed land, and it became known as Crow's Nest Farm. After Wollstonecraft's death, his partner and brother-in-law, Alexander Berry (1781–1873) worked the property. After Berry's death the land was sold and resold until subdivided and used for home-sites. North Sydney Demonstration School was built on the site of the house itself.

A cable tram ran from Crows Nest to Milsons Point to connect with the ferry service from Sydney in 1893 and was replaced in 1898 by an electric tram. Today buses have taken over from the trams, and the shopping area has been extended and developed. During the 1920s there were just a few small businesses, most of which closed during the Depression. Possibly the last to go was a large

drapery store owned by a Mr Isaacs, the corner site of which is now occupied by the Crows Nest Hotel. One of the main streets of this suburb, Falcon Street, also immortalises a bird, the falcon, a member of the hawk family, and it is possible that these birds of prey were found in Crows Nest at the time of Wollstonecraft's grant. Nearby Berry Street and the suburb of Wollstonecraft commemorate these two early land-owners.

# CROYDON

*Municipalities of Burwood, Ashfield and Canterbury*
Location: 11 kilometres south-west of Sydney between Parramatta Road and the Hume Highway, on the Main Suburban Line

This suburb, between Ashfield and Burwood, began with a grant to a convict's wife. Isaac Nelson was transported for seven years, and his innocent wife, Sarah, decided to follow as a free settler. She arranged her own passage and

arrived in 1791. Three years later she received a grant of 15 acres on what is now known as Malvern Hill.

Other early grants included two 25 acre grants to James Eades and James Brackenrig in 1794 and 30 acres to Dennis Connor in 1796. All of these were in the area north of the present Queen Street. John Townson's 1793 grant (see Five Dock) extended into modern Croydon, and so did Thomas Rowley's Burwood estate (see Burwood) and William Faithful's 1,000 acre grant (see Enfield). By 1920 much of the area was included in Joseph Underwood's Ashfield Park estate, which extended west as far as Croydon station. In 1834 the western part of the area (formerly the Burwood estate) was held by John Lucas, who divided 113 of his 213 acres into small allotments and sold them.

Where the railway station now stands was Hermitage Farm, a 100 acre grant made in 1794 to Baron Augustus Alt (1731–1815). He arrived with Governor Phillip in the First Fleet and was the colony's first surveyor-general. Alt Street, Ashfield, bears his name.

From the 1860s to 1890s Croydon was a small village surrounded by the homes of wealthy businessmen. One survivor of this period remains. The third Anthony Hordern, the retail baron, began in 1868 to build a property on 30 acres in Croydon. A splendid home, called Shubra Hall, it was completed in late 1869. It was sold in the 1880s to J. Coghlan and in 1890 was acquired by the Presbyterian Church. The Presbyterian Ladies College, established in 1888, transferred there, where it remains today.

From 1867, when William Bottle had a small brickworks in Lucas Road, brickmaking was an important local activity. By the 1910s three such firms were operating in the area.

The area was known as Burwood or Ashfield, but when the railway station opened in 1875 it was called Five Dock. In August 1876, however, the name was changed to Croydon. This name, after the London suburb, was suggested by Ashfield Council in 1874 because Five Dock was a long way to the north of the new station and some confusion had ensued.

Subdivision followed the coming of the railway, and Croydon and its neighbouring suburbs were known for their attractive Federation-style bungalows and two-storey, free-standing Victorian terraces. The latter usually have Australian cedar staircases with delicate carving and stained-glass windows. Renovation of some of these Victorian gems has uncovered original sandstock bricks used to decorate fireplaces and verandah areas. But times and trends have changed and many of the old houses have been demolished to make way for high-rise dwellings, which have altered the character of Croydon.

The first school opened in January 1884, and the first post office on 1 January 1880.

## CROYDON PARK
*Municipalities of Canterbury, Ashfield and Burwood*
Location: 12 kilometres south-west of Sydney between Georges River Road and the Hume Highway

This small neighbourhood, on the edge of Croydon proper, and close to Dulwich Hill and Enfield, achieved a separate identity because of the dissatisfaction of its residents. The public school's Parents' and Citizens' Association considered that residents were rather left out of regular and efficient postal deliveries. A petition was prepared for their member of parliament, asking that a post office be opened in the area, named Croydon Park post office. In 1914 their efforts were successful. The area was made a separate neighbourhood and took the name of its new post office.

The north-western part of the suburb was part of William Faithful's grant (see Enfield). Today Croydon Park Reserve, bounded by Brighton Avenue, Albert Road and Croydon Avenue on the Cooks River, is a well-known and attractive park. A public school, an important memorial perhaps to that early group of parents who established Croydon Park, stands in Georges River Road. The post office is in Dunmore Street, which honours John Dunmore Lang (1799–1878), the first Presbyterian clergyman in Sydney.

## CURL CURL
*Shire of Warringah*
Location: 18 kilometres north-east of Sydney, facing the Pacific Ocean

This Aboriginal name, thought to mean "a lagoon", was originally applied to nearby Manly Lagoon, and the reason for its being given to the ocean beach is not known. The name has been used for a number of localities. Curl Curl Head lies to the south of Harbord, beside Manly Lagoon. Curl Curl Heights was the name for the area behind Queenscliff until the 1930s. The beach is north of that suburb, and the first recorded use of the name Curl Curl here was in 1899. Now Curl Curl is used to describe the area around the beach. Curl Curl North, which has been renamed Wingala, lies north of Dee Why Head.

The suburb of Curl Curl was slower to develop than Harbord to the south, and in the early part of this century it still held only holiday camps and weekenders. Today Curl Curl is well-known for Stewart House, a holiday home and education centre for under-privileged children. It was established in 1931 and is maintained by children from public schools in New South Wales.

This part of the coastline is clear and open to the ocean, and, at Curl Curl, Harbord Lagoon at the northern end of the beach, with its adjacent parks, lends a sense of unspoiled natural unity between land and sea.

## DACEYVILLE
*Municipality of Botany*
Location: 7 kilometres south of Sydney just north of Botany

The beginnings of this neighbourhood, south of Kensington and adjoining Kingsford, were inspired by the dream of an Englishman, Ebenezer Howard, who first conceived a plan for a garden city outside London.

Daceyville was named after John Rowland Dacey (1884–1912), a state parliamentarian for the area from 1895 to 1912, who urged the government to create a model suburb, reminiscent of Letchworth in England, with low-cost housing for working-class people. The idea found favour after Dacey had died,

J. R. Dacey said of Daceyville that it was to be a "city beautiful" of which Australians could be proud. Started in 1895, the Dacey Garden Suburb was not completed till 1981, and even then the boundaries were less extensive than originally envisaged. This photograph was taken in 1915

and 336 acres were resumed for the project; Daceyville became Australia's first garden city experiment. Sir John Sulman (1849–1934) was given the work of planning the housing estate, and the scrubby crown land that had been reserved in eastern Mascot as a water conservation site became a new-style suburb between 1912 and 1924.

John Rowland Dacey

# DARLINGHURST

*City of Sydney*
Location: 2 kilometres east of Sydney between William Street and Oxford Street

This suburb was once known as Eastern Hill because of its geographical position east of the city. By 1800 several large windmills were situated on the heights of this area, using the stiff breezes to grind much-needed grain. The area began its suburban life under the name Henrietta Town, being called after Mrs

Four main roads meet in this suburb, as specified in Sulman's plan: Gardeners Road, Anzac Parade, Rainbow Street and Bunnerong Road. To the south of this point, known as the Nine Ways, are a series of semi-circular streets. The plans provided for nearly 15,000 cottages, as well as shops and public buildings, such as schools and churches, and parks and open spaces. Daceyville Public School was opened in 1921.

Macquarie, whose second name was Henrietta. At that time it was an Aboriginal reserve. Loyalties changed with governors, however, and when Governor Darling assumed office, the suburb changed its name to Darlinghurst, in honour of his popular wife. "Hurst" is an old English word for wooded hill.

Darlinghurst was once quite a fashionable suburb and it housed some famous people. One of the grandest houses was Craigend, built by New South Wales surveyor-general, Sir Thomas Mitchell, in 1828–31. It stood on about 4 hectares of land in the area now bordered by Kings Cross Road, Surrey Street and Victoria Street. Mitchell and his family lived in this neoclassical mansion with the facade of a Greek temple for only five or six years. It then passed to several owners and was demolished in 1921, but Craigend Street is a permanent reminder.

David Scott Mitchell (1836–1907), the wealthy bachelor who endowed the Mitchell Library with £70,000 and his valuable collection of books and documents relating to Australia and the Pacific region, was a longer term

A bleak scene—Darlinghurst terraces in the early 1900s

resident. He moved from the family home in Cumberland Street in the Rocks on the death of his mother in 1871. He then lived unostentatiously at 17 Darlinghurst Road, indulging his interest in and talent for book collecting, until his death in 1907.

The gilt went off the suburb when Darlinghurst Gaol, designed by architect Mortimer Lewis, (1796–1879), was built in 1841. It was not the style of the building, but the significance of its erection that was the reason for the decline in Darlinghurst's popularity. The gaol buildings in Forbes Street are a fine example of the stonemason's craft. Governor Brisbane had reserved 3½ acres on the outskirts of Sydney for a new gaol to replace the earlier lock-up in George Street. In 1823 a stockade was erected. Convicts quarried the

stone from nearby William Street and hauled it to the hilltop, where other convict gangs shaped it by hand into blocks. The completed enclosure was known as Woolloomooloo Stockade. Construction of the gaol commenced in 1836, and by 1841 it was complete, and prisoners from the George Street prison were marched in chains to Darlinghurst, to the jeers and catcalls of the watching crowd.

The first public hanging took place at the new gaol on 29 October 1841, when Robert Hands and George Stroud faced the hangman's noose. John Videle, a Frenchman, was the fourth man hanged at the gaol. In 1844, he was party to the murder of a debt collector, Thomas Warne, and disposed of the body by sawing it in half, then trying to burn it, and finally packing it into a sea-chest to be dumped on the north side of the

harbour. Unhappily for Videle, the boatman hired to take the chest and Videle across the harbour "smelt a rat". The chest was thrown back onto the Quay, spilt open and scattered its gory contents in front of the public gaze. Four thousand citizens watched this murderer go to his end, kneeling at his request as his head was placed in the noose.

The case of the infamous John Knatchbull has gone down in Australia's criminal history. He was charged with murdering his landlady, Mrs Jamieson, the proprietress of a boarding house in Margaret Street, Sydney. Knatchbull was defended by Robert Lowe, a notable lawyer who later became Earl of Sherbrooke. He pleaded a case of monomania on behalf of his client, but the evidence was too strongly against Knatchbull, who was hanged for his crime at

Darlinghurst Gaol on 13 February 1844, before a crowd of 10,000 — almost the total population of Sydney at that time. The last hanging in Sydney was in 1907.

The gaol was closed as a prison in June 1914 and became a security house for German refugees during the First World War. In 1921 the building changed character completely when it became the East Sydney Technical College. The grim silence of the gaol has been replaced by an air of creativity and success. The only evidence of the convict builders are their marks on the eastern and southern walls, as no convict labour was used in the construction of the buildings themselves.

The courthouse standing conveniently beside the gaol, and facing Taylor Square, was also designed by Mortimer Lewis. It was opened in 1842, and fulfils the same function today.

The suburb's main thoroughfare, William Street, was named after King William IV, who reigned from 1830 to 1837 and was often scathingly referred to as Sailor Bill, or even Silly Billy.

*The portico of Craigend from the garden. After the house was demolished the property was subdivided into eleven lots*

# DARLING POINT
*Municipality of Woollahra*
Location: 4 kilometres east of Sydney on New South Head Road reaching down to Port Jackson

Originally known by its Aboriginal name Yarranabbee, this suburb is on the south side of the harbour. It was called Mrs Darling's Point in honour of his wife by Ralph Darling, the colony's often criticised governor of 1825 to 1831. At the time, the area was heavily timbered, but after New South Head Road was built in 1831 timber cutters felled many of the trees, and the land was subdivided. Most of the plots, covering 9 to 15 acres in this area, were taken up between 1833 and 1838. The Mrs was lost from its name and the suburb and point became Darling Point.

The water supply was always a problem in early Sydney, and in the long, hot summers, many people ran short. Darling Point was, therefore, specially favoured, because it had two fresh-water streams at the end of the point. It was here that Sir Thomas Mitchell (1792–1855), colonial surveyor-general, built his second family home. He named it Carthona which derives from a Spanish phrase meaning "the meeting of the waters". It was, from the outset, a special home to the Mitchell family, Major Mitchell himself having carved some of the ornamental stonework and many of the keystones of the window arches and doors. The house had fine cedar staircases, lofty ceilings and glorious views to the Harbour. It was in his beloved house that this great man died on 5 October 1855.

The estate passed to Mitchell's daughter but with considerable debts hanging over it. In 1861 it

Governor Ralph Darling

Sketch of St Mark's Church, Darling Point, by an unknown artist

was leased to the Cooksey sisters who for the next ten years used the premises as a school for young ladies. Much later, it was purchased and modernised by Philip Bushell, who set up Bushell's Tea Warehouse, in George Street North, and began importing tea and coffee. In 1960, when Mrs Bushell died, the estate was valued at £2.5 million.

Darling Point, situated between Rushcutters Bay and Double Bay, has always been noted as a suburb for the prominent and wealthy. About the middle of last century residents included Thomas Sutcliffe Mort (1816−78), who lived at Greenoaks, pioneer of exporting frozen meat (see Mortdale); the Reverend George Fairfowl Macarthur (1825−90), one-time rector at St Mark's, Darling Point, and later headmaster of The King's School, Parramatta; members of the Tooth family, brewers; and Samuel Hordern (1849−1909), the retail king. Some of the beautiful homes still survive, despite the modern tendency to demolish and erect high-rise buildings. As well as Carthona, there are The Swifts, willed to the Catholic Church by the founder of Resch's Brewery, and Bishopscourt, residence of the Anglican archbishop of Sydney. The Anglican church of St Mark was designed by Edmund Blacket (1817−83), and its foundation stone was laid in 1848. As in past times, it is a fashionable and popular church for society weddings.

Sydney newspapers of the mid-1850s give reports of the social activities of the era and of the hostesses who entertained with charm and élan, which make fascinating reading. One of the famous venues was the Gothic-style mansion Lindesay. Now owned by the National Trust, it is possibly one of their most popular properties. It was standing in 1836 when Charles Darwin visited these shores and was once occupied by Sir Thomas Mitchell and his family, and later by William Bradley, a wealthy pastoralist, who reared his motherless daughters in the house. It was named in honour of Colonel Patrick Lindesay (1778−1839), who was acting governor of the colony from 22 October to 2 December 1831, between the departure of Governor Ralph Darling and the arrival of the next governor, Major-General Sir Richard Bourke.

Today Darling Point is a delightful combination of the essence of a past age and of modern convenience, being only 4

kilometres from the city, yet isolated for its rush and bustle. There is a small shopping centre at the junction of New South Head Road and Darling Point Road. The latter leads from the modern to the traditional, past the old church, to the peace of the harbour foreshore. The beloved Australian poet Dorothea Mackellar lived at 155 Darling Point Road, and her funeral service was held at St Mark's on 14 October 1968.

## DARLINGTON
*City of Sydney*
Location: 3 kilometres south of Sydney between the University of Sydney and Redfern

Darlington's first settler was William Shepherd, a botanist, who in 1827 was offered 200 acres of Grose's Farm, later the University Paddock in what is now Camperdown. Shepherd refused the grant, saying he would prefer a block "closer to the Town", and accordingly he was given land to the north-east. By 1835 he held 28½ acres here and had cultivated a thriving nursery garden which he called the Darling Nursery, in honour of Governor Darling. Later the borough took the name and added "town", which was gradually corrupted to Darlington. Street names in the area recall Shepherd's venture — Rose, Myrtle, Ivy, Vine and Pine all appear, as well as Shepherd.

In 1835 James Chisholm was granted 62 acres in the area, on which he built Calder House, which he enjoyed for only a short time before his death in 1837. The land was resumed by the government in 1878 and now forms part of the Eveleigh Railway Workshops.

Another grant, which came to a Mr O'Brien in 1833, was disposed of at the time of the Crimean War (1854–56). The street names in that subdivision include Raglan and Codrington, which commemorate two British generals, and Alma, which was a famous battle. In 1844, when Darlington was created a municipality, it covered only 44 acres, had 700 residents, and there were no parks. A further subdivision was made in 1855.

In 1872 the Deaf and Dumb and the Blind Institutions were moved from Paddington to a site on City Road, Darlington. The buildings were enlarged in 1891. In 1942 they were requisitioned by defence authorities, and they later became part of the University of Sydney.

In 1948 Darlington municipality was amalgamated with the city of Sydney, and eventually a large part of the suburb was absorbed by the university. Many residents were forced to moved, and much of this small inner-city area has been lost for residential purposes.

## DAVIDSON
*Shire of Warringah*
Location: 20 kilometres north of Sydney just west of Frenchs Forest

In 1923 a park was dedicated in this new suburb and named after a governor of New South Wales, Sir Walter Davidson (in office 1918–23). The suburb, on the upper reaches of Middle Harbour and adjoining Frenchs Forest, took the same name from that date.

Davidson, developed in the 1960s, is still an area of natural bushland. The park from which the suburb took its name is extensive and unspoiled, with walking tracks threading through

it. Pony clubs also use it regularly for trekking. Mona Vale Road separates Davidson Park from Ku-ring-gai Chase.

Houses in the area have been built to blend in with the bushland surroundings, and the result is restful and truly Australian. Some street names commemorate famous early Australians, including surveyors Sir Thomas Mitchell and William Govett; Laurence Halloran, an early nineteenth-century schoolmaster and journalist; and Sir Gerald Strickland, governor of New South Wales from 1913 to 1917. Other streets are named after native plants and trees, such as Hakea, Jarrah, Blackbutt and Mimosa.

## DAWES POINT
*City of Sydney*
Location: 2 kilometres north of Sydney near the southern pylon of the Harbour Bridge

This historic point, which is just under the southern end of Sydney Harbour Bridge, has known at least three name changes. The first names were Aboriginal, Tarra, and Tullagulla, which were later changed to Point Maskelyne, in honour of the Reverend Dr Nevil Maskelyne, astronomer royal. Maskelyne sent out to the colony the first astronomical instruments, which were established on the point in 1788 by Lieutenant William Dawes (1762–1836) in the country's first observatory. The present domed building on Observatory Hill was not completed until 1858. Later the point was renamed Dawes Point in his honour.

Dawes was interested in scientific matters and in the Aborigines, and he became an

Hickson Road, Dawes Point, 1921. The old fort at left was demolished to make way for the Harbour Bridge

expert on their languages. Although he had hoped to settle in New South Wales to farm, the marines, with whom he was serving, were ordered home and no suitable position in the colony was offered. He left the colony in 1791, and in 1792 he became governor of Sierra Leone.

The point has other historical associations. It was the site of the first guns mounted in Sydney (by Dawes in 1788); and the first salt was refined from sea water there in 1790. The first slaughterhouse in the settlement was located there, the point sometimes being called Slaughter House Point. At one time there was also a small burial ground.

## DEE WHY

*Shire of Warringah*

Location: 18 kilometres north-east of Sydney on Pittwater Road facing the Pacific Ocean

Between Collaroy and Curl Curl on the Barrenjoey Peninsula north of Sydney, Dee Why has a fine ocean beach, a salt-water pool, and a lagoon rich in bird life. The origin of the suburb's name is not clear. It could well have been derived from an Aboriginal word, "Diwai", applied to a bird that frequented the lagoon. The historical claim, however, is that James Meehan (1774–1826), who surveyed the area in 1818, recorded on his map "Dy Beach, marked a honeysuckle near beach". The "DY" could be an abbreviation for

the Greek word "dyspropositos", which means "difficult to reach", a feasible explanation since the beach would have been shielded by thick undergrowth and swamp surrounding Dee Why lagoon.

In the 1820s and 1830s Dee Why was part of James Jenkins's property (see Narrabeen). In 1900 this land passed to the Salvation Army and in about 1906 they subdivided the area between Pacific and Dee Why Parades. Harper's estate was also subdivided in 1906, and once these two estates were broken up, the area began to develop. The Salvation Army has homes in the area, and it periodically sells some of its land.

A peaceful seaside suburb until after the Second World War, when it became a residential area and a rash of high-rise unit buildings increased the population dramatically, Dee Why is now heavily populated. The shopping centre on both sides of the main road, Pittwater Road, flowed into side streets and it now offers a wide range of merchandise. A good bus service connects Dee Why with Sydney, an important factor for people who live here.

A beauty spot well worth a visit, especially in spring, is the Stony Range Flora Reserve. Situated on Pittwater Road just south of Dee Why, it has a collection of native flora in a controlled but natural bush garden.

On 27 September 1979, a small area on the south-east side of Dee Why Lagoon was dedicated as the James Meehan Reserve. Meehan worked as a surveyor in New South Wales and Van Diemen's Land from the time of his arrival in Sydney in 1800 until his retirement in 1823. The park honours the claim that Meehan, a former convict, put Dee Why's name "on the map" and was one of the first white men to explore the area.

## DENISTONE
*Municipality of Ryde*
Location: 16 kilometres
north-west of Sydney between
Victoria Road and Blaxland Road,
on the Main Northern Line

Denistone's name was derived from
the property of a doctor settler,
Thomas Forster, who came to the
area in 1830 and six months later
issued a warning to trespassers that
he "had taken possession of his
farm now called Deniston".

The history of Forster's land
goes back to the early days of the
colony. Grants in the area had been
made in 1795 to John Parnice (45
acres), Humphrey Evans (45 acres)
and William Ternan (30 acres). The
Reverend Richard Johnson
acquired all of these grants only a
month later, and in 1800 the land
passed to the Connor family and
then into Forster's hands.

Forster married into an old
pioneering family when he wed
Eliza Blaxland, explorer Gregory
Blaxland's daughter.
Unfortunately the house the doctor
built on the property was
destroyed by a bushfire, and in
1840 the land was leased for twelve
years to Major Edward Darvall.
When Darvall died, the property,
advertised as Glen Ryde, was sold
in two lots. Richard Rouse Terry,
brother of Edward Terry, first
mayor of Ryde, bought the estate
in 1872, and built a splendid stone
house, which he called Denistone
House, now the maternity wing of
the Ryde Soldiers Memorial
Hospital in Denistone Road. Near
the railway station, which opened
in 1937, is Darvall Park, which
was named after Major Darvall.

A village named Deniston is
located 25 kilometres north-east of
Stafford in England, and it is
possible that Forster named his
property after that faraway but
well-remembered place.

## DHARRUK
*City of Blacktown*
Location: 46 kilometres
north-west of Sydney and north of
Mount Druitt

This suburb lies south of
Blacktown, among the recently
developed areas of Blackett,
Emerton and Hebersham. It has an
Aboriginal name, purported to be
that of a local tribe who frequented
this area of Sydney. The Dharruk
were the first inhabitants of the
Blue Mountains, but no member
of the tribe survives today. A rock
carving of the flight of the great
grey kangaroo, at the foot of the
Hawkesbury Lookout near
Springwood, is the work of
members of this tribe. The legend
about the Three Sisters at Echo
Point, Katoomba, also came from
this tribe.

## DOONSIDE
*City of Blacktown*
Location: 40 kilometres
north-west of Sydney on
Richmond Road, on the Main
Western Line

Originally known as Crawford,
after the family that had holdings
here in the district's earliest days,
this suburb's name was changed to
Doonside in 1886, when the
railway line came through the area.
The name, chosen by Robert
Crawford, on whose property the

Bungarribee House as it was in the early
1900s

new station was built, was the name of an estate owned by his father in Scotland.

A Robert Crawford had received a grant of 197 acres in the area in the early nineteenth century and had called his property Hill-end. Another early grant was of 2,000 acres to John Campbell, who built Bungarribee House on it in 1825. After he died in 1828, the property passed through many hands until purchased by the Overseas Telecommunications Commission, which demolished the house in 1958. OTC owns a large area in the south of the suburb.

The railway construction camp in 1880 was known by the Aboriginal name of Wolkara, and this name was given to the first post office when it opened in 1921.

*Left to deteriorate in the 1940s and 1950s, Bungarribee became the focus of many a haunted-house story, boasting no less than two ghosts downstairs and one upstairs*

But in April 1929, its name was also changed to Doonside.

A Scottish influence was evident in this first small hamlet, as shown by street names Knox, Cameron, Kildare and Graham.

Doonside's early days saw poultry farmers and orchardists in this area. When the railway line to Penrith came through, some subdivision made home-sites available, but the area has only gone ahead in the last few years when Doonside's low to medium house prices have attracted home-buyers.

Situated on the periphery of Blacktown, the suburb has all the advantages offered by that satellite city. A modern public school is situated in Kildare Street, and a high school stands in Power Street. A pleasant reserve is located in Woodstock Avenue, on the eastern side of Eastern Creek.

## DOUBLE BAY
*Municipality of Woollahra*
Location: 4 kilometres east of Sydney on New South Head Road on the south side of Port Jackson

Early charts show the first recorded name of the bay between Darling Point and Point Piper as Keltie or Keltie's Bay. It honoured James Keltie, a master in the Royal Navy, who had sailed with the First Fleet as mate of the storeship *Fishburn*. During the voyage, Micah Morton, master of the *Sirius*, was injured, and Arthur Phillip transferred Keltie from the *Fishburn* to take Morton's place. As master of the *Sirius* James Keltie entered Port Jackson, and in the course of the harbour survey his name became attached to the inlet now known as Double Bay. Somewhere between 1796, when Keltie's name was recorded on a map, and the 1820s the name was

View from Double Bay looking toward
Port Jackson, early 1900s

changed to Double Bay, the sandy
shoreline being interrupted by a
miniature point. The second
(eastern) bay, earlier known as
Blackburn Bay, after David
Blackburn, master of HMS *Supply*,
is still called Blackburn Cove.

The name Double Bay appears
in Governor Macquarie's journal
for 4 September 1821, when he
reported a visit there, and wrote of
his plan to establish botanic gardens.
Although this plan did not
eventuate, a well-known botanist,
Michael Guilfoyle, who migrated
here in 1853, introduced some
exotic plants into the area, and
established a nursery on the corner
of Ocean Avenue and South
Avenue known as Exotic Nursery.
He grew date palms from Asia,
coconuts from Brazil, tea and
coffee trees from Arabia and
cinnamon trees from Ceylon,
all only 5 kilometres from the

obelisk in Macquarie Place.

The area Macquarie had set
aside for the gardens was held by
the government until 1834. It was
then laid out as a village when
New South Head Road was being
constructed, and occupied by
fishermen and gardeners. By 1836
the name Double Bay was in full
use.

The suburb today offers two
swimming areas. One is the
beachfront known as Seven
Shillings Beach, so named when a
Mrs Busby gave an Aboriginal 7
shillings compensation for his
fishing rights. The second is
Redleaf Pool on the bay, named
after the local house Redleaf.

Double Bay Creek, a
watercourse about 1 kilometre
long, rises in Cooper Park and
flows generally north into Double
Bay. The park on the bay, a
favourite spot for local residents
and their children, has a large
tree which is beautifully decorated

during Christmas week.

One interesting house in this
suburb has had many owners, all
of whom seemed to delight in
renaming it. Since 1913, however,
it has been called Gladswood. Built
about 1856, it was the home of
Samuel Deane Gordon (1811–82),
a merchant, businessman,
land-owner and finally a member
of the New South Wales
Legislative Council. Gordon
delighted in his home and suburb,
where he died in 1882. In those
days there was a bus drawn by two
horses, and it ran from Double
Bay to Kings Cross; another ran
from Edgecliff, on the hill above
Double Bay, to Macquarie Place.

Double Bay today has cultivated
its image as an exclusive shopping
centre, offering imported and local
furniture, clothing and food. It is
somewhat continental in character
and has endeavoured to retain its
village atmosphere.

## DOVER HEIGHTS

*Municipality of Waverley*
Location: 9 kilometres east of
Sydney on Old South Head Road
facing the Pacific Ocean

This tiny area high on the coast
between Watsons Bay and North
Bondi, was named after Dover
Street (now Dover Road), which
joined it to Rose Bay. It is not
known who gave it this name, or
whether it was called after the
English white cliffs of Dover.

The first mention of Dover
Heights appears in the municipal
records of 1886. Like Rose Bay and
Watsons Bay, Dover Heights was
at first an area of market gardens.

Early subdivision plans for Dover Heights.
Hardie & Gorman, established in 1873, is
one of the oldest real estate agencies in
Australia

In 1830 land was owned in the area
by Daniel Cooper (1785–1853), a
partner in the firm of Cooper and
Levey, which owned the Waterloo
Stores. This retailing emporium
stood in George Street, Sydney, on
the site of the present Gowings at
the corner of Market and George
Streets. Waterloo Stores was
named after their mill at Waterloo,
which was named after the Battle
of Waterloo, fought in 1815. Many
veterans of the battle were in
Sydney in the early twenties and
patronised Waterloo Stores.

In the 1860s large homes with
spacious gardens were built
throughout the Eastern Suburbs,
including Dover Heights. One
early house gave Fernleigh Avenue
its name. Fernleigh, in New South
Head Road, was set in splendid
gardens and was almost hidden by

trees. It was built between 1881
and 1892, by Frank Bennett,
whose father, Samuel, founded the
*Evening News*, Sydney's first
evening paper, in 1867. The house
was built in stages and its style
modelled on another famous
mansion, called Mundarra Towers,
at Little Coogee (now called
Clovelly). Fernleigh was built on
the site of an earlier house,
completed in 1874 for J. C.
Roberts, mayor of Sydney in 1874.

In 1913 Dover Heights Estate
was subdivided and the land sold
for home-sites. Once prospective
home-builders realised the
potential of this high, breezy area,
with its splendid views, they were
eager to buy.

From the early days in the
colony's development, the cliffs
from Watsons Bay and South Head
extending past Dover Heights had
been used as observation posts.
During the Second World War the
army had installations on Dover
Heights, built on unused
Commonwealth land, facing the
ocean, which had become
overgrown with low bushes. After
the war, the area was reclaimed
and converted into a park, known
today as Rodney Reserve.

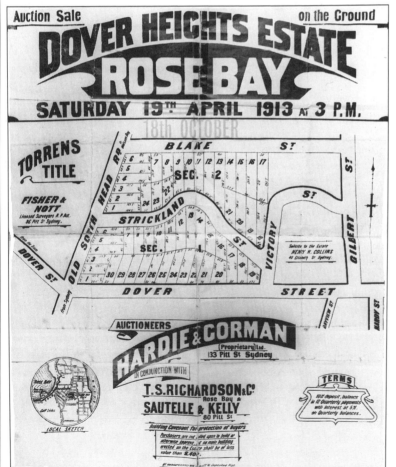

## DRUMMOYNE

*Municipality of Drummoyne*
Location: 6 kilometres west of
Sydney on the south side of the
Parramatta River

Surrounded by water on three
sides, Drummoyne was described
in the 1920s as "a picturesque
suburb which has made rapid
strides since the tram route was
opened". Trams are no more in
Drummoyne, but in spite of
changes in building styles, many

Above: Undated postcard of Drummoyne Bridge

Right: A strictly supervised gardening class at Drummoyne Public School, c. 1905

residents still have wonderful views of the Parramatta River.

Governor King's grant to Surgeon John Harris, Five Dock Farm, included this area (see Five Dock). Part of it, the area between Thompson and Millar Streets, was subdivided in 1841 and advertised as "Bourke Town within forty minutes row of Sydney", boats being the colony's main means of transport at that date. William Wright, a merchant who was also a whaler and sealer, bought land in the northern part of the area in 1853 and named it Drummoyne Park after his family home at Drummoyne on the Clyde in Scotland. Drummoyne is Gaelic for "flat-topped ridge". Drummoyne abounds in streets named after people from British and Australian history, such as Queen Victoria, Alexandra, Wolseley, Gipps, Therry, Polding, Broughton and Marlborough. Wrights Road honours the man responsible for the suburb's name,

and, at the northern end of the suburb, on Wright's Point, a flight of sandstone stairs, known as Wright's Steps, lead to a river-landing once in the grounds of his home, Drummoyne House.

Spectacle Island can be seen from the eastern part of Drummoyne. Used by the navy, the island was so named because it is shaped like a pair of spectacles. The island has been used for storage of armaments since 1865.

The original Gladesville and Iron

Cove bridges, which connect the suburb to the north and south banks of the Parramatta River, were ready for use by 1884. The Gladesville Bridge, built in 1881, had an opening span to let through the colliers carrying coal from Newcastle to the gasworks at Mortlake. But the opening disrupted road traffic to such an extent that a new bridge was built with a raised centre high enough to allow shipping to pass underneath. This is the attractive bridge

Wolseley Street Wharf, Drummoyne, fronting an impressive backdrop of houses, c. 1930

spanning the Parramatta River today, connecting Drummoyne and Gladesville.

The old road north had run through Abbotsford, but when the new bridges and a new road to Gladesville were built in the 1880s, the area boomed. Many subdivisions were made in the following years, including the Drummoyne estate, and several hotels were established along the road.

Drummoyne Bay, on the Parramatta River, was once known by the Aboriginal name Warrembah, meaning "where sweet waters meet". The south-east section of this suburb is known as Birkenhead, after an English town on the Mersey. It was first applied to the area in an 1854 subdivision.

Today Birkenhead Point is the site of a modern shopping centre built in the remodelled Dunlop rubber factory, with a marina and the Sydney Maritime Museum alongside. Another subdivision in the area was the Tranmere estate.

## DUFFYS FOREST

*Shire of Warringah*
Location: 28 kilometres north of Sydney bordered by Ku-ring-gai Chase National Park

Suburb names often come from one of the three sources: the original Aboriginal name may be retained; a name may be chosen to honour a person of note; or an early resident may be remembered.

The last is the case for Duffys Forest, a northern suburb at the upper reaches of Cowan Creek, adjoining Ku-ring-gai Chase National Park.

In 1857 a land grant was made to Irishman Patrick Duffy in a thickly wooded part of Warringah shire. Duffy, who became a timber-cutter, cleared a road through bushland so that he could move timber by bullock waggon to a stone wharf that he built on the creek at Cowan. His land, and later the surrounding bushland, became known as Duffy's Forest. The wharf, still known as Duffy's Wharf, remains.

In recent years proposals were made to build Sydney's second airport in this area, but fortunately for the flora and fauna, the inhabitants and the natural peace of the bush area, the plans were abandoned.

# DULWICH HILL

*Municipality of Marrickville*
Location: 9 kilometres south-west of Sydney on New Canterbury Road, on the Bankstown Line

This suburb, between Marrickville and Hurlstone Park, takes its name from Dulwich, a suburb of London. The name means "meadow where dill grows". A number of different names were used for the area before Dulwich Hill was chosen. First it was Petersham Hill, then Sarah Dell, followed by Wardell's Bush, South Petersham and Fern Hill, and finally Dulwich Hill. When the railway line opened on 1 February 1895, it was known as Wardell Road, but in July 1920 it became Dulwich Hill.

One of the largest land-owners in this district was a prominent citizen, lawyer Dr Robert Wardell (1793–1834). His estate extended into Dulwich Hill (see Petersham). Wardell Road, a main thoroughfare running from the station north to New Canterbury Road, commemorates this pioneer.

The school at Dulwich Hill opened in January 1885, and the first official post office followed on 5 May 1887. The area developed quickly after the steam tram lines were extended to the suburb in about 1900. In the following years villas were constructed on the spacious allotments that characterised the area.

# DUNDAS

*City of Parramatta, Shire of Baulkham Hills*
Location: 22 kilometres north-west of Sydney between Kissing Point Road and Pennant Hills Road, on the local Carlingford Line

This district north-east of Parramatta was part of the Field of Mars. Settlement of The Ponds, in the eastern part of Dundas, began in 1791 when a group of ex-convicts settled on 30 to 50 acre grants, which were gradually incorporated into larger estates in the area. Grants of 25 to 100 acres were made later to settlers including the Reverend James Bain, a chaplain of the New South Wales Corps, who received his grant of 100 acres, where the Dundas council chambers now stand, on 2 October 1794. He later sold to John Macarthur.

The Reverend Samuel Marsden (1764–1838), selected 100 acres in 1796 at Thompson's Corner. He called his property Dundas Farm, in honour of Henry Dundas, principal secretary of state for the home department in London from 1791 to 1794. The name was not used for the suburb now known as Dundas until nearly a century later, the little settlement being known originally as Adderton Road.

When the post office opened in 1861 on Kissing Point Road, it was called Pennant Hills. In 1867 the name was changed to Field of Mars, and in 1890 it was changed yet again, this time to Dundas. When the railway station on the line being extended from Clyde to Carlingford opened on 20 April 1896, it was called Kissing Point Road. On 1 August 1901, when the line became part of the government railway system, the recognised name was Dundas.

Dundas was part of a wide area known as Pennant Hills in the early years, and the site of Pennant Hills Quarry is actually in Dundas Valley. This source of blue metal was exploited for road-building from early in the nineteenth century until the quarry was abandoned in 1902.

The area was one of Sydney's main fruit-growing areas from the 1830s until two disasters intervened in the 1860s. The orange trees were attacked by a small white insect, and had to be grubbed out and burnt. Hardly an orchard escaped. A severe drought followed this first disaster, and it was six to seven years before the district was free of its troubles.

After the railway line came through, Dundas began to develop rapidly. In 1902 and 1905 the orchard land was subdivided and sold as building blocks. Today all evidence of the early orchards has vanished. In 1955, the Housing Commission began to subdivide 300 acres in the beautiful Dundas Valley. Much of the native timber had to be cut down in order to make way for roads and housing, and one of Sydney's largest housing estates was born.

The municipality of Dundas was formed in 1889, but in 1948 it was amalgamated with the City of Parramatta.

# DUNHEVED

*City of Penrith*
Location: 48 kilometres north-west of Sydney north of St Marys

The first land-owner of importance in the area north of St Marys was Governor Philip Gidley King (1758–1808), who obtained 600 acres there in 1806. He called his property Dunhaved, the name of

Governor Philip Gidley King

the keep of the old castle at
Launceston, in Cornwall. The
name remained unaltered until the
suburb began to develop, when it
was commonly spelled
Dunheaved. Still later, in the
1950s, regular usage altered the
spelling to the current Dunheved.

South Creek, a tributary flowing
north to the Hawkesbury River,
forms the boundary between
Dunheved and Werrington County
to the west. The whole stretch of
land from St Marys north towards
Windsor was used for grain
growing, orchards and sheep
raising in the early days.

Until the Second World War this
was a sparsely populated area
without any special significance.
However, the war changed all that.
A large munitions factory was
built and in 1942 a railway station
opened to accommodate hundreds
of workers employed in an
essential industry. After the war
the St Marys munitions factory
area, immediately south of
Dunheved, became an industrial
subdivision. Land close to Sydney
was in increasingly short supply in
the 1960s and 1970s. The open
grasslands around Dunheved —
from Blacktown west to Penrith —
rapidly disappeared as extensive
housing estates were built.

## DURAL
*Shires of Hornsby and Baulkham
Hills*
Location: 36 kilometres
north-west of Sydney on Old
Northern Road

Originally called Dooral-dooral, its
name being Aboriginal for "a
smoking hollow tree", this area
west of Hornsby originally
covered present Glenorie, Galston
and Arcadia. Surveyor James
Meehan's map of April 1817 shows
the name spelled as Dooral. For
many years this peaceful area was
the scene of timber getting and
fruit growing. In 1802 Governor
King included the area in a
government reserve, but the first
grant in the area was made to
George Hall in 1819.

Some well-known names from
the early records of the colony
were associated with Dural. The
Suttor family, having first held
land in the Parramatta area, had a
property there where they grew
citrus fruit that was marketed in
Sydney. Two other well-known
families were those of Thomas
Best and James Roughley. These
two settlers were closely associated
with the beautiful sandstone
Anglican Church of St Jude's,
situated on the Old Northern
Road, 260 metres above sea level.
Edmund Blacket (1817–83) is
believed to have been the architect,
as many elements are typical of his
designs. The foundation stone was
laid by Bishop Broughton on 11
November 1846, when the walls of
the church were already partly
erected. It was built using free
labour. In 1976 a new rectory was
constructed next to St Jude's, and
the existing garage was converted
into a kindergarten room to
accommodate the growing
numbers of children attending the
Sunday school.

Dural is an ideal area for a

Sunday drive, with its semi-rural
atmosphere and roadside stalls of
fresh flowers and produce that are
well worth inspection.

## EARLWOOD
*Municipality of Canterbury*
Location: 12 kilometres
south-west of Sydney on the south
side of the Cooks River

This suburb began its life as a
farming area known as Forest Hill,
and as late as 1923 Wilson's street
directory states that it was still
part of the Canterbury
municipality. The name had been
changed in 1905–06 to Parkstown,
but in 1918 it was changed again,
to its present name. Earl
commemorated a former mayor of
Canterbury, and Wood, the two
Wood brothers who had a poultry
and pig farm on Wolli Creek.
Other settlers in this forested area
included F. and A. Martin, who
had a grant in the eastern area, and
Joshua Thorpe whose 80 acre
property, Thorpe's Farm, was in
the west, stretching from Cooks
River to Wolli Creek. A prominent
early land-owner was Abraham B.
Polack, who in the 1830s acquired
eight grants, totalling 790 acres,
which covered most of Earlwood
and extended into Undercliffe.

Subdivision in most of the area
began in the 1880s. After the First
World War a war service homes
subdivision was made west of
Wardell Road, and many returned
soldiers and their families settled in
the cottages erected. The streets of
that subdivision recall the names of
many famous men and battles
connected with the war: Kitchener
(who appeared on recruitment
posters), Hamilton, Vimy, Hamel,
Fricourt and Guedecourt. For
streets in other parts of the suburb,

names of Australian historical figures were chosen, such as Bass, Flinders and Wardell; Beaman Park and Parry Steps immortalise an Earlwood alderman and a Canterbury mayor respectively.

By the 1920s Earlwood had made rapid strides as a residential suburb. At that time it was serviced by trams and the trains on the Bankstown line, and its extensive views to Botany Bay and Illawarra, and to the Blue Mountains were enticing sales points.

Today Earlwood is serviced by bus transport. Its air of homely comfort still exists and the parklands and golf links along the Cooks River to the north and east invite nearby residents to stop and rest a while, away from the demands of modern living.

## EASTERN CREEK
*City of Blacktown*
Location: 38 kilometres west of Sydney between the Great Western Highway and the Western Freeway

The origin of the name of this suburb of Blacktown is unknown. In 1820 William Dean was granted a licence for the Corporation Inn, at the bridge where Western Road crossed Eastern Creek. The area was later one of market gardens and dairies along the creek and there were blue metal quarries north of the Western Road. The post office had opened by 1866.

## EAST HILLS
*City of Bankstown*
Location: 26 kilometres south-west of Sydney on the Georges River, on the East Hills Line

The name of this suburb on the northern shore of the Georges River was first applied to the whole area between The River Road, running south from Bankstown, and the river; it was first mentioned in the *Sydney Gazette* in 1810. George Johnston junior (1790–1820) received 500 acres here as a grant in 1804, which he called New Jerusalem. It covered an area west of the present River Road, between Bansgrove and Tompson Streets. His tenant farmer, Robert Gardiner, called his farm East Hills, perhaps after the region of that name near Liverpool in England.

In 1828 Thomas Graham was promised 640 acres south of Johnston's, and in 1835 he sold it to Charles Tompson. The area to the west was bought by George Nicholas Weston in 1837. All of the area was heavily timbered and, although it was all alienated by about 1840, it remained sparsely occupied until the end of the century. In 1893 the area of the former Johnston and Weston grants (bounded approximately by The River Road and Tower, Weston and Polo Streets, now in Panania and Revesby) was subdivided, and named East Hills after the farm. The name was also given to the station at the end of the line when the railway came through in 1931.

Today East Hills retains an air of natural peace. It has a state primary school and boys and girls high schools. East Hills Park, a reserve between the Georges River and Cook Crescent, is a popular local spot for weekend relaxation.

## EASTLAKES
*Municipality of Botany*
Location: 8 kilometres south of Sydney off Southern Cross Drive

This southern suburb, east of Mascot and south of Kensington, covers the area once known as Botany Swamps. This was Sydney's third source of fresh water. From 1859 water was pumped from here to a reservoir in Paddington, but after the Nepean scheme was instituted in 1888, the Water Board leased the water rights to various industrial concerns, such as the Sydney Hydraulic Presses, which ran lifts and wool presses in Sydney from the 1880s to the 1950s. The lakes that gave the suburb its name were later partly reclaimed for the Lakes Golf Course and airport extensions, but the area is still described as swampy.

Part of this residential suburb is on the 62 acres of the former Rosebery Racecourse. In 1960 the land was purchased by a real estate company and subdivided. Cottages and home units were built, along with the Lakes Drive-in Shopping Centre, one of the first of its kind in the inner southern suburbs. A primary school, Eastlakes Public School, is situated in Florence Street, Mascot.

## EAST SYDNEY
*City of Sydney*
Location: 1 kilometre east of Sydney between William Street and Oxford Street

This neighbourhood in the parish of Alexandria was the site of early dairies and market gardens, scattered about the flats of Alexandria, part of East Sydney. Today this area, to the east of the city's Hyde Park, has educational institutions, offices, light industry, services and shops, as well as surviving terrace residences.

The first structure on the site of the Australian Museum, at the corner of College and William Streets, was built in 1849, although a curator had been appointed and the collections begun in 1827. In recent years displays of its wide-ranging collections have been refurbished and reorganised. Alongside the museum in College Street is Sydney Grammar School, established here since 1857, on the site once occupied by the Sydney College, a private high school which opened there in 1835. East Sydney Technical College is in Darlinghurst, on the site of Darlinghurst Gaol.

Blaxland Road, Eastwood, c. 1910. It is now known as Rowe Street

# EASTWOOD

*City of Parramatta, Municipality of Ryde*

Location: 17 kilometres north-west of Sydney between Blaxland Road and Marsden Road, on the Main Northern Line

The area north-west of Ryde now known as Eastwood was originally part of the Field of Mars. The railway station and shopping centre stand on a grant of 90 acres made in 1795 to John Love, a private in the New South Wales Corps. The grant was described as "North Brush, in the Field of Mars". The area was covered with dense timber, and the first industry was timber-getting. Later a Captain Kent acquired the land and sold it for a mere £288 in 1835, to William Rutledge, who named the property Eastwood in 1840, and his house, Eastwood House. Rutledge, known as Terrible Billy was a government contractor and director of the Commercial Banking Company of Sydney.

The suburb found fame of a sort when a new industry, sericulture, the production of raw silk, was introduced. James de Beuzeville, an Englishman of Huguenot extraction, migrated to New South Wales in 1848, determined to begin silk production. He addressed a meeting in Sydney in July 1848 and won the interest and support of several influential businessmen. An expert in his field, and from a family business in England, James de Beuzeville intended to import silkworm eggs from China and India. After examining several likely localities, he decided "Eastwood in the Kissing Point district" was the most favourable. To feed the silkworms, mulberry trees were to be planted near the village of Ryde. Eastwood House was approved as a residence for de Beuzeville and his family, and the spare rooms were seen as adequate to house both the silkworms and the workers. A plan was mooted to employ orphans from Liverpool and Parramatta orphan schools to

Built in a disused stone quarry, Eastwood freshwater swimming baths (and viewing stage). This photo was a memento of a visit to the baths in March 1931 by the Allen family

wind the silk, but the principals of these institutions decided that no orphans were available — "disposable" was the word actually used in the reply. Sadly, the whole venture failed. De Beuzeville was forced to spend his own money to try to save the business, and finally he had to seek employment at The King's School, Parramatta. He died at Enfield in 1887, the instigator of a scheme too advanced for the age.

In 1851 Rutledge sold Eastwood House to Dr William Sherwin from Parramatta, who refurbished the property, adding an orchard before selling it to John Ross. When Edward Terry purchased the property in 1863, the orchard contained nearly 3,000 trees, mainly apple and plum. Terry lived at Eastwood House for over forty years and died there in 1907. He had been the first mayor of Ryde, serving a total of three

Edward Terry

terms, and was elected twice as member of the Legislative Assembly for the district. Very keen on hunting, Terry was master of the Sydney Hunt Club, and one of the group who hunted wild dogs on the Dog Trap Road (see Guildford).

In June 1929, Eastwood House was purchased for a Catholic presbytery and was blessed by Archbishop Kelly.

Eastwood's more substantial claim to fame is the Granny Smith apple. Granny was Maria Ann Smith, who lived in Eastwood in

the 1860s. Her famous apple was the result of a lucky accident, after she had thrown the remains of some Tasmanian apples near a creek. The apple seeds took root, and the soil and moisture produced a large green apple with a fine texture and tart taste. In 1895 the *Agricultural Gazette* referred to the apple as "Granny Smith's Seedling, a New South Wales variety raised from the seed of a French Crab, near Ryde".

The area became a hive of industry when the northern railway line from Strathfield to Hornsby was being built from 1884. A large number of workers were accommodated under canvas, at what was known as Main Camp. The Darvall family, a name commemorated by Darvall Road, Eastwood, owned the land on the western side of the railway line from West Ryde to the borders of Eastwood, and part of the Main Camp was located on Darvall land. When the station opened it was called Dundas, but this was soon discarded in favour of Eastwood.

The convenience of the railway

began to make its mark on Eastwood. Land sales for home-building increased. In 1906 building blocks in Clanwilliam Street, Wentworth Road, Rutledge Street and Tarrants Avenue (then known as Railway Road) were offered for sale. The shopping centre was small, limited to Herbert McDonald's Eastwood Hotel and a few shops, although a plan was afoot to build a School of Arts in Rowe Street, still the main street through the village.

Happily the suburb retains much of its old world charm. There are still many large Federation-style houses, and St Phillip's Church of England and St Andrew's Presbyterian Church blend well with modern buildings. Curzon Hall, built by Harry Curzon-Smith from stone quarried on its original 35-acre estate, is an example of the stately style of buildings from Eastwood's past. Completed in 1900, it was later used by a Catholic religious order and is now a centre for seminars, receptions and other social events.

Eastwood Oval, the venue for many exciting football and cricket matches, was once a lake, fed by Terry Creek, an arm of the Lane Cove River. It was large enough for sailing boats, but when the creek was diverted to accommodate the construction of the railway, the lake dried up. Terry Creek was named after Edward Terry, and Lakeside Avenue recalls that early span of water.

Today Eastwood is serviced by fast electric trains as well as buses. The modern shopping area extends along Rowe Street and into Hillview Street and Progress Avenue, where Westfield Shoppingtown stands. The area's first public school opened in 1884, and today the Eastwood Public School in Rowe Street is also used by Eastwood Evening College, which has a large attendance. Eastwood Bowling Club in Second Avenue, was officially opened in March 1930.

## EDGECLIFF
*Municipality of Woollahra*
Location: 3.5 kilometres east of Sydney on New South Head Road, on the Eastern Suburbs Line

Literally clinging to the edge of a cliff, Edgecliff sits elegantly on the crest of New South Head Road between Rushcutters Bay and Double Bay. The rocky cliff has been extensively quarried.

A cable tram service from King Street, city, to Ocean Street, Edgecliff, opened in September 1894, the powerhouse driving the underground cable being at Rushcutters Bay. Unlike the trams used in other districts at this time, which were driven by steam, the Edgecliff cable tram was pulled along by a wire cable that ran in a gutter between the tracks. Each car had a grip that grabbed this moving cable and released it to stop. Like all things new, the system had its teething troubles. Waiting passengers often stood open-mouthed as the tram flew past without stopping — the helpless driver was still learning the controls of the monster! In fact clergymen were known to pray for the safety of passengers using the new cable trams.

The tram trip became very popular with our grandparents, who would ride from the city to Edgecliff Post Office and back for pleasure. The Edgecliff cable trams remained in service, becoming one of Sydney's curiosities, until 1905, when the line was electrified.

The Eastern Suburbs Railway, a half-built hope for many years, was opened in 1979 and now carries thousands of residents and visitors between the city and Edgecliff and on to Bondi

Edgecliff Post Office, on the corner of New South Head Road and Edgecliff Road, was built in the 1890s and stands in the same place today. This photo was taken in 1926

Junction — perhaps a more reliable and convenient means of travel, but lacking the excitement of bygone days.

Trumper Park, in a hollow south of Edgecliff, was named after Victor Trumper (1877–1915), a brilliant Australian cricketer who once scored eleven centuries in one season. Ill-health cut short his career and he died in Sydney at the age of 38.

## ELANORA HEIGHTS
*Shire of Warringah*
Location: 27 kilometres north of Sydney off the Wakehurst Parkway overlooking Narrabeen Lakes

The meaning of this suburb's Aboriginal name is "home (or camp) by the sea", a perfect designation as the high ground west of Narrabeen on the northern beaches affords some splendid views. The area was sighted by Governor Phillip as early as 1788 during his local explorations. George Caley (1770–1829), a young botanist sent to the colony in 1800 to collect plant specimens for Sir Joseph Banks named the lake south of Elanora Heights (now Narrabeen Lakes) Cabbage Tree Lagoon. Cabbage trees provided strong waterproof leaves, which were used to thatch the roofs of early huts. They were also woven into the famous cabbage tree hats worn by many young men in the colony.

The district opened up in 1810 with grants that were worked as small farms. In 1888 a new aspect of the area was discovered when a drill was sunk for coal nearly a kilometre up Deep Creek, south of Elanora Heights. Twenty-seven metres down a bed of oyster shells three metres thick was discovered, indicating that the land had subsided thousands of years earlier. At 370 metres natural gas was discovered and piped to nearby cottages; at 580 metres the drill met a seam of coal, but this was non-bituminous.

Street names reveal much in this suburb. Powder Works Road recalls an attempt to maintain a factory (at Ingleside) making gunpowder for rockets (see Ingleside), while Woorarra, Weeroona, Coolangatta, and Warraba are a few of the many Aboriginal names given to streets and roads. Some are hard to pronounce accurately, so it is a happy relief to find Care Free Road near Narrabeen Lakes! One place for shedding care is the well-known Elanora Golf Club, much used by both residents and visitors to this suburb.

## ELIZABETH BAY
*City of Sydney*
Location: 3 kilometres east of Sydney on the south side of Port Jackson

Originally known by the Aboriginal names Jerrewon (Macleay Point), and Yarrandabby, this delightful suburb was named in honour of Governor Macquarie's wife, Elizabeth. Situated on the eastern side of Potts Point, the suburb has breathtaking views across Sydney Harbour, especially from Elizabeth Bay House.

This Regency-style home was built on a 54 acre grant made in 1828 to Alexander Macleay (1767–1848), who came to New

View from Elizabeth Bay toward Potts Point. The couple appear to be rowing toward the landing stage with the domed pavilion belonging to Tarmons house

Elizabeth Henrietta Macquarie

South Wales to become colonial secretary. In 1833 he commissioned architect John Verge (1782−1861), to build the house, which was completed in 1837. Like Verge's masterpiece, Camden Park, it has been restored and opened for public inspection. There were seventeen children in the Macleay family, and visiting Elizabeth Bay House today one can easily imagine it as a busy family home, complete with several large cellars. Many interesting people visited this house and in 1834 Captain Charles Sturt, a close friend of Macleay's son George, rowed across the harbour from his moored ship with his bride, to stay with the Macleays. In 1829 George had accompanied Sturt on his expedition to the Murray and Murrumbidgee Rivers, for which George had received a grant of 2,650 acres between Goulburn and Yass.

The garden surrounding Elizabeth Bay House was a riot of overseas plants brought to the colony by Alexander Macleay who was a keen student of natural history. His specimens, displays and scientific papers became the nucleus of the Macleay Museum of Natural History at the University of Sydney, later augmented by his sons William and George and his nephew William, where it remains a valuable asset to scholars. The land was subdivided by Macleay's son George Macleay after he had inherited it from his brother William.

The residential build-up in Elizabeth Bay today has crowded the winding streets with houses and home units. It is hard to imagine those early days when the homes, including Elizabeth Bay House, had undulating grounds sloping down to the water's edge. Nowadays the famous house has only a small patch of velvet lawn surviving from its former horticultural glory.

# EMERTON

*City of Blacktown*
Location: 46 kilometres north-west of Sydney and just north-west of Mount Druitt

In 1853, William Emert, a native of Siglingen, Germany, arrived as a free settler in New South Wales. He bought land in the Mount Druitt area in 1861. Emert opened a store in this small settlement of timber-getters and later became the postmaster for the district. He also took a leading part in founding the first Wesleyan Church. When the state housing commission extended the residential area of Mount Druitt, they called the new neighbourhood Emerton after this industrious early settler. Streets in the suburb have been given the names of great composers and include Hindemith Avenue, Bach Avenue, Handel Avenue, Weber Crescent and Offenbach Crescent.

# ENFIELD

*Municipalities of Burwood and Strathfield*
Location: 13 kilometres south-west of Sydney at the junction of Coronation Parade and the Hume Highway

In 1808 a grant of 1,000 acres, in this area between Strathfield and the Cooks River, was made to William Faithful (1774−1847), who began farming the land. Excellent timber covered the area, and all the timber on Faithful's land was reserved by the government for naval use. About 1813−14 Liverpool Road was opened, and ran through Faithful's land, which extended from the present Coronation Parade to near Croydon Avenue and from Burwood Farm to the Cooks River. Later Faithful exchanged the balance of his land for a similar area at South Creek, in St Marys. The deed stated that "William Faithful agrees to exchange the whole of the grant of 1,000 acres at Burwood [as the total area was then known] made in 1810, and through which a road to Liverpool has since been opened, to Alexander Riley, for an area of 1,200 acres at South Creek." The date of exchange was 1815, but the land continued to be known for some time as Faithful's Farm.

In 1816 the area south of Liverpool Road was regranted to Simeon Lord (1771−1840), and this area, which he called Brighton, with some smaller grants between Liverpool Road and Cooks River, made up what is now known as Enfield. The western part of the suburb was in a grant made to James Wilshire (see Strathfield). Other early land-owners were Father Therry (1790−1864), the fiery Catholic priest who received a 47 acre grant, which he had wanted for its timber, needed for the construction of St Mary's Cathedral in the city, and William H. Moore, a wealthy merchant, who cleared his land in 1822 for farming. In 1824 Simeon Lord sold Brighton estate to him. About 1842 a number of the Canadian exiles who had been in the stockade at Concord came to live at Enfield and started a large market garden.

Meanwhile, Thomas Hyndes, who was to have such an influence on this suburb, had begun a sawmilling business on the upper North Shore. In 1815 he was firmly entrenched on a grant made to Robert Pymble who, arriving with his wife and six children, was astonished to find Hyndes living

St Thomas's Church of England, Enfield, in 1907

on his land (see Pymble).

Hyndes moved to the north of Pymble's grant, where he leased 2,000 acres. In 1833 this astute businessman purchased 10 acres of land near the water at Lane Cove, where he built a wharf, enabling him and neighbour Pymble to ferry their timber to Sydney. In 1838 he added 640 acres to his lease and two years later obtained a further grant. During this time Hyndes had also established a stone quarry.

In 1843, Thomas Hyndes purchased land in the suburb now known as Enfield, calling his estate Adelaide Park. He set aside 5 acres of land for a church, but first he erected a schoolhouse, which he called Adelaide Park Free School (instituted in 1847). He then began to build the church that was to

become St Thomas's, Enfield, using stone from his own quarry. The school building eventually became the Sunday school hall. St Thomas's was designed in Gothic style, with a square Norman tower topped by a spire originally covered with shingles. All the interior fittings were of Australian cedar, from Hyndes's timber-felling, but eventually the seats were replaced with polished pine. The arches in the roof are especially beautiful, ending in delicately carved angels' heads. St Thomas's was consecrated in 1849.

In the graveyard adjacent to the church, one may find many names of early pioneers in the surrounding district. Near the church gates, and marked by elaborate stonework, are the graves of Thomas Hyndes's first wife,

buried here in 1849, and Hyndes himself, who was interred in 1855.

Once the timber was cleared, subdivision of the area began in the 1840s, when the nucleus of a small village had been formed, and small farms were created. The area was slower to develop than neighbouring Burwood because of its distance from the railway. Subdivision increased in the 1880s, and the municipality was formed in 1889. In 1948 it was, however, divided between Burwood and Strathfield municipalities.

In the New South Wales Gazetteer for 1865, Enfield was described as "a small postal village in the parish of St George, the district being chiefly agricultural, dairy farming, and market gardening. There are four hotels — The New Inn, The Enfield, The Woodcutter's Arms, and the Royal Arms, the population is 400 persons."

The suburb became a comfortable, residential area, its original settlers mostly being free immigrants, who, like those of Strathfield, came to seek a new life in the colony. Its later connection with industrial life stemmed from the department of railways, which built steam locomotive workshops; the main marshalling yards were between Enfield and what is now Chullora, providing work for hundreds of local residents.

The area was known as Enfield in the 1850s; the first known use of the name was in 1853, when the post office was opened with that name. Enfield is named after an early market town in Middlesex, England. The British government had a small arms factory there during the First World War and the town was known for its old church and sixteenth century grammar school. It is not known who named Sydney's Enfield, but there may be a connection with the early inn, The Enfield.

# ENGADINE
*Shire of Sutherland*
Location: 33 kilometres south-west of Sydney on the Princes Highway and the Illawarra Line

This area on the southern outskirts of Sydney first opened up when Governor Sir Thomas Brisbane granted 150 acres of land to John Lucas on 18 November 1825, so that he might build a water mill and establish a flour-milling business. The land was located on a tributary of the Georges River that was to become known as the Woronora River, from an Aboriginal word meaning "black rock". At that time the land was heavily timbered, and there was no road access to Sydney. All Lucas's transport was by water, and vessels would carry grain to the mill for grinding by Lucas, and pick up the flour ready for the Sydney market. At an unknown date the mill caught fire and was razed to the ground.

In 1843 the new Illawarra line of road was being discussed, and the site, called Woronora Mill Estate, was put up for sale. It was suggested that it would suit a woollen cloth manufacturer. Road-building commenced the following year under the supervision of Surveyor Darke, who took a convict gang with him. Their job was to clear the line of the road, which would later be built by contractors. Many relics of the road-building have been found in this part of Engadine, including a convict-built baker's oven, and convict chains.

Large areas of this suburb had been reserved for a national park in 1879, but about 1890, Charles McAlister was able to buy a large piece of land on which he built a house and established gardens. The estate was known as McAlister's,

and the suburb became known by this name. After an overseas trip later in the decade, the family renamed their property Engadine after the beautiful Engadine district in Switzerland, where the hills and valleys were full of wildflowers. The suburb also took the new name — appropriately, since wildflowers are prolific in the Royal National Park to the east and Heathcote National Park, south-west of Engadine.

After 1900 Charles McAlister subdivided his land and sold home-sites to other families, whose names are some of the oldest in the district. He continued to live in Engadine for some time, eventually moving to Cronulla, where he died in 1915.

Although only 33 kilometres from Sydney, Engadine remained rather isolated until 1920, when a railway station was opened and the suburb became more easily accessible. Many ex-soldiers from the First World War settled there, and several street names recall not only that war but others as well. There are streets named Nelson, (after Trafalgar), Bullecourt, Amiens, Villers Brett, Anzac and Tobruk, as well as Australian historical personalities, Parkes, Strickland, Copeland and Dalley. Others were named after composers, such as Bach, Beethoven and Grieg. And McAlister Street immortalises the settler who gave Engadine its name.

In the western part of this suburb is Boys Town, a remarkable venture modelled on an institution in the United States. Founded in 1939 by Father T. V. Dunlea, who remained principal from 1939 until his retirement in 1951, the institution caters for boys, irrespective of their religious beliefs, who have not been able to conform to the rules of society. Their ages range between 9 and 15 years, and their temporary citizenship in Boys Town has saved many from a term in a reformatory. The scheme has its own self-government, and an annually elected mayor and eight aldermen, drawn from the boys, are responsible for the welfare of the citizens of this unique town. The town was "still going strong" in the 1980s under the priest in charge, Father Wenting.

The official post office opened on 1 January 1927, and Engadine public school took in its first pupils in September 1932.

There are several parks and reserves in Engadine itself, and Engadine Waterfall on Engadine Creek in the Royal National Park is a beauty spot enjoyed by both residents and visitors.

Enmore Road looking north-east from Stanmore Road, early 1900s

# ENMORE
*Municipality of Marrickville*
Location: 5.5 kilometres south-west of Sydney on Enmore Road

This suburb was named after a grand mansion, Enmore House, which was built in the 1830s by Captain Sylvester Brown, who had been an officer in the British East India Company. Designed by architect John Verge (1782–1861), who had also designed Elizabeth Bay House for Alexander Macleay and Camden Park for John Macarthur, it was surrounded by gardens and orchards, and included its own farm buildings and stables. Produce grown on the property made it practically self-supporting. Enmore House was bought by Judge Joshua Josephson, who had formed the Camdenville Estate by purchasing a number of small grants in the area that had originally been made in 1794. He

Rolf Boldrewood

sold Enmore House in 1871, and it was demolished in the 1880s. The Enmore Estate had been subdivided in 1841.

At this time this suburb was known as Stanmore Road, after a main thoroughfare leading to Enmore Road, but on 1 November 1895 it was officially designated Enmore.

Captain Brown's son, Thomas Alexander Browne (1826–1915), who added the "e" to his name,

became famous as Rolf Boldrewood, writing seventeen Australian novels, including the classic *Robbery Under Arms*. He spent part of his boyhood in Enmore House, which is said to have been located opposite the present post office.

Today Enmore is a busy inner city suburb, a mixture of older-style houses and light industry. The move by many young couples towards city living has brought a wave of renovation to the area, and many old workers' cottages and terrace houses now wear bright colours in a new lease of life.

## EPPING

*Shire of Hornsby, City of Parramatta*
Location: 18 kilometres north-east of Sydney at the junction of Beecroft, Epping and Carlingford Roads, on the Main Northern Line

The area now called Epping was once part of the originally extensive Pennant Hills area and the Field of Mars, one of the earliest districts named in New South Wales. Land in Epping was originally granted to two naval officers, Captain William Kent (1751–1812) and his nephew, Lieutenant William Kent (b.1788). Their land was on the north-west part of what became the Field of Mars Common. The elder Kent received 170 acres on 12 May 1796, and young Kent was given 460 acres north of his uncle's grant on 19 April 1803, the property extending as far as Devlin's Creek. Kent Street, Epping, commemorates these two men.

A very undesirable class of person had collected in Epping by 1804 — gaol escapees, sly groggers, smugglers and others — and honest settlers avoided the area. Many people squatted on the Field of Mars Common, built humpies, planted small orchards, and stayed until the government subdivided the common and sold the blocks to private buyers.

The area was an important source of timber, and in Governor Macquarie's time the Pennant

Epping Station, c. 1900

Hills sawing establishment was set up in what is now Oxford Street, Epping.

William Farm, owned by the Kents, was bought in 1835 by one of Ryde's pioneers, James Devlin. He is commemorated by Devlin Street and Devlin's Creek, which runs into the upper reaches of the Lane Cove River, forms part of the boundary between Epping and Beecroft, and is crossed by Beecroft Road, the major artery running north.

The first subdivision in the area, in 1883, began the suburb's change of character from bushland and orchards to residential. Mobbs Orangery, one of the colony's showplaces of the 1830s, was one of the properties affected (see Carlingford).

The railway line opened up the area. Many people squatted on the Field of Mars Common, built humpies, planted small orchards, and stayed until the government subdivided the common and sold the blocks to private buyers.

The suburb's name changed to

Epping only after much debate. When the first post office opened in 1890, it was called East Carlingford, but the station at that time was named Carlingford. The postal department found this very confusing and suggested that the station name be changed, so that both would be known as East Carlingford. Strong opposition led to many other names being suggested, including East Lynn and Corella. Finally, William Midson, whose father had been born in Epping, in Essex, England, suggested Epping, and the new name was officially accepted in 1899. Essex Street and Midson Road further commemorate this resident's influence in the district. The name Epping is said to mean "people of the look-out place", possibly referring to an Iron Age hill fort on a ridge in Epping Forest, in England. Epping Forest today retains its air of peace and beauty. It seems a very apt name for Australia's Epping, which is built on ridges and hills, and was once a heavily timbered area.

# ERMINGTON

*City of Parramatta*
Location: 19 kilometres west of Sydney on the north bank of the Parramatta River

Ermington was named by Major Edmund Lockyer (1784–1860), who came to New South Wales in 1825 as commander of a detachment of the 57th Regiment. In 1826 he went to the west coast of Australia to form a settlement on King George's Sound, to prevent a possible French occupation. He returned to New South Wales in 1827, sold his army commission to take up farming,

Major Edmund Lockyer

and was appointed police magistrate at Parramatta, the first of a number of public appointments. He was, for example, the first usher of the Black Rod under responsible government in the parliament of New South Wales in 1856. Lockyer had already bought up earlier grants in this area and in 1828 he built an elegant stone house with a wide Indian verandah, which he called Ermington. The suburb took its name from the house.

The first settlement in the area had been formed in February 1792, when eight marines received grants of land close to the river. By the end of the year these Field of Mars settlers had cultivated 48½ acres with various grains, and another 33 acres had been cleared but not planted out. The farming scheme failed, however, as the soil was too poor to continue to produce flourishing crops.

Orchards and nurseries were the main land uses in the 1870s. One of the largest enterprises, covering 17 acres, was the Mount Pleasant Nursery, owned by W. Atkins and his son, who raised citrus, apple, peach and apricot trees.

Ermington remained a

semi-rural suburb until the 1920s, partly because of poor transport. The nearest railway station was Ryde.

The closure of the Ermington garbage tip, which had been a problem for residents for many years, was one of the district's biggest improvements. Modern methods now cope with garbage service in a clean, efficient manner. Several factories, however have appeared since the 1960s, and former orchard land is now the site of many homes of differing styles. The old quiet life has gone as this once peaceful area moves ahead.

# ERSKINE PARK

*City of Penrith*
Location: 44 kilometres west of Sydney south of St Marys and the Western Freeway

When this suburb was created in 1980–81 there was much controversy over its name. Some people thought that St Clair was a more attractive name than the historical Erskine Park. The problem was solved by creating not one, but two suburbs, so that now both St Clair and Erskine Park are suburbs of the city of Penrith.

Erskine Park was the name of a 3,000 acre property held in 1818 by James Erskine (1765–1825). As the colony's lieutenant-governor, he took up office in 1817. In 1819–20 he was also president of the Native Institution, one of Governor Macquarie's projects. He was interested in the welfare of the Aborigines and the poor of Sydney and was patron of the Benevolent Society. Commissioner Bigge reported favourably on Erskine's treatment of his convict servants on his property, which extended from St Marys to the present St Clair and Erskine Park. Erskine Street, Sydney, also commemorates this early official, who returned to England in 1823 and died shortly after rejoining his regiment in India.

## ERSKINEVILLE
*City of Sydney*
Location: 5.5 kilometres south-west of Sydney off Erskineville Road, on the Illawarra Line

Some of the earliest grants in this area, a few kilometres south of Central Station, were made in 1794 and 1799 to Nicholas Devine, a superintendent of convicts. Devine built a house called Burren Farm near the corner of the present George Street and Erskineville Road, and on his death in 1830, aged 104, the property passed to Bernard Rochford and his wife, who had cared for Devine in his old age. This fitting conclusion to a humane story does not end there. Rochford subdivided and sold the estate, and some of the land was bought by a Wesleyan Minister, the Reverend George Erskine. Here, in 1830, he built a house, which he called Erskine Villa.

By 1852 the suburb was developing well, with industrial as well as residential areas, when a John Devine arrived in the colony. He made a claim for the whole area, which was dismissed. Devine appealed again, and lengthy and costly litigation ensued, continuing until 1857 when Devine again was the loser. Convinced of his rights, this tireless man was set to appeal a third time, but the owners of the Erskineville land established a fund to pay him a compensation for his loss.

The Reverend George Erskine, the buyer of one of the subdivided parcels of land, did not live long to enjoy the home he had built. He died there in 1834 and was buried in the grounds. Mr Robert Henderson, a naturalist, was Erskine Villa's next owner, followed by William Toogood, a Sydney inn-keeper. When Toogood died, he left the property to the Church of England, and it became the rectory for Holy Trinity Church, Macdonaldtown.

In 1893, parliament passed the Borough of Erskineville Naming Act, and part of what had until then been Macdonaldtown, including the area on which the Methodist minister had built his home, became a brand new suburb. Sixteen years later the church connection was not forgotten when electric trams began to run to Erskinville in 1909. The destination sign on the front of the tram showed a green diamond on a white background, chosen because this was the symbol of trinity and honouring the parish church for which Erskine Villa was the rectory.

By 1920 the suburb had become the home of many workers, some employed locally in brickmaking, bootmaking and hat-

manufacturing. Today, Erskineville is a busy inner-city suburb, but Devine Street, Burren Street and Rochford Street are reminders of the story of its early turbulent history.

## FAIRFIELD
*City of Fairfield*
Location: 29 kilometres of Sydney off the Horsley Drive, on the Main Southern Line

Fairfield was probably first seen by Europeans when Watkin Tench (1758–1835), officer of marines and a keen explorer, climbed Prospect Hill. The property that gave Fairfield its name was originally owned by Gabriel Louis Marie Huon de Kerrileau (1769–1828). Fleeing from France during the French Revolution, he enlisted in the New South Wales Corps and arrived in the colony in 1793. He was granted a discharge in 1807 and became tutor to the sons of John Macarthur. He was already married to Louise Le Sage, who followed her husband to the colony, where they went through

Steam train pulling out of Fairfield Station, c. 1900

another wedding ceremony to satisfy colonial law. In 1807 Huon de Kerrileau received a grant of 100 acres in the centre of present Fairfield, which he called Castel Paul. In 1840 Captain John Horsley bought Castel Paul and renamed the property Fairfield, after the family estate in Somerset. Later, a state treasurer, Thomas Ware Smart (1810–81), bought part of Fairfield, and in the 1860s the mansion Fairfield House was built there.

In 1803 Governor King's land grant for the Orphan Institution (see Cabramatta) extended into the area of Fairfield, and it is commemorated by Orphan School Creek.

In 1895 Symons Bros Pty Ltd began manufacturing roof tiles in Fairfield, taking advantage of the district's good quality clay.

The municipality of Fairfield was proclaimed in 1888, under the name of the municipality of Smithfield and Fairfield, but in 1920 Smithfield was dropped from its title. On 18 May it was proclaimed a city at a ceremony conducted by the then governor, Sir Roden Cutler.

Fairfield railway station opened in 1856 and is one of the oldest in the state. A private railway line, laid by the Sydney and Suburban Blue Metal Company, began running in 1924 from Widemere Quarry on Prospect Hill to Fairfield goods yard. It remained in use until 1945. The route followed Horsley Drive, named in honour of the district pioneer.

Fairfield today is a busy residential area, with a considerable migrant population, as many newcomers from Europe and Asia have settled there. As well as Fairfield Public School, there are primary schools in Fairfield Heights, Fairfield West, and Fairvale. Three high schools have also been built for Fairfield, Fairvale and Fairfield West students. Fairfield Heights Park, Tarrawarra Reserve and West Fairfield Park offer pleasant leisure spots in the area. The much larger Fairfield Park, near the station, also has a swimming centre and oval and adjoins an athletic field. Fairfield Showground and Fairfield Golf Course are on adjoining sites in the municipality, but lie 5 kilometres from Fairfield station in the suburb of Bossley Park.

Cambridge House, a well-known landmark in Fairfield, was demolished amid widespread controversy in 1975, after it was extensively damaged by fire. The site is now occupied by a block of home units and a tavern

# FAIRLIGHT

*Municipality of Manly*
Location: 13 kilometres north-east
of Sydney overlooking North
Harbour

This small suburb between Manly
and Balgowlah was named after a
house built by Henry Gilbert
Smith (1802–86), who is known as
the father of Manly (see Manly). In
1853 Smith bought a grant made to
John Parker in 1837, for which he
paid £8 an acre. The following year
Smith built a sandstone house,
which he named Fairlight, after an
historic village near Hastings on
England's south coast. Smith sold
his Fairlight property to John
Woods in 1880, and in 1885 it was
partly sold in allotments. More
sales were made in 1902, and in
1939 Smith's Fairlight House was
demolished.

The higher streets in this
attractive residential area command
splendid views of both North
Harbour and the harbour waters
beyond Manly Cove. Many high-
rise buildings have been erected
during the past twenty years, but
the entire waterfront is now a
reserve, Esplanade Park, which
gives access to Fairlight Pool and
Delwood Beach.

# FIVE DOCK

*Municipality of Drummoyne*
Location: 10 kilometres west of
Sydney between Iron Cove and
Hen and Chicken Bay

The suburb is named after a farm
that covered the whole of the
peninsula west of the city on the
southern shore of the Parramatta
River between Iron Cove and Hen
and Chicken Bay. It was so named
because of five rocky inlets, or
docks, in the Bay. They are no
longer all visible since three of
them were affected by the
construction of the southern
approaches to the Gladesville
Bridge. The name was perhaps
known as early as 1797 and was
certainly in use by 1805.

Five Dock Farm was the name
given to his 1,500 acre grant of
1806 by Surgeon John Harris
(1754–1838). Seven earlier grants
had been made in the area, but
they had reverted to the crown by
the time Governor King made the
grant. Five Dock Farm spread
over the sites of the present-day
suburbs of Abbotsford,
Drummoyne, Chiswick and Five
Dock.

In 1828, Surveyor-General Sir
Thomas Mitchell marked out a
new line of road, passing through
Five Dock Farm, which was to
become the Great North Road;
part of it retains that name today.
When the convict gangs began
work, the whole area was covered
with trees and bush, but the land
was cleared and a road eventually
constructed from its junction with
Parramatta Road, running north
towards present-day Abbotsford.

In 1836, Dr Harris sold Five
Dock Farm to Samuel Lyons, the
leading Sydney auctioneer of the
time. He in turn subdivided the
land into 30 and 60 acre allotments,
allowing for the construction of
large residences. Lyons Road,
Fivedock commemorates him.

Later occupants of the area of
Five Dock Farm gave their names
to parts of the district. Rodd Point
was named after the Rodd family,
who built Barnstaple Manor there
in 1845. Russell Lea was named
after the property of Russell
Banton (1830–1916), a pastoral
and mining magnate who bought
the 60 acre property of C.
Abercrombie. Erina Avenue, a

Cashman's Corner at the junction of Great
North Road and Ramsay Road, Five Dock,
as it looked in 1921. Although Cashman &
Co. no longer operate, the corner has
retained the name of the once-prominent
real estate company

short cul-de-sac near Five Dock Park, was named after a fine residence known as Erina House, owned by an outstanding legal man of his day, Peter Faucett (1814–94). Born in Dublin, Faucett came to the colony in 1852. He was solicitor-general from 1863 until 1865 and made Erina House his home. The house, which has now been restored, was surrounded by spacious grounds, including a vineyard.

Five Dock retained its rural character longer than neighbouring Drummoyne, as the 1880s land boom concentrated on the areas around bridges and main roads. In 1871 it was incorporated as a municipality and in 1901 was amalgamated with Drummoyne. During the 1920s the suburb became popular with young couples when further subdivisions enabled them to build attractive brick homes. Trams ran direct to the city. The fifty minutes journey cost fourpence. Today the suburb is busy with cars and buses, but the charm of the bay with its access to the Parramatta River has not been totally lost.

# FLEMINGTON

*Municipality of Strathfield*
Location: 16 kilometres west of Sydney on Parramatta Road, on the Main Western, Main Southern and Bankstown Lines

Lying west of Strathfield the suburb of Flemington stands in the area originally known as Liberty Plains (see Homebush). A 200 acre grant was made in the area in 1806 to John Fleming, a free settler who gave his grant his own name. The area was then virgin bush, but as it was cleared by settlers it was used for cattle grazing and resting

paddocks. Later, when a cattle saleyard was established there, the suburb became officially known as Flemington, the name being used by the cattleyards, the markets, and the new railway station. In the 1970s the cattle saleyard south of Parramatta Road became the site of a new fruit and vegetable market to relieve the Haymarket site in the city.

The area south of the railway was part of the Church Lands from 1823 to 1841, when part of the area was acquired by Joseph Hyde Potts, after whom Potts Point and Potts Street, Flemington, are named; Bates Street commemorates his wife, who was born Emily or Elizabeth Bates. Other streets have been named after members of Strathfield council, such as Mackenzie, Kessell and Austin Streets, after former mayors; Kerruish Street, after a town clerk; and Badgery Street after a council alderman.

Flemington is bordered by Rookwood Cemetery, the largest graveyard in the world. The remains of many famous people of all denominations have been interred there. In the 1920s when some large industries were sited in Flemington monumental masons were among them, providing headstones for graves. Runcorn and Lea was a well-known firm, and A. Larcombe and Company, established in 1870, were located at both Flemington and Lidcombe. Much of the area's real estate was subdivided by Arthur Rickard, an estate agent.

# FOREST LODGE

*Municipality of Leichhardt*
Location: 4 kilometres south-west of Sydney just north of Sydney University

Sandwiched between Glebe and Parramatta Road, Forest Lodge is a small residential suburb that took its name from a house. Mr Ambrose Foss, a well-known chemist and druggist in Sydney, built a home here in 1836, which he called Forest Lodge. It stood on a site at about the present 208–210 Bridge Road, until demolished in 1912. Mr Foss and a colleague, Edward Hunt, were instrumental in founding the Congregational Church in New South Wales.

Originally the land in the area was part of the Church Lands reserved in 1789 (see Glebe), but in 1806 the area west of Orphan School Creek was included in a grant made to William Bligh. In 1795, 20 acres on the eastern side of the creek and between Bridge and Parramatta Roads were granted to Catherine King, and the property was named Catherine Farm.

By the middle of the nineteenth century the suburb was beginning to develop as a residential area. Some of the homes of the wealthy were being built on various scales of grandeur, and the near-city suburbs, such as Forest Lodge and The Glebe, were popular areas. Forest Lodge's street names are historical reminders of people of those times and Foss Street recalls the resident who named the suburb. The Royal Alexandra Hospital for Children in Pyrmont Bridge Road was moved here in 1907 from Glebe, where it had been established in 1880.

# FORESTVILLE

*Shire of Warringah*
Location: 15 kilometres north of
Sydney on Warringah Road

As its name suggests this suburb
on the north side of Middle
Harbour was once a thickly
wooded forest. In 1856, when
James Ffrench began felling timber
in the area, he built a small wharf
on what is now Bantry Bay, from
where he shipped the timber down
the harbour to Sydney. At that
time wood was in great demand
for all types of construction. The
name Forestville means "house in
the forest" and possibly refers to
Ffrench's dwelling.

In 1915 the state lands
department made 200 acres here
available for soldier settlement
farms, and groups of voluntary
workers cleared the land and built
cottages. One of the settlers was
the writer Frank Clune
(1893–1971). The land was poor,
most of the settlers were unskilled,
and the area was isolated, all of
which contributed to the failure of
the scheme. Most of the settlers
left their land and only a few farms
survived until the years after the
Second World War when suburban
spread caused the area to be
resettled. The area's isolation was
greatly reduced when the first
Roseville Bridge over Middle
Harbour opened in 1924, but it
remained semi-rural until the
1950s, when many residential
subdivisions were created, and the
suburb spread out on either side of
Warringah Road.

Today the suburb is residential,
but retains its natural bush setting,
reflected by street names such as
Redwood Place, Bushland Avenue,
Glentrees Avenue, and Willow
Way.

# FRENCHS FOREST

*Shire of Warringah*
Location: 16 kilometres north of
Sydney at the junction of
Warringah Road and Forest Way

Governor Phillip and his exploring
party took two days to walk
north-west from Manly through
this area, and they were greatly
impressed by the size and strength
of the trees there. In 1853 Simeon
Henry Pearce (1821–86) and his
brother James acquired 200 acres in
the area (bounded by the present
Fitzpatrick Avenue, Rabbett Street,
Frenchs Forest Road and Allambie
Road). The property, known as
Pearce's 200 acres, and later as
Rodborough, was acquired by
James Ffrench, who was so
important for the development of
Forestville. Ffrench, a special
constable and crown lands ranger,
came to the Forest in 1856 and
acquired 46 acres, bounded by
Fitzpatrick Avenue, Bantry Bay
Road and Yarraman Avenue,
adjoining the Pearce property that
he later bought. Pearce's job was
to supervise the timber-getters. He
also set up two sawmills, one on

Frenchs Forest Road. All the
timber was cut and split by hand,
then bullocks hauled it to a wharf
on Bantry Bay, from where barges
floated it down the harbour. As
late as 1974 the old bullock track
was still visible.

In 1885 the Hews family
established a brickworks on land
bought from Ffrench.

From the 1880s to the First
World War much of the land here
was taken up by farmers.
Churches, a school and shops to
service the area were established at
the junction of Forest Way and
Warringah Road (then called
Pymble and Rodborough Roads).
After the First World War the area
began to develop, but progress was
slow.

The government used the
Bantry Bay area as an explosives
depot from 1908 until 1974. An
interesting enterprise in the area
was begun by the actor George
Sorlie. In 1945 he initiated an
ambitious land and housing
development around Sorlie Road,

The unveiling ceremony at the opening of
the Wakehurst Parkway by the then
Premier of New South Wales, the Hon.
W. J. McKell

the Village of Sorlie, but it was a financial disaster. He died in 1948, and today the name of this road is all that remains of his dream.

Frenchs Forest Cemetery is an early burial ground between Kambora Avenue, Hakea Avenue and Ashworth Avenue in the west of the suburb. The district showground on Blackbutts Road adjoins a large reserve, Lionel Watts Park. The suburb also has a modern high school and a public school. In addition, there is Frenchs Forest West Primary School, which is known by the delightful name of Mimosa Public School. Bushland flourishes in the area and wildflowers grow abundantly during springtime. Horse-riding is a favourite pastime for visitors as well as residents.

## GALSTON
*Shire of Hornsby*
Location: 36 kilometres north-west of Sydney on Galston Road

A delightful semi-rural suburb at the northern edge of Sydney, Galston was originally known as Upper Dural. It was first settled in the early years of the last century, when it was an area of orchards. In 1886, when the local school was built, Alex Hutchinson suggested that the small hamlet, about 3 kilometres north of Dural, should have a change of name to give it an identity of its own. He named it Galston, after a Scottish town near Kilmarnock, an area famous for its coal output.

In spite of some building development, Galston has managed to retain its serenity and peaceful atmosphere. Rumours disturbing this peace circulated in 1973 when a government proposal

to put Sydney's second international airport in the area became public. Fortunately — from the residents' point of view — nothing came of it.

A road that winds its way through the steep Galston Gorge (see Hornsby) connects the suburb with Hornsby to the east.

## GEORGES HALL
*City of Bankstown*
Location: 24 kilometres south-west of Sydney north of Bankstown Airport

This suburb was originally part of Bankstown and Bankstown Airport is its nearest neighbour. George Bass (1771–1803) and Matthew Flinders (1774–1829) sailed the *Tom Thumb* up the Georges River as far as this suburb's boundary in 1795. In 1798 Bass was given a grant of 100 acres, in the area of the present Hazel Street and Flinders Road, alongside Prospect Creek, by Governor Hunter, and Bass Hill, a neighbouring suburb, honours his name. The grant later reverted to the Crown. Bass's fellow explorer, Matthew Flinders, received a grant south of Bass's bounded by Marion Street, Bellevue Avenue, Flinders Road and Prospect Creek. He bought more land until he had 300 acres, but he did not farm it.

Captain (later Colonel) George Johnston (1764–1823), later a resident of Annandale, built his first home, a farmhouse, in this area, on a grant of 172 acres dated 1798. It was situated on Prospect Creek near the present Henry Lawson Drive and Beatty Parade. He named it George's Hall. His third son, David, became a grazier on this property, which was a farming area in its early days, and

the suburb takes its name from the Johnston farm. David Johnston was appointed by Governor Macquarie as superintendent of herds and stock. His elder brother, George junior, had held this position until his death in 1820 following a riding accident on the Macarthur property at Camden Park. In 1809 the farmhouse of George's Hall was used as an administration centre, and when convicts gathered at the centre to have a census taken, a military guard was posted there.

In 1837 another home was built by the Johnston family. This time it was on higher ground in Bankstown, in present Lionel Street, and well away from the danger of the Georges River floods. The Homestead, as they called it, is one of the oldest houses in Bankstown. Its design was simple but elegant, with wide verandahs, and the interior of the house featured cedar woodwork. Johnston's wife, Esther (1771–1846), came to live permanently at The Homestead in 1829. The family is commemorated by Johnston Road.

In later years The Homestead was owned by a Mr Ashcroft, and still later it was purchased for use as a convalescent home. The National Trust has classified this house, although it is not open for public inspection.

Street names in Georges Hall commemorate two First World War soldiers: Lord Birdwood is immortalised by Birdwood Avenue and another great soldier, Haig, by Haig Avenue.

Adjacent to this suburb are the Liverpool Golf Links and a well-known recreation place the Hollywood Picnic Ground. Years ago before world travel was the norm teenagers could startle their friends by saying "I've been to Hollywood".

# GEORGES HEIGHTS

*Municipality of Mosman*
Location: 8 kilometres north of
Sydney overlooking Port Jackson

This neighbourhood, on a
headland between Balmoral Beach
and Clifton Gardens, is known
mainly for its military reserve but
it is also an area with fantastic
views of Sydney Harbour. Its
name honours George III, who
reigned from 1760 to 1820 and so
was king when the First Fleet left
Portsmouth in 1788. Many places
in New South Wales were named
after him, including George Street,
Sydney.

The military associations of the
area go back to the early days of
the colony. A battery was
established on Georges Head,
within the area of the present
military reserve, by Governor
King, and construction was begun
in 1801. In 1870, when there were
fears of a Russian invasion,
improved defence works were
carried out. A casemate battery
was constructed in 1872 and a store
barracks in 1873. In 1886 another
casemate battery was erected.
Today the reserve covers nearly
the whole peninsula on the
seaward side from just north of the
Clifton Gardens Park to the point
of Middle Head. A naval depot
stands on the bay side in Middle
Harbour.

# GIRRAWEEN

*Municipality of Holroyd*
Location: 30 kilometres west of
Sydney on the Great Western
Highway between Parramatta and
St Marys

The Aboriginal name of this
suburb means "the place where the
flowers grow". It was part of Dr

D'Arcy Wentworth's estate (see
Wentworthville), granted in 1799.
Situated south of Toongabbie, it
retains the air of a country village,
although it was built on part of the
site of the notorious Toongabbie
convict camp (see Toongabbie),
where Irish prisoners suffered
some of the harshest treatment in
the colony. An early resident was
William Brown, whose dairy was
situated in Tungarra Road.

In the early part of this century
the area was described as "a
delightfully peaceful place". Its
development as an independent
suburb began in 1910, when land
was subdivided, and sold by
Arthur Rickard, a well-known real
estate developer. The lots sold
rapidly, some to be later resold at
much higher prices. Girraween
was originally a street name in that
subdivision, which had been
named Toongabbie Park, but when
the post office opened, it took the
name of Girraween, which also
became the suburb's name.

An old tramway, operating in
the 1920s from Toongabbie station
to the blue metal quarry at
Prospect, travelled around the
outskirts of Girraween and crossed
the Great Western Highway.

Girraween's residents have
always had a progressive attitude,
and the Girraween Ratepayers and
Electors Association was
instrumental in having public
swimming baths constructed in the
district. It also agitated for road
maintenance and more work on
water supplies in the area.

The School of Arts was founded
in 1918, and its building has played
an important part in the social life
of Girraween. The Anglican and
Catholic Churches held their first
services in it, as were the
Girraween school's first classes. In
1925 land was acquired for
Girraween Park, and a playing area
was laid out soon afterwards.

# GLADESVILLE

*Municipalities of Ryde and Hunters
Hill*
Location: 10 kilometres west of
Sydney on the north side of the
Parramatta River between Hunters
Hill and Ryde

Part of this area was first known as
Doody's Bay, after John Doody, a
convict artist who was granted 30
acres on the waterfront in March
1795. Doody had produced a series
of drawings of Australian native
plants, which were sent to Sir
Joseph Banks by Captain William
Paterson, himself a keen naturalist.
When Paterson later became
administrator of the colony in
1794–95, he granted the land to
Doody as a reward for his work.

John Glade, after whom
Gladesville is named, arrived in the
colony as a convict in 1791. He had
a farm in the area from about 1806,
although the deeds were not issued
until 1836, and he bought Doody's
grant in 1817. The farm, which
stood on the waterfront that
became known as Glade's bay,
prospered, but it was eventually
subdivided and sold in 1841. One
of the purchasers was a Sydney
lawyer, William Whaley Billyard.
He bought 150 acres of Glade's
land for £300 and built a wharf and
a road, which opened up the area.
The name Gladesville first
appeared on one of the subdivision
titles in 1856, when Billyard began
to sell lots of his land.

One of John Glade's near
neighbours was a James Squire,
who gave his address in 1820 as
"Bethlem Point". In the 1820s,
when a semaphore station stood on
the point to relay messages
between Sydney and Parramatta
the telegraph assistants were among
the few occupants of the area.
When a hospital for the insane, the
Tarban Creek Asylum, completed

in 1838, was built at Gladesville it is thought the name was changed to the present Bedlam Point. A large mental hospital in England, in existence since the fifteenth century, was known as Bedlam (a corruption of Bethlehem Hospital). The Gladesville building, designed by the colonial architect, Mortimer Lewis (1796–1879) housed sixty patients. A new wing was added in 1866, and the building was later called Gladesville Hospital or Asylum.

In 1828 residents of the Hunter Valley and the Hawkesbury River began to agitate for a new direct road to Sydney. In 1826 a road north from Castle Hill, which crossed the Hawkesbury at Wiseman's Ferry, had been completed, but the route to Sydney went via Parramatta, because there was no vehicular ferry at any point on the Parramatta River. Residents illegally used their own boats, but a public punt was urgently needed. Surveyor-General Sir Thomas Mitchell eventually proposed a new road and a punt to link Kissing Point with Sydney, which would join Sydney with Ryde and all points north. In 1829 it was finally decided that the road would cross the river at Bedlam Point. In 1830 a ferry house was built in readiness for the punt that would join the two sections of the Great North Road. The ferry was in use by 1832.

In March 1878 work commenced on the building of the Gladesville Bridge and a new way of transporting the public was about to begin. The bridge, completed in 1881, was replaced in 1964.

By the turn of the century the public had two ways of crossing the Parramatta River from Sydney: by a steamer operating from No. 6 wharf Circular Quay, or by trams running every ten minutes via George Street, through Pyrmont, Balmain, Drummoyne and Gladesville, and terminating at Hatton's Flat, Ryde. The tram fare to Gladesville was fourpence.

Punt Road recalls the time when travellers on the Great Northern Road crossed the Parramatta River by punt from Abbotsford to Bedlam Point. Linsley Street commemorates John R. Linsley, mayor of Ryde from 1877 to 1879, and Bateman's Road is named after Robert Bateman, who ran the punt from Bedlam Point. John Glade, who gave his name to this busy residential suburb, was buried in St Anne's Church of England graveyard, Ryde.

## GLEBE

*Municipality of Leichhardt*
Location: 3 kilometres south-west of Sydney north of Parramatta Road

This suburb, the correct title of which is The Glebe, was at first regarded as part of the Kangaroo Grounds, or Petersham district. In 1789 the Glebe area was reserved as church land by Governor Phillip, and the Reverend Richard Johnson (1753–1827) started to clear the 400 acres granted. The Glebe means church land for the maintenance of the incumbent of a parish. The land was rough and heavily timbered, however, and insufficient convict labour was available for clearing, so Johnson gave up attempts to cultivate it. The area mostly remained unused except for the encroachment of some small grants near the present Parramatta Road. In 1828 the church lands, except for the area between Parramatta Road, St John's Road, Mount Vernon Street and Cowper Street, were sold, and

soon substantial houses with pleasant gardens had been established.

One of the earliest was Toxteth House, in what is now Toxteth Street. This was designed by the eminent architect John Verge (1772–1861) for George Allen (1800–77) and later occupied by his son George Wigram Allen, who lived there until 1885. Completed in 1834, the house was named after the home of the family's friend Sir Robert Wigram. After this it became a boarding-house, and still later part of the educational complex maintained by the sisters of the Order of the Good Samaritan, when it was named St Scholastica's. Two street names recall the first owners of the home — Wigram and Allen.

Another estate, of 32 acres, was Lyndhurst Estate, the site of a beautiful Georgian mansion, Lyndhurst House. This was built in 1833–36, again to the design of John Verge, for Dr James Bowman (1784–1846), the inspector of colonial hospitals, who helped found Sydney's Rum Hospital. From 1847 it was the site of an Anglican divinity school and from 1852 a Catholic school. The once elegant house was later used as a laundry, an ice-cream factory and flats. Sadly Lyndhurst House, with gardens that once stretched to the then heavily wooded land fronting Blackwattle Bay, became derelict after being taken over by the Main Roads Department when it was planning to use the area for the north-western expressway. In the 1970s the house was saved from demolition at the last moment, and it has since been restored. It is now the headquarters of the New South Wales Historic Houses Trust and the ground-floor rooms are open to the public.

Another of these early homes

The restored verandah and portico of
Lyndhurst, 1987. Photo by Max Dupain

was Hereford House, completed in
1829, on the corner of Glebe Point
Road and Pyrmont Bridge Road.
From 1910 to 1924 it was a teacher
training college. Later the house
was demolished and today only a
plaque marks its site. Part of its
land was used for a baby health
centre and public recreation area.
Most of Glebe's large estates had,
however, been broken up in the
1880s, when numerous workers'
cottages and terraces were built.

The Presbyterian manse in
Bridge Road is a fine example of
Victorian architecture of the 1870s,
which favoured gables and bay
windows. An architect, Edward
Halloran, lived there in 1871, but
in 1879 the house became the
Presbyterian manse and was
occupied by the Reverend Andrew
Gardiner.

St John's Bishopthorpe, on the
corner of St John's and Glebe Point
Roads, was designed by Edmund
Blacket (1817–83), who lived in
Glebe for nineteen years and was a
member of its first council in 1859,
a position he held for eleven years.
It was built from stone quarried at
Pyrmont. The foundation stone
was laid in 1868, and the church
opened on 21 December 1870. The
church furnishings were also
designed by Blacket.

The area known as Bishopthorpe
Estate, which includes Derwent,
Westmoreland and Mount Vernon
Streets, was originally chosen as a
home-site for the Bishop of
Sydney, and all revenue from this
land was to become the bishop's
personal income. In April 1857,
Edmund Blacket began to design
the area; the cottages and terrace
houses erected then, and later,
show the variety of architectural
styles of Sydney's houses in the
1860s and 1870s.

Glebe is bounded on the north
by Blackwattle Bay and Rozelle
Bay, and to the east by Wentworth
Park, famous for greyhound-
racing and trotting races. Once a
swamp area, it was filled in and
grassed over, although heavy rains
will always reveal its watery
origin, usually on the busiest
nights of the racing carnivals.

Glebe Point juts into Rozelle
Bay in the north of the suburb.
Just opposite, across the bay, is
Glebe Island, which is no longer a
true island. It was joined to the
mainland by a causeway when the
first Gladesville Bridge was built.
Today the area houses the Balmain
coal loader, the wheat loader,
container terminals and ICI's soda
ash berth. Glebe Island Bridge
connects the island to Pyrmont.
The original bridge, with a swing
span, was built in 1857, but it was
replaced in 1901 by a two steel
truss design with an electrically
operated central swing span.

Glebe was proclaimed a borough
in 1859 and is now part of the
municipality of Leichhardt. After
its early years as a fashionable area,
Glebe later became a working-class
suburb, and its architecture now
reflects the suburb's changing
fortunes. Today a complete range
of house styles can still be seen in
the suburb, from small cottages to
large mansions, many of them

restored in recent years as the suburb's location, near the city and the University of Sydney, has again made it popular.

# GLENFIELD
*City of Campbelltown*
Location: 39 kilometres south-west of Sydney between the Hume Highway and the Georges River, on the Main Southern Line

Dr Charles Throsby (1777–1828) arrived in the colony in 1802 as surgeon on the convict ship *Coromandel*. He was commandant at the Newcastle settlement from 1804 to 1809, when he retired to a grant of 950 acres south of Liverpool. It extended from Georges River to the present Glenfield, which had been the name of the village near Leicester, England, where he was born. In 1816 Throsby built a home here, which he called Glenfield House. Between 1816 and 1821 Throsby took part in several exploration trips, including one with Hamilton Hume, a family friend. He went to Jervis Bay with Surveyor-General James Meehan, and to Bathurst, Goulburn and the area around Canberra. He was rewarded with a

Dr Charles Throsby

1,000 acre grant by Governor Macquarie, who named Throsby's estate, in the new land he found near Goulburn, Throsby Park. He died in 1828 and the property was inherited by his nephew, Charles, who had come to New South Wales in 1820 with his wife, Betsy Broughton, who as a child was the only survivor of crew and passengers massacred when their ship berthed in New Zealand.

The township developed during the 1880s and the first school opened in the area in April 1882. It was followed by the first official post office on 9 October 1899. Glenfield is the site of three well-known institutions: Hurlstone Agricultural High School (see Hurlstone Park), Glenfield Veterinary Research Station, and the Frank Whiddon Masonic Homes, one of a group of homes for the aged.

Glenfield is on the Main Southern railway line, between Casula and Macquarie Fields, but when the extension to the East Hills line reaches Glenfield, forty-five minutes will be cut from the travelling time to Sydney for Glenfield and the suburbs south to Camden. It is bounded to the west by the Ingleburn military reserve, and to the east by Holsworthy military reserve.

# GLENHAVEN
*Shire of Baulkham Hills*
Location: 32 kilometres north-west of Sydney between Castle Hill and Dural

Like neighbouring Dural, Kenthurst and Kellyville, this small suburb has retained a tranquil setting of bush and open grassland. Originally called Sandhurst by early settlers, the name was changed at a public meeting in 1894, because of confusion with a similar name in Melbourne. The small settlement lies in a valley, of which the peaceful, southern part was known as The Haven and the combination of glen and haven seems appropriate.

The Great North Road between Sydney and Newcastle, the surveys for which began in 1826, opened in 1833, when convict gangs were working from dawn to dark towards its completion. As the Old Northern Road it now passes through the suburbs that have grown around early settlements, like Glenhaven. Today Glenhaven is still a semi-rural area, but while some market gardens survive, it is increasingly residential.

# GLENORIE
*Shires of Baulkham Hills and Hornsby*
Location: 44 kilometres north-west of Sydney on Old Northern Road

This suburb, on the road to Wiseman's Ferry, between Dural and North Maroota, is one of a group that began life as part of Dural. Formerly known as North Dural, it was on part of the 34,000 acres of land reserved in 1802 by Governor King, and opened up by timber-cutters from 1817. The

area proved excellent for orchards, which were being established from the 1860s, and especially for citrus fruits. As the district developed, the name North Dural caused much confusion for the post office, so it suggested the name be changed and submitted a list of possible names. Finally the choice was between two suggested by William Black, a well-known local identity: Glenorie and Hazeldene. The local progress association chose Glenorie, a Scottish name. From 1894 the suburb was known by this name and soon developed an identity of its own.

Preliminary surveys were made in 1826 for the road passing west of St Jude's Church, Dural, now called the Old Northern Road, when John Oxley (1785?–1828) was surveyor-general. It was the main road to Newcastle, but many travellers still preferred to travel to Newcastle by sea. An inn was established by Thomas Best soon after the road opened, near today's Middle Dural. Best was one of the first residents, and the Roughley family were also early settlers in this delightful area (see Dural).

## GORDON

*Municipality of Ku-ring-gai*
Location: 16 kilometres north-west of Sydney on the Pacific Highway and the North Shore Line

In the 1920s Gordon was considered to be one of the healthiest suburbs on the North Shore line. Situated 116 metres above sea level, and at that time in a bushland area, it attracted people who wanted to build their homes in a peaceful, away-from-it-all atmosphere, and yet be close to the city.

Historians are not really certain about the origin of its name. Like Willoughby, it probably commemorates General Sir James Willoughby Gordon who, as the quartermaster-general in England when the First Fleet sailed for the colony in 1787, would have been responsible for outfitting the fleet.

One of Gordon's pioneer settlers was Robert McIntosh, who is commemorated by McIntosh Street. In 1832 he planted an orchard, which was situated opposite today's St John's Anglican Church, on the corner of St John's Avenue and the Pacific Highway. Another pioneer was John Brown, known as the Squire, who, through his trade as a timber-cutter, became prosperous, although he could neither read nor write. He first acquired land in the 1850s on the site of the present Ravenswood Methodist Ladies College. This was also the site of the first post office, which opened in 1860, and the brick cottage that housed it still stands in the school grounds. Because the suburb was part of the area known as Lane Cove, this was the name given to the first post office. The confusion that resulted, however, caused it to be renamed Gordon in 1879, and the site of the post office was also changed.

Brown's ambition was to own a square mile of land, and to this end he acquired several parcels of land, until by 1870 he had bought land as far down the North Shore as St Leonards, where he had a large timber yard. John Brown had five sons and six daughters, who all

Empire Day celebrations at Gordon Public School, 1907

worked in the enterprises begun by their father, who also made sure his children all received a good education.

St John's Church of England at Gordon is another historic point of interest in this charming suburb. It was built in 1872, and the rectory was built in the 1890s. In 1817 Governor Lachlan Macquarie donated £10 towards the building of a small wooden structure, which came to be used as a church, community centre and general meeting place. There was no regular vicar living in the area, so a visiting clergyman came on horseback to hold services for the small group of early settlers. A larger church built in 1832 was destroyed by bushfire in 1862, and ten years later a church building designed by Edmund Blacket (1817–83) was begun. This beautiful building was later extended as the congregation grew with the growth of the district. The church's graveyard is the last resting place of many well-known pioneers, as well as settlers from those first days in Gordon.

Gordon's railway station opened in 1890. A shire encompassing the area from Willoughby to Hornsby was formed in 1906 and called Ku-ring-gai, after the Chase, which had been established in 1894. In 1928 it became a municipality with its headquarters at Gordon.

A well-known house in Gordon today is Eryldene, designed by William Hardy Wilson (1881–1955) for Professor Waterhouse, and expert on camellias. The house has beautiful gardens and is particularly worth visiting when the camellias are in flower.

# GORE HILL
*Municipality of Willoughby*
Location: 7 kilometres north-west of Sydney on the Pacific Highway

Originally called Huntershill in 1794 by Thomas Muir, after his home in Glasgow, it became Gore Hill after William Gore (1756–1845) took up land in the area in 1810. Gore had been appointed provost-marshall and became friendly with the new governor, William Bligh, on his voyage to Australia. The colonists immediately associated the two men, and as Bligh became unpopular so Gore's life became difficult. Rebels against Bligh's rule arrested Gore in 1808 and made false accusations against him. The unfortunate man was dismissed from his position and sentenced to work in the Newcastle coal mines for seven years. This was just the beginning of increasing difficulties in his career in New South Wales until he retired to his property in 1825 (see Artarmon).

The old Gore Hill Cemetery, now recognised as a "headstone history book", where many early Australian notables are interred, is an important historic site in the suburb. The cemetery covers nearly 6 hectares and fronts onto the Pacific Highway, known as Lane Cove Road last century. The first known burial here was in 1877, but some of the headstones from the Devonshire Street Cemetery, once on the site of Central Railway, were also brought here. Lousia King, the first woman pharmacist in Sydney, and Sir John Sulman, architect, are among those buried here.

Three television towers are also located on Gore Hill, and the Australian Broadcasting Commission's Channel 2 has a main office block on the site. Gore Street, near River Road, and a small park, Gore's Creek Reserve, as well as Gore's Creek, which flows into the Lane Cove River, all commemorate William Gore.

Gore Hill Cemetery, resting place for many notable Australians including Bernard "Varney" Kieran, a national swimming hero who died tragically in 1905 at the age of 19. His funeral, attended by 30,000 people, was one of the most remarkable Australia has ever seen

# GRANVILLE

*City of Parramatta*

Location: 22 kilometres west of
Sydney at the junction of
Woodville Road and the Great
Western Highway, a junction
station for the Main Western Line
and the Main Southern Line

In 1855, Granville was known as
Parramatta Junction, because it was
then the end of the railway line
from Sydney to Parramatta. It
retained that name until 1880,
when two public meetings voted
that the name be changed. Some
very strange names were
suggested, including Drainwell,
Vauxhall, Nobbsville and
Swagsville, but finally the name of
Granville, in honour of the Earl of
Granville, a former colonial
secretary, was selected. Even then
the voice of protest was raised,
declaring the name was "too
French", but the dissenter was
ignored. George Leveson-Gower,
second Earl of Granville, had been
England's colonial secretary in
1851 and foreign minister in
1870–74 and 1880–85.

Almost one hundred years
before, Governor Phillip had
visited the area during his
exploration of the Duck River in
February 1788, so the suburb has
some of the oldest connections
with Australian history. The road
from Parramatta to Sydney passed
through the suburb, and by 1791 a
rough track had already been
cleared.

The present suburb stands on
grants once issued to John Harris,
Garnham Blaxcell, William
Lawson and W. C. Wentworth.
The most important was Blaxcell's
grant of 1,125 acres, which he
received in 1806. Called the
Drainwell Estate, it covered the
area between Clyde Street and
Woodville Road, with Rawson

Street forming the southern
boundary. Garnham Blaxcell
(1778–1817) had arrived in Sydney
as a naval officer in 1802 and held a
number of official positions. A
partner of John Macarthur's, he
was more interested in trade than
public office or farming. Despite
early success, some ambitious
ventures later brought him into
debt and he left the colony in 1817
and died on the journey to
England.

Blaxcell's property passed to Sir
John Jamison (1776–1844), the son
of surgeon Thomas Jamison, who
used the estate for grazing.
Educated as a surgeon, he was
responsible for the successful
treatment of an outbreak of scurvy
in the Swedish army and received a
knighthood from the Swedes; in
1813 he was also knighted by
England's Prince Regent, later
George IV. He inherited
Regentville on the Nepean where
he built an elegant mansion. He
became one of the leading colonists
and among the many offices he
held was first president of the
Agricultural Society of New South
Wales, to which he was elected in
1822.

An early governor, Charles
FitzRoy, in the 1840s set up a hunt
club in Granville to pursue the
wild dogs that infested the area.
The main road in the area was
called Dog Trap Road until 1879,
when it became Woodville Road.
Another pest of the highway was
the bushranger, preying upon
settlers.

The first industry in Granville
was timber getting, as the
surrounding country was heavily
covered with gum, box and
ironbark trees. The timber, cut by
pit-sawyers, was used in many
buildings erected around
Parramatta, and quantities were
also transported to Sydney via
Duck River and the Parramatta

River. The largest saw pit was
located at the corner of Robertson
Street and Guildford Road.
Charcoal-burners were also active
in the early years, providing fuel
for householders and blacksmiths'
forges.

Subdivision of the area began
after the railway came through in
1855, and from 1862 the Drainwell
Estate was being subdivided.
Orchards and small farms were
then characteristic of the area, but
by 1871 the local population was
still less than a hundred. The first
official post office opened in March
1878, and the public school took in
its first pupils in 1880, at about the
time that Granville began to
develop rapidly. An early inn, the
Vauxhall Hotel, was licensed in
1856, soon after the railway came
through the area. This hotel sold a
bucket of rum for a penny — but
the trick bucket was small and
solid except for the slight
depression on the top that held the
rum.

Several industries developed in
this period and became the nucleus
of one of Sydney's principal
industrial areas. One of these was
James Bergan's woollen mill,
established in 1870, where cloth
was manufactured. William
Ritchie's agricultural machinery
business, in Parramatta in the
1870s, transferred to Granville in
the following decade. Tanneries
were also established in the area at
an early date.

In the 1920s Houston's produce
store stood at the corner of
Blaxcell and William Streets,
selling not only produce, but also
petrol. At the rear of the store a
large iron shed housed the local
gymnasium where some of
Australia's boxing champions —
Micky Miller (lightweight
champion of Australia), Don Day,
"Tiger" Donnelly, Dave Short —
and the wrestler Phil May trained.

Although the coming of the railway had made a vast difference to Granville's development, it was also associated with the suburb's most tragic event. In January 1977, the Bold Street Bridge collapsed onto and crushed a peak-hour electric train, which had hit one of the bridge's pylons. A memorial garden planted with roses and many other flowers reminds passers-by of the eightly-three lives lost in that dreadful accident.

Today Granville is still an important railway junction, a busy industrial suburb, and a residential area for hundreds of people who are rearing their families in this historically interesting place.

## GRAY'S POINT

*Shire of Sutherland*

Location: 29 kilometres south of Sydney on the peninsula between the North West Arm of Port Hacking and the Hacking River

Situated on the North West Arm of Port Hacking, Gray's Point abuts the Royal National Park south of the city. It is a peaceful suburb, once rich in bird life, as street names Heron, Kookaburra, Plover, Kingfisher, Swallow and Cormorant, all indicate. But it has a meagre recorded history and the origin of its name is unknown. It may have been named after Samuel William Gray, who owned land on the point, or perhaps after John Edward Gray, who was a resident ranger in the national park in the late 1800s and was a well-known local identity.

A pleasant reserve known as Gray's Point Oval is located towards Audley, and a local public school is sited in Angle Road, Gray's Point.

## GREENACRE

*City of Bankstown*

Location: 17 kilometres south-west of Sydney at the junction of Boronia Road and the Hume Highway

Once known as East Bankstown, this suburb is situated between Bankstown and Strathfield. There was a novel reason for its new name. An acre of ground was cleared for cultivation near the first road through the area, and its contrast with its surroundings led to it being referred to as Green Acre; the name used for an early subdivision near Bankstown railway station. Greenacre Park Estate was, in 1909, one of the first subdivisions in the area.

An early resident of the Greenacre area was Michael Ryan, who bought land north of Liverpool Road, where he operated an inn called the Harp of Ould Erin.

Greenacre is now a busy residential area with two public schools. Street names, always interesting because they tell of historic events and people, recall both people, and native flora and fauna: Macquarie Street and Napoleon Road exist side by side with Acacia Avenue, Banksia and Mimosa Roads, and Koala Road represents our native fauna.

## GREEN VALLEY

*City of Liverpool*

Location: 39 kilometres south-west of Sydney, west of Liverpool

The Housing Commission's development of the Green Valley housing estate near Liverpool, between 1961 and 1965, was the largest single housing scheme ever attempted to that date. The new districts of the scheme were Ashcroft, Busby, Cartwright, Heckenberg, Miller, Mount Pritchard and Sadlier. Within the space of a few years 7,464 cottages, flats and units were built and, by 1966, over 24,000 people were living in an area that had been occupied by market gardeners, dairymen and poultry farmers. It was, however, a long time before residents were provided with adequate services such as public transport, health services, shopping centres and other necessary facilities, and before 1970 there were no pre-school centres. The Liverpool city council had to provide sporting and leisure facilities, shopping complexes, baby health centres and libraries to help the population to settle in a totally new environment.

Unlike older suburbs of Sydney, where streets often run parallel in a grid pattern, newer suburbs, such as Green Valley have been designed to follow the contours of the area, so that many streets are curved and follow an almost semi-circular pattern. Many of the streets in the suburb of Green Valley have Aboriginal names, such as Arunta, Kinkuna, and Naranghi.

Today the area is busily residential, populated by many families with young children. Green Valley Creek skirts the edge of the suburb and Green Valley Public School stands in Green Valley Road. The Liverpool Speedway is at the corner of Wilson and Liverpool Roads.

# GREENWICH
*Municipality of Lane Cove*
Location: 7 kilometres north-west of Sydney on the Lane Cove River where it joins the Parramatta River

The Parramatta River was known to early settlers as the Thames of the Antipodes, perhaps because it reminded them of the English Thames, which at that time flowed through areas of natural beauty. Greenwich on the Thames in England is known for its hospital, the Royal Observatory completed in 1675, and the famous naval training school, which Arthur Phillip attended from the age of thirteen. It is not certain whether this suburb was named by an early grantee, George Green, or after Greenwich on the Thames. Perhaps the latter, since other Parramatta River suburbs were named after Thames-side localities, such as Henley, Woolwich and Putney.

Greenwich House, built in 1836, still stands on the corner of George and St Lawrence Streets. It stood on a 20 acre grant originally owned by George Green, a boatbuilder active in the area in the 1830s. He had the property divided into allotments and sold in 1840.

A punt service ran from the city to Greenwich in the 1840s, but lack of customers caused it to be cancelled. In the 1850s, when the demand increased, it was reinstated.

During the 1880s there were many subdivisions in the area, and by the middle years of the decade Greenwich was a small village with about sixteen houses, a school, a shop and a post office near the junction of George and St Lawrence Streets. Several of the houses have survived to the present. It was not until after 1900 that settlement moved away from the point, and the school and post office were both moved further north.

The Shell Company's installation at Gore Cove in Greenwich is a storage and distribution centre for petrol.

Greenwich is conveniently close to Sydney and is characterised by gracious homes and an old-world charm, despite the increase in high-rise housing over the past fifteen years.

# GREYSTANES
*Municipality of Holroyd*
Location: 29 kilometres west of Sydney south of the Great Western Highway

This suburb, north of Fairfield, takes its name from a mansion built by Nelson Lawson, the third son of explorer William Lawson (1774–1850). Nelson married Honoria Mary Dickinson and before 1837 he built Greystanes House as their future family home on the crest of Prospect Hill. He had received the land from his father, who had been granted 500 acres here by the illegal government that followed the overthrow of Governor Bligh in 1808. Governor Macquarie confirmed the grant, where William Lawson had built a house, which he called Veteran Hall, because he had a commission in the New South Wales Veterans Company. The house was demolished in 1926 and the site is now partly covered by the waters of Prospect Reservoir.

Greystanes House was approached by a long drive lined with an avenue of English trees — elms, hawthorns, holly and woodbine — mingling with jacarandas. It had a wide, semi-circular front verandah supported by four pillars. The foundations were of stone, the roof of slate, and the doors and architraves were heavy cedar. It was richly furnished with articles and furnishings of the best quality available, and was the scene of many glittering soirées attended by the elite of the colony.

Honoria Lawson died in 1845. Nelson remarried a year later, but he died in 1849, and the property reverted to his father. Greystanes House remained standing until late in the 1940s, when it was demolished.

The suburb of Greystanes kept a country air until the 1950s, when developers began to build moderately priced houses on what had formerly been grazing land and orchards. This attracted young families to the area, which today is part of the suburban sprawl away from Sydney. A number of small parks are scattered through the area; the Greystanes Sports Centre stands in the south; and the Cumberland Golf Course is in the centre of the suburb. Streets have been named after cricketers, such as Bradman, Simpson and Benaud; flowers, such as Hyacinth, Nemesia and Lupin; girls' names such as Elvina, Rowena and Esther; boys' names, such as Ivan, Hector and Jasper; and the names of New South Wales country towns, such as Ballina, Casino and Orange. The suburb has a primary school in Merrylands Road and a modern high school in Beresford Road. Today it is a busy progressive suburb with improved local bus services to Merrylands, Parramatta and the city.

Greystanes House, a fine example of early colonial architecture, was unfortunately demolished in the late 1940s

# GUILDFORD

*Municipality of Holroyd, Cities of Parramatta and Fairfield*

Location: 23 kilometres west of Sydney between Parramatta and Fairfield, on the Main Southern Line

Guildford, which lies between Merrylands and Yennora, was named in 1837 in honour of the Earl of Guildford. A connection of his, retired army officer Lieutenant Samuel North, was in 1817 granted 640 acres where this suburb now stands, and he named his property Guildford. In 1843 it was bought by Henry Whittaker, who acquired several properties nearby and called his estate Orchardleigh.

An area of 1,000 acres in the northern part of the suburb, west of the present Woodville Road, was reserved by Governor Phillip and then passed to the Church and Schools Corporation to be used to support clergy and teachers. It was subdivided in 1871–72. The area west of Woodville Road and south of Rawson Road was a grant of 1,000 acres made to John Thomas Campbell (1770?–1830), administrative assistant to Governor Macquarie, in 1823. It was called the Quid Pro Quo Estate, and in 1832 it was divided into four blocks and sold.

William and John Lackey also received grants in the area in 1838, and their property was known as Woodville. One of the first inns, owned by William Lackey, opened in 1840. It was the Sir Maurice O'Connell, situated on the Dog Trap Road (now Woodville Road). Here, too, a small hamlet developed and by 1870 there was a

school here and, by the 1880s, a church.

Land was subdivided in the 1860s and 1870s and the names of Holroyd and Sherwin came into the area. Another pioneer was Mr Joseph Kenyon, who bought the properties of Benjamin and Joseph Herbert in the 1820s. His home and orchard, Woodlands, were showplaces in those early days.

When Guildford railway station opened in 1876, a new settlement developed around it, and the former settlement was called Old Guildford. But it was not until 1913 that Guildford became a busy suburb. A brickworks, established in 1915, and the building industry here contributed to the suburb's growth. Soon shops and houses were occupied by new residents, and the building boom continued into the 1920s.

When the first public school opened it was constructed of slab and bark, and housed

117

twenty-seven pupils. In 1877 Edward Whittaker gave land on which a new school and a teacher's residence was built, and this school remained in use until 1915. A new post office, built in 1924, replaced the 1867 building, and 1915 saw the first fire station in the district.

A man of whom the district may be proud was George McCredie. A builder, architect and consulting engineer, he became a magistrate in 1892 and in the same year was elected mayor of Prospect and Sherwood. He was re-elected each year until 1894, when he became a member of the Legislative Assembly. In 1891 McCredie built his home, Lynwood, in Byron Road. It is still standing and has been beautifully restored. All the material used in the house was imported from England. It had the first telephone in the district, and the first Presbyterian church service was held there. McCredie is commemorated by McCredie Park off West Guildford Road, in the block behind Lynwood Hall.

Guildford in the mid-1980s is a modern suburb, with a wide choice of community activities and an active Chamber of Commerce representing 114 businesses. Its aim is to increase housing for the population, while ensuring that the new medium-density housing blends with the old world charm of the suburb's interesting past. Bowling is popular in this suburb, and the Country Women's Association has a very active group working with the Red Cross and Rotary in the district.

## GYMEA
*Shire of Sutherland*
Location: 26 kilometres south-west of Sydney and east of Sutherland on the northern side of Port Hacking, on the Cronulla Line

How delightful to find a suburb named after a flower! Mr W. A. B. Greaves, a government surveyor, chose the name in 1855 because of the large, tall-stalked lilies growing in the area. The giant-sized flower of this unusual plant forms a head of red petals with a base of green and yellow fronds. Building in the suburb has eliminated most of the lilies, although some survive in nature strips and in the Royal National Park, a few kilometres to the south.

Gymea stretches down to the Port Hacking waterfront between North West Arm and Gymea Bay. Like neighbouring areas, it was slow to develop, mainly because of poor transport. Whereas the western suburbs opened up with the coming of the railway from the 1850s, even in the early 1920s there were no stations here serving Miranda or Gymea, which relied on the steam tram from Sutherland station to Cronulla, or, as indicated in a 1920s street directory, on "vehicles of all descriptions".

Progress has changed the scene today — transport and shopping facilities are right up-to-date. The railway station, on the Cronulla line, opened in 1939. Three schools accommodate local children: Gymea Bay and Gymea North public schools, and Gymea High School. Gymea Technical College caters for tertiary students.

So Gymea has seen many changes, but fortunately no one wants to change the suburb's name to its botanical equivalent — *Doryanthes excelsa*.

## HABERFIELD
*Municipality of Ashfield*
Location: 9 kilometres south-west of Sydney between Parramatta Road and the head of Iron Cove

This residential suburb was part of a grant of 480 acres originally made in 1803 to Nicholas Bayly (1770–1823), former officer of the New South Wales Corps. Bayly called the grant Sunning Hill Farm. As Iron Cove Creek and Hawthorne Canal flow through this area, Bayly's grant may have been rather swampy. It is said that he planted the first Norfolk pines seen in the area.

In 1826 the land was acquired by Simeon Lord (1771–1840), who was transported for stealing some pieces of cloth and became one of the wealthiest commercial men in Sydney. He renamed it Dobroyde Farm, after the village in Yorkshire, England, where he was born. In 1825, Simeon Lord's daughter, Sarah Ann Lord, married Dr David Ramsay, and they received Dobroyde Farm as Sarah's dowry. As their family grew (they had ten children) David Ramsay enlarged the original house. At that time locals called the area Ramsay's Bush and an early directory states that "Dobroyde is the residence of Dr Ramsay". He established a plant nursery at the farm — "the orchard alone being worth £100 a year" — and is said to have grown some of the best oranges in New South Wales. In 1818 he built the Plough Inn, and gradually areas of land between Haberfield and Five Dock were added to the property.

The Ramsay family was responsible for the establishment of the Presbyterian church in Haberfield, and in 1840, the first Sunday school was established by the Ramsay daughters, held at first in Dobroyde House, on Parramatta Road, between later Rogers Avenue and Dalhousie Street. In 1862 a school building, Yasmar (Ramsay spelled backwards), was erected. St David's Hall was also built by the family, and like the church, it is still in use today. In 1868, Mrs Ramsay laid the foundation stone of St David's Presbyterian Church, which opened in 1869. The family gave £1,000 towards the construction costs. Yasmar House on Parramatta Road was built in 1873 by David and Sarah Ramsay's daughter, Mary Louisa Learmonth, who also taught at the Sunday school.

Although subdivision began in a small way in the 1880s, the area was mostly bush until, in the early 1900s, a famous real estate personality, Richard Stanton, acquired much of the land and set about creating a garden suburb, engaging an architect who made individual plans for over 10,000 houses. Stanton called the suburb Haberfield, after the English branch of his family who bore that name. Buyers could acquire properties on a low deposit with repayment on a long-term mortgage. Covenants were placed on the titles to protect the single-storeyed character of the area, and houses were to be set in gardens. Permission had to be obtained from Richard Stanton, or, after his death, from his family, to alter properties.

By 1903 a directory commented that "Haberfield is growing and the dwellings being erected there are of the most modern design." The average price of a home in 1985 was $85,000, compared with £780 in 1903. The Federation character of this suburb has largely been preserved, as has Stanton's idea of maintaining gardens in the streets and around the houses, and

of achieving a sense of national pride by giving streets and roads Australian names. Deakin and Barton Streets are named after prominent Federation politicians. Dobroyd Point, Dobroyd Parade, and Dobroyd Lane (the final "e" has been lost over the years) recall the days of the Lord—Ramsay family ownership, as do Ramsay Road, Yasmar Avenue and Lord Street. Stanton Road commemorates the man who determined the present character of the suburb. Dalhousie Street was named after a frigate that was wrecked off Beachy Head during a violent storm on 7 October 1848 on the journey from London to Sydney. Of the sixty-one persons on board, only one survived.

# HAMMONDVILLE
*City of Liverpool*
Location: 31 kilometres south-west of Sydney, south-east of Liverpool on Heathcote Road

One of the earliest settlers in the area south-east of Liverpool was George Evans (1780–1852), who surveyed the road over the Blue Mountains. In 1809 he was granted 140 acres along Harris Creek, but in 1819 he sold the property to John Connell. The area remained rural until over a hundred years later.

During the Depression of the 1930s, the present suburb was created by Canon R. B. S. Hammond (1870–1946), a member of the Anglican clergy. At that time Canon Hammond was the rector of St Barnabas Church, Broadway, where he instituted the "sermon in a sentence" on the noticeboard at the front of the church, which continues today. His idea in developing the suburb

was to provide reasonably priced housing for young families who were suffering because of unemployment. The conditions for entering Hammondville reflected the plight of many of the families at that time. Both parents had to be unemployed, with a family of at least three young children, and under threat of immediate eviction, or already evicted from their home.

At Hammondville, begun in 1937 on 13 acres (later expanded to 225 acres), each family was housed in a new cottage, which they would own at the end of seven years if they paid 5 shillings a week rent for three years and 7s 6d a week for the remaining four years, for a total cost of £234. Many couples took advantage of this scheme, and 110 cottages were erected and occupied, the cost of building each one being about £100.

Hammondville's second honorary managing director was the Reverend Bernard G. Judd, who in 1947 was the rector of St Peter's church, East Sydney. He became aware of the plight of the ageing population of Sydney's suburbs, and decided to "get Hammondville going again" by integrating the impoverished elderly with the existing occupants of Hammondville. Cottages were built for aged pensioner couples and disabled ex-servicemen with families.

A committee was formed to raise funds by public appeal, first for a fifty-three bed nursing home to accommodate the chronically ill. The idea seemed a splendid one, but the Reverend Mr Judd found that the donors to the first Hammondville scheme were no longer able or interested in giving again, and new donors had to be found. It was not until 1953–54 that a committee was formed and the vision of the Reverend Bernard Judd and his wife could gradually become a reality.

Today Hammondville is a suburb of Sydney, on the route of the new railway line from East Hills to Glenfield. Anzac Village and Holsworthy Village and Barracks, built during and after the Second World War, are its nearest neighbours.

## HARBORD
*Shire of Warringah*
Location: 17 kilometres north-east of Sydney facing the Pacific Ocean

This suburb, situated between Curl Curl and Queenscliff, was named as a compliment to the wife of the governor of New South Wales, Lord Carrington, who held office in New South Wales from 1885 to 1890. Before her marriage, his wife was the Honourable Cecilia Harbord.

This area had been first explored by Governor Phillip in April 1788, when the governor and his party had set out from Manly planning to trace Manly Creek to its source. Finding their path blocked by swampy scrub, they turned coastward, following the beaches to Curl Curl. The black swans on Harbord Lagoon caused them to pause in amazement. Surveys were made by James Meehan between 1811 and 1821, when he was appointed to check the area and discover land suitable for farming.

The first land grant was made in 1818 to Thomas Bruin, a 50 acre lot opposite the beach, which he fenced with post and wire. Other land divisions followed, and by 1845 many parts of the present suburb were under cultivation. Land west of Harbord was for sale

in 1878, and at that time the maps showed the area's name as Freshwater Heights to the north and Curl Curl Heights to the south. In 1884, Bruin's estate, by then called Freshwater, was subdivided, and the Harbord Estate was subdivided in 1886. The boom of the 1880s collapsed, however, and the area did not regain its popularity until 1913, when daytime sea-bathing became legal (see Manly). At that time the area became popular as a worker's holiday resort. Tents and primitive huts provided shelter and shops were soon established to cater for the holiday-makers.

By this time the area was known as Freshwater, but its residents wanted to change the image of the suburb from a holiday to a residential area, particularly because they believed that, although Freshwater was one of the safest of the northern beaches, the reputation of the suburb had deteriorated because of "people of doubtful and riotous character, who frequent the place at weekends in the summer time". Manly Council petitioned the postmaster general's department on behalf of local people requesting a change of name. Agitation for the name change began in 1912, but it was not until 1923 that Harbord became the official name of the area and the post office's name was changed. But it didn't rest there. Agitation to retain Freshwater as the name of the beach set off more correspondence, which explains why today Sydney street directories list the suburb as Harbord, and its beach as Freshwater.

## HARRIS PARK
*City of Parramatta*
Location: 23 kilometres west of Sydney on the Great Western Highway and the Main Western Line

On the railway line between Granville and Parramatta, Harris Park is part of an estate that belonged to the surgeon of the New South Wales Corps, John Harris (1754–1838), who arrived in the colony in 1790. Harris's estate, made up of two grants, 100 acres from 1793 and 30 acres from 1805, was near James Ruse's Experiment Farm, which Harris later purchased (see Parramatta). Harris was an explorer at heart and went on an expedition to Bathurst with the surveyor and explorer John Oxley (1785?–1828). Harris's fearless nature and medical skill made him a valuable member of the party. Among his many official appointments was that of magistrate, and when he died, having lived fifty years in this country, he was described as the colony's oldest magistrate. He died in 1838, twelve months after his wife, Eliza, and is buried with her, in Parramatta. In the 1870s his land was subdivided, under the name

Dr John Harris

Harris Park, when the railway line came through the area and Harris Park station was established.

Many old weatherboard houses are found in the streets of Harris Park, rubbing shoulders with more modern styles, and showing the residential development of this old area. Many Lebanese families have settled in this suburb, and a large number of their children attend the convent school Blessed Oliver Plunkett, in Allen Street, which has operated in the district for over fifty years.

# HASSALL

*City of Blacktown*
Location: 46 kilometres north-west of Sydney between the Great Western Highway and Richmond Road

This suburb, situated north of Mount Druitt, is one of the areas created from part of the original suburb of Blacktown, which has expanded and been subdivided during the past ten years.

In 1798 the family of Thomas Hassall (1794–1868), later a clergyman, grazier and magistrate, arrived in the colony and settled at Camden. In 1822 Hassall married Anne, the eldest daughter of the Reverend Samuel Marsden. Their two sons, James Samuel (b.1822) and Rowland (b.1819), were among the earliest pupils enrolled at The King's School, Parramatta. James Hassall also became a clergyman, and a daughter, Eliza Marsden Hassall, founded a training school for women missionaries in Ashfield. Thomas Hassall in 1813 had started the first Sunday school in Australia in his father's house, and when he sailed for England in 1817, he became the first Australian candidate for

ordination. He was the Church of England clergyman in this area until 1829.

The housing commission has made a great difference to the area with its programme of residential development. Blacktown now boasts a splendid shopping centre, which is accessible to Hassall, although local transport is still poor.

At present, action is taking place to change this suburb's name to Oakhurst, so eventually the Hassall family may well be forgotten in the western suburbs.

# HEATHCOTE

*Shire of Sutherland*
Location: 36 kilometres south of Sydney on the Princes Highway and the Illawarra Line

A small suburb close to the Royal National Park, Heathcote was once known as Bottle Forest. It was surveyed in 1835 by the surveyor-general, Sir Thomas Mitchell, who named it Heathcote in honour of an officer who had fought with him during the Peninsular Wars against Napoleon.

In 1842 fourteen town allotments were laid out in Bottle Forest, in what is now Heathcote East. A house known as Heathcote Hall was built there in 1887 by Isaac Harber, who was a brick manufacturer. Its architecture was typically Victorian, and its tower, the accepted symbol of wealth at the time, could be seen through the surrounding trees. Sadly, Harber's pleasure in his grand house was short-lived, as he suffered heavy financial losses in another enterprise — the construction of the Imperial Arcade in Sydney. The clouds of the 1892 depression did nothing to help Harber's

efforts to dispose of his property. Eventually the Financial Institution, which became the house's legal possessor, arranged with George Adams of Tattersalls to organise a sweepstake with the house as the prize. Mr S. Gillett, a Sydney builder, won the prize, proving the value of having "a ticket in Tatts". Later the property was sold to E. R. Brown in 1901, and Heathcote Hall is still standing.

This area, like its neighbours, has always been popular with hikers, bushwalkers and nature lovers. In the 1930s the walk from Heathcote to Waterfall was a favourite day's outing with young people. The Boy Scouts Association has a camping area near Boundary Road, and nearer to Waterfall is Waterfall State Sanatorium, established in 1909 for the treatment of patients with tuberculosis. It is now a rehabilitation hospital for the treatment of drug addicts.

Street names such as Dillwynnia, Boronia and Grevillea reflect the suburb's bushland setting, rich in

Heathcote Hall, still privately owned, is also National Trust listed

Australian wildflowers in springtime, while others honour historic figures, including Dalley, Blacket, Strickland, Hunter and Parkes. Bottle Forest Road recalls the area's early name.

Heathcote railway station was opened for traffic in 1886, but the construction names for the station were Bottle Forest and National Park. The suburb has two primary schools and a high school.

# HEBERSHAM

*City of Blacktown*
Location: 47 kilometres
north-west of Sydney north of
Mount Druitt

This suburb, like its neighbours Dharruk and Hassall, was once part of Blacktown proper, but subdivision has given it an identity of its own.

The name was first used as early as 1829, when a village, to be called Hebersham, was planned by the trustees of the Church and School Lands in New South Wales. It was to be situated on 3,122 acres near Rooty Hill in the Eastern Creek area. The name Hebersham was to honour Bishop Reginald Heber, of Calcutta, whose diocese included the colony of New South Wales. The village did not, however, eventuate.

Today the area is developing rapidly, almost outstripping the facilities needed in a busy suburb, particularly in public transport, always a problem in places well away from the centre of the city. A public school, which stands in Welwyn Road, is a busy site of learning as Hebersham, like its neighbours, has many first-home owners with young children.

# HECKENBERG

*City of Liverpool*
Location: 36 kilometres
south-west of Sydney between
Elizabeth Drive and the Hume
Highway

Another of the south-western suburbs that was part of the Green Valley housing settlement initiated in the 1960s, Heckenberg was named after a pioneer family who settled in the area before 1840. The eight Heckenberg brothers were all noted for their strength and height. Their average height was 6 feet 1 inch (186 centimetres) and none weighed less than 16 stone (about 100 kilograms). They had one sister, and she, too, was tall, measuring 5 feet 11 inches (180 centimetres) in height.

Today this is a busy residential area of young families. Children are catered for by two schools, Heckenberg Public School and Fadden High School. Mannix Park remembers an early Catholic archbishop of that name. The streets, which curve around the natural contours of the area, were named after places in the Snowy Mountains: Cabramurra, Jindabyne, Kiandra, Monaro, Thredbo and Guthega, and Snowy Park added for good measure.

# HENLEY

*Municipality of Hunters Hill*
Location: 9 kilometres west of
Sydney between Victoria Road and
the Parramatta River

This small, picturesque suburb on the northern banks of the Parramatta River opposite Abbotsford Bay is a near neighbour to Huntleys Point. Described in the directories of 1925 as "a quiet place, thinly

Dr William Bland

populated", it derives its name from the English Henley-on-Thames, where famous sculling and rowing races are held. Many of the Parramatta River suburbs received their names during the Victorian era, when a wave of nostalgia for the Old Country swept over the new settlers. In the case of Henley, the name is believed to be due to a spark of national pride when an Australian competitor was successful in the sculling championship in England in the 1880s.

Henley was originally known as Blandville, after Dr William Bland (1789–1868), who was transported for killing a fellow naval officer in a duel. Bland arrived in Sydney in 1814, but was pardoned in 1815 and began a private practice in the city. Found guilty in 1818 of libelling Governor Lachlan Macquarie, he served twelve months in gaol at Parramatta. When released he resumed his medical practice and purchased the land on which History House, 133 Macquarie Street, Sydney, now stands, but later he sold it. He took a serious interest in the administration of justice, government, education and the

Benevolent Society, and was one of the founders of the Australian Medical Association. Bland resided in Pitt Street in the city in the 1850s and 1860s, but he seems to have bought the area that became Blandville and subdivided it in about 1866.

Today Henley is a peaceful backwater with one of the most beautiful waterfront locations in Sydney. The Parramatta River is popular for water sports, and many boats are moored along the shoreline. For others there's popular Henley Bowling Club, and Gladesville Reserve adjoins Henley to the east. Once a year the residents of Henley get together to enjoy the Henley Happening, a big "family" picnic on the grassy river bank.

## HILLSDALE
*Municipality of Botany*
Location: 10 kilometres south-east of Sydney between Bunnerong Road and Botany Road

This small inner southern suburb was part of the suburb of Matraville until the 1960s. All of the Matraville area was originally part of the land reserved for the Church and Schools Corporation, the income from which was intended to support clergy and teachers. It later reverted to the crown, and when, in 1917, it was allocated for a settlement for soldiers returning from the First World War, the area was divided between Randwick and Botany municipalities. Problems later arose from the division, and so in 1961 Botany Council decided to rename its section Gilmore, after the Australian poet Dame Mary Gilmore (1864–1962). The postmaster general's department

pointed out that there was already a Gilmore in New South Wales, so the council chose Hillsdale, to honour Patrick Darcy Hills, then the New South Wales minister for local government. There was some criticism of the choice as many people considered that a name that reflected Botany's early importance in Australian history should have been chosen.

Many of the houses in the area were built in the years after the Second World War, some by the Housing Commission. A large area of high-density housing was built during the 1960s and 1970s in the area between Bunnerong Road and Denison Street, where there had been vacant land and poultry farms into the 1950s. The suburb had also supported market gardens and, in earlier times, pig farms. The western part of the suburb has some industry, and a shopping centre was built on Bunnerong Road in the early 1960s.

The Hensley Athletic Field, which had the first olympic standard all-weather track in New South Wales, stands in the north-western corner of the suburb. It was built by the Randwick–Botany athletic club on land leased from the council and was first used in the 1968–69 season.

## HOLSWORTHY
*City of Liverpool*
Location: 31 kilometres south-west of Sydney south of Heathcote Road

Many former soldiers will automatically stand to attention when they hear the name of this suburb. Situated near Liverpool, it was acquired by the army in 1913 and since then has been very much an army establishment, with

barracks, a firing range and a school of artillery. Its village houses the families of soldiers and, as would seem appropriate, many of the street names recall battles in which Australian soldiers were engaged. The village evolved after the Second World War and the barracks lie to the south.

The origin of its name implies a more romantic background. The original Holsworthy is a charming village in a quiet backwater of Devon, in England. Lachlan Macquarie married his second wife, Elizabeth Campbell, in the ancient church of St Peter and St Paul in Devonshire's Holsworthy in November 1807. In 1810, Macquarie, as governor of New South Wales, and his wife arrived in the colony. Both had a marked influence on its progress, and many landmarks were named after them and events in their lives. Holsworthy has been known by that name since Macquarie's time.

The streets are named after places and battles that were household words during the Second World War, such as Tarakan, Bardia, Wewak, Anzac, Lae, Brunei, Finschhafen, Madang and Gona. Things military are represented by Sabre Crescent, Gunner's Row, Cavalry Crescent, Infantry and Light Horse Streets, and Trooper Row. In Anzac Village, around the north-eastern corner of the military reserve, streets record the names of Australian generals, such as Birdwood, Monash, Bridges and Blamey.

# HOMEBUSH

*Municipalities of Strathfield and Concord*

Location: 15 kilometres west of Sydney on Parramatta Road and the Main Suburban Line

Eleven days after the first British flag was raised at Sydney Cove, in 1788, Captain John Hunter and Lieutenant William Bradley, First Fleet officers from HMS *Sirius*, explored the Parramatta River as far as the present Homebush Bay. It was a shallow swampy area, flooded at high tide, at the junction of what are now Powell's and Haslam's Creeks. Hunter did not fully explore the bay, but he added it to his charts.

The present suburb is in the area originally known as Liberty Plains, because the colony's first free settlers received grants there in 1793. They received small grants of 60 to 80 acres, but because it was a poor area for agriculture, grants were later increased and also changed hands over the following years. The area was chosen for occupation in order to provide a settlement between Sydney and Parramatta, and it became the last overnight stop before Sydney for teams travelling from the west.

Edward Powell (1762-1814) was one of those who was granted 80 acres here in 1793. In 1807 he established the Halfway House on an additional grant fronting Parramatta Road. His son sold the inn to his brother-in-law James Underwood (1776?–1844) in about 1825, who leased it to James Kerwin, known as Jimmy the Jockey. The inn was reopened as the Horse and Jockey and this early landmark is still operating today. Underwood's property in the area was not subdivided until 1878, when lots were described as being in the Village of Homebush. The streets laid out in 1878, in what had been open country, are virtually identical to those still existing.

Another early settler was D'Arcy Wentworth (1762?–1827), who arrived with the Second Fleet in 1790 as ship's surgeon on the *Neptune*. After Macquarie became governor, Wentworth was made principal surgeon and chief magistrate in the colony. He received a grant of 920 acres at the head of the present Homebush Bay and adopted the colloquial name Home Bush for his estate. The name was loosely applied to the whole area until it was officially adopted in the 1878 subdivision.

Wentworth had some influence on the affairs of the colony. He established the first police force in

A fleet of Arnott's delivery vehicles in the early 1920s. The trucks would have been the same vibrant red as they are today

this country, he was in charge of the money-minding side of the first bank in Parramatta, and had much to do with managing the affairs in that city. He and his son, William Charles, who became an explorer and statesman, were both keen on horse-racing. They were instrumental in establishing a racecourse at Homebush in 1842. The course continued in use until Randwick Racecourse opened in 1859–60.

Homebush saleyards were opened in 1882 by John Harris, then the mayor of Sydney. In 1906 a large area north of Parramatta Road was resumed for the construction of the state abattoirs. The installations were completed by 1915, and the abbatoirs were transferred from Glebe Island.

The municipality was incorporated on 6 June 1906 and amalgamated with Strathfield in 1947.

An important recent addition to Homebush is the State Sports Centre in Underwood Road. It was opened officially in 1984 by the premier of New South Wales, Neville Wran. This multi-purpose venue has facilities for at least twenty-five different sports. Sports and sporting events of international, state and national standard, as well as conventions, concerts, and other public entertainments can be presented there. It also has a training centre for athletes and a sports education centre. The facilities may be used by schools, state and national sporting bodies, community organisations, and individual athletes. The second stage of the project — the State Hockey Centre — was opened in 1985. The 40 hectare site at Homebush Bay is planned, over the next ten years, to provide similar facilities for track and field sports, aquatics, rowing and canoeing.

## HORNSBY

*Shire of Hornsby*
Location: 24 kilometres north-west of Sydney on the Pacific Highway, a junction station for the North Shore and Main Northern Lines

The name Hornsby was first applied to the area that is now Normanhurst; present-day Hornsby was originally known as Jack's Island. A grant of 320 acres was made to Constable Samuel Henry Horne in 1831, lying between the present Thornleigh and Pearce's Corner. It became known as Horne's Grant, or Hornsby Place, and finally as Hornsby. He had been given the land as a reward for his work in helping to capture two bushrangers, one of whom was the notorious John Macnamara.

The district is on the high ridge that separates the upper waters of Berowra and Cowan Creeks and surrounding bushland. Hornsby Valley, which includes Galston Gorge, has long been a favourite area for bushwalking and was originally known as Old Man Valley, because of the huge old man kangaroos found there. An early settler in the Galston Gorge area was Thomas Edward Higgins, who settled down on 250 acres granted to him by Governor Bourke in 1836.

The North Shore railway line terminates at Hornsby, where it connects with the Northern line going to Brooklyn, Gosford, Newcastle and eventually to the north coast and Brisbane. The Northern line, which was extended in 1886 from Strathfield to the Hawkesbury, passed through present Hornsby. The station was over 2 miles from the village of Hornsby (modern Normanhurst), so in 1895 the station was called

Hornsby Junction to avoid confusion. In 1900 the word Junction was dropped and the area around the station became known as Hornsby; Old Hornsby was the name adopted for the present Normanhurst. The first post office was known as Hornsby Junction when it opened in September 1887, but also became Hornsby in 1900.

Three notable Australians who made their marks in widely varied fields have lived in Hornsby — Sir Edgeworth David, a geologist; J. J. Hilder, a painter; and James Bancks, the creator of Ginger Meggs. Sir Edgeworth David (1858–1934) had a distinguished career as professor of geology at the University of Sydney and as a soldier during the First World War. In the 1880s he discovered the rich tin-bearing leads of New England, and he traced the Maitland–Cessnock coal seams. He took part in Shackleton's Antarctic expedition of 1907 and in 1916 was a major in the Australian Tunnellers, an Australian army battalion of miners and mining engineers raised through his efforts for service in France. Edgeworth David Avenue remembers this brilliant man.

J. J. (Jesse) Hilder (1881–1916) was a painter who came to live in the northern suburbs in 1906 and became associated with the Hornsby district in 1910 through Adolph W. Albers, a prominent Sydney art dealer, who acted as his selling agent. Over 250 paintings were sold over the ten years before his death in 1916, many of them of the Hornsby area. Altogether, Jesse Hilder produced about 400 paintings, some of which now hang in the Australian National Gallery.

The cartoonist James (Jim) Bancks (1889–1952) found his model for Ginger Meggs in the person of young Charlie

Somerville, a resident of Hornsby and a member of a prominent local family, and areas in the district inspired the setting for his adventures. When Bancks became a cartoonist for the *Sunday Sun* and was commissioned to draw a series involving the adventures of a small boy, memories of Charlie Somerville flowed through the artist's pen, and in 1921, Sunday readers met Ginger. Although Jimmy Bancks is no longer alive, the comic strip lives on, drawn by other artists.

Hornsby is now a major regional shopping centre, and has public and high schools and a district hospital.

## HORSLEY PARK
*City of Fairfield*
Location: 41 kilometres west of Sydney, south of Blacktown

As a reward for subduing the Irish Rebellion of Castle Hill in March 1804, Major (later Lieutenant-Colonel) George Johnston (1764–1823) received a 2,000 acre grant west of what is now Fairfield. Originally known as The King's Gift, the land may have been named Horsley Park by Johnston, possibly after a colleague who was associate to Judge Jeffrey Hart Bent, after whom Bent Street in Sydney is named.

Johnston left the land idle until his daughter, Blanche, married Edward Nicholas Weston at St James's church, King Street, on 21 May 1829. The young couple settled at Horsley Park, and Horsley homestead, built 1831–34, became their home. Edward Weston had been in the service of the East India Company, and the house showed a distinct influence of Indian colonial architecture, with wide verandahs and shuttered doors and windows. It is still standing in Horsley Drive. It has been suggested that it was Johnston's son-in-law who named the property after his home in England.

There is still a lot of vacant land in Horsley Park and the area is rather flat, but its semi-rural character is rapidly changing to outer suburban. The Sydney water supply channel flows through the western part of the suburb from Prospect Reservoir. Its main thoroughfares are Wallgrove Road and Horsley Road, which run south from the Great Western Highway, and Horsley Drive, which runs east to Fairfield. There are two parks for residential use, one called Horsley Park, and Horsley Public School is in Horsley Drive.

Although this suburb is isolated in some respects, the main roads are well planned, and residents rely on road transport for contact with Parramatta and Fairfield, the two nearest developed areas.

## HOXTON PARK
*City of Liverpool*
Location: 38 kilometres south-west of Sydney between Cabramatta Creek and Cowpasture Road

Still in a state of development, Hoxton Park lies west of Liverpool and south of the Green Valley housing estate. Originally part of the area known as Cabramatta, Hoxton Park received its name in 1887 when Phillips & Co., a land syndicate, subdivided much of the area under that name.

An early settler here was Thomas Setrop Amos, a London solicitor who arrived in Sydney in 1816, and was granted 800 acres of land here in June 1818. Other grants in the area include one made in 1819 to George Williams, who called his property Sarahville, which became an early name for the suburb.

This flat area was previously semi-rural, and was reserved for industrial development, although government housing projects have since developed nearby suburbs, such as Miller and Cartwright, which adjoin the boundary of Liverpool.

A public school, established in 1882, and a high school cater for young people, while Hoxton Park Reserve is located at the junction of Wilson Street and Hoxton Park Road. Hoxton Park Aerodrome, maintained by the department of civil aviation, is situated north-east of Hoxton Park. The Hoxton Park Flying School is located there and the aerodrome is used for civilian flights, joy flights and gliding.

## HUNTERS HILL
*Municipality of Hunters Hill*
Location: 9 kilometres west of Sydney of the peninsula separating the Parramatta and Lane Cove Rivers

The smallest and one of the oldest municipalities in Sydney, Hunters Hill is thought to have been named after Captain John Hunter (1737–1821), who came to New South Wales as captain of the *Sirius* in the First Fleet and was later appointed governor (1795–1800). The area's Aboriginal name, Mookaboola or Moocooboola, means "meeting of the waters", an apt name for this point where the waters of the Parramatta and Lane Cove Rivers meet.

Another theory about the origin

Line engraving of Thomas Muir by F. Bonneville, 1796

of the name of this suburb is that it was called after Huntershill, the name of a property on the lower North Shore owned by one of the Scottish Martyrs, Thomas Muir (1765–99). Today Muir would be tolerated in our society, but in 1792, with the rumbling of the French Revolution ringing in their ears, British parliamentarians took a poor view of a lawyer who was an advocate of democracy and parliamentary reform when both were unpopular. Muir and four companions were sentenced to transportation. Authorities in Sydney Town were rather embarrassed by these "convicts who were not convicts". The Scottish Martyrs, as they became known, considered themselves free men, merely banished from their homeland for what were then seen as radical ideas. Eventually they asked Hunter, by then governor of New South Wales, to petition the British government on their behalf, but to no avail. Two of them developed fatal illnesses and died within a few years. Muir, however, was allowed to buy land and build a house. In 1794 he chose land near the north-east pylon of the Harbour Bridge and named it Huntershill, after his boyhood home. In 1796 Muir escaped from the colony and made his way, via Spanish California, Mexico City, Havana and Spain, to Paris, where he died in poverty in 1799, much weakened by wounds received when he was involved in an English–Spanish naval engagement on the way to Spain. The name of his property, however, continued to be applied to the area, but was soon used for all the area north of the harbour and west to Lane Cove, until it became particularly attached to the present Hunters Hill when parishes were defined in the 1830s.

The area of the present Hunters Hill was not occupied until 1835, and one of the earliest settlers was Mary Reiby, the first woman

Fig Tree Wharf and Bridge, 1915, looking up the Lane Cove River

retailer in Sydney, who that year bought land with a frontage to the Lane Cove River and built a cottage near a huge fig tree. Reiby Street still commemorates her name. Between 1835 and 1843 the land on the peninsula was sold.

During the 1840s, Hunters Hill was a haven for bushrangers and convicts escaped from the penal settlement on adjacent Cockatoo Island. It was a small matter for the most daring and desperate to swim across the intervening water when the tide was right, scramble over the rocks at the shore's edge and hide there in the thick bush.

Today the area is noted for its delightful stone houses, several of which were built by the Frenchman Didier Numa Joubert (1816–81). Joubert came to Sydney in 1837 and bought 200 acres of land from Mary Reiby in the years after 1847. He engaged seventy stonemasons from Italy, which may well account for the solid artistic construction of the houses he built. He lived in a small cottage while he built St Malo, which he named after his mother's birthplace. Before 1858, he also built Passy for the first French consul-general, M. Sentis. Built in classic French style, the house

Mary Reibey

stood in 30 acres of ground. The number of French settlers here led to the area being known as the French Village during the 1850s.

A later mayor of Hunters Hill, Charles Edward Jeanneret, also built a mansion nearby, and Leonard Etienne Bordier began importing timber houses from Paris. Soon these gracious houses made Hunters Hill a showplace, and the bushland setting, coupled with harbour views, gave it a reputation that has never been lost.

A Sydney newspaper reporting on the development of Hunters Hill struck an almost humorous note. It described a house erected in 1850 as having been "designed in Germany, bought in Paris, transported and erected at Hunter's Hill, Australia, and occupied by an Irishman". Quite a feat in 1850!

Hunters Hill became a municipality on 5 January 1861, after long arguments about its extent. Jules Joubert (1824–1907), brother of Didier, was elected first chairman and Didier became the first mayor in 1867–69 — appropriately, since the brothers had petitioned for incorporation. Jules, as secretary of the state's Agricultural Society, moved its annual show from Parramatta to Sydney and included non-agricultural exhibits. He also started a ferry service, which Didier's son, Numa, continued running from Hunters Hill to the city, but Numa sold it in 1906. Joubert descendants continued to live in this suburb for many years.

The construction of Fig Tree Bridge and Tarban Creek Bridge to link up to the new Gladesville Bridge and main roadway meant demolition for many early houses, including St Malo. Mary Reiby's cottage was removed and re-erected in Tarban Creek Road, but Hunters Hill still has a rich heritage of early stone houses.

# HUNTLEYS POINT
*Municipality of Hunters Hill*
Location: 9 kilometres west of Sydney on the northern side of the Parramatta River

This riverside suburb, on the peninsula between Tarban Creek and the Parramatta River, next-door to Henley, was purchased by Alfred, the son of Dr Robert Huntley, who arrived in the colony with his family in 1836. Dr Huntley first occupied land in Braidwood that is still known as Huntleys Flats. When his labourers went to the Victorian goldfields the family returned to Sydney and settled in Balmain.

Alfred Huntley opened Turkish baths in Bligh Street in the city, on the present site of Adyar Hall, and later he became the Australian Gas Light Company's chief engineer. He bought land on the river and called it Huntley's Point, where he built Point House, and went to live there in 1851. His son and only child, also named Alfred, a brilliant scholar at The King's School, Parramatta, later became an architect and civil engineer, and built some of the stone houses at Hunters Hill.

In 1847 Marist missionaries established a centre here beside Tarban Creek. Known as The Priory, it was eventually absorbed into Gladesville Hospital, which extends into this area.

The construction of the Gladesville Bridge brought this formerly quiet peninsula onto the main road, at the junction of Victoria Road, running north-west, and Burns Bay Road running north.

Aerial photograph of the Gladesville Bridge which spans the Parramatta River linking Drummoyne to Huntleys Point. Further north lies Tarban Creek Bridge connecting Huntleys Point and Hunters Hill. Fig Tree Bridge can be seen at the top of the photo

# HURLSTONE PARK
*Municipalities of Canterbury, Marrickville and Ashfield*
Location: 10 kilometres south-west of Sydney between Marrickville and Canterbury, on the Bankstown Line

Cooks River flows through this inner south-western suburb, described in the 1920s as "convenient and progressive". Originally part of the Canterbury Estate (see Ashbury), it had earlier been known by the names Wattle Hill and Fernhill, which was the name given to the railway station, both describing its hilly bushland character. The present name derives from the name of a school, Hurlstone College, founded by John Kinloch in 1878 on the site of present-day Trinity College. He named the school after his mother, who had been Miss Helen Hurlstone before her marriage. In 1911 a local referendum chose Hurlstone as the suburb's name to replace Fernhill, which the post office had objected to so strongly that they wouldn't open a post office there until the name was changed. The railway station had Park added to the name to avoid confusion with Hillstone, a town in western New South Wales.

The Kinloch property was acquired by the department of education in 1882 and became a training college for women teachers. Two men well known in educational circles, Messrs Turner and Board, influenced the next move in the property's history. Mr Turner had the idea of opening special schools to prepare students for farm work, and in 1906 Mr Board opened an agricultural school at Hurlstone Park, with an initial intake of forty-five boarders. This school was the first of four established to train secondary students who planned to go on the land, in response to the recognition of the importance of agricultural science in Australia. At that time it was seen as the great grain bin of the world. Such schools provided a link between primary school and an agricultural college or university faculty of agriculture. The schools offered a sound secondary education as well as teaching the practical aspects of agriculture. The first school, known as Hurlstone Agricultural High School, provided a two-year course to prepare students for admission to Hawkesbury Agricultural College. Later it was moved from Hurlstone Park to Glenfield, which provided large areas of land for practical work.

The coming of the Bankstown line through the area in 1895 opened up its home-building possibilities and young couples moved in. The first post office opened in 1911, and the first public school started in 1918. Today Hurlstone Park, like its neighbours Canterbury and Earlwood, is a busy residential suburb. Canterbury Racecourse is on its western boundary, and Beaman Park, with an adjoining oval and golf links, is on its eastern side.

Opened as Fernhill Station in 1894, this station was subsequently renamed Hurlstone Park in 1911

# HURSTVILLE

*Municipalities of Hurstville and Kogarah*

Location: 17 kilometres south-west of Sydney on Forest Road and the Illawarra Line

This suburb was formed within the 1,950 acre grant, stretching from King Georges Road to Stoney Creek Road to beyond Kogarah railway station, made to Captain John Townson (1760–1835) in 1808 (a further 250 acres north of Stoney Creek Road were added in 1810). In 1812 the original grant was sold to Simeon Lord (1771–1840), who was transported for seven years for the theft of some cloth. He arrived in the colony in 1791, but after an early pardon he set up as a trader and by 1798 was living in Macquarie Place and on the way to becoming a wealthy businessman. By 1822 he owned over 5,000 acres outside Sydney. His land in Hurstville gave the name Lord's Bush to the suburb. After Lord's death, however, this land was sold to Michael Gannon (1800–61), and the centre of present Hurstville was known as Gannon's Forest. Finally the suburb was named Hurstville, after the town of Hurst in Lancashire, England.

Michael Gannon arrived in Sydney as a convict, transported for life, in December 1820, with his brother James. In 1824, Michael married Mary Parsonage, and she later applied to Governor Darling to have her husband assigned to her as a servant. When Gannon was pardoned, by 1826, he began to work independently as a builder and undertaker, and to purchase land, but because his brother suffered business losses, Michael's business credibility also suffered. Nonetheless, by 1850 Gannon was able to purchase, for £732, the 1,905 acres of forest land that had been John Townson's grant.

The first road from Cooks River to the settlements in the Illawarra district passed through Gannon's estate, and the road was called Gannon's Forest Road; later the Gannon's was dropped, and today the thoroughfare is known as Forest Road. The land in those early days was heavily timbered and so was occupied by timber-getters. Later it became an agricultural and pastoral area, and boasted a tobacco manufacturer.

Another early settler was Alfred Barden, who came from Sussex to the colony in 1827. Aged 14 years, he was apprenticed to a Cooks

Department of Main Roads workmen
"ballast packing" on Forest Road,
Hurstville, 1927

River butcher, and when he grew
older he opened his own business
at Gannon's Forest. He did so well
that in 1862 he became a squatter
on the Castlereagh River,
gradually acquiring land until he
owned a total of 64,000 acres.
Eventually he returned to
Hurstville, where he lived for
thirty years and was active in local
affairs. Barden Streets in Arncliffe
and Tempe remember this man.

Older Sydneysiders will
remember the Hurstville train
crash on 3 August 1920, in which
five people were killed and fifty
injured. Two steam trains on the
Illawarra line left Central Station
within a few minutes of each
other. When the first train, bound
for Sutherland, arrived at
Hurstville the signal was against it,
so it could not proceed.

Meanwhile, the second train,
which was to terminate at
Hurstville, was approaching the
station. It was a dark evening, and
without warning, the second train
crashed into the back of the
stationary Sutherland train. The
train lights went out; the station
was plunged into darkness; and the
cries of the injured and dying were
pitiful. At that time, St George
Hospital was a cottage hospital
with only limited accommodation,
but every available doctor rushed to
assist, struggling in the darkness to
find and treat the injured. There
were no instant radio flashes in
those days, and many families sat
waiting for missing members,
unaware of the disaster. There
were emotional scenes as later
trains arrived at Hurstville from
Sydney: one father alighted from
a train, to see his son lying on
a stretcher. Neither driver
was injured, and fortunately

neither train left the line.

Hurstville railway station
opened on 15 October 1884, and
Hurstville is today an important
station on the Illawarra line for
suburban, inter-urban,
Wollongong and far South Coast
trains. As in other areas, the
coming of the railway encouraged
land subdivisions, and Hurstville
municipality was incorporated in
1887. The modern shopping centre
is extensive and serves a large,
progressive district. The old
station, which once accommodated
steam trains and their passengers,
has given way to one of the most
convenient station-cum-shopping
complexes in the Sydney suburban
area.

# ILLAWONG
*Shire of Sutherland*
Location: 27 kilometres
south-west of Sydney between the
Georges and Woronora Rivers

This neighbourhood of Sutherland
was once known as East Menai. In
1960, when the public school was
built, at the corner of Austin Street
and Fowler Road, the name was
changed to Illawong. This
Aboriginal word means "between
two waters", appropriate for this
peninsula suburb between the
Georges and Woronora Rivers.
The area has kept much of its
natural bushland setting.

# INGLEBURN
*Cities of Campbelltown and Liverpool*
Location: 43 kilometres
south-west of Sydney on the
Hume Highway and the Main
Southern Line

This suburb, north-east of
Campbelltown, was first known as
part of Macquarie Fields, and it
took that name when in 1869 the
railway station opened. The station
name was changed in 1883, when
suburban development of the area
began, and it became Ingleburn,
although the area to the north was
still known as Macquarie Fields.
The first school in the area opened
in 1887 and the post office
followed in 1889.

There is some difference of
opinion as to the origin and
meaning of this suburb's name.
One suggestion is that it was
named after an English town by
Richard Atkins (1745–1820), who
received the first grant in this area
in 1793. Atkins became judge-
advocate after David Collins, the
great colonial diarist. He farmed

the land and in 1810 sold it to
Captain Richard Brooks
(1765?–1833), a partner of Robert
Campbell. Brooks built a family
residence on the land, which was
near Liverpool, and called it
Denham Court. He continued
his trading voyages, and as he
became well known his home
evolved into a centre of social life.
Friends arrived from Sydney in a
miscellany of vehicles, some with
liveried postilions. Captain Brooks
died at Denham Court in October
1833.

The other opinion is that the
suburb's name is from the Gaelic
"inge", meaning "bend", and
"burn", meaning "in the river".
Since Bunburry Curran Creek flows
through Ingleburn and Georges
River forms its eastern boundary,
and both waterways have many
curves and bends, this explanation
seems the most likely.

The names of many of
Ingleburn's streets have English
associations, such as George, Pitt,
and Sackville, Cambridge,
Oxford, Norfolk, Suffolk, Chester
and Wellington. The streets north
and east of the modern high
school, however, are named after
birds, such as Kestall, Heron and
Bronzewing.

The main Southern railway line,
the Hume Highway and Bunburry
Curran Creek, which all run from
north-east to south-west, divide
Ingleburn in two. The residential
area is to the east, and to the west
is Ingleburn military camp, where
thousands of young Australians
were trained during the Second
World War.

There are three major parks in
the suburb: Ingleburn Memorial
Park in Memorial Avenue,
Ingleburn Park, between
Ingleburn and Macquarie Fields
railway stations, and Ingleburn
Reserve, towards Long Point.

# INGLESIDE
*Shire of Warringah*
Location: 28 kilometres north of
Sydney on Mona Vale Road

In the 1880s Baron Von Beiren, an
industrial chemist of Dutch and
American extraction, built a
mansion called Ingleside House in
the high, forested area west of
Mona Vale. His specialties were
gunpowder and explosives, and he
founded a factory which he called
the Australian Gunpowder and
Explosives Manufacturing
Company. Powder Works Road,
which runs east from Mona Vale
Road to Narrabeen, took its name
from these works, and the suburb,
its name from the house. The
chemist's story, however, has a sad
ending. People began to regard his
experiments with some suspicion,
which had a detrimental effect on
his business. In 1924 he was tried
as a fraudulent bankrupt and
sentenced to a prison term of two
years and ten months. He died
before his term was completed.

The Baha'i Temple was built at
Ingleside in the early 1960s, and its
dome is an architectural landmark
visible from many parts of Sydney.
Monash Golf Links and Elanora
Golf Links are in this area, offering
an almost country club atmosphere
to players. Ingleside Park lies in the
eastern part of this suburb.

# JAMISONTOWN
*City of Penrith*
Location: 56 kilometres west of
Sydney south of the Western
Freeway

A neighbourhood within the
Penrith area, Jamisontown was
named in honour of Thomas
Jamison (1745–1811), surgeon's
assistant on the *Sirius* in 1788. By

1805 Jamison was surgeon-general of New South Wales and, as such, in 1809 received a grant of 1,000 acres on the south side of today's Jamison Road, stretching west to the Nepean River.

The property was inherited by Thomas Jamison's son, Sir John Jamison (1776–1844), a colourful character, a splendid host, and a gracious gentleman, who was also a surgeon. While serving in the navy in 1807, he curbed a serious outbreak of scurvy in the Swedish navy, and was rewarded with a Swedish knighthood; in 1813 he also received an English knighthood. He came to New South Wales in 1814, having inherited his father's land, and built there, in about 1825, the imposing mansion, Regentville, which is still standing. Sir John encouraged a group of talented convicts at Emu Plains government farm to form a drama group. They wrote plays and made costumes and scenery, and Sir John invited them to Regentville to entertain his guests. He became a leading colonist and was elected the first president of the Agricultural Society of New South Wales in 1822.

# JANNALI
*Shire of Sutherland*
Location: 28 kilometres south-west of Sydney just north of Sutherland, on the Illawarra Line

South of the Georges River, Jannali is on the Illawarra railway line between Sutherland and Como. The district began to develop with the coming of the railway in 1884, but there was no station at Jannali until 1931. The construction of the station was the dual responsibility of the department of railways and the local council, who each paid

half of the costs. The council's share was for the road bridge over the railway station and the entry ramps.

Home-building increased in the 1930s and received another boost after the Second World War when blocks of land were offered to help returned servicemen and their families. Jannali — an Aboriginal word meaning "beautiful moonrise" — is now a pleasant residential area. Parklands extend down to the Woronora River on its western boundary. Backing onto the park are one of two public schools and Jannali Girls High School; immediately to the east are Jannali Oval and the boys high school.

# KAREELA
*Shire of Sutherland*
Location: 24 kilometres south-west of Sydney west of Princes Highway

In 1968 the Geographical Names Board gave this small suburb on the Oyster Bay waterfront on the Georges River the Aboriginal name Kareela, which is derived from "kari-kari" and means "fast". The name seems to refer appropriately to the area's strong south winds. Perhaps a street on the point, Tradewinds Place, gives further proof of strong breezes in the area.

The suburb has a golf course in Bates Drive, and on the opposite side of the road is Kareela Oval. A reserve extends from here down to Oyster Bay. A public school stands in Freya Street, while Gymea High School and Technical College nearby accommodate older students.

# KELLYVILLE
*Shire of Baulkham Hills and City of Blacktown*
Location: 36 kilometres north-west of Sydney on Windsor Road

This small suburb, with its rural atmosphere, is bounded by Baulkham Hills, Blacktown, Rouse Hill and Glenhaven. Population is low because properties here are large, and many accommodate orchards, or support horses kept for riding, or cultivate native-plant nurseries.

In 1884 a large subdivision of fifteen old grants created 100 acre lots. It was called the Kellyville Estate as much of it had been owned by Hugh Kelly, hence the suburb's name. Previously it had been known as Irishtown, a logical enough title since a large clan of the Kellys inhabited the area, and after Kelly's death disputed the apportionment of his land among them.

Hugh Kelly had a hotel on the Windsor Road known as the Bird-in-Hand where coaches made a refreshment stop. Another hotel further along the Windsor Road, known as the White Hart Hotel, was owned by a man named Cross. Two other inns were run by John Hillas who received two grants on the present Old Windsor Road in 1802 and 1804. He farmed the land as well as operating the inns, the Stanhope Arms and the Nowhere Here — apparently this was the standard reply to authorities looking for people who had no business to be in the area!

Another important early land-owner in the district was the Macarthur family. They purchased the grant of Joseph Foveaux in about 1802. Elizabeth Macarthur (1766?–1850) bred merino sheep on this Seven Hills Farm, which

was situated in what is now the Old Windsor Road, opposite Meurants Lane, until 1820, when it was returned to the government by the Macarthurs in a land exchange. It passed through other hands and by the late nineteenth century the whole area was one of vineyards and orchards.

Kellyville Park in Memorial Avenue provides a pleasant stopping place for today's picnicking motorists. Kellyville Public School, established in 1873, is set in a pleasant area in Windsor Road.

# KENSINGTON
*Municipality of Randwick*
Location: 5 kilometres south-east of Sydney on Anzac Parade

This suburb was named after the Royal Borough of Kensington, London, one of England's most interesting city areas. The name goes back to the 1880s when the idea of first planning a site for a suburb or town was new. Until then most new settlements "just

growed", like storybook Topsy, or were subdivided by real estate agents, who wanted to realise a profit from the area, and cared little about attractive layout. Civic authorities in London designed the model suburb of Bedford Park near English Kensington about ten years before a group of Sydney businessmen planned a new suburb on what was then the outskirts of Sydney. Because their inspiration came from London's Kensington, our Kensington received the same name.

The land was part of an estate formerly owned by Daniel Cooper (1785–1853), an ex-convict, who acquired the land in 1825 with his partner Solomon Levey, whom he later bought out. Cooper's nephew Daniel (1821–1902) planned a subdivision and township here, but in 1865 all industry and development was forbidden; the land was crossed by the Lachlan Stream and was part of the catchment for the Lachlan Swamps, in what is now Centennial Park, which provided Sydney's domestic water supply. From 1888 Prospect Dam fulfilled

Bella Vista homestead at Kellyville was built in the late 1800s but the estate dates back to the first years of settlement and is thought to have been part of Elizabeth Macarthur's Seven Hills Farm

that service, so the land now known as Kensington became available for occupation. A group of astute businessmen formed the Kensington Freehold Corporation, which organised a competition with a prize of £250 for the best design for the new settlement. This first town planning contest in Sydney's history aroused a great deal of interest, and the winning designs chosen from the twenty entries were displayed at Sydney Town Hall in June 1889.

The main feature in the winning design was a wide boulevarde, now the main traffic artery Anzac Parade, which set Kensington well ahead of other Sydney suburbs. It also provided for a railway, which has so far not eventuated.

Kensington Racecourse, in High Street on the present site of the University of New South Wales, opened in 1893 on 63 acres of government land leased by the

Kensington Recreation Grounds Company. It did not compete with the adjacent Randwick Racecourse as it mostly held midweek meetings for pony racing and hosted related sports, such as polo, as well as football, cricket and hockey. The course was used to house troops and horses in the Boer War and First World War. It did not survive the Second World War and in 1950 the land was resumed for construction of Sydney's second university.

The University of Technology was incorporated by an Act of Parliament in 1949, to meet the urgent demand in Australia for applied scientists and technologists. Its name was changed to the University of New South Wales in 1955, following the report of a body known as the Murray Committee, which inquired into the future development of all New South Wales universities. Since then, the university has grown and increased the number of areas of

Bushmen's Contingent encampment at Kensington Racecourse in 1900 at the time of the Boer War

study available, although there is still an emphasis on scientific and commercial studies. Today the university has over 18,000 students.

Kensington today is a quiet residential suburb. Like its neighbour Randwick, it was the site of many elegant homes during the years when the racing fraternity patronised the area. Many of those homes today are nursing homes or have been replaced by flats and home units. But the sport of kings still flourishes, and neighbouring Randwick is still Sydney's principal home of horse-racing.

# KENTHURST

*Shire of Baulkham Hills*
Location: 39 kilometres north-west of Sydney off Old Northern Road

Originally known as Little Dural, this suburb lies north-west of present Dural in the Baulkham

Hills area. In 1886 a public meeting was held to discuss a change of name for the area. The main agitator for the change was Charles Gibb, who declared that the developing settlement merited a more elegant title. Kent Forest was suggested, possibly because several Kentishmen had settled in the area, but it was considered ungainly and finally the name Kenthurst was chosen. The meeting applied to the ministry for public instruction for permission to change the suburb's name, and the *Cumberland Mercury* covered the story of the residents' revolt. The answer was obviously favourable as by 1887 Kenthurst was in general use.

The first land grants were made here in 1823, when John O'Hara received 50 acres near the corner of the future Kenthurst and Annangrove Roads; Michael Cantwell also received 50 acres and Thomas Sanders was granted 60 acres further north. At this time loggers were busily denuding the splendid forest of its glory, and by 1858 a survey reported that all the good timber had been felled. In

1861 the Robertson Land Act enabled prospective land-buyers to select acres before they were surveyed and to purchase on a deposit of 5 shillings an acre. The price per acre was £1, and not less than 40 acres and not more then 320 acres had to be acquired. The Act encouraged settlement in this area, and the new residents took up fruit-growing and farming.

In 1883 Kenthurst's public school was opened. In 1888 the post office was established and in 1889 the School of Arts was opened.

Today this suburb retains its rural atmosphere and new houses are built to blend with the natural charm of the area.

# KENTLYN
*City of Campbelltown*
Location: 53 kilometres south-west of Sydney on the northern side of the Georges River

Kentlyn, an area north-east of what is now the city of Campbelltown, was originally known as Kent Farms. In 1933 the local agricultural bureau decided to give the area a new name, and of the many suggested, Kentlyn was finally chosen.

In the first decade of this century settlers crossed the hills north-east of Campbelltown proper and established themselves in this area extending to the Georges River. Once the area's thick forest was cleared, they established market gardens, orchards and poultry farms.

# KILLARA
*Municipality of Ku-ring-gai*
Location: 14 kilometres north-west of Sydney on the Pacific Highway and the North Shore Line

This Aboriginal word meaning "permanent" or "always there" became the suburb's name when it was chosen by the railways commission for this station on the North Shore line, opened in 1899. Wilson's directory of 1925 summed up the area well: "this suburb may justly claim to be both attractive and select. There are many substantial residences, the homes of the well-to-do citizen; and altogether the dwellings are of a superior class." Although the residential style today has changed to include blocks of home units, town-houses and retirement apartments, Killara can still claim to be "attractive and select". It remains a completely residential area with just a small shopping centre. The centre of the suburb, including the railway station, stands on a grant of 160 acres made in 1839 to a Mr McGillivray, which he called Springdale.

One of the first settlers in the area was gunsmith Joseph Fiddens, a convict who arrived in the colony in 1801. By 1821 he had been granted 40 acres of land on the south side of the later Fiddens Wharf Road. He became a boatman and began transporting timber along the Lane Cove River, which forms Killara's south-western boundary, from Fiddens Wharf to Sydney. On the journey back, he brought supplies for the area's early settlers as well as providing transport for them to and from the city. He died in 1856, aged over 90 years, having resided nearly sixty years in this country.

One of the first hotels on the

North Shore was the Green Gate Hotel in Killara. Its licence was issued to John Johnson in 1832, by which time there were several hotels in the area, and the hotel has been serving customers ever since. The first customers of the Green Gate were early pit-sawyers and timber-getters who were felling the huge trees from Wahroonga to Killara. These men were great drinkers, and there were many illegal stills in the area. The licence for the hotel was granted in an attempt to put an end to these illicit bush stills. The original Green Gate was just a stone cottage with four rooms and large stables.

In 1853 Thomas Waterhouse (1810–84), bought the licence and enlarged the premises. After his death his son, John Waterhouse, who promoted boxing, horse-racing, and cock fights, took over the running of the hotel. Peter Jackson, a Negro ship-deserter who later became a heavyweight champion of the world, worked at the Greengate Hotel at that time. On the death of John Waterhouse in 1903 two women became the owners of the property. First, a Mrs Bartholomew, and later her daughter, Mrs McIntosh, held the licence. In 1939 Mrs McIntosh sold the hotel to Tooth and Company, which built the present Greengate Hotel.

At an important meeting at the Greengate in 1875, a group of residents gathered to request that a railway line be constructed on the upper North Shore. At this meeting James George Edwards (1843–1927) was elected representative for the people of the whole of the Lane Cove area, and in 1899 he was the strength behind the request to the commission of railways to provide a new station at Killara. In 1860 Edwards had petitioned for the opening of a post office in the district, so that mail would not have to be collected from the post office at St Leonards (North Sydney). His sister was first postmistress of what became Gordon post office. He was also instrumental in having 10 acres set aside for recreation purposes in 1892 when the area was being subdivided. This is now Killara Park. J. G. Edwards was buried in St John's cemetery at Gordon. Edwards, the first headmaster of Gordon Public School, was a grandson of Robert Pymble, who settled in the area that later took his name (see Pymble). He took a great interest in writing the history of the suburbs on the North Shore. Marian Street, Killara, remembers the name of one of his daughters.

Killara's official post office opened in 1904 and the public school in 1938. The suburb also has a modern high school.

## KILLARNEY HEIGHTS
*Shire of Warringah*
Location: 15 kilometres north of Sydney east of Warringah Road and overlooking Middle Harbour

A pleasant, bushland suburb south of Forestville, Killarney Heights is bounded on two sides by water. It overlooks Middle Harbour to the south, and Bates Creek is to the north-east. The Middle Harbour foreshores are natural bushland, forming part of the Davidson State Recreation Area. Killarney Point is a sharply shaped piece of land jutting into Middle Harbour. An attempt to auction land here in 1886, as Heidelberg, was unsuccessful. The suburb's name, after Killarney in Ireland, was given when estate agents subdivided the area in the 1960s. It was probably taken from the area's popular Killarney Picnic Ground.

Killarney Castle, a house in the area, is supposed to be a replica of the castle of that name in Ireland. The Irish theme is carried on with many street names, such as Blarney, Shamrock, Sligo, Londonderry and Galway.

Two schools cater for the young people living in the area. Killarney Heights High School stands in Starkey Street, and the infants and primary school is in Tralee Avenue.

In December 1979 this suburb was the scene of some devastating bushfires, but nature has since restored the burnt-out areas so the suburb's parks and reserves are once more places for pleasure.

## KINGS CROSS
*City of Sydney*
Location: 2 kilometres east of Sydney, on the Eastern Suburbs Line

This small area on the ridge between Woolloomooloo and Rushcutters Bay just east of the city has an individual character. The name Queen's Cross became attached to the area in the 1890s, in honour of Queen Victoria's Diamond Jubilee, but because it was often confused with Queen's Square at the top end of King Street in the city, the name was changed to Kings Cross in 1905. Victoria Street commemorates this queen.

Sometimes compared to London's Soho, Kings Cross can also claim to have its share of history. The first penetration of the area was when a road was put through to South Head during Macquarie's governorship (1810–21). Before it became a residential area, the ridge boasted six windmills. Many of the old

Blanche Mitchell

historic landmarks have now gone, making way for high-rise buildings.

On his 1831 grant the then surveyor-general, Sir Thomas Mitchell (1792–1855), erected a house which he called Craigend, with a frontage to Victoria Street, opposite the present fire station (see Darlinghurst). Behind the house stood a windmill, then reputed to be the largest in New South Wales; it measured 105 feet from the top of the sails to the ground. The diaries of his youngest daughter, Blanche, describe life in this area last century.

Another house of interest was Kellett House in Kellett Street, the home of Sir Stuart Alexander Donaldson, who in 1856 became the first premier of New South Wales. S. Clair Donaldson, an archbishop of Brisbane, was born in this house. The house was later demolished, and terraces were built on the site.

Goderich Lodge, in Bayswater Road, was named after an English cabinet minister. Later the site of a private hotel, in the 1840s it was the home of the bishop of Australia, Dr William Grant Broughton. Students preparing for the clergy at St James's College

The Kings Cross tunnel under construction, December 1974

## KINGSFORD

*Municipality of Randwick*
Location: 8 kilometres south-east of Sydney, south of Randwick Racecourse

often visited the bishop at this house to get advice on their sermons; they were then driven back to the college in the bishop's carriage. The house was built on an 1831 grant by the sheriff of the day, Mr Thomas McQuoid. Frederick Tooth, the brewer, owned it in the 1850s and lived there before building Buckhurst at Point Piper.

The first official post office opened on 11 August 1873, as William Street Post Office; the name was changed on 1 January 1965, to Kings Cross post office.

The Cross, as it is popularly known, has two lives — its night life, when anything goes, and its streets and eating places throng with visitors and noise, and its daytime hours when residents and

visitors browse through its interesting shops. Once a Bohemian area, the Cross gained much of its present character from the transformation wrought in the 1960s, when it was the favoured area for United States servicemen on rest and recreation leave from the war in Vietnam.

The Eastern Suburbs Railway gave Kings Cross an underground railway station and quick access to the city proper for this high-density residential area. The suburb's charm probably lies in its contradictions, but soft, green-leafed trees in spring and summer, water sparkling in the El Alamein fountain, and the aroma of coffee could well be the part of its character most favoured by its residents, who for many years referred to the area as Topwilliamstreet.

Formerly known as South Kensington, the suburb was renamed in honour of Sir Charles Kingsford Smith (1897–1935), one of Australia's greatest pioneer aviators.

In 1922 Kingsford Smith made a mail flight between Broome and Port Hedland in Western Australia in record time. From that day his ambition to be a first-class flyer never wavered. His first main aim, to fly the Pacific, was eventually achieved with his colleague and co-pilot Charles Ulm. On 31 May 1928, their Fokker aircraft, the Southern Cross, left the United States to travel through fair and foul weather until, 83 hours later, it touched down in Brisbane. In 1933 Kingsford Smith made a record-breaking solo flight from England to Australia in 7 days and 4 hours and 43 minutes. He disappeared in 1935 while flying the Lady Southern Cross between Calcutta and Singapore.

Kingsford remained undeveloped until the land boom of the 1920s. Previously it had been the site of stables, because of its proximity to Kensington Racecourse, and poultry and pig farms. There were only scattered dwellings and a number of people living in shacks made of flattened kerosene tins.

In the 1940s many Greeks settled in the area, particularly migrants from the small island of Castellorizo, near the Turkish coast. Many opened businesses in the area and in 1973 they built the Castellorizian Club, in Anzac Parade, as a local point for socialising and celebrations.

Anzac Parade, named in honour of the Anzacs of the First World War, is the main thoroughfare through this suburb, which is a crossroads for bus services to Eastlakes, Matraville, La Perouse, Maroubra, Randwick, Bondi Junction, Rose Bay, Double Bay and the city. It was originally intended to be the terminus for the Eastern Suburbs Railway, but in 1979 the line was terminated at Bondi Junction.

Today Kingsford is a residential suburb, with a shopping centre extending along Anzac Parade. It is home to many students attending the nearby University of New South Wales, but children attend schools in the adjoining suburbs of Daceyville, Maroubra and Moore Park.

Publicity shot of Charles Kingsford Smith and company and the Southern Cross, April 1929

# KINGSGROVE
*Municipalities of Rockdale, Hurstville and Canterbury*
Location: 16 kilometres south-west of Sydney between Bexley North and Beverly Hills on the East Hills Line

This busy residential suburb derives its name from an early land grant. On 11 August 1804 Governor Philip Gidley King granted 500 acres of land to Hannah Laycock (1758–1831), the wife of Quartermaster Thomas Laycock (1756–1809). She called the farm, in the area now bounded by Kingsgrove and Bexley Roads and William Street, King's Grove in honour of the governor. Later, as the district progressed and developed, the name came to be spelled as one word.

Thomas Laycock was well

thought of by Governor Phillip, who pronounced him "an officer of merit" and recommended him to fill the vacancy of an ensign in the New South Wales Corps. Two of their sons, William and Samuel Laycock, were also given grants in the district of 100 acres each in 1804, which extended the family farm holdings. In 1812 Hannah received another 120 acres. The 820 acres, extending from South Campsie and Clemton Park to Stoney Creek Road, that finally made up Kingsgrove Farm, were sold to Simeon Lord in 1829.

The first inn built in the area was called the Man of Kent. Licensee Evans, formerly a sea captain, erected a saw pit to cut native timber for the inn's construction. His daughter Maria married Thomas Smithson, who manufactured snuff and tobacco in premises in Stoney Creek Road. Smithson also had a vineyard on the site of today's Bexley Golf Links, on the southern side of the present Stoney Creek Road.

Kingsgrove High School stands on the corner of Stoney Creek Road and Kingsgrove Road, and a primary school is situated in Kingsgrove Road. The official post office was built in King George's Road, Kingsgrove. A number of small parks are scattered through the suburb.

# KINGS LANGLEY
*City of Blacktown*
Location: 39 kilometres west of Sydney just north-east of Blacktown

Early settlers granted 160 acres of land in this area were Matthew Pearce and his wife, who began a farm here in 1795. They called it King's Langley after the manor house in the village of that name south of London, England, where Matthew Pearce was said to have been born. The land covered an area today bounded by the Old Windsor Road, Seven Hills Road and Toongabbie Creek.

The Pearce fortunes flourished and eventually the family owned several farms in the area which was known as Seven Hills. The name of the Pearce farm was resurrected for one of the new suburbs developed around Seven Hills. The housing scheme here was initiated by real estate agents L. J. Hooker in the 1970s. The Pearce family is commemorated by Pearce Reserve, between Whitley Road and Joseph Banks Drive.

The early rural character of this orcharding and poultry farm area has been replaced by residential development. A modern public school stands in Sutherland Avenue.

## KINGSWOOD
*City of Penrith*
Location: 51 kilometres west of Sydney at the junction of Parker Street and the Great Western Highway

This suburb, a near neighbour to Penrith, was named after Philip Gidley King's family, which held land in the area. King was the governor of New South Wales from 1800 to 1806, the third naval governor to have charge of the colony. He had formerly been superintendent and commandant of the convict settlement on Norfolk Island. In 1881 the area was known as Cross Roads, possibly because two main roads, The Northern Road (now Parker Street) and the Great Western Highway, intersected here. This name was changed to Kingswood on 20

August 1887.

Originally heavily forested, the land was later used for farming, particularly in the later part of the nineteenth century, when subdivision began after the railway came through the area in 1862. Although there was a temporary siding in the area for a short time after that, Kingswood siding was not opened until 1887. Subdivision continued until about 1914, when the St Stephen's Estate was being sold, but residential development did not begin until the 1960s and 1970s. Since then the population has increased dramatically, and many residents travel to work in Sydney each day on the Main Western railway line.

The first official post office opened on 16 June 1891, and the public school followed a year later, in September 1892. There are now two primary schools, Kingswood Park Public School and Kingswood South Public School. Kingswood High School and the Nepean College of Advanced Education enable Kingswood students to complete their entire education in their home suburb.

Farm site on the north side of the railway at Kingswood, c. 1900

## KINGSWOOD PARK
*City of Penrith*
Location: 54 kilometres west of Sydney

This is the name for a neighbourhood north of Penrith, between Cambridge Park and Mount Pleasant. An extension of the suburb of Kingswood, it developed with the opening up of land adjacent to the earlier suburb. It lies in the vicinity of Parker Street and Richmond Road, Coreen Avenue and Illawong Avenue.

## KIRRAWEE
*Shire of Sutherland*
Location: 25 kilometres south-west of Sydney off the Princes Highway, on the Cronulla Line

This suburb between Sutherland and Gymea received its name when the electric railway line came through from Sutherland to Cronulla. The name is Aboriginal and means "lengthy". The area had previously been called Bladesville, apparently because of a

connection with a family of the name of Blade.

The suburb's early days were connected with the development of Sutherland. Streets in Kirrawee today commemorate famous Australians, such as Putland and Bligh, after the Rum Rebellion governor and his daughter, Mrs Putland; Meehan, after an early surveyor; Johnston, after a First Fleet lieutenant and first settler in Annandale; Kemp, after a notorious captain in charge of early government stores; and Gilmore, after Australian-born poet Dame Mary Gilmore. Other names such as Orana and Weemala, or Nyrang, Mundakal and Wanganui, are Aboriginal in origin. Other street names recall plants and animals, such as Flora Street, Acacia Road and Fauna Place.

The two schools in the area are the public school in Clements Parade and Kirrawee High School in Hunter Street. Saville's Creek forms the southern boundary of the suburb, separating it from the Royal National Park and Port Hacking.

## KIRRIBILLI

*Municipality of North Sydney*
Location: 3 kilometres north of Sydney just east of the northern exit of the Harbour Bridge

When Russians on a scientific voyage visited Sydney in the 1820s, they built an observatory on Kirribilli Point — opposite the site of the Sydney Opera House — which they referred to as Russian Cape. They repaired their ships, which were anchored in Neutral Bay, and refurbished their stores before departing.

This suburb was part of a grant to James Milson (1783–1872), after

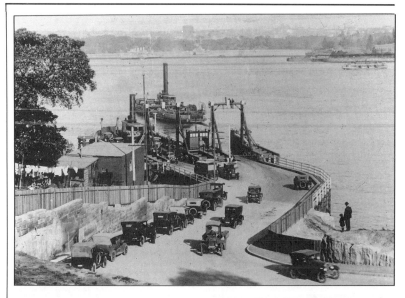

whom Milsons Point was named. He built a number of houses on the land, including Carabella, where he died in 1872. Carabella may have been a mispronunciation of Kirribilli or a similar Aboriginal name for the area. The house is remembered by Carabella Street, a major thoroughfare in the area.

In 1800 Robert Ryan, a marine, was granted 120 acres between Lavender Bay and Careening Cove. He sold it in 1806 to Robert Campbell (1769–1846), who in 1842 leased 5 acres to J. G. N. Gibbes (1787–1873), the collector of customs, and agreed to pay him for any improvements he made. By 1845 Gibbes had built a substantial home, and in 1849 the house and 5 acres of land were sold to him for £700. Over the following years it had many

Above: The vehicle ferry docks at Jeffrey Street, Kirribilli. The docks were first used in 1925 when the Milsons Point docks were closed to make way for the Harbour Bridge

Below: Sketch of Beulah in Kirribilli, 1855, by Rebecca Martens. During the 1860s the house was leased by Frederick Lassetter, the owner of a large retail store in George Street called Lassetter's

occupants, some of whom made alterations and additions. In 1885 the New South Wales government decided to acquire the property and use it as an official residence for the admiral commanding the British squadron in Australia, rather than continue using a house at Potts Point. At that time the house at Kirribilli, known as Wotanga, was owned by Thomas Cadell. The government renamed it Admiralty House. The house was considered ideal for the purpose, as the down-harbour views from all the front rooms made it easy to spot enemy ships entering the harbour. It was used as the admiral's residence until 1913, when its last occupant was Rear-Admiral Sir George E. Patey, RN. After his departure it was loaned to the federal government as a residence for the governor-general, but after his residence was moved to Canberra, it reverted to the state government.

Kirribilli House, next door to Admiralty House, was erected about 1855 and privately owned until acquired by the Commonwealth government in 1920. Its first owner was Mr Adolph Feez, a businessman who built Kirribilli House on the 1 acre of Admiralty House land which he had acquired in 1854.

The Royal Sydney Yacht Squadron is another important establishment in Kirribilli. The first colonists brought with them a great love of sport, and both horse-racing and yachting were soon established in New South Wales. The first yacht race of any note took place in 1831; the flag ship on that day was the paddle-steamer *Australian*, and the commodore, Mr Burton Bradley. The first race was won by *North Star*, owned by a Mr Sawyer. Yachting became an established part of the Sydney Harbour scene, and 18 July 1862 saw the birth of the Royal Sydney Yacht Squadron. The first vice-commodore of the Squadron was James Milson (1814–1903), son of the original land-holder in the area, who was also a keen yachtsman. James junior's 25-ton yacht, *Era*, was well-known on the Harbour in the 1860s.

Today Kirribilli remains an attractive residential suburb, and despite an increasing number of high-rise buildings in the area, many homes retain wonderful

harbour views. The Loreto Convent School and St Aloysius College are the area's only educational institutions.

# KOGARAH

*Municipalities of Kogarah and Rockdale*

Location: 14 kilometres south of Sydney on the Princes Highway extending to Kogarah Bay on the Georges River, on the Illawarra Line

This area, west of Botany Bay and the present Brighton-le-Sands, was originally a swampy tract of land, where rushes grew in great profusion. Its name is derived from the Aboriginal word for rushes, "coggera" or "cogerah". The present spelling was settled when the railway came through in the 1880s and a station was built.

An early land grant here was made to Captain John Townson (1760–1835), who received a total of 2,250 acres centred on the Hurstville area in 1808–10. This and a neighbouring grant made to

James Chandler extended into what is now Kogarah (see Bexley). Subdivision of the area began in about 1848. In 1869 William Wolfen gave the 2 acres of land on which St Paul's Church of England, Rocky Point Road, Kogarah, was built, and the suburb soon grew up around the buildings that followed. The municipality was incorporated in 1885.

Today the suburb is a busy residential area, with a good train service on the Sutherland line, which is now linked to the Eastern Suburbs Railway. Kogarah was served by silent, double-decker, electric trolley buses from 1937 to 1959. They were popular with passengers, but despite an outcry when the transport department tried to cut them out, they were replaced by diesel buses on the old route from Rockdale to Dolls Point.

The St George District Hospital is a focal point in this district. Set in gardens, it covers a large area with an administration block, wards, rehabilitation units,

Corner of Belgrade Street and Railway Parade, Kogarah, 1918. Built in 1892, the turreted building was occupied by the Post Office until 1974 and now houses a community health centre

casualty and special training areas. Education is well served by Kogarah Public School and no less than four high schools: Kogarah, St George Girls, Moorefield Girls and James Cook Boys. The last two stand on properties adjoining the St George Technical College on the Princes Highway opposite the hospital. In the southern part of the suburb stand Jubilee Oval and Kogarah Park.

The former neighourhood of Moorefield, once well patronised, today is part of Kogarah and is remembered by name only.

On 28 August 1812, Governor Lachlan Macquarie made a land grant of 60 acres to Patrick Moore, "to be called Moorefield". A fine house was built on the grant, and later Patrick J. Moore, a descendant of the first Patrick, built a racecourse, opened in 1888, which took its name from the grant. The Moorefield Course was later taken over by the Sydney Turf Club and continued to operate until July 1951.

In the 1950s the Moorefield estate was subdivided, and 300 buyers built homes in this historic area. The Department of Education purchased 19 acres fronting the Princes Highway and President Avenue, Kogarah, where the first Patrick Moore's farm had once stood, and Moorefield Girls High School was erected on this site in 1955. The name also lives on in the names of Moorefield Bowling Club, the Moorefield Squash and Exercise Centre, and Moorefield Pharmacy.

An early inn was located near "that well-known property, Pat Moore's Farm". Known as Rocky Point Hotel, it was a wooden building with a shingle roof, and a long front verandah.

# KURNELL

*Shire of Sutherland*

Location: 32 kilometres south of Sydney on the southern headland of Botany Bay

This suburb north-east of Cronulla on the Kurnell Peninsula, the southern headland of Botany Bay, was Captain James Cook's landing place on 29 April 1770. Its name is believed to be an English pronunciation of an Aboriginal word, Collonel, although it has also been suggested that the name came from an early settler in the area, John Connell.

The first land grant, of 700 acres, was made in 1815 to James Birnie, who established Alpha Farm, although there is no record of his having lived in the area. In 1821 John Connell Junior was granted land here and he added to it by purchase, using his property mainly for timber gettings. His father bought Alpha Farm but in 1860 sold it to Thomas Holt (see Sutherland). In 1827 Surveyor

The Solander Monument at Kurnell was built by the Swedish community in honour of Dr D. C. Solander, a botanist aboard the HMS *Endeavour*

Dixon worked out the boundaries of Connell's land and by 1842 his holding amounted to 1,000 acres.

Several historically significant names are found at Kurnell. Sutherland Point remembers one of Captain Cook's crew, Forby Sutherland, who died of tuberculosis and was buried at Kurnell. Cape Solander was named after Joseph Bank's colleague, Swedish botanist Daniel Solander. Inscription Point was so called by the Australian Philosophical Society in 1822 when they secured a plaque to the cliff face to mark the point of the *Endeavour* crew's first landing.

Today the northern part of the peninsula is an historic site, and three memorials have been erected there: a Captain Cook Memorial Obelisk, a Sir Joseph Banks Memorial and a Solander Monument to honour three men whose names are engraved on our history. There is also a splendid Visitors Centre, presenting interesting information as well as relics from those first days in Kurnell's history. Kurnell Lookout nearby gives a clear view over the bay. This well-cared-for area is known as Captain Cook's Landing Place.

The Endeavour Heights area is a recreation reserve extending from the Landing Place in the north along the coast. On the landward side is a large industrial area, the site of an oil refinery and a lubricating refinery. Refined petrol is piped to the other side of the bay in an underwater pipeline. A small residential area stands to the north of the industrial area, behind Kurnell Beach. Its public school stands at the corner of Dampier and Tasman Streets, which commemorate two other navigators of early Australian history.

Before the 1920s Kurnell was the

haunt of fishermen, as schools of several varieties of fish inhabited the foreshores of the bay. Shacks sheltered them during a weekend's happy and peaceful fishing. During the 1920s, when the Depression severely affected low income families, many took up residence in the area in makeshift shacks. This was one of a number of settlements in Sutherland, Randwick and Botany that became known as Happy Valley.

# KURRABA POINT
*Municipality of North Sydney*
Location: Locality in Neutral Bay, 5 kilometres north of Sydney on Port Jackson

The small residential area known as Kurraba Point, which separates Neutral Bay from Shell Cove on the northern harbour shores, had a romantic origin. When Captain John Piper's daughter married Alfred Thrupp, the captain gave the young couple the gift of 700 acres of land facing into Neutral Bay. Kurraba Point was part of this land. The farm they established there was known as Thrupp's Farm, and the headland was called Thrupp's Point. However, the Aboriginal name of Kurraba, possibly a tribal name, eventually became the point's official title.

The stone used to build Fort Denison was quarried from Kurraba Point, and the two freshwater springs on the tip of the point were used to replenish supplies of drinking water on sailing ships anchored in Neutral Bay. In the 1860s it was not an unusual sight to see large vessels waiting off Kurraba Point for casks of fresh water to be ferried from the shore. When cargo ships were returning empty to Britain and other ports, the necessary ballast was often collected from the rocky shore of Kurraba Point, and providing ballast became quite a lucrative occupation. For a time, the peninsula was known as Ballast Point.

The three children playing in this rather ramshackle backyard are seemingly oblivious to the impressive backdrop of Port Jackson at Kurraba Point

# KYEEMAGH
*Municipality of Rockdale*
Location: 12 kilometres south of
Sydney at the mouth of the Cooks
River

Situated on the southern bank of
Cooks River, south of Sydney
Airport, this suburb began its life
as a grant of land. In 1837 John
Webb was granted 300 acres in the
area, but he did not settle on the
land because its scrubby and arid
nature made farming a risky
business.

In 1882, 309 acres of the land in
this district were resumed for a
sewerage farm, and later another
311 acres were taken over for the
same purpose. This rather slowed
the progress of the area, and it was
not until 1916, when an ocean
outfall was built, that any
substantial subdivision of land took
place. At that time the New South
Wales Polo Association bought 56
acres of the old sewerage farm on
which to establish a polo ground,
and the association officials gave
the area the name Kyeemagh, an
Aboriginal word meaning
"beautiful dawn".

Two men are remembered in
Kyeemagh's history for their
enthusiastic efforts on the suburb's
behalf. The first, John Goode, had
a property in West Botany Street,
from which he built a private road
to Seven Mile Beach, as Lady
Robinsons Beach was then known.
Goode Street was named in his
honour, although it has since been
renamed Bestic Street. Alderman
E. G. Barton also worked to
develop the district. He devoted
his mayoral term to the
reclamation of 120 acres of
low-lying swampland. Barton
Park, adjacent to the Kogarah Golf
Links and fronting Cooks River
opposite Sydney Airport, is his
monument today.

General Holmes Drive and Lady
Robinsons Beach are two other
well-known local names in this
suburb which had uncertain
beginnings. The public school
stands at the corner of Jacobson
Avenue and Beehag Street, the
latter named for James Beehag,
who owned land in the district in
the 1850s and became one of
Rockdale's early mayors (see
Rockdale).

# LAKEMBA
*Municipality of Canterbury*
Location: 15 kilometres
south-west of Sydney, and east of
Bankstown, on the Bankstown
Line

In 1810 Samuel Hockley, a
member of the 102nd Regiment of
the New South Wales Corps, was
granted 50 acres south of the
present Punchbowl Road on which
most of Lakemba now stands. He
called the area Essex Hill Farm
after his home county in England.
The area had previously been
known as Potato Hill because
potato crops were grown there.
Later Benjamin Taylor, an
entomologist and town clerk of
Canterbury, bought a large portion
of the land, and built his home
near the site of the present
Lakemba railway station. He called
the cottage Lakemba Cottage after
the mission station Lakemba in
Fiji, which was conducted by his
father-in-law. At that time the
suburb was heavily timbered and
developing slowly.

In about 1880 John Fenwick
bought 100 acres between
Canterbury, Canary and Bonds
Roads, an area first granted in 1842
to H. R. Morgan. Fenwick's
Belmore House, built on this land,
was demolished for the

construction of Roselands
Shopping Centre.

The suburb did not go ahead
until the coming of the railway in
1909. When the station was being
built, it was known as Haldon
Street; it opened on 14 April 1909.
The suburb was called South
Belmore until June 1910, when the
railway station's name was
changed to Lakemba, after Ben
Taylor's home. By then, Taylor
had been laid to rest in St
Thomas's cemetery at Enfield.

The area's first school opened as
Belmore School in April 1869,
then became Belmore South
School in September 1907. In June
1910 the name was changed again,
this time to Lakemba Public
School. The first post office began
on 1 July 1879 and was known as
Belmore post office; in August
1907, it became South Belmore
post office. Like the station and the
school, its official name became
Lakemba, on 1 June 1910.

Two rival estate agents had a
great influence on the growth of
Lakemba. They were the firms of
Raine and Horne, and Hardie and
Gorman. Both of these real estate
giants sold home blocks on "a
deposit down, and
pay-as-you-live" basis, which
meant people on low incomes were
able to secure a home-site and
build a house, which particularly
suited newly arrived migrants.

# LALOR PARK
*City of Blacktown*
Location: 3 kilometres north-west
of Sydney just north-east of
Blacktown

This suburb was developed by the
housing commission in 1959 on
land formerly known as Seven
Hills West. The suburb was named

145

after a family called Lalor who owned land in the district, or after Peter Lalor (1827–89), who was elected leader of the rebellious miners in November 1854 at the Eureka Stockade.

This suburb has a large population, which benefits from several parks and from its proximity to Blacktown with its large modern shopping complex. The main thoroughfare, Northcott Road, was named in honour of a distinguished soldier and former governor of New South Wales, Sir John Northcott. Heffron Road was named after a former state premier. Other famous Australians are also recalled in street names: Moncrieff and Melba Roads represent musical notables; Lawson Street, Gilmore and Gunn Roads and Harpur Place represent Australian literature; and thoroughfares named Landy, Jackson, Charlton, Cartwright and Dalray (winner of the 1952 Melbourne Cup) recall sporting greats. Early explorers are also commemorated, such as Blaxland, Lawson, Leichhardt, Oxley, Kennedy and Wills.

Below and right: Part of a panorama taken of Longueville Road, Lane Cove, c. 1920, showing Lane Cove tram terminus

# LANE COVE
*Municipalities of Lane Cove and Willoughby*
Location: 9 kilometres north-west of Sydney off Epping Road and the Pacific Highway reaching down to the Lane Cove River

This suburb received its name from the cove and river, which legend says were so named because the heavily wooded shores, viewed from the opening of the Lane Cove River onto the Parramatta River, gave it the appearance of a laneway. The waterway was originally thought to be simply a cove, and the river was only later discovered. The name originally covered the whole area of the North Shore from Gordon to Greenwich.

This area north of the harbour was explored on several occasions from 1788. Grants of land were made in the area in 1794–96, when thirty-two grants were made in the area stretching across the eastern part of the present Lane Cove and west Artarmon. The area was heavily timbered and government saw pits were operated here in the early nineteenth century. In the early years there were many

conflicts with local Aborigines, and in 1796 a constable, James Everitt, was appointed.

Two early residents were a German, Albert Radke (1828–99), and John Charles Ludowici (1836–1916), from Denmark. The men, trading as Ludowici and Company, occupied 16 acres of land at the head of Burns Bay Creek in 1860 where they had the first tannery on the North Shore. In 1860 Radke and Ludowici dissolved their partnership; Radke became a leather-belt manufacturer and Ludowici and Sons took over the tannery. The Ludowici home in Burns Bay Road was on the site of the land first occupied by the two partners. Later a smaller house was built there, possibly for a son who married. Today the Caroline Chisholm Retirement Village occupies part of the area.

Materials and goods in the early days were transported by water, as roads came to the area much later. By 1829 a line of road was established from Blues Point northwards. It was properly constructed to Pearce's Corner at Wahroonga in the early 1850s, when it was known as Lane Cove Road. Today it is the Pacific Highway.

As early as 1859 attempts were made to establish a ferry service on the Lane Cove River, but there were no takers for this service, and it was not until 1871 that the *Womerah* began to run to the city from the Lane Cove side of the Parramatta River. By 1880 a ferry service was running five trips a day to and from the Lane Cover River wharves.

From 1865 Lane Cove was part of the borough of North Willoughby, but in 1895 it became independent as the Borough of Lane Cove. Residential development here was later than most of the lower North Shore, which was being more intensively occupied, because this area had such poor transport.

Carisbrook, at 334 Burns Bay Road, Lane Cove, was built in 1861. The second oldest house in Lane Cove, today it is a historical museum, furnished in the style of the nineteenth century, and is open to the public.

The Lane Cove area today is largely residential, with some light industry and a modern shopping centre.

# LANSDOWNE
*City of Fairfield*
Location: 27 kilometres south-west of Sydney between Henry Lawson Drive and the Hume Highway

The hardwood bridges built in the early days of the colony soon proved unsafe, so David Lennox (1788–1873), a Scottish stonemason who arrived in Sydney in 1832, was made superintendent of bridges in 1833 with the particular task of building a series of stone bridges. One of his finest works

David Lennox

was the Lansdowne Bridge over Prospect Creek near Liverpool. Still standing today, the bridge was built in 1834–35 of stone quarried 10 kilometres away on the bank of the Georges River. Governor Bourke named the bridge in honour of Henry Petti-Fitzmaurice, third Marquis of Lansdowne (1783–1863), a Whig politician. This small suburb west of Bankstown, between the Hume Highway and Prospect Creek, took its name from the bridge. The previous bridge on the site had been called Bowler's Bridge because it led to Bowler's Inn, but it had frequently been swept away in floods.

One of the first land grants in the Bankstown area was made to Lieutenant John Shortland (1769–1810). The land he received in 1800 was in the area of the later Lansdowne Bridge and Woodville Road. In the early 1900s Lansdowne House was built for John V. Tillett, crown solicitor of New South Wales, for whom Tillett Parade, Lansdowne, is named.

In 1962 the World Scout Jamboree was held at Lansdowne, and the site, now Mirambeena Regional Park, was reserved for a

future recreation area. Money for the project was supplied by the federal and state governments and by Bankstown Council. Today the park is a people's playground, with a lake, Lake Gillawarna, and ponds full of wildlife, native walks and a pedestrian and cycle way. The picnic area has barbecues and all kinds of play equipment for children.

## LANSVALE
*City of Fairfield*
Location: 28 kilometres south-west of Sydney on the Hume Highway and fronting the Georges River

Sandwiched between the Georges River and Prospect Creek, this suburb seems to have taken its name from its neighbours: Canley Vale to the north-west and Lansdowne to the east.

The suburb developed in the 1950s when the peripheral areas of Bankstown municipality assumed identities of their own. One popular housing estate is known as River Heights, where stylishly designed houses with every modern detail and a luxurious finish have been built. Lansvale East Public School stands near the Georges River and Lansvale Public School is in Chancery Street.

## LA PEROUSE
*Municipality of Randwick*
Location: 14 kilometres south of Sydney at the southernmost end of Bunnerong Road, near the entrance to Botany Bay

In 1788 ships of two great nations were sailing towards Botany Bay, in the Great South Land. One group was from Britain under the care of Captain Arthur Phillip (1738–1814), who was bringing the First Fleet of convicts to establish a colony. The other was a French exploration fleet led by a renowned French navigator, Jean-François de Galaup, Comte de La Pérouse (1741–88), who was seeking shelter in a peaceful bay after his men had been attacked by Samoans. The French ships, *La Boussole* and *L' Astrolabe* (French names of navigation instruments), entered the bay on 26 January 1788 and saw, to their surprise, British ships riding at anchor. Phillip had already left to find a more suitable harbour, but John Hunter had remained with the *Sirius* and the transports. The French camped on the northern shore, where the crew members who had been wounded in the attack in Samoa received attention. A scientist on the expedition, Father Receveur, died in February and was buried at what has since been called La Perouse. The French ships sailed out of Botany Bay, to vanish completely, and no members of their crews were ever seen again. In 1826 the mystery of the French ships was solved when their wrecks were found on an island in the Santa Cruz group.

Frenchmen visiting Australia

View of Frenchmans Bay, La Perouse, c. 1885

A snake charmer at La Perouse, c. 1914, entertains a captive audience

sometimes make a pilgrimage to La Perouse, considering it a small part of France in Australia. Today there are two French memorials in the suburb of La Perouse: the grave of Father Receveur and the large La Perouse monument erected in 1825 by the French, commemorating the great French navigator. In 1825 Governor Brisbane proposed that the land on which these two memorials stand should be made over to France, but this was never done, and the land remains the property of Australia.

Captain Cook's map of Botany Bay shows a stream of fresh water running into the bay on the site of today's La Perouse beach. This stream, described by Cook as "a very fine stream in the first sandy cove within the island", was used by Cook, La Pérouse and Phillip.

The first building in the area was the round tower erected during the governorship of Macquarie in 1820–21 as part of the accommodation for a small guard stationed there to prevent smuggling. The stone tower is still standing in the suburb.

By 1885 a reserve for the use of Aborigines had been established in the suburb and a number of missions were successively operated in the area. The original church here was dismantled and moved from its site on sand dunes near the beach and reconstructed on the corner of Elaroo and Adina Streets, where it now stands. There is still a large Aboriginal community in the area and craftwork and boomerangs have long been produced here for tourists.

The Loop, the circular track terminus for trams coming from the city, was for many years a focal point in La Perouse. A kiosk was built here in 1896 to provide for tourists. Many came to see the "snake men", who held exhibitions of snake-handling from the early years of the century. John Cann still works the pit at the Loop, as did his father George (1897–1965) before him. George

Jean François de Galaup, Comte de La Pérouse

Cann was advertised as a "master snake man who fears not the bite of python, asp, tiger snake or death adder". Many of the early snake men also sold snake antidotes, which they demonstrated, reptile oils and even crystallised venom, but today educating the public about snakes is seen as more important than displays of bravado.

During the depression of the 1930s unemployment camps known as Happy Valley, Frog Hollow and Hill 60 were established at La Perouse on land leased by the New South Wales Golf Club and adjacent to the Aboriginal reserve. Frog Hollow and Hill 60 survived into the late 1950s, when some of the shacks were occupied by post-war immigrants.

Just inside the heads of Botany Bay near La Perouse and now linked to the mainland by a bridge, James Cook mentioned in his reports "a small bare island".

Bare Island was fortified in 1885 to a design by the colonial architect, James Barnet (1827–1904), who had been made responsible for building defence works at Port Jackson and Newcastle as well as Botany Bay. As well as building lighthouses, court-houses and police stations throughout the state, he designed several important buildings in Sydney, including the General Post Office, the Colonial Secretary's Office, Customs House, the Public Library and the medical school at the University of Sydney.

In 1912 Bare Island was made into a retirement home for war veterans. The home was established and maintained by voluntary women workers, members of the British Empire League, one of whom also presented each veteran with a navy blue military-style uniform. The home continued until about 1963, after which the island was handed over to the New South Wales National Parks and Wildlife Service. The island and its museum today attract many tourists.

## LAVENDER BAY
*Municipality of North Sydney*
Location: 3.5 kilometres north of Sydney just west of the Harbour Bridge

Lavender Bay, a small suburb at the head of the bay between Blues Point and Milsons Point, began its life under the ugly name of Hulk Bay. This was because the old hulk (a ship that is no longer seaworthy), *Phoenix* was anchored there early in the 1800s, holding convicts awaiting retransportation to Norfolk Island, where convicts who caused trouble in the colony were sent.

The best-known official on the *Phoenix* was the bosun, George Lavender, whose name was later given to the bay. He lived on 14 acres fronting the harbour, adjacent to Billy Blue's land (see Blues Point) and from 1837 ran a ferry from Dawe's Battery to what was then called Billy Blue's Point. He married Susannah, the daughter of Billy Blue, in 1834. George Lavender had a sad end. He sold his house on Lavender Point and went to live in the old

Commodore Hotel in Blues Point Road. In 1857 while there, he shot himself and Susannah was left a widow. Later she married a Mr Chuter.

On 30 May 1915 a temporary railway station was established at Lavender Bay to take the place of Milsons Point Station during the proposed building of the Sydney Harbour Bridge, which it was anticipated would soon begin. The scheme lasted seven weeks, before the day came when passengers refused to alight and demanded to be taken on to Milsons Point. This was the end of Lavender Bay's railway glory, and Milsons Point station came back into use.

Today the suburb has a gentle quality. The bay itself faces the Harbour Bridge and shelters many sailing craft for those lovers of yachting who reside in the area.

Lavender Bay swimming baths, c. 1910. The old baths closest to the camera became the "ladies baths" after the larger new baths, behind, opened in 1905. Naturally the newer baths, complete with forty-five foot diving tower, were christened the "gentlemen's baths". The train line along the foreshore ceased to be used after the construction of the Harbour Bridge

# LEICHHARDT
*Municipality of Leichhardt*
Location: 7 kilometres south-west
of Sydney on Parramatta Road

This inner western suburb was
originally known as Piperston, as
Captain Piper and Ensign Hugh
Piper received large grants of land
here in 1811. The land, which lay
east of Balmain Road between the
present Brenan and Styles Streets,
was sold to Walter Beames, who
chose the name Leichhardt, in
honour of his friend, the famous
explorer. He subdivided the area in
1842. Piper Street in Annandale
recalls these settlers.

In its early days the area was the
site of many splendid estates where
some of the wealthiest and
best-known families in Sydney had
homes surrounded by extensive
gardens and large paddocks. A trip
to Leichhardt in the 1850s and
1860s was likened to a day in the
country. Some of these estates
were Elswick House, owned by
James Norton, MLC, from 1834
until his death in 1862; Broughton
Hall, originally built by Bishop
Broughton in the area of
Leichhardt Park and in the 1860s
and 1870s the residence of Robert
Scott-Ross, a son-in-law to the
original David Jones; and Annesley,
the estate at one time owned by the
tea and coffee merchant William
Inglis (of W. Inglis and Son).
Elswick House had been built on
the first land grant in the district,
which was given to John Thomas
Elswick in 1794. With few
exceptions each of these wealthy
residents had his own horse and
carriage, and a line of horse-drawn
buses ran from the city to this area.
There were also brickyards and
stockyards owned by Messrs Flood
and Oatley on Taverner's Hill.

On both sides of the present
Balmain Road stood Garryowen,

the estate of John Ryan Brenan
(1798?–1868), magistrate and
coroner. The mansion he built
there was later demolished. The
northern part of the estate was
taken over by Callan Park Mental
Hospital, now the Rozelle
Hospital.

Other colourful characters in the
district were Charles Hearn, who
moved about 1850 from his hotel
the Bald Faced Stag in the
Haymarket, to Leichhardt. Here he
opened another Bald Faced Stag on
the corner of Balmain and
Parramatta Roads. William
Taverner (remembered by steep
Taverner's Hill) also built a hotel
here, the Bay Horse.

The suburb's idyllic situation
changed with the building of the
railway station at Petersham,
which gave easy access to
Leichhardt. Soon the population
increased markedly, and the estate
owners became dissatisfied. Mr
Norton, the then owner of Elswick
House, died in 1862, and the
family sold the property to John
Wetherill, a well-known city
draper, who resold to the Excelsior
Building Society. The land was
subdivided and major changes
in housing and life-style became
evident. Cottages were built where
once the large gardens had given
beauty to the district, which soon
evolved into a working-class
suburb. The primary school
opened in 1862, but was called
Petersham Public School until
1874.

On 14 October 1871, Leichhardt
was proclaimed a municipality,
and the name Leichhardt was
adopted for the area. Ludwig
Leichhardt (1814–48), who gave
his name to the suburb, is
particularly remembered for his
expedition from Brisbane to Port
Essington, which covered 4,800
kilometres. He had migrated to
New South Wales from Germany in

1841 and became an expert botanist
and geologist. The members of his
second expedition attempting to
cross the continent from east to
west disappeared, and this has
remained one of the great
mysteries of Australian inland
exploration. Although other
exploration parties went out in
search of the group, no trace of it
was ever found.

Leichhardt was famous for its
council horse-and-cart garbage
service. The service continued
right up to 1975, when the
animals, who had endeared
themselves to Leichhardt's
residents, were pensioned off.
Motor trucks took over, and
another reminder of early days in
this suburb ended.

# LEMONGROVE
*City of Penrith*
Location: 53 kilometres west of
Sydney on the Great Western
Highway just north of Penrith

The present neighbourhood of
Lemongrove is an area north of
Penrith centred on Lemon Grove
Road. It was developed
particularly in the years after 1976
when new suburbs of Penrith were
growing fast.

The original land grant in the
area, which gave the suburb its
name, was fraught with
disappointment. The name
Lemongrove first appeared on a
map dated 1827. Free settlers John
and Sarah McHenry were
promised 100 acres here, and
although allowed to build a house,
which they called Lemongrove, the
land was not formally theirs until
1834. By this time John had died
and Sarah had no wish to stay in
the house without him, so the
property was shared by Sarah, her

151

father, the Reverend Mr Rulton, and a friend, Alexander Fraser.

Later these new owners sold Lemongrove House, so named because it was built on the site of the McHenrys' lemon orchard, to Robert and Margaret Thurston. When they died, a court petition in 1881 requested that the property be held in trust for the two Thurston children and that William Hemming, the commissioner of stamps, be appointed as their guardian.

The case-at-law ran for some time, concluding with a decision to demolish Lemongrove House and subdivide the land. The 249 lots on the estate offered for sale in January 1885 sold quickly. Some of the street names remember the principal people in that court case, such as Robert, Thurston, Haynes and Hemming Streets.

## LETHBRIDGE PARK
*City of Blacktown*
Location: 47 kilometres west of Sydney, north-west of Mount Druitt

This suburb is named after the home and estate of early settlers, the Lethbridge family. It is one of the Mount Druitt housing development suburbs that came into being near Penrith between 1960 and 1970. Its history goes back to the district's pioneering days when the King and Lethbridge families were united by marriage. Captain Phillip Parker King (1791–1856) married Harriet Lethbridge, and Robert Copeland Lethbridge married King's sister Mary in 1826. Captain King was granted 1,500 acres west of Rope's Creek in 1806, and settled there with Harriet. The Lethbridge family were well known in Mulgoa and St Marys, and the

family vault is the largest in St Mary Magdalene graveyard at St Marys.

Many of the suburb's streets are named after Pacific Islands, including Samoa, Bougainville, Tahiti, Papeete, Pitcairn, and Manila and Luzon, and places in New Zealand, such as Rotorua and Taranaki. The modern public school stands in Bougainville Road.

## LEUMEAH
*City of Campbelltown*
Location: 49 kilometres south-west of Sydney off Campbelltown Road, on the Main Southern Line

An Aboriginal word, meaning "here I rest", is the name of this new suburb north-east of the city of Campbelltown. The name was originally given to a farm near Campbelltown established by a Mr Fowler in 1876. When the railway platform was opened, John Davis, who lived close by, suggested that the name of that early farm be recalled in the suburb's name. Davis had inherited a 60 acre farm and hotel owned by another early resident, John Ray.

The local hotel was an important part of early settlement in these outlying areas. In fact, Governor Macquarie encouraged the establishment of hotels, as they formed a focal point for district settlers, alleviating loneliness, and providing a contact when help was urgently needed.

Smiths Creek runs through the centre of the suburb and reserves have been maintained along much of its length. Aboriginal words, such as Menindee, Wyangala and Warragamba, have been used for street names in the suburb.

## LEWISHAM
*Municipality of Marrickville*
Location: 8 kilometres south-west of Sydney off Stanmore Road, on the Main Suburban Line

The suburb, like its neighbours, Petersham and Summer Hill, developed with the construction of the Main Western railway line in the 1850s. The first station opened in 1886 and a new one was opened in 1891. It was named after Judge Joshua Josephson's residence, which he had called Lewisham after the borough of that name near London.

An early grantee in the area was John Gambling, who received 40 acres in 1810 on Gambling Creek, which is now a covered drain.

The suburb has always been residential and well-populated. One of its landmarks is Lewisham Hospital, conducted by the Catholic Church. An order of nursing nuns staffed the hospital, which served Lewisham residents and those of surrounding suburbs until 1987. The hospital was well known for its modern sports medicine clinic. Lewisham Public School is in The Boulevarde.

## LIDCOMBE
*Municipality of Auburn*
Location: 17 kilometres west of Sydney off Parramatta Road and Olympic Drive, a junction station for the Main Western, Main Southern and Bankstown Lines

A station known as Haslam's Creek was opened in 1859 on the railway line built in 1855 from Sydney to Parramatta. From 1804 Samuel Haslam, who owned various grants adjacent to the creek, held a beer licence on his farm, which stood within the area

Lewisham Hospital, c. 1905

bounded by today's Parramatta Road, Nyrang and Boorea Streets, and Haslam's Creek storm-water canal.

In July 1858, Haslam's Creek railway station was the scene of the first railway disaster in New South Wales, which resulted in two deaths.

Subdivision of the area around the station began in 1867. In 1870 the Sydney Meat Preserving Company was founded and acquired 146 acres between the station and Parramatta Road.

When the necropolis, which means "city of the dead", was opened near here in 1867, it was called Haslam's Creek Cemetery, but because residents disliked the association of the suburb with a burial ground, in 1876 it was renamed Rookwood, from a title of a novel by William Harrison Ainsworth (1805–82) which had enjoyed great popularity about forty years before. In 1878 the

station name was changed to Rookwood. By the mid-1880s shops were established in the area and in 1891 the municipality of Rookwood was incorporated. From 1898 there was again agitation to change the suburb's name because of the association with the cemetery. In 1913 a new name was suggested, this time honouring two men who had served the community: Mr Lidbury, the current mayor, and Mr Larcombe, a former mayor. On 1 January 1914 the station name was changed to Lidcombe.

Each time the suburb's name changed, so did the titles of the post office and the public school. The first post office opened as Haslam's Creek post office on 16 October 1868, to become Rookwood post office in July 1876, and finally Lidcombe post office on 15 December 1913. In February 1879, the first public school opened as Rookwood, but its name was changed to Lidcombe in November 1913. The

municipality was amalgamated with Auburn in 1949.

The earliest land grants in the area south of the main road were made in 1810 to Edward Gould (30 acres), Henry Marr (30 acres) and Sophia East (50 acres). The area of central Lidcombe was first granted in 1823, when nine grantees received 60 or 100 acres each. In 1833 Joseph Hyde Potts, an accountant in the Bank of New South Wales, received 1,100 acres, which he called Hyde Park. By 1835 he had increased his holdings to 2,564 acres. Potts Hill, south of Lidcombe, and nearby Potts Park were named after him. The two reservoirs there, built between 1888 and 1923, are part of the Sydney water supply system.

North-west of the station is Wyatt Park which includes within its boundaries a swimming pool and Lidcombe Oval. Rookwood Cemetery lies south-east of Lidcombe railway station, and nearby is the large Lidcombe Hospital, built on a site acquired by the government in 1878. The government intended to use the 1,300 acres, cleared by unemployed relief workers in 1884, for a model farm. In 1887, however, it was decided to build a hospital here instead, and this had been done by 1893. In 1896 the government decided to use the institution to house the aged male poor.

## LILLI PILLI

*Shire of Sutherland*
Location: 26 kilometres south of Sydney on the northern shore of Port Hacking

The earliest description of this peninsula on Port Hacking between Yowie Bay and Burraneer Bay was in a report by Robert Cooper Walker in 1868, in which he described Thomas Holt's Sutherland estate. Holt (1811–88), a wealthy wool merchant and politician, owned a large parcel of land in the Sutherland Shire (see Sutherland). Cooper wrote: "towards the South West, there is another small point, called 'Lilly Pilly Point' on account of the native myrtles that grow there, in rich black soil". The parish map of this area shows a property of 20 acres on the point held by Francis Mitchell in 1840, with the name "Great Turriell" or "Lilli Pilly Point". On the same map the large adjoining grant is marked as belonging to Thomas Holt, some of that land being marked as "Lilli Pilli" in the village of Port Hacking. Francis Mitchell gradually disappears from the history of this area, and who he was or where he went is not recorded.

A public school did not open in the suburb until 1957. Today the

Lilli Pilli Point on the Port Hacking River, c. 1930

suburb is a pleasant residential area, taking its name from the early name of Lilly Pilly. The lilly pilly tree was possibly a fairly common species on the foreshores of harbours and inlets. The tree is beautiful when in bloom, and attractive when covered with berries, which provided a food for Aborigines and early settlers.

## LILYFIELD

*Municipality of Leichhardt*
Location: 6 kilometres west of Sydney between Parramatta Road and Iron Cove

The first official use of the name of this small inner western suburb between Leichhardt and Rozelle was in the 1893 Sands Directory, when Lilyfield Post Office was entered at "53 Lamb Street, Leichhardt". Robert Ralph, a draper, was the postmaster. A document relating to a sale of land in 1896 gives the name of a

"Robert Millett of Lilyfield, Leichhardt", further evidence that before the end of the century Lilyfield was a recognised area of Leichhardt.

The name may have been in use before this, but its meaning and origin are obscure. There are several versions of how the suburb was named, the most likely being that lilies — perhaps a self-sown wild variety — grew in a field in the area. Another suggestion is that the area was owned by a Mr Lily, but neither theory can be proved.

## LINDFIELD

*Municipality of Ku-ring-gai*
Location: 13 kilometres north-west of Sydney on the Pacific Highway and the North Shore Line

This North Shore suburb was named by a Mr List, who was born in Lindfield, a suburb of Hayward's Heath, in England. He owned a property named Lindfield, which means "lime-tree field", near the present railway station. When the North Shore railway line came through the area and a station was built in 1890, his property provided the name for this new station.

In the 1920s Lindfield was described as "a rising suburb 322 feet above sea level. There are numerous fine dwellings, and the business thoroughfare, which faces the railway station, contains modern and well-stocked shops of all descriptions." Many of the large Federation-style houses of this period still remain.

The first school in this suburb opened in April 1903, and the official Lindfield post office began operating on 5 January 1895.

Isaac Nichols (1770–1819), an ex-convict who became a superintendent of convicts and later the first postmaster in the colony (see Chatswood), had property extending north into East Lindfield. This was near Mr Archbold's grant, which is remembered by Archbold Road, between Tryon Road and Boundary Street.

Some of the streets in East Lindfield are named after Australia's state capitals: Brisbane, Adelaide, Perth and Hobart Avenues are happily bounded by Sydney Road at one end and, all rivalries forgotten, Melbourne Road at the other. Canberra is also represented with a nearby crescent bearing its name. East Lindfield is a small residential suburb tucked between Lindfield's Soldiers Memorial Park, surrounding Gordon Creek, and Roseville Chase on the shores of Middle Harbour.

West of the Pacific Highway, the National Measurements Laboratory and Ku-ring-gai College of Advanced Education occupy sites overlooking natural bushland along the Lane Cove River.

## LITTLE BAY
*Municipality of Randwick*
Location: 14 kilometres south of Sydney east of Bunnerong Road facing the Pacific Ocean

This neighbourhood, situated between Cape Banks and Malabar, came into being during Sydney's smallpox epidemic of 1881–82. A makeshift camp was established on the beach here to isolate sufferers from the disease. After 1885, further outbreaks of smallpox and a typhoid epidemic convinced the government that a permanent hospital to treat infectious diseases was needed. The Little Bay site was a perfect choice, as it was close to Sydney, but isolated from the settlement. The hospital proved its value during the outbreak of bubonic plague in Sydney in 1900, and again in 1919, when soldiers returning from Europe brought an influenza virus that attacked between 20 and 50 per cent of Sydney's population. In those days, before the development of drugs we take for granted today, little could be done to prevent the spread of the virus or help its

victims. The Coast Hospital continued to admit patients until the epidemic had exhausted itself by 1920.

The Coast Hospital, which became Prince Henry Hospital in 1934, and later part of the Prince of Wales Hospital group still serves the community, but today as a general hospital as well as being used for the treatment of infectious diseases.

## LIVERPOOL
*City of Liverpool*
Location: 32 kilometres south-west of Sydney on the Hume Highway and the Main Southern Line

This interesting old city was the first of the early towns founded by Governor Lachlan Macquarie (1810–21). Macquarie, very impressed by the area, was determined to erect a town there, and on 7 November 1810, accompanied by Captain Antill,

St Luke's Church, Liverpool, is the oldest Anglican church still in use in Australia. The first service was held in 1819

Moore Theological College, Liverpool, c. 1880. The chapel at the front of the building was dismantled and re-erected in Newtown in 1891 but the rest of the building, including Thomas Moore's house (on the far right), was demolished in the 1920s

James Meehan, Mr Moore and Dr Redfern, he set out to view and survey the land where the new township was to be built. The group travelled by boat along the Georges River, and about mid-afternoon arrived at a site that pleased the governor. He named it Liverpool, in honour of Robert Jenkinson, the Earl of Liverpool, at that time secretary of state for the colonies and later prime minister of England. By 1814 the population of the area was 832 and by 1819 the town had about thirty houses.

The early history of this city is very evident in some of the older streets with their brick and stone buildings. One of its most historic and pleasing buildings is St Luke's Church of England in Elizabeth Drive. Australia's great architect Francis Greenway (1777–1837) designed this church, the foundation stone of which was laid

by Governor Macquarie on 7 April 1818.

Another building of historic interest is Liverpool Technical College. It is thought that it was designed by Francis Greenway as a convict hospital. An earlier hospital had been condemned by Commissioner Bigge when he came to the colony to evaluate the work being carried out by Macquarie. The date on the technical college building is 1825, but it was not completed until 1830. Architect Morton Herman once described it as one of the finest colonial buildings remaining from that period.

From 1851 to 1862, it was held by the Benevolent Society, which had already established a considerable capacity for caring for the destitute and the unfortunate. Later the government resumed responsibility for the building and its inmates, using it as a hospital for the destitute and infirm until 1958, when the Liverpool District Hospital was erected nearby. In 1960 the building became the Liverpool Technical College, officially opening on 10 July 1961.

Moore Theological College was established at Liverpool, in 1856, with a legacy from Thomas Moore (1762–1840), boatbuilder, farmer and philanthropist, for training youths "of the Protestant persuasion". When the college, which had been moved to near the University of Sydney in 1891, held its centenary celebrations in 1956, historians discovered that the Church of St Luke had never been consecrated, so steps were taken at the celebrations to unveil a tablet in the church to record its (late) consecration. Moore had worshipped in St Luke's and helped raise money to complete it, as it still lacked pews and a gallery by 1823.

In its early years Liverpool was a dairy-farming area. There were also a woolwash, a slaughtering and boiling-down works (owned by Mr Atkinson) and by 1866, a paper mill had been established by the Australian Paper Company, which employed many local residents. When the railway line reached Liverpool in 1856, there was an influx of residents. The public school was established in

1863, and in 1872 the municipality of Liverpool was formed.

This city, proclaimed on 9 November 1960, is now a flourishing commercial centre that has grown tremendously since the Second World War, particularly with the housing developments of the 1960s and 1970s (see Green Valley). Parts of it retain the quiet dignity of that earlier age, however, and street names are reminders of colonial days. One of these is Bigge Street, which recalls Commissioner J. T. Bigge (1780–1843).

## LOFTUS

*Shire of Sutherland*

Location: 29 kilometres south of Sydney on the Princes Highway and the Illawarra Line

A small residential suburb on Sydney's southern outskirts, Loftus was named after a former governor of New South Wales, Lord Augustus William Spencer Loftus. Born near Bristol, England, in 1817, Lord Loftus served in Russia during the Crimean War. He was governor from 1878 to 1885, after which he returned to England, to write his memoirs, and died there in 1904.

The Illawarra railway line from Sydney reached Sutherland in 1885. The next station to the south, Loftus Junction, was opened on 9 March 1886. Ten years later the name was changed to Loftus, and in 1979 the station moved to its present site.

A rural area for many years, residential development began late. A public school opened in January 1953, and an official post office in July of the same year, but the latter was closed in 1980. Many streets in the suburb are named after plants,

Lord Augustus Loftus

such as Mistletoe, Viburnum, Gorse, Broom, Cranberry and Cassia.

Loftus is protected from large-scale residential development, and its peaceful bushland atmosphere assured for all time, by the Royal National Park on its eastern boundary, and the Woronora Cemetery and Prince Edward Park to the north. Loftus Creek, which flows north to join Forbes Creek and the Woronora River, forms the western boundary. Loftus Ridge, which divides the waters of Engadine Creek and Platypus Gully in the Royal National Park, extends south-east from the Princes Highway to a point overlooking the junction of Platypus Gully and Kangaroo Creek.

The Sydney Tramway Museum in the Royal National Park close to Princes Highway is well worth a visit. Run by volunteers, this is an operating museum that offers visitors rides on restored electric tramcars that once ran along Sydney streets.

## LONGUEVILLE

*Municipality of Lane Cove*

Location: 8 kilometres north-west of Sydney on the Lane Cove River

The land on which this residential suburb is sited was originally an estate of 120 acres owned by Robert Kirk. It lies between Tambourine Bay and Woodford Bay on the Lane Cove River, and its near neighbour is Northwood. The origin of its name is somewhat hazy, although it is thought to be called after a French nobleman, the Duc de Longueville.

In 1884, when there were still only two houses on the point, owned by Joseph Palmer and Henry Lamb, a well-known land speculator, Richard Hayes Harnett, acquired some of the land and subdivided it into home-sites. By 1923 a street directory described Longueville as "being fast built upon, the dwellings being of a superior class and attractive design". The directory further predicted that the suburb's future would be as one of the most popular residential areas and a large business centre. Today Longueville may truthfully claim to be still a picturesque suburb.

Three pleasant reserves are found in Longueville. Longueville Park is situated in Stuart Street, on the shores of the Lane Cove River; Aquatic Park is near the Longueville Wharf on Yacht Bay; and Kingsford Smith Oval recalls the famous Australian airman who helped create early distance flying records.

Longueville Wharf is located on the Lane Cove River opposite Woolwich. A peak-hour ferry service brings residents into the city to work, and home again.

# LUCAS HEIGHTS

*Shire of Sutherland*
Location: 31 kilometres south of Sydney west of the Woronora River

This neighbourhood, situated on the Woronora River, which flows north into the Georges River, owes its name to John Lucas, who received a grant of 150 acres here in 1825. A miller by trade, Lucas built a water-driven machine to grind grain grown by the farmers in the district. The location suited his purpose admirably, as small boats could come up the river to collect the bags of milled grain, and return via Georges River to Botany Bay. The mill was destroyed by fire in the 1830s.

Lucas Heights is notable today for its nuclear reactor, used mainly for medical research. The nuclear reactor and display centre are under the care of the Atomic Energy Commission, and visits by tourist parties are encouraged.

# LUGARNO

*Municipality of Hurstville*
Location: 23 kilometres south-west of Sydney on the northern bank of the Georges River

This suburb on the peninsula between Salt Pan Creek and Lime Kiln Bay still has an air of spaciousness about it. It was named after the beautiful Swiss lake, Lugano, which lies between the lakes Maggiore and Como, on the Italian frontier. The surveyors of the first coastal road to the Illawarra district, Major Sir Thomas Mitchell and his assistant William Govett, named the area in 1843, obviously reminded of the Swiss lake by the water views from this point. No explanation is available for the added "r" in its name.

The earliest land grant in the area was of 120 acres, given to Thomas Lawrence in 1831, on the western side of the peninsula near the junction of Salt Pan Creek and the Georges River. The area to the east and north was granted in 1856 to T. G. Lee (113 acres), J. P. Henning (40 acres), John Lushy (41 acres) and Frewin Sleath (45 acres). The whole area as far as Arncliffe was heavily timbered then, and timber-getters were active.

Old Illawarra Road, built by

Looking from the north to Lugarno Ferry, 1948

convicts in 1841, ran through Gannon's Forest, and down to the punt across the Georges River. Today this is called Forest Road and has its beginning in Arncliffe. From 1843 a punt transported people from Lugarno across the river, but the service was discontinued when Alfords Bridge was built just west of Lugarno and opened in 1974.

In the late 1960s large blocks of land were released by the crown for sale as home-sites. The suburb has moved swiftly ahead since that time, to become popular and modern. Lugarno infants school is in Lugarno Parade and the primary school is in Old Forest Road.

Promotional poster for a forthcoming land auction at Lugarno, 1913

## LURNEA
*City of Liverpool*
Location: 33 kilometres south-west of Sydney west of the Hume Highway

This suburb, south of Liverpool, was once known as Hillview. It became Lurnea, meaning "a resting place", when veterans from the First World War were settled on land there to start poultry farms and orchards. This was the first of the great rehousing schemes around Liverpool, and its suburbs have since made that city one of the busiest and most rapidly expanding areas outside the city of Sydney. That first soldier housing scheme at Lurnea provided the nucleus of a working-class suburb, and by the 1960s the Housing Commission was providing homes for soldiers who were veterans of more recent campaigns, as well as many other people. In the 1970s the European immigrants were making a new life here or in the neighbouring Green Valley housing scheme.

Although somewhat isolated from Sydney, the suburbs of Liverpool have developed a self-sufficiency and a dependence on the development of that city, which now provides shopping and leisure facilities for the region. Local employment remains a problem for the large population of the district and nearby industry and increased transport facilities will be needed to overcome the problems for those who have to travel into Sydney for work.

Everyday life in Lurnea is family based, with an accent on children and young adults. Young Lurneans are catered for with a public school on the corner of West and Reilly Streets and a high school in Hillview Parade — a street name that recalls that first district title. Other street names in that area recall the ships that brought the first colonists, such as Supply and Lady Penryn, and early governors, Bligh, Darling and Brisbane.

## MACDONALDTOWN
*City of Sydney*
Location: 4 kilometres south-west of Sydney on the Main Suburban Line

This suburb, first incorporated as a local government area in 1872, was originally part of a grant made to a Irishman, Nicholas Devine. It is only a short walk from Newtown, which first appeared on the map of Sydney as Devine's Farm.

Devine built his homestead near the corner of the present Erskineville Road and George Street, Macdonaldtown, and the farm became quite a landmark as the area opened up. Wealthy families began to build in the suburb, considering it to be "near-country". At that time Macdonaldtown covered a large area that included today's Erskineville.

A Mr Macdonald, who had a large ironmongery store at the corner of George and Market Streets in Sydney, was a major property owner in the area, living in a house near the present Macdonaldtown station. He must have had considerable standing, for when the railway went through to Parramatta in 1855, the station was named Macdonaldtown. In 1893 Erskineville became a separate suburb, and Macdonaldtown became smaller and more industrial.

Macdonaldtown is now a busy inner-city suburb surrounded by industry. It still has many examples of terrace houses and small corner shops, many colourfully renovated, which tell an architectural story of the suburb's early days.

## MCMAHONS POINT
*Municipality of North Sydney*
Location: 5 kilometres north of Sydney on Port Jackson

The first resident of this quaint and almost continental style suburb west of Lavender Bay gave it his name. He was Maurice McMahon, a brush and comb manufacturer who settled in the area in 1864. At that time it was referred to as Mr McMahon's Point, but gradually constant use dropped the formal Mister and it became officially known as McMahons Point. This gentleman was obviously someone of importance as he was a member of North Sydney Council and an early mayor.

By the 1920s McMahons Point ranked as an important tram terminus for the Crows Nest (via Lane Cove Road), Chatswood, Willoughby, Gore Hill and Lane Cove trams, which all began their journeys from McMahons Point. Trams were timed to meet the ferries running direct from Circular Quay. Residents could travel to Circular Quay for the sum of twopence, but the fare on the all-night ferries was sixpence. These days McMahons Point retains its popularity with many flat and unit dwellers, even if the fares have gone up!

The ferry depot in the small bay between McMahons Point and Blues Point, c. 1930. The McMahons Point tramline can be seen at the extreme left of the picture

# MACQUARIE FIELDS
*City of Campbelltown*
Location: 41 kilometres
south-west of Sydney between the
Hume Highway and the Georges
River, on the Main Southern Line

This suburb between Glenfield and
Ingleburn was named after
Macquarie Fields House, built by
James Meehan (1774–1826) on his
1810 grant of 1,400 acres at
Ingleburn. Macquarie Fields House
was named in honour of his
benefactor, although Governor
Macquarie referred to it as
Meehan's Castle. In 1812 Meehan,
an emancipated Irish convict, was
appointed deputy-surveyor of
lands, and later superintendent of
roads and bridges. He remained a
valued settler, and·when his health
declined, he was given a pension.
He retired to live at Macquarie
Fields House, where he died on 21
April 1826. Meehan is
remembered by James Meehan
High School and the adjacent
James Meehan Park in Harold
Street.

A new Macquarie Fields House,
which is still standing, was ordered
in the 1840s by the second owner
of the property, Samuel Terry
(1776?–1838), a wealthy
emancipist merchant. The estate
was given to his daughter Martha,
who married John Hosking, later
first mayor of Sydney, in 1829.
The house has been restored and is
on the National Trust Register.

In 1869 the Reverend George
Fairfowl Macarthur (1825–90), a
former rector of St Marks, Darling
Point, was invited to be
headmaster at The King's School,
Parramatta. He had been
conducting a school at Macquarie
Fields House since 1858, where
he established a cadet corps, which
formed the basis of The King's
School cadets.

Macquarie Fields House, now restored and
privately owned, narrowly escaped
demolition in 1958 after being used for over
a decade by the Department of Agriculture
for fodder storage

Ingleburn military camp is
adjacent to Macquarie Fields, and
Glenfield's Hurlstone Agricultural
Research Station and Glenfield
Veterinary Research Station are
near neighbours.

This residential suburb is now
more easily accessible because of
frequent electric train services, so
that young people and their
families are able to work in Sydney
and travel home in the evening to
this pleasant suburb with the
historical background.

# MALABAR
*Municipality of Randwick*
Location: 12 kilometres south-east
of Sydney facing the Pacific Ocean

This coastal suburb, south of
Maroubra and north of the
entrance to Botany Bay, was
named after a place near Bombay,
India, where at one time Governor
Macquarie's 73rd Regiment was
stationed. In 1855, before its
renaming, it had been known as

Long Bay, the name of the narrow
bay between the Anzac Rifle Range
and the Randwick Golf Links.

The area was originally part of
the Church and School Lands, set
aside to support clergy and
teachers in the early days of the
colony, but it later reverted to the
Crown. At the end of last century
there was a small fishing village
here and at the beginning of this
century it became a popular picnic
and weekend resort for
city-dwellers. Today, however,
pollution has made the beach
unusable. During the Depression
the suburb, like its neighbour La
Perouse, had an unemployment
camp of huts made of scrap
materials.

Long Bay Penitentiary is in this
district. The first gaol here opened
in 1909 as the State Reformatory
for Women. In 1914 the State
Penitentiary was opened alongside
the earlier institution, its 2 metre
walls erected entirely by prison
labour. In the late 1950s the old
reformatory became part of the
male prison, and the new women's
prison built at Long Bay was
vacated in 1969 when the Mulawa
Training and Detention Centre
was opened.

Anzac Rifle Range, originally

called Long Bay Rifle Range, occupies most of the headland between Maroubra Bay and Long Bay. In 1968 it closed, and rifle shooting practice was transferred to Holsworthy near Liverpool. However, in March 1970, it was reopened and renamed in honour of the First World War soldiers.

By a strange coincidence a ship named *Malabar* came to grief in the area on 2 April 1931. At about 6.40 am in thick fog, the *Malabar*, a Burns Philp motor vessel, drifted towards the rocks off shore and became stranded. A fishing fleet operating from Long Bay brought the stricken ship's passengers and crew to safety, but nothing could be done to save the *Malabar* which was a total loss.

Copy of a postcard, c. 1900, showing Steyne Reserve at Ocean Beach, Manly

# MANLY
*Municipality of Manly*
Location: 14 kilometres north-east of Sydney bordered by Port Jackson and the Pacific Ocean

The name of this suburb just north of North Head, extending between North Harbour and the ocean, was descriptive of the people rather than the place. Governor Arthur Phillip, visiting the area for the first time in January 1788, was impressed with the noble and manly bearing of the male Aborigines, and called the place Manly Cove. On a later visit, Phillip was speared by a native, named Willomering, whilst speaking with Bennelong, Phillip's protegé. Phillip refused to punish the offender, no doubt considering the reason for the attack to be fear of the white men. Bennelong, however, gave his fellow tribesman a severe hiding.

One of the earliest settlers in the

area was John Whaley, who received permission to buy 20 acres near Manly Lagoon in 1836—37. Two of the earliest grants were made on 1 January 1810, by the illegal Rum Rebellion government, to Richard Chears (100 acres) and Gilbert Baker, who received 30 acres between the ocean and harbour beaches, north of Chears's grant. D'Arcy Wentworth (1762?—1827) later bought the properties and also received another grant of 380 acres, all of which were inherited by his daughter, Katherine, in 1827. There was some doubt as to the titles, but an Act of Parliament of 1877 empowered the trustees to sell. All the land, much of it still in its virgin state, was subdivided and auctioned in 1877—79.

In 1841 the population of the area was sixty-one, and there were only ten houses; in the 1850s and early 1860s Manly was still bushland. The birdlife was varied

and beautiful: gillbirds, rosellas, and whipbirds called where there are now streets full of houses. The Corso was a sandy track, fringed by bottlebrush trees and wildflowers, and today's Manly Pier was a wide sandy beach.

John Thompson, the deputy surveyor-general, had received a grant of 100 acres at Manly in 1842, which he sold to Henry Gilbert Smith in 1853 for £1,000. In 1854 Smith built a home which he called Fairlight. Fairlight, a small suburb on the heights west of Manly, remembers Smith's house. In 1854 Smith started a ferry service to Sydney. He built a pier and hotels and cleared a street, which he named The Corso after a street he remembered in Rome. Smith bought up a great deal of property, which from 1855 he subdivided to create the town of Manly. He also laid the foundation stone of the first Church of England church, St Matthew's, and gave land for other public buildings and parks.

The Norfolk Island pines, some of which still stand in regal magnificence along the ocean front, are said to have been planted by Henry Gilbert Smith, who also planted trees on the harbour foreshores and established the idea of planting trees in Manly's streets. The pines on the oceanfront, however, may have been the idea of Tom Rowe, who, as Manly's first mayor in 1877 established a tree planting beautification scheme.

Transport by land in and out of Manly was a problem from its earliest days and in 1891 a move was made to establish a reliable tram service running between Manly Wharf and Ocean Beach. The Manly to Pittwater Tramway League was established and was influential in establishing a tram service from Manly to as far as

Black and white copy of a coloured glass negative slide advertising a forthcoming swimming carnival

Narrabeen. Trams met the needs of travellers to Manly and surrounding districts until replaced by buses in 1939.

In the 1830s the New South Wales government passed Acts forbidding bathing in a public place between 6 am and 8 pm, and bathing boxes on wheels were used at several beaches, including Manly's Ocean Beach in the 1860s (see Coogee). In 1902 William Gocher, editor of the *Manly and North Sydney News*, the forerunner of the *Manly Daily*, decided to challenge the laws. He swam unmolested twice, but on the third occasion he was arrested. On 2 November 1903 Manly Council rescinded the by-law prohibiting swimming after 7 am. In 1980 the historic spot of Gocher's swim was marked by a plaque. It is said that in 1907 Gocher received a gold watch and a purse containing fifty sovereigns, so obviously the residents applauded his "manly" action, and have been swimming ever since!

In 1907 the Manly Sea Bathers Club was formed, forerunner of the Manly Surf Life Saving Association.

One of Manly's landmarks today is St Patrick's College, where students are trained for the Catholic priesthood. The land on which the college stands, granted to Archbishop Polding to establish an episcopal residence, was unused until 1884 when construction of the college began. The college adjoins North Head Military Reserve and alongside it on the harbour side, is the site of the former quarantine station established there in about 1836. Manly District Hospital is also on North Head, in the southern part of the suburb. In the north, fronting Manly Lagoon, is Manly Golf Course. On the harbour side are also Manly Amusement Pier and Marineland, and in Esplanade Park stands Manly Art Gallery.

# MANLY VALE
*Shire of Warringah*
Location: 14 kilometres north of
Sydney on Condamine Street

This small suburb between
Balgowlah and North Manly is
tucked between reserves on Curl
Curl Creek and two golf courses
fronting Manly Lagoon. Two of
the reserves, separated by Sloane
Crescent, are David Thomas
Reserve and Millers Reserve.
Condamine Street, dropping
sharply from its junction with
Sydney Road at Balgowlah, lies in
a small valley or vale, which
accounts for the suburb's name.

The area is closely allied to the
life of its near neighbours, and the
houses reflect suburban family life
in house style and gardens. Young
members of the family are catered
for by a public school in Sunshine
Street, opened in 1955, and
Mackellar Girls High School stands
in Campbell Parade. Manly and
The Mall at Brookvale provide the
nearest main shopping centres.

# MARAYONG
*City of Blacktown*
Location: 38 kilometres
north-west of Sydney just north of
Blacktown, on the Richmond Line

This suburb immediately north of
Blacktown was named when the
railway station was opened in
1922. Marayong is an Aboriginal
word for emu or "place of the
cranes"; it is thought that there
were large numbers of these birds
here before land was cleared for
building. Like many other suburbs
in the Blacktown area, Marayong
was a planned housing
development catering for low-
income families. Some streets here
bear the names of islands such as

Timor, Madagascar and Falkland.
Two neighbourhoods in this
suburb are Marayong Heights and
Marayong South, each of which
has its own public school.
Marayong Public School is in
Davis Road.

# MAROUBRA
*Municipality of Randwick*
Location: 10 kilometres south-east
of Sydney facing the Pacific Ocean

The name Maroubra — an
Aboriginal word for "like
thunder" — aptly describes the
sound of heavy surf pounding
against the beach and nearby rocks.
But as a suburb it had a quiet
beginning. In fact Maroubra, south
of Coogee, was not even recorded
on the 1892 map that showed the
great progress Sydney had made in
the hundred years since settlement.
At that time very few visitors went
there, and the small group of
inhabitants were mostly employees
of the wool scouring works at the
northern end of the bay,
established in the 1870s.

However, 6 May 1898 brought
the area right into the news. For
two days the coast of New South
Wales had been lashed by a violent
gale, remembered as the Maitland
gale, because the steamship *Maitland*
was wrecked near Broken Bay
with heavy loss of life. The
*Hereward*, a full-rigged iron ship of
1,893 tons, was heading north
towards Newcastle when the
storm caught it and drove it ashore
at the northern end of Maroubra
beach. It remained there for some
time, attracting sightseers from
Sydney and putting Maroubra on
the map. Later a coffer dam was
built around the *Hereward*, and an
attempt made to refloat it. But the
vessel broke loose from the tow
rope and was wrecked on the
rocky shoreline. The wreck is
recalled by Hereward Street,
Maroubra.

The area was originally part of
the Church and School Lands, set
aside in the early days of the
colony to support clergy and
teachers. The land later reverted to
the Crown and Maroubra remained
an isolated area, visited only at

Cooper Street, Maroubra, 1925

weekends or by those who walked there from Randwick or Coogee, which was as far as the trams went. A house built here in 1861 by Humphrey McKeon remained in isolation until residential development began in the second decade of this century, when Herbert Dudley, a real estate developer, subdivided land in what had been seen as a resort area. In the 1920s, releases of crown land spurred on development, which was made easier once trams ran to the beach from 1921. Dudley was also responsible for bringing the first tramway to Maroubra Junction in 1912, where he had built Dudley's Emporium, incorporating Dudley's Theatre, in Anzac Parade.

The beach is one of Maroubra's greatest attractions; its horse-shoe shape protects it and makes swimming safe. The Anzac Rifle Range is on the southern headland, and Arthur Byrne Reserve stands alongside it at the southern end of the beach.

Maroubra Junction, until 1961 a tramway junction on the La Perouse line where trams turned off to the beach, is the commercial area, where shopping facilities are modern and well patronised by a large residential community. Even in the 1920s the junction was described as having "numerous modern business establishments which supply every requirement". In recent years South Maroubra has been an area of considerable medium-density residential development.

At one time Maroubra had a speedway, opened in 1925, but the concrete track was steeply graded and there were several fatal accidents. It closed in 1934 after a time as a motor cycle track. The land, at the corner of Fitzgerald Avenue and Anzac Parade, was resumed by the Housing Commission in 1947 and developed as a residential area.

Coral Sea Park, near the beach, is a memorial to the sea battle fought during the Second World War. It took place in the Coral Sea north of Australia in May 1942, when Australian and American ships and aircraft turned back a determined assault by the Japanese. The park is a constant reminder of the bravery of Australian seamen involved in the fierce fight.

The area has a number of schools: Maroubra Bay Primary School and Maroubra Junction Public School, and Maroubra Bay, Maroubra Junction and South Sydney High Schools.

## MARRICKVILLE
*Municipality of Marrickville*
Location: 8 kilometres south-west of Sydney between Sydenham and Dulwich Hill on the Bankstown Line

Once part of the parish of Petersham, the area on which Marrickville now stands was included in some of the early grants in the colony. The first was the 100 acres given to William Beckwith in 1794. In 1799 Governor Hunter made a second grant, this time of 470 acres to Thomas Moore, who four years later received another 700 acres from Governor King. These three grants covered most of present-day Marrickville, which is bordered in the south by Cooks River.

Dr Robert Wardell (1793–1834), who was murdered by escaped convicts at Petersham in September 1834, purchased most of this land from the grantees or their heirs and included it in his estate (see Petersham), which was broken up after his death. Wardell Road is named after him.

Another man who had a big influence on Marrickville was Thomas Chalder. He acquired a 60 acre subdivision of land, which he advertised for auction in 1855. He called it Marrick, after his native village in Yorkshire; this (with the addition of the "ville" suggested by another resident, William Dean) was adopted for the municipality when it was gazetted in 1861.

A landmark in the district for many years was the castellated mansion overlooking the Cooks River known as The Warren, built by Thomas Holt (1811–88), a Sydney business tycoon who made a fortune from wool (see

During the First World War the Warren was converted into an artillery training centre. It was demolished in 1922

Sutherland). Holt gave his home this name because he bred rabbits there for hunting. All that now remains to remind us that the house once existed is Warren Park on the Cooks River and Warren Road, Marrickville. His estate of about 100 acres south of Wardell's property covered the area bounded today by Unwin's Bridge, Illawarra and Warren Roads.

Until 1860 the area was covered in scrub and timber, but the 1866 *New South Wales Gazetteer* recorded that industries had been established in the suburb: two soap and candle factories, three brickyards and a tannery. Much of the district, however, was laid out in market gardens, taking advantage of the fine alluvial soil.

The estate of The Warren was subdivided in 1886, and the buyer began to erect a home on part of the property. Completed in 1887, it was known as Ferncourt. The house was noted for its beautiful stained-glass windows, which featured a pattern of birds, and the fanlight over the front door, which showed a scene with the first wooden bridge built over the Cooks River by Frederick Unwin in 1836 (see Tempe). The original bridge was replaced by a more substantial structure in 1889. When the original owners left, an order of French Carmelite nuns moved into the Warren in 1886, and Ferncourt became a primary school. After the First World War Ferncourt was demolished and the grounds were subdivided.

When the railway line to Bankstown came through this district in 1895, the construction name for the station was Illawarra Road. Later it was renamed Marrickville.

The first school opened in August 1864, and the post office a year later in January 1865.

# MARSFIELD

*Municipality of Ryde*
Location: 16 kilometres north-west of Sydney between Epping Road and Blaxland Road

Although not historically recorded as such, it is believed that Marsfield is a corruption of the name Field of Mars, which was applied at various times to areas from Ermington to Epping. The present Marsfield, which adjoins Macquarie University in North Ryde, stands on what was Field of Mars Common, established in 1804 for the use of settlers in the Field of Mars and Kissing Point areas. In 1848 the Common covered 6,235 acres. In the 1880s the land was cleared and the first land sale was held in 1885.

In the 1890s Harry Curzon Smith built Curzon Hall on land between Balaclava and Sabraon Roads, and now facing Agincourt Road. The house was bought in 1922 by the Vincentian Brothers and St Joseph's Seminary was established there. Today the house has been restored and is used as a restaurant and a centre for conferences and social occasions.

Another early settler in the area was Robert Christie, who bought 22 acres from Smith and ran an orchard and poultry farm there.

As Mars was the ancient Roman god of war, it is fitting that many streets in Marsfield have names associated with battles, such as Balaclava, Agincourt, Culloden, Waterloo, Crimea and Corunna. Sobraon Road is a reminder of the training ship, anchored in Sydney Harbour near Snapper Island, on which young lads were put through the naval ropes.

Curzon Hall, Marsfield, as it looks today

# MASCOT

*Municipality of Botany*
Location: 7 kilometres south of
Sydney on the northern side of
Botany Bay

A racecourse, operated as the main
venue for unregistered racing and
known as Ascot, after its famous
counterpart in England, was
established in 1904 on land
formerly held by the Australian
Golf Club. The area at that time
was known as North Botany, but
residents wanted a new name and
an individual identity. In 1911 a
referendum was held to choose
between Mascot, Boronia and
Booralee, and the suburb's name
was decided.

The first land grants in the area
were made in 1835 and subdivision
followed the construction of
Botany Road in 1875. The main
land-use in the early days was
market gardening. A municipality
was formed here in 1888 as North
Botany.

Houses with neat gardens began
to appear in the suburb, which at
first promised to be totally
residential, but there were several
Chinese market gardens. In 1920,
however, a suitable site was being
sought for a large, public airfield,
and Mascot proved to be suitable.
The need was recognised when
two pilots from South Australia
won a competition for the first
flight from England to Australia in
thirty days. Ross and Keith Smith,
flew the route in a twin-engined
Vickers Vimy, a machine used in
the bombing of Berlin in the First
World War, making the journey in
twenty-eight days. In 1920 Nigel
Love leased 400 acres from the
Kensington Race Club for use as
an airport and in 1921 the
Commonwealth government
purchased 161 acres for the same
purpose. Cooks River, which

flowed through the area, was
diverted in 1947–52 to give extra
land, and today as a result of good
planning and hard work, Mascot
has an airport of world standard.

As the airport has grown, more
houses have given way to its
progress. Millions of dollars have
been spent to expand and add to
the original airport, and one of the
runways has been extended to
Botany Bay. The first regular
flights began in 1924, and by 1938
there were 120 flights a week, then
handled by a staff of eleven. Today
planes arrive and depart constantly
on domestic and international
flights. The airport is known as
Kingsford Smith Airport, in
honour of aviator Sir Charles
Kingsford Smith (1897–1935) —
"Smithy" to all Australians —
who, with Charles Ulm, made a
record flight around Australia in
just over ten days. His 1933 flight
from Sydney to London was
another record.

It is natural that a suburb so
involved with flying should have
several streets close to the airport
named after people connected with
flying and planes. Keith Smith,
Ross Smith and Shiers (the
mechanic who flew with the Smith
brothers on their epic flight)
Avenues, recall the "magnificent
men" and streets named Lancaster,
Catalina, Constellation, Boeing
and Vickers, the "flying
machines". Qantas Drive is named
after Australia's international
airline, originally the Queensland
and Northern Territory Aerial
Service, founded in 1920.

Today Mascot and its industries
and services revolve around the
airport. It is hard to imagine
conditions in the early stages of its
development when stock from
nearby paddocks strayed across the
runway, and the public bought
tickets for aerial joy rides from a
wooden ticket box.

The J. J. Cahill Memorial High
School in Mascot, opened in 1961,
was the Botany municipality's first
high school. Ten acres had been
resumed for a high school in
Sutherland Street in 1951 and local
parents lobbied hard from 1957 for
the school to be built.
Construction began in 1959 and
the first pupils were admitted in
1960. The high school, named after
John Joseph Cahill, a premier of
New South Wales (1952–59), was
the third high school in the
metropolitan area to have its own
swimming pool, built in 1968 with
funds raised by the Parents and
Citizens Association.

# MATRAVILLE

*Municipality of Randwick*
Location: 11 kilometres south-east
of Sydney between Maroubra and
Malabar

This suburb, a near neighbour of
Maroubra, owes its name to a
school established in the area in
1904, thanks to the efforts of J. R.
Dacey, the state member for
Botany at that time, after whom
nearby Daceyville is named.

The school's historical
significance in honouring James
Mario Matra is also interesting.
Matra sailed as a midshipman in
the *Endeavour* on Captain James
Cook's epic voyage to Botany
Bay. Matra was obviously a man
of intellect, as he became British
consul at Tenerife in 1772, and
served Britain at the embassy in
Turkey in 1778. An appointment
as British consul at Tangiers
followed. Matra was born in New
York but later settled in England.
In his journal, Captain Cook wrote
Matra's name as Magra, a spelling
Matra himself used in the early
years of his life, although later he
signed himself Matra. Many

Seventeen schools took part in the operation to build cottages at Matraville for returning First World War soldiers. This photo of one band of builders in front of their handiwork was taken in 1920

migrant McGraths, who settled in America, spelled their surnames as Magra, but there is no record of James Matra being originally a McGrath. He was a close friend of Sir Joseph Banks, and he proposed in 1783 that the British government establish a colony at Botany Bay, which he envisaged as a place where American Loyalists could settle. Banks had also been captivated by the bay, and these two favourable opinions were very convincing, but Prime Minister William Pitt's government decided to make it a penal colony, since England's prisons were over-crowded.

The tiny settlement on the sandy dunes where the new school had been built had the uninspiring name of Cross Roads. The ingenious Mr Dacey wrote to the Department of Education, suggesting the name Matra would be more appropriate, as Matra had walked over the area with Cook

and Banks in 1770. The request was granted, and the school and the suburb became known as Matraville.

Originally the area, like neighbouring suburbs, was part of the Church and School Lands set aside in the early days of the colony to support clergy and teachers, but it later reverted to the Crown. The crown land was subdivided in 1917 after the state government passed legislation to make cheap land available for soldiers returning from the First World War. A Voluntary Workers Association was formed to build homes in this suburb for the soldiers and their families, or their widows. Skilled stonemasons, carpenters and bricklayers gave weekends to the project, and many unskilled men and women worked side-by-side with them. Some materials were found locally, such as sandstone quarried from the end of Beauchamp Road, near Bunnerong Road. Other materials were brought by tram along Anzac Parade.

By February 1919, the first cottage was finished, and it was

occupied by Charles Gross. This new residential area was known as Matraville Soldiers Garden Village, or more popularly simply as The Settlement. More recently legislation was passed to allow redevelopment of the estate and in 1977 demolition began, despite the protests of the residents, who take pride in the history of their neighbourhood.

Residential development has extended the occupied area of Matraville, which has a small shopping centre and some industry, although the area's market gardens lasted until recent years. The suburb has two primary schools, Matraville Soldier Settlement Public School in Menin Road and Matraville Public School in Bunnerong Road; Matraville High School is in Anzac Parade. Heffron Park, named after R. J. Heffron, premier of New South Wales from 1959 to 1964 and formerly the state member for the area, is a large reserve extending to the borders of neighbouring Maroubra. It occupies the site of a Second World War naval stores area and a later hostel, which housed some of the immigrants who came to Australia in the decades after the war.

## MAYS HILL
*Municipality of Holroyd, City of Parramatta*
Location: A locality 25 kilometres west of Sydney on the Great Western Highway

A neighbourhood adjacent to Parramatta and south of Westmead station, Mays Hill was named after Thomas May. He bought land here in 1859 when the first subdivision was made of the governor's domain, surrounding Government House at Parramata, and built his house on a hill on the property. The area in those days was characterised by citrus orchards.

In 1890, James Sulman of Mays Hill suggested to the authorities in Parrramatta that a cavalry corps should be established in Parramatta. Accordingly, about fifty mounted men and horses presented themselves for service, with Colonel James Burns as captain, and James Sulman as lieutenant.

In 1909 the junior house of The King's School moved to this area while extensions were being made to school buildings in Parramatta.

## MEADOWBANK
*Municipality of Ryde*
Location: 17 kilometres north-west of Sydney on the Parramatta River and the Main Northern Line

In 1799 Surgeon William Balmain (1762–1803) was given a grant of land at the Field of Mars with a frontage onto the Parramatta River, and he named it Meadowbank. Records show that a family named Bennett was farming this land in the 1820s; one member of the family, John, was transported in 1795 and his relative William, arrived as a free settler in 1820. Willam was a sea captain by profession and brought his ship to Charity Point, opposite Homebush Bay, for refitting. It is thought that he acquired the original Balmain grant. In 1855, 100 acres of the Meadowbank property were purchased by Major Edward Darvall whose name is linked with the history of Eastwood and Denistone, to the north.

In its early days Meadowbank was best known as part of the surrounding fruit-growing area,

which earned the title "the fruit bowl of the colony". The area developed quickly after the Main Northern railway line went through in the 1880s. The station opened here was first known as Hellenic, but its name was later changed to Meadowbank.

Today the suburb is notable for its extensive technical college, which stands on the site of the machine works established by the Mellor brothers in 1890, the Ryde area's first large industrial installation. Mellor Street, near Meadowbank Boys High School, recalls their name.

Although a school known as Meadowbank Public School opened in 1917, it was in West Ryde and its name was later changed to Ryde West. A school in Meadowbank was opened in August 1950. The first official post office had opened on 16 January 1894. Meadowbank Park is a large reserve on the northern bank of the Parramatta River.

## MELROSE PARK
*Municipality of Ryde*
Location: A locality 18 kilometres north-west of Sydney between Victoria Road and the Parramatta River

Ryde–Parramatta Golf Links separate this neighbourhood from Meadowbank on the north bank of the Parramatta River. It was established in 1937 as a large housing estate and named in honour of aviator Charles James (Jimmy) Melrose (1913–36). He was the only solo flyer to finish the Melbourne Centenary Air Race in 1934, held a number of early flying records, and helped in the unsuccessful search for Sir Charles Kingsford Smith. He died when

his plane broke up in turbulence on a charter flight from Melbourne to Darwin.

Before the estate was planned and given its name, the whole area had been known as Walumetta, and its soil was reputed to be some of the richest near Sydney. Today the gardens of the homes built on the land benefit from that good earth. Streets recall the names of those who flew the skyways — Cobham, (after Sir Arthur Cobham), Batten (after Jean Batten) and Johnson (after Amy Johnson) among them.

## MENAI
*Shire of Sutherland*
Location: 29 kilometres south of Sydney west of Sutherland

Owen Jones, a Welsh settler, called this place Bangor, after a well-known town in Wales, when he came to the area south of the Georges River in 1895. Confusion arose, because there was already a suburb named Bangor in Tasmania. The postmaster general's department changed the name in 1910 to Menai, after the Menai Straits between the Isle of Anglesey and Bangor, on the Welsh mainland. So although the original name was altered, the Welsh sentiment was maintained. The area retained its rural character until the 1970s. A modern public school has been opened in Hall Drive.

The eastern part of the original area of this suburb was subdivided in the years after the opening up of land to the west of the Woronora River and the building of the Lucas Heights Atomic Energy Commission in the 1950s. This suburb has been named Bangor, despite the possibility of confusion.

Menai Public School and its students, 1908

## MERRYLANDS
*Municipality of Holroyd, City of Parramatta*
Location: 25 kilometres west of Sydney south of Parramatta on the Main Southern Line

Merrylands was named after the former English home of an early settler. Arthur Todd Holroyd (1806–1887), who had a marked influence on the beginning of this suburb, was born in London, and trained as a physician but later studied law. He migrated to New Zealand and in 1845 came to Sydney. In 1861 he entered parliament, in 1863 was appointed minister for works, and sixteen years later he became a Supreme Court judge.

Holroyd acquired land south-west of Parramatta in 1855, which was part of the Sherwood Estate. This was a property of

1,165 acres consolidated by Dr William Sherwin on 25 June 1831, from his original grant and purchases and named after Robin Hood's famous forest in England. Holroyd, who named it Sherwood Scrubs, established a pottery and brickworks there and operated a dairy, which he called Merrylands, after a family property in England. He also experimented with fodder plants, cultivated an orangery, and

Arthur Todd Holroyd

had his own bowling green on the property.

North of the present railway station land was granted to Richard Atkins (1745–1820), judge-advocate in the colony. He received 100 acres in 1793 and 145 acres in 1798. This property, which he called Denham Court, was later bought by John Bowman, who added it to the 150 acres he had been granted in 1812. The land remained in the family until 1875, when it was subdivided, as were many properties in the 1870s and 1880s. The land south of the railway station, originally part of the Church and School Lands, set aside in the early days of the colony to support clergy and teachers, was subdivided in 1871–72.

When the Southern railway line from Granville to Liverpool came through the area the residential population began to increase. The station opened on 6 July 1878. The first school opened as Goughton School in March 1886, but the name was changed to Merrylands

Public School in Janury 1912. The first official post office opened in January 1885.

Merrylands is a healthy district, and it has become a busy residential area. Its settlement first grew up around Holroyd's property, about 2 kilometres west of the railway station.

Holroyd High School at nearby Wentworthville commemorates this district pioneer, who was the first mayor of the municipality, formed in 1872 as Prospect and Sherwood municipality and renamed in his honour in 1927. He died on 15 June 1887, at his home, Sherwood Scrubs, in Merrylands and was buried at Rookwood Cemetery. The house passed through several hands after his death and is now a Marist Sisters Convent.

# MIDDLE COVE
*Municipality of Willoughby*
Location: 9 kilometres north of Sydney on Middle Harbour

Middle Cove is a small suburb encompassed by the North Arm and South Arm of Sugarloaf Bay, a western inlet of Middle Harbour. Sugarloaf Bay and Sugarloaf Point are so named because of the shape of the land on the headland.

The Harold Reid Reserve on the headland remembers "the untiring work of Mr H. J. Reid [a town clerk] for the people of the Municipality of Willoughby over a period of more than fifty years". This tribute to Reid was paid at the official dedication of the park by a colleague, H. A. W. Ashton. The 35 hectare reserve, with its circular roadway to the lookout and its picnic facilities, retains much of its original wildflower beauty, and gives splendid views over the bay.

# MILLER
*City of Liverpool*
Location: 36 kilometres south-west of Sydney west of Liverpool

Lying between Hoxton Park and Sadleir, this suburb is named after an early land-holder, Peter Miller. It is one of several new suburbs developed west of Liverpool by the Housing Commission in 1961–65 (see Green Valley).

Miller seems to have retained more of its natural treescape than some of the older suburbs that are part of the Green Valley housing scheme. Streets have an Australian flavour, with names related to the sheep industry, starting with Wool Place: Merino, Corriedale, Suffolk, Southdown, Dorset and Romney recalling famous breeds; while Haddon Rig and Boonoke highlight famous sheep properties.

Miller Public School, in Miller Street, and Miller High School, in Cabramatta Avenue, cater for local children's education. Reserves stand along the south-eastern boundary of the suburb, fringing Cabramatta Creek, including Miller Park and Romney Park. The Michael Wenden Community Pool, named after the olympic swimmer, stands in Romney Park.

# MILLERS POINT AND THE ROCKS
*City of Sydney*
Location: 1 kilometre north-west of Sydney on Port Jackson beneath the southern approaches of the Harbour Bridge

This area west of Sydney Cove was occupied in the earliest years of settlement and much of historical interest has been preserved here. A mill was built in 1795 on the present site of the Observatory, on the point separating Walsh Bay and Darling Harbour. A small mill, it was owned by Jack Leighton and the area became known as Jack the Miller's Point. Millers Point today has many quaint old houses dating from the Macquarie period and through the Victorian era.

A huge fire at Millers Point in 1890 was probably the reason that Sydney became fire conscious. The difficulty in fighting it made firemen realise how inadequate their fire-fighting resources were. The Millers Point fire was no ordinary blaze. It was Sydney's first large oil fire, against which water was worse than useless. It began in the bond store owned by Gibbs Bright and Company, who in December 1890 had stored about 35,000 cases of tinned kerosene pending payment of customs duty. Moored nearby were other ships in the process of discharging cargo, among which was the barque *Australia* with 18,000 cases of kerosene from New York. At 5.30 pm unloading ceased, the bond store was locked, and night watchman Proctor came on duty. All seemed to be in order until 8.40 pm, when a seaman on a ship tied up at the wharf saw sparks coming from the warehouse roof. Telephones were still a novelty, but they proved their worth in such an emergency by quickly summoning help. Two months earlier another Sydney fire had caused great changes in fire services, which in those days depended on horse-drawn fire engines: horses were now kept in the engine room instead of stabled, so that within minutes they could be harnessed and away. The alarm passed along to other stations as far away as Marrickville and all went full speed to Millers Point.

In 1890 foam for fighting oil fires had not been invented. The

Kent Street, Millers Point, from Observatory Hill, c. 1880. The Lord Nelson Hotel is still trading today

firemen, realising water just rolled off the oil fire, thought of sand, but the 35,000 cases of oil were burning too fiercely to approach with sand buckets. The bond store and the wharf were doomed. The building collapsed, a mass of molten fire. Fortunately no wind was blowing so sparks did not fly onto nearby ships or buildings. Nonetheless, gallons of blazing kerosene flowed into the harbour and it was feared that the tide would carry the blaze across to the northern shore. The fire burnt all night and throughout the next day, drawing huge crowds of spectators. When the fire had burnt itself out, the exhausted fire stations were in disarray for days.

Millers Point is perhaps best known today as the location of the district known as The Rocks, which was settled very early in the colony's history. The rising land of rocky ridges on the west side of Circular Quay was the natural habitat for emancipated convicts, some free settlers of doubtful means, and visiting sailors ashore

on leave. It gradually became notable for its hotels, many of which remain, and also became an area of dubious repute. The Hero of Waterloo, one of the oldest hotels standing in Sydney, was built in 1843–44 of sandstone from the quarries in Kent Street. The block of land on which it stands in Windmill Street was bought in 1840 by stonemason George Payten, who received his licence in 1845. Next door was another hotel the Shipwrights Arms, built during Macquarie's governorship (1810–21). The Lord Nelson, in Kent Street near the waterfront, is said to be Sydney's oldest hotel, as it opened in 1834.

Also in Kent Street is the Ark, a rough stone terrace of two houses built by stonemason Thomas Glover before 1820, making this the oldest terrace in Sydney. Nearby is Richmond Villa, built in 1849 by colonial architect Mortimer Lewis (1796–1879) for his own home. Campbell's Storehouse in Circular Quay West was begun in 1842 by Robert Campbell (1769–1846), one of Sydney's wealthiest and most successful early merchants. His

son, also called Robert (1804–59), occupied Bligh House, which was built for him in 1833. It is still standing in Lower Fort Street. A less elegant house in The Rocks is four-roomed Cadman's Cottage in Lower George Street, originally built on the beach in 1815–16 as barracks for boatmen. John Cadman, superintendent of government craft, lived here from 1827 until 1845. A group of fine examples of Victorian terrace houses, called Sergeant Major's Row, stand in George Street on the site of the first street in Sydney, the name of which they commemorate. Also in the area are two historic churches: Holy Trinity, or the Garrison Church, built in 1840 for the nearby garrison; and St Patrick's Church, Sydney's oldest surviving Catholic church, consecrated in 1844.

In 1967 the state government appointed Sydney Cove Redevelopment Authority to consider preservation and redevelopment of the historic Rocks area. By December 1969 the first six members of the authority had been chosen and in January 1970 they began their important work which was to preserve and restore buildings architecturally and historically valuable; to create open spaces for leisure activities of residents in The Rocks, and to produce suitable housing for higher income residents in what had become a depressed area. The main idea was to prevent new buildings intruding on the shoreline so that the original atmosphere of the area, with its low- to medium-height buildings, would not be swamped and the flavour of the early years of The Rocks development would still be reflected.

The area they administer comprises about 23 hectares of The Rocks extending north from Grosvenor Street to Dawes Point, and east from the Bradfield Highway to George Street. It includes the Sydney Cove

Gloucester Street, The Rocks, looking north in the early 1900s — the girls were probably on their way to school

shoreline but excludes properties and land held by the Catholic Church and state and Commonwealth agencies.

In the early days of Millers Point rocks on its shores were used for ballast in ships travelling back to England without a cargo. By the 1830s The Rocks had become respectable — the pushes, or gangs and rioters had dispersed and by 1858 its buildings already blended together to form a special tourist attraction, in what has remained, until recent years, a working-class area.

# MILPERRA

*City of Bankstown*
Location: 24 kilometres south-west of Sydney between Bankstown Airport and the Georges River

Residential development of this satellite suburb of Bankstown, like that of the historically notable old city, began after the Second World War. In fact, Milperra has been influenced by both world wars, as soldiers returning after the 1914–18 conflict settled in the area. They established forty-eight poultry farms and eight vegetable gardens. Each farm was equipped with a house, sheds and fences, and had a town water supply. The farms have gone but evidence of a few of the vegetable gardens still remains. Street names of Pozieres, Lone Pine, Nieuport, Amiens, Flanders and Sinai are some of those that recall the First War and the area's soldier settlers.

Henry Lawson Drive, named as a tribute to the writer beloved of the Aussie battlers, is a main road running through this suburb. The area's importance has increased since 1975, when the Milperra College of Advanced Education was established. It provided a much-needed service to the community, and planning for a multi-discipline college began in 1972, when a 50 acre site adjoining the Milperra Public School was chosen. The building was finished in 1975, and on 16 July of that year 270 students enrolled. It is now a campus of the Macarthur Institute of Higher Education, whose other campus is at Campbelltown. How appropriate that this suburb's name, Aboriginal in origin, means "a gathering of people" when we consider the college's importance to the area.

## MILSONS POINT

*Municipality of North Sydney*
Location: 3 kilometres north of Sydney just off the northern exit of the Harbour Bridge, on the North Shore Line

The early history of Milsons Point, the peninsula between Lavender Bay and Kirribilli Point, is closely linked with North Sydney, but there are some unique elements in its history.

In about 1809 James Milson (1783–1872), who gave his name to the suburb, began to exploit his land in the northern part of the area. He quarried stone and also established a farm and dairy. The land was originally held by Robert Ryan, but the grant made to him in 1800 had lapsed.

Before the Sydney Harbour Bridge was built passengers had to be ferried across the harbour, and

Publicity photograph of North Sydney Olympic Pool, c. 1930. It was promoted as the finest saltwater swimming pool in the Southern Hemisphere

as early as 1863 five enterprising individuals, one of whom was James Milson the younger (1814–1903), son of the area's first settler, formed a ferry company. The Milsons Point Ferry Company operated steam ferries, which had the appropriate names of *Kirribilli*, *Alexander*, *Waratah*, and *Cammeray*. Each one carried about sixty passengers.

After the North Shore railway line extended to Milsons Point in 1893, a busy fleet of vehicular ferries laboured endlessly between Bennelong Point and Milsons Point. The point became the

terminus and the station named Milsons Point was built. At the time of its construction the railways department was going to call the new station Kirribilli, but the Milson descendants objected.

On 5 March 1878, the ferry company was purchased by another group of businessmen for the sum of £20,100. The service was renamed and its working power increased, and the North Shore Steam Ferry Company Limited was born.

In 1886, Milsons Point boasted a cable-tram, which ran from the harbour to present-day Ridge Street. Later the service extended to Crows Nest. The site of the first tram depot is now marked by the former Independent Theatre, which the late Doris Fitton, OBE, created.

A house connected with James Milson still stands in Winslow Street, Kirribilli. A two-storey building built in the 1870s by Milson's eldest son, James, it is a copy of a house known as Fern Lodge that James Milson senior built in the early 1840s. The first Fern Lodge, in common with most houses built during the 1840s, was sandstone, but the second was built of weatherboard with cypress and cedar elements. Fern Lodge is now occupied by a commercial firm. Both the elder and younger James Milsons were keen yachtsmen, and the younger James was, in 1863, one of the first commodores of the Royal Sydney Yacht Squadron.

# MINTO
*City of Campbelltown*
Location: 47 kilometres south-west of Sydney east of Campbelltown Road, on the Main Southern Line

Known as Campbellfields in 1874, this district north of Campbelltown was renamed eight years later in honour of Gilbert Kyngmount, Earl of Minto, then governor-general of India.

A still countrified area between Ingleburn and Leumeah, it was considered by Governor Lachlan Macquarie in 1810 as a possible alternative to the settlement in the Hawkesbury Valley, which had been severely flooded following violent storms. He rode around the periphery of Minto, crossing the Georges River twice to return to Liverpool. In 1811 Dr William Redfern (1774?–1833) was granted 800 acres here, on which he built a Georgian style farmhouse. Redfern was the first doctor in charge of

the famous Rum Hospital, later named Sydney Hospital, which was built by three merchants in return for exclusive liquor import licences approved by Macquarie. Redfern's property was to the west of Pembroke Road, and he retired to this farm, called Campbellfields, in 1818. Redfern Road is named after him, and street names such as Minto, Pembroke, Warwick, Sussex, Essex, Nelson and Derby recall the English aristocracy of the times.

When the southern railway line came to the area, and the railway station opened in 1874, the population increased. The line itself passed through the original Redfern grant.

The first school, which opened in 1867, was known as Taggart Field School, but in May 1884 the name was changed to Minto Public School. The Sarah Redfern primary and high schools, named after William Redfern's wife, opened in 1979. The first official post office opened in January 1885.

These early granted areas have a charm of their own, particularly in the naming of schools or post offices. Studying parish maps often reveals that the person who gave the land on which the school was built also gave the family's name to the school, while the post office may have operated under the name of the postmaster. A study of these early names can often reveal the identity of the first residents in what were then isolated and lonely areas.

# MIRANDA
*Shire of Sutherland*
Location: 24 kilometres south of Sydney between Sutherland and Cronulla on the Cronulla Line

This suburb, built on the oldest settled portion of the Sutherland shire, was named by the manager of the Holt estate, James Murphy, after a town in Spain. Land was originally promised to Gregory Blaxland for discovering a route across the Blue Mountains in 1813, and in 1816 he sold the promise to merchant John Connell for £250. Blaxland did not choose the site of his land until 1831, and after he chose this area, Connell claimed it. In 1835 the courts recognised Connell as the owner. In the 1860s the land was purchased by Thomas Holt (1811–88), who planned a model sheep and cattle farm on the site (see Sutherland), but the plan failed and the fertile ground was leased to market gardeners.

By the 1920s Miranda was served by steam trams travelling from Cronulla to Sutherland every hour. In the 1980s tramless days, it is difficult to understand the important part they played in the earlier life of Sydney and its suburbs. For threepence residents could travel from Miranda to Sutherland in fifteen minutes.

By 1923 there were three stores in Miranda, and a post office and a butcher's shop at the junction of the main road from Sutherland with Port Hacking Road. Today there is a large, modern shopping centre at Miranda Fair. In the 1920s settlements of returned First World War soldiers were well established in Miranda, which at that time was considered one of the best fruit-growing and poultry-farming areas in the state. Today Miranda is a residential suburb with easy access to Port Hacking to the south and Cronulla Beach to the east.

Before the days of Miranda Fair, the general store serviced most people's needs. This picture was taken around 1950

# MONA VALE
*Shire of Warringah*
Location: 28 kilometres north of Sydney at the junction of Pittwater, Mona Vale and Barrenjoey Roads

This northern beach between Warriewood and Newport was called Bongin-Bongin by Aborigines, but the township was named Mona Vale after a 700 acre farm surveyed in 1814 for Robert Campbell (1769–1846), which had passed into other hands by the 1840s. There is a Mona Vale in Scotland which may have inspired Campbell's choice of name for his property.

The suburb became well known for its fine beach and baths. A boarding house that later became popular in the area as La Corniche originally belonged to Mr Brock, a Newtown resident, who inherited a fortune. He spent the money in the late 1890s building a

magnificent house, with lodges and recreation facilities to create a Riviera-style resort. But it proved to be ahead of its time, business was poor, and Brock was bankrupted. The state government took it over, and sold it in 1907. The site was then used as a hydro until it was destroyed by fire in 1912. The land, however, had already been subdivided in 1911. Mr Rainaud rebuilt the house and renamed it La Corniche. In the 1920s La Corniche became a fashionable boarding house, patronised by visitors from all over the state. However, it fell into disuse before the Second World War and was eventually demolished.

The name Foley is well known as that of an early resident in Mona Vale; he was a tenant at the farm originally owned by Campbell from 1843 to 1849, when he was murdered in a dispute with a neighbouring family called Collins. Mrs Foley was no mean hand at the skills of a farmer's wife, being reputed to make the finest quality butter in the district. Foley's successor on the property, James

Therry, had his house burnt, and a series of tenants followed until it was bought by George Brock in the 1890s.

The Rock Lily Inn was built in 1886 on the road north from Narrabeen by Leon Houreux, who bought the property originally owned by the Collins family. This important coach stop operated until 1913 and later reopened in 1947.

The public school and post office both opened in 1906. Even in the years after the Second World War this was still a market gardening area, specialising in tomatoes grown in glasshouses. A violent hailstorm in 1947 damaged many of the glasshouses and, when this happened again in the early 1970s, many were completely destroyed and market gardening ceased.

Today Mona Vale is a pleasant residential suburb with the Mona Vale District Hospital, which became Mona Vale Hospital and Warringah Health Service in 1983–84, and Mona Vale Golf Course in the southern part of the suburb.

## MONTEREY

*Municipality of Rockdale*
Location: 15 kilometres south of
Sydney on the western shore of
Botany Bay

For a long time this
neighbourhood between Brighton-
le-Sands and Ramsgate was a
suburb without a name. For many
years a post office with the name
of Monterey stood on the corner of
Scarborough Street, and the local
residents knew the small shopping
centre as Monterey shops. Official
blessing was, however, missing,
and in 1972 Rockdale Council
decided to clear up confusion by
creating a new suburb named
Monterey. Not everyone agreed
with the choice of name. Some
thought that it was too American,
especially with streets named
Hollywood, Pasadena, Monterey
and Culver already in the area. But
most people favoured Monterey.

This tiny suburb between Lady
Robinsons Beach and Scarborough
Park is a comfortable and attractive
area, and, in spite of its American
title, it has a dinkum Aussie feeling
in the friendliness of its residents.

## MOOREBANK

*City of Liverpool*
Location: 29 kilometres
south-west of Sydney between
Heathcote Road and Newbridge
Road

Land grants were made in this
area, east of Liverpool, as early as
1798, but the largest land-owner
was the man after whom the
suburb was named. An
enterprising and generous man,
Thomas Moore (1762–1840) was
an industrious ship's carpenter,
who became a government
boatbuilder. He received a grant of

Thomas Moore

750 acres in 1805 on the Georges
River near Liverpool, which he
named Moorebank. Governor
Macquarie made many journeys
through Liverpool to the
Cowpastures, probably riding his
favourite horse, Cato, and always
referred to this area as Moore
Bank. By 1840, the year of his
death, Moore had built up his
estate to 7,300 acres, extending to
Liverpool and the borders of
Warwick Farm Racecourse. He left
the house and grounds to establish
a college to train young men "of
the Protestant persuasion". Moore
Theological College opened first at
Liverpool, but at the end of the
century was moved to a site near
the University of Sydney. The
original Moorebank, the site of
Thomas Moore's grant, lies
towards today's Chipping Norton.
A tablet to his memory is to be
found in St Luke's church,
Liverpool (see Liverpool).

In the early days of orchards and
vineyards at Moorebank, a seam of
coal about 2 metres wide was
discovered, and the rumour flew
around the district that it was
going to become a British
Newcastle. However, the coal
seam was too deep for mining, and
nothing came of the discovery.

Moorebank has been associated
with the army since the First

World War, and Kitchener's
Cottage still stands in Moorebank
Avenue, as part of the army's
married quarters. This cottage was
built and furnished for Lord
Kitchener's use during the few
days he spent at Liverpool in 1910.
He came to Australia to advise on
defence matters, and in the course
of the visit came to Liverpool to
inspect the troops in the area.

Over time Moorebank has
developed from being a country
farming area to its present mixture
of light industry and residential
use. Many of the business people
live close to their places of work in
nearby Chipping Norton,
Hammondville, Warwick Farm
and Casula.

## MOORE PARK

*City of Sydney*
Location: A locality 3 kilometres
south-east of Sydney on Anzac
Parade

This neighbourhood south of
Paddington was named after the
mayor of Sydney in 1867–69,
Charles Moore, who fought for
the right of the city council to use
the land as a leisure area for the
people of Sydney and its suburbs.
Land here had been set aside as part
of 1,000 acres of common
pasturage in 1810 by Governor
Macquarie.

The area is still dedicated to
pleasure, with the Moore Park
Municipal Golf Links, Sydney
Cricket Ground, bowling greens,
the Royal Agricultural Society's
Showground and the E. S. Marks
Athletic Ground located there.
Moore Park itself houses tennis
courts and other sports fields as
well as Kippax Lake in the north.
To the east is Centennial Park, and
on the Moore Park golf course are

Moore Park Zoological Gardens, 1912

Sydney's only mountains, Mt Steele and Mt Rennie.

Sydney's second water supply runs beneath the showground. Known as Busby's Bore, it began in Lachlan Swamps, in the area of the later Centennial Park, and was connected with an underground tunnel, cut by convict labour between 1827 and 1837, ending in Hyde Park, opposite the David Jones store in Elizabeth Street. This water supply filled the city's freshwater needs until 1849. The tunnel is intact and no less than nine entrance shafts still exist in the showground area. John Busby (1765–1857), an English civil engineer, devised the scheme. In 1962 a fountain was erected in Hyde Park to commemorate this man's brilliant piece of engineering.

Sydney's first public zoo was established in the Moore Park area, being 7 acres then known as Billygoat Swamp, in 1879. By

1906 the zoological gardens covered 15 acres, but the zoo now known as Taronga, was moved to Bradley's Head in 1916. In 1920 Sydney Girls High School was officially opened on the site, and the pupils transferred from the old school, on the present site of David Jones, Elizabeth Street, in 1921. Sydney Boys High School opened on some of the remaining zoo land in 1928. Some remnants of the zoo buildings survive in the grounds of the school.

## MORTDALE
*Municipalities of Hurstville and Kogarah*
Location: 20 kilometres south of Sydney between Penshurst and Oatley on the Illawarra Line

Originally known as Mort's Hill, the name Mortdale was accepted as the official title of this suburb

when the first railway station opened on 20 March 1897. Twenty-five years later, on 14 September 1922, a station on the present site replaced the earlier one, but the name Mortdale remained. Some early residents of this suburb south-west of Hurstville did not take kindly to its name. They thought the "Mort" signified death and with "dale" meant "the valley of death"! Instead this suburb takes its name from one of the most enterprising Australian industrialists — Thomas Sutcliffe Mort (1816–78). He had large land holdings in this district before 1861, having acquired the south-western section of a grant originally owned by Dr Robert Townson (1763–1827), an early botanist, and brother of John Townson (see Penshurst).

Mort's achievements are worth noting. He pioneered weekly wool auctions and the refrigeration of food, was involved in moves for the first railway in New South

Thomas Mort

## MORTLAKE
*Municipality of Concord*
Location: 17 kilometres west of
Sydney on the southern bank of
the Parramatta River

In an age when preventive
medicine and inoculations have
controlled children's diseases, it is
strange to recall that parents in the
1930s took children who had
whooping cough to inhale the

fumes from the gasworks at
Mortlake. The efficacy of this cure
is doubtful but the Australian Gas
Light Company certainly came
into the suburb in 1883 with its
first purchase of land. Since those
early days the company has
increased its land holding to over
100 acres. Colliers carrying the

When real estate agents advertised land for
sale at Mortlake in 1884, "near the
gasworks" was a good selling point

Wales, and was also one of the
founders of the AMP Society.
Mort was instrumental in the
construction of Mort's Dock at
Balmain in 1854, which gave
Sydney a dry dock for repairing
ships. (Fitzroy dock on Cockatoo
Island was begun in 1847 but not
finished for some time.) Morts
Road is also called after him.

When the district was known as
Mort's Hill, there was a small
farming community. The
Hurstville Steam Brick Company
was established in 1884, the year
the railway came through the area.
Two main farms, Kemp's orange
orchard and Parkes's farm near
Victoria Avenue, were cut in half,
and by 1894 the land had been
subdivided and sold for home
building blocks. This led to a big
increase in Mortdale's population
which had numbered about forty
in 1885. The first district school
opened in January 1889, and an
official post office, combined with
a grocery store, followed in
November of the same year.

Mortdale, 3 kilometres from
Hurstville, became a popular
residential suburb in the 1920s
when houses were being built by
soldiers returning from the First
World War.

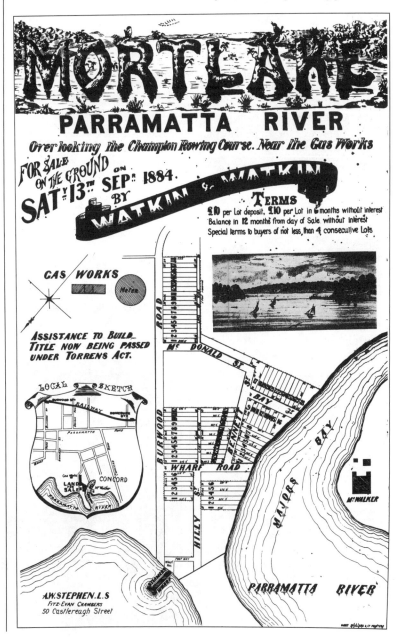

coal for gasmaking from the Newcastle collieries were the main reason for the construction of the new Gladesville Bridge with its high arched roadway. The old bridge had to open and let the colliers through, causing frequent traffic delays on Victoria Road, one of the main roads to the city.

At one time Mortlake was known as Bottle Point, and it is thought that the suburb was later named Mortlake in memory of the place of that name on the Thames, in England. Many of the suburbs bordering on the Parramatta River followed this pattern, possibly from memories of home; even Governor Arthur Phillip succumbed to nostalgia and called Parramatta River "the Thames of the Antipodes". The actual date of naming this suburb is obscure. When the Australian Gas Light Company first purchased land there in 1883, it was referred to as "Parramatta land opposite Gladesville". A township grew up around the gasworks, and in the 1920s an attractive park and swimming baths were situated on the river, and weekends and school holidays found it crowded with people from surrounding areas. The pleasure ground has now disappeared, and with it the laughter of those lost yesterdays at Mortlake. The gasworks also went out of operation with the introduction of natural gas but no decision has yet been made on the future use of the site.

# MOSMAN
*Municipality of Mosman*
Location: 10 kilometres north-west of Sydney between Middle Harbour and Port Jackson

Archibald Mosman (1799–1863) and his twin brother, George, arrived in Sydney in 1828. In 1831 they moved onto a 4 acre grant in this area and became engaged in the shipping and whaling industries, using as headquarters a deep, sheltered bay on the north side of the harbour, which became known as Mosman's Bay. Brother George soon took up grazing, but Archibald continued with his whaling activities. By 1838, when he owned 108 acres along the Mosman waterfront, he decided to sell his whaling interests and retire to a country property near Glen Innes. On his death in Randwick in 1863 he was buried at St Jude's cemetery, Randwick, in a grave now maintained by the Mosman Council.

Mosman Bay had been explored by Captain John Hunter as early as 1789. He mentions the bay as Careening Cove, and Charles

Archibald Mosman

Grimes, an early surveyor, notes it as such on his map of 1796, apparently because HMS *Sirius* was careened in the bay in 1789. In the following years the name of the Bay varied. A survey by Roe in 1822 marked it as Careening Cove, but a map by Cross in 1825 called it Sirius Cove. A grant made in the area was called "land at Great Sirius Cove", while the parish map of 1871 registers the name Great and Littler Sirius Cove. The name Little Sirius Cove is today applied to the inlet immediately east of Mosman Bay. It became a popular picnic area in the 1920s. Careening Cove now applies to the inlet east of Kirribilli.

In 1839 James King bought the largest single property in Mosman. His 150 acres extended from Mosman Junction to the site of the present zoo. He named the property Silex, because of his pottery and glass-making operations, and the estate is recalled by Silex Street today. In 1853 the estate was divided and sold. One part was bought by Richard Hayes Harnett, who built Buena Vista there in 1875. A block of flats with the same name stands on the site now. In 1878 Harnett opened a quarry, which provided stone for many Sydney buildings until it closed down in 1889.

Mosman's public school was opened in 1880. In 1893 Mosman became a municipality, having previously been part of North Sydney municipality.

A famous Australian who lived in Mosman was the beloved writer Ethel Turner (1872–1958), author of *Seven Little Australians*. Her honeymoon was spent in a tiny house known as The Chalet, overlooking Little Sirius Cove. She had married Herbert Curlewis, and later had a daughter, Jean, and a son, Adrian, who in adult years followed his father into the legal

A favourite spot for walks and picnics in the 1880s, Mosman's Bay Falls

profession, and became a judge. The Turners' first home was Avenel, at 17 Warringah Road, and the family later moved to a house known as The Neuk, at 5 Moruben Road, which was demolished in the late 1930s. It is hard to imagine the area as almost total bushland, as Ethel Turner recalls it.

Alongside Little Sirius Cove and at Mosman's southern edge is Taronga Park Zoo. This now world-famous zoo was created in 1912 and opened on 7 October 1916. Its Aboriginal name means "beautiful view". Enthusiastic citizens of note had banded together to provide animals for a zoo built at Moore Park, which was in use from 1884 to 1916, now the site of the Sydney Girls and Sydney Boys high schools. The

move across the harbour was prompted by lack of space at Moore Park, and when their new home was ready, the old zoo's animal residents were transferred to Taronga. One of the legends of Moore Park and Taronga Park was Jessie the Indian elephant, beloved by thousands. In 1916 she was transported on a pontoon across the harbour to her new home, alighting and walking through the gates like the gentle lady she always was. Nowadays members of the public may "adopt" an animal, paying annually for its upkeep.

Mosman today is a charming suburb. Its shopping centre, stretching along each side of the main street, Bradleys Head Road, encourages window shopping by the quality and individuality of the goods displayed. Small arcades,

restaurants and boutiques give an almost village atmosphere, although the area feels very much alive. Attractive modern townhouses rub shoulders with Federation-style houses. On the northern side of Military Road the streets afford glimpses of Middle Harbour and its surrounding bushland.

From Spit Junction, north of Mosman shopping centre, Spit Road leads down to The Spit Bridge — one of two bridges crossing Middle Harbour, the older being Roseville Bridge some kilometres upstream. Until 1924 people, arriving by trams running down Parriwi Road, and vehicles were ferried across the stretch of water by a punt.

## MOUNT COLAH
*Shire of Hornsby*
Location: 29 kilometres
north-west of Sydney on the
Pacific Highway and the Main
Northern Line

Mount Colah lies beyond Asquith
on the Northern railway line to
Newcastle. Its boundaries are Ku-
ring-gai Chase National Park to
the east and a very steep hillside
leading to Wall's Gully on the
west. The name has been in use
since early last century, as the
parish of South Colah, which
originally stretched over much of
the present Hornsby shire from
Hornsby northwards. The
meaning of the name is, however,
unknown.

## MOUNT DRUITT
*City of Blacktown*
Location: 43 kilometres west of
Sydney on the Great Western
Highway and the Main Western
Line

Mount Druitt, east of St Marys,
was named after Major George
Druitt (1775–1842), who was chief
engineer of roads in 1819 during
Governor Macquarie's term of
office (1810–21). He came to New
South Wales as an officer of the
48th Regiment, and met his future
wife on the journey from England
in 1817. Margaret Lynch was a
stowaway who married Private
Terry Burns on the ship. In
Sydney they parted, and she lived
with Druitt for some time before
their marriage in 1825, which was
to become an extremely happy
union.

George Druitt became a notable
figure in the life of the colony.
Macquarie appointed him colonial
engineer and inspector of public
works, and he supervised the
construction of many of architect
Francis Greenway's buildings,
including the Government House
stables, now the Conservatorium
of Music. Druitt also planned and
supervised the building of Fort
Macquarie on Bennelong Point.

In 1821 Druitt acquired 1,000
acres of land that covered the
major portion of the Mount Druitt
township. In 1842, after his death,
the estate was sold, and in 1849 his
old home was destroyed by fire.
Druitt Street, which runs alongside
Sydney's Town Hall, and Mount
Druitt Road are named after this
early settler in the district.

In 1966 a new housing area was
planned at the original settlement
of Mount Druitt. Using Mount
Druitt itself as the centre for major
shopping, entertainment and other
facilities, the scheme planned to
create new suburbs. Extra
shopping complexes were
envisaged, as it was realised that
Mount Druitt would not be able to
cope with the needs of a greatly
increased population. But as
building of the houses went ahead,
construction of other necessary
buildings slowed down, and they
were not finished until 1973,
although the houses in the
meantime were filling rapidly with
young family groups, which meant
a young, growing population,
needing transport, shops,
entertainment, health and baby
care centres, and parkland and
sporting facilities.

In spite of all the early problems,
the deficiencies are fast
disappearing. The once poor train
service to the city has been
remedied, and now there is a good
peak hour service for workers.
Instead of a few overloaded schools
there are now six government high
schools and fourteen primary
schools in the district, each with an
average of 1,000 pupils. A super-
modern shopping centre, covering
28,000 square metres, now caters
for the population. Recreation
centres and playing areas are also
available for older children and
young adults.

See the separate entries on
Bidwill, Blackett, Dharruk,
Emerton, Hebersham, Lethbridge
Park, Shalvey, Tregear, Whalan
and Wilmot for the history of these
suburbs.

## MOUNT KU-RING-GAI
*Shire of Hornsby*
Location: 31 kilometres
north-west of Sydney on the
Pacific Highway and the Main
Northern Line

After the northern railway line had
been extended from Hornsby to
the Hawkesbury River in the
1880s, a railway station between
Mount Colah and Berowra was
opened in August 1903 and named
Kuring-gai. In 1933 Mount was
added to the name, and today the
spelling has again altered. The area
was once the home and hunting
ground of the Ku-ring-gai
Aborigines, and this Aboriginal
word means "hunting ground of
the men" (of that tribe).

It is a relatively small residential
suburb, bounded on the east by
Ku-ring-gai Chase National Park
and on the west by steep, rocky
cliffs, and a number of small
streams leading to Calna Creek.
The area has a peaceful beauty,
much favoured by weekend
picnickers and bushwalkers.

## MOUNT LEWIS
*City of Bankstown*
Location: 18 kilometres
south-west of Sydney just north of
Bankstown

Sandwiched between Bankstown
and Greenacre, Mount Lewis is
the highest land in the district.
Wattle Street is the main road in
this suburb. There is an infants
school close to the highest point.

## MOUNT PLEASANT
*City of Penrith*
Location: 58 kilometres west of
Sydney off The Northern Road

Samuel Terry (1776?–1838), who
arrived in the colony as a convict
in June 1801, became a land-owner
on a grand scale after gaining his
freedom in 1807. One of his
properties was Mount Pleasant,
where after 1820 he built a house
overlooking the two pieces of land,
totalling 210 acres, granted to his
wife, Rosette, in 1809. The house
was demolished in the mid 1950s.
When Terry died in 1838, he was
worth £500,000 in real estate in
Eastwood.

In 1976 the neighbourhood of
Mount Pleasant was chosen as a
new residential development of the
city of Penrith. It is close to the
area known as Cranebrook, also a
suburb of Penrith.

## MOUNT PRITCHARD
*Cities of Fairfield and Liverpool*
Location: 33 kilometres
south-west of Sydney between
Cabramatta Road and Elizabeth
Drive

Part of the Green Valley housing
development of the early 1960s,
Mount Pritchard lies to the west of
Cabramatta. The suburb's streets
follow the contours of the land and
their names honour many famous
Australians: Florey, who
contributed to the discovery of
penicillin, and Oliphant, the
physicist and governor of South
Australia; Dargie, Dobell,
Streeton, Roberts, Meldrum and
Lambert recall famous artists; and
composers such as Antill and
Grainger, and musicians such as
Verbrugghen, and Heinze are also
represented. Parks lie along the
bank of Cabramatta Creek, which
forms the suburb's south-eastern
boundary, and Cabramatta Golf
Club and Orange Grove Golf
Course are nearby.

In its early days the area was one
of small land grants given to

convicts who had been transported
after the 1798 Irish Rebellion. One
of these was Joseph Holt's 40 acre
property, in the area of the present
Oliphant Street.

## NAREMBURN
*Municipality of Willoughby*
Location: 6 kilometres north of
Sydney on Willoughby Road

A small suburb between Crows
Nest and Willoughby, Naremburn
was known in its earliest days as
Central Township. The origin of
its present name remains a
mystery, although a Scottish
influence could account for the
"burn" in the neighbourhood's
name.

One of the most historic and
imposing buildings in the district is
St Leonard's church, which was
dedicated in 1916 with Father
Sherwin as its first incumbent. The

The aftermath of a freak tornado that swept
through Naremburn, 27 March 1906. Its
path was roughly three kilometres long and
up to one kilometre wide

church catered not only for the Naremburn residents but also responded to sick calls from the Royal North Shore Hospital. Another notable church building is the Church of Christ, in Central Street, Naremburn, which was built in 1923, with additions made in 1924 and finally in 1960. But older than both these well-known buildings is Naremburn Public School, built in 1887 for the princely sum of £1,250.

# NARRABEEN

*Shire of Warringah*
Location: 23 kilometres north of Sydney on Pittwater Road facing the Pacific Ocean

The origin of Narrabeen's name is confused. One theory is that it was the Aboriginal name of a bird common near Narrabeen Lakes, rich in birdlife in those first days. The other tells of a marine drummer called Reynolds of the First Fleet who lived in, or led a party into, the area and befriended local Aborigines. When a woman called Narrabin overheard a group of convicts planning to kill Reynolds or his party, it is said she walked to Parramatta to tell the authorities of the plot. Reynolds was killed, but the convicts were apprehended, and the district was named in the woman's honour. Lest legend became fact, it is well to consider the distance from Narrabeen to Parramatta. The suburb's name appears on the maps of Surveyor James Meehan in 1814–15 as Narrabang in 1814–15, and in 1830 the lakes were called Narrabine Lagoon.

One of the earliest land grants in the area was made to John Ramsay in 1818. This farm which was known as Mount Ramsay, had

been acquired by James Jenkins by 1824. Jenkins received other grants in the area in 1831 and bought more land until he held over 600 acres. The property remained in the family until 1900, when Elizabeth Jenkins willed it to the Salvation Army, despite the opposition of her family, who accused the Army of undue influence. The Salvation Army still owns land in the area, although it has sold portions of the estate since receiving it. Other land grants were made in the area in the 1820s and 1830s and the area gradually became sparsely occupied. The post office opened in 1898.

In December 1909, on a day of great excitement, George Taylor (1872–1928), a young man experimenting with the ideas of aerial travel, made the first Australian flight in a 28-foot motorless biplane along Narrabeen Beach.

By the 1920s the area was being advertised to potential residents as being "7 miles from Manly by tram, with a good hotel and the usual week-end accommodation cottages. Narrabeen has, amongst other attractions, one of the finest and most accessible surfing beaches in this state, being over two miles in length from Collaroy Point to Narrabeen Heads. Fish are plentiful in the Lake ... the district is eminently suited for Orchards, Flower and Vegetable Gardens, and Poultry Farms."

Today most of the weekenders have been replaced by high-rise units and substantial houses occupied by permanent residents; the flower and poultry farms have gradually vanished; the old trams and bathing sheds are no more. But that glorious long stretch of beach is still there, and Narrabeen Lakes are still a haven for birdlife and a delight for anglers.

# NARRAWEENA

*Shire of Warringah*
Location: 18 kilometres north of Sydney north of Warringah Road

The Aboriginal name for this suburb, between Dee Why and Brookvale means "a quiet place in the hills", which describes the area very accurately, although the quietness can be shattered by the busyness of life.

The suburb developed after the Second World War when land was subdivided for Housing Commission homes. Close to Dee Why, residents can enjoy the surfing facilities there, and the extensive shopping centre along the main road. Narraweena Public School stands in McIntosh Road.

# NARWEE

*Municipalities of Hurstville and Canterbury*
Location: 18 kilometres south-west of Sydney between King Georges Road and Forest Road, on the East Hills Line

This suburb was first settled when Richard Podmore received a land grant of 100 acres in the 1820s. The area was bounded by Broadarrow and Penshurst roads, Shorter Avenue and Karne Street, an area which today includes Narwee Station. Podmore named his property Sunning Hill Farm, when he cleared the heavy timber and established a comfortable home and a productive farm. The area south of Broadarrow Road was part of Robert Townson's grant (see Penshurst).

In 1900 the Podmore grant was subdivided and, as the Graham Park Estate, became a residential area of individually styled homes. The railway station opened on 21

December 1931. During construction it was known as Podmore, after the original grantee, but the Tempe-East Hills Railway League's Grand Council, which was interested and involved in the district's development, suggested the name Graham Park. The station was named Narwee, however, from the Aboriginal word meaning "the sun".

The official post office opened in October 1948, and a public school was established two years later.

## NEUTRAL BAY
*Municipality of North Sydney*
Location: 5 kilometres north of Sydney on the northern side of Port Jackson

The name of this suburb can be traced back to the colony's first governor, Arthur Phillip, who needed to be sure the settlement at Sydney Cove was protected from any foreign ships arriving in Port Jackson. In 1789 he chose the bay on the north side of the harbour now known as Neutral Bay as an anchorage for foreign ships where they could wait on neutral territory until their country's attitude to England could be checked, although news often took six months to arrive in the colony. The bay's suitability was enhanced by the position of Kirribilli Point, around which any ships waiting in Neutral Bay would have to manoeuvre to attack Sydney Cove.

In 1830, 4 acre allotments were laid out between Careening Cove and Neutral Bay and set aside for the whaling industry. The area's timber was used for shipbuilding, and already in 1831 Millard of Neutral Bay was able to launch a 40 ton vessel.

Benjamin Boyd (1803?–51), who arrived in the colony in 1842 and by 1844 was one of its largest land-holders, set up a woolwash in the suburb. It was south of the present Mann Avenue, and here he prepared wool for shipment to England. He is remembered by the name Ben Boyd Road.

Patrick Hayes acquired two of Ben Boyd's iron boilers, once used for woolwashing, to begin a soap and tallow factory. Hayes built a house, called The Towers, on the hill above his works, said to be the first home in Sydney made entirely from concrete. In 1880 Hayes ventured into the real estate business, building four houses on the point, which he endeavoured to sell. But buyers were not keen. The area was isolated from the city and was heavily wooded, and the threat of bushfires in the area did nothing to encourage settlers. In fact, summer fires were known to burn right down to the water's edge, destroying everything in their path.

In 1882 the North Shore Gas Company Limited was formed and established works at Neutral Bay. The main works were transferred to Wollstonecraft in 1917.

Houses in the area today are usually large and two-storeyed, and many have been converted to flats. In recent years a great many blocks of units have been built. An attractive, modern shopping centre has developed at Neutral Bay Junction. This is a tree-softened suburb, where wharves known as Kirribilli, High Street, Hayes Street and Kurraba dip their wooden piles into Neutral Bay.

## NEWPORT
*Shire of Warringah*
Location: 31 kilometres north of Sydney on the Barrenjoey Peninsula

Newport and Newport Beach stretch from the surf to the calm beauty of Pittwater. The origin of the name is simple — this was a new port for steamers carrying passengers and cargo, and sailing away with quantities of local shell lime and firewood.

Newport Beach is a curving ocean beach with a splendid surf, and Newport itself enjoys the quiet, eye-catching splendour of Pittwater. Governor Arthur Phillip saw the area on one of his trips of exploration and considered it to be one of the most beautiful lake-like places he had seen. A site north of the present Royal Motor Yacht Club, known as Saltpan Cove, was used to produce salt for domestic use in the colony, salt being essential for preservation of raw meat. An interesting building, on Bungan Head south of Newport Beach, is a "medieval" stone castle, Bungan Castle, built in 1919 by a German art dealer, Adolph Albers. The views from the headland are breathtaking.

Haystack Point, opposite Green Point which today is the site of the Royal Prince Alfred Yacht Club, received its name from a great flood in 1873. A haystack from a Hawkesbury farm was caught up in the floodwaters of the river, and, as it was attached to a framework of logs, it floated up Pittwater and came to rest at the place just below the Newport township, now known as Haystack Point. Some pigs that travelled down with the hay were later rescued by a passing fisherman.

Early land grants in the area included 60 acres at Long Beach,

Newport, given to James Farrell on 18 May 1843; he was convicted of stealing cattle in 1864. Other early land-holders were a Mr Bolton and Thomas Warner, who received 50 acres in the district in 1833. In 1867 the Royal Prince Alfred Yacht Club was established, one of several clubs now in the suburb.

Coastal excursions by the ships *Maitland*, *City of Grafton* and *Namoi* were a feature of the 1890s at Newport. The day-trippers were family groups who came with picnic baskets for a day by the sea. There was much of interest to see, as coastal luggers anchored at the port to unload or for repairs, and many overseas clippers tied up on Pittwater. Smuggling was rife in those days, but nothing was so frightening as the invasion of the Sydney larrikins who soon found the advantage of a sea trip to Newport. For some years these Sydney Push boys and their girlfriends descended on the little seaside village to engage in fights with the locals, rob orchards and fowl runs, and drink bootleg beer brewed across the river near McCarr's Creek. Finally the local residents formed retaliatory forces, and after the loss of the *Maitland* in a storm in 1898 and the Newport jetty being declared unsafe in 1902, the day-trips came to an end and Newport returned to its peaceful life.

Although a telegraph office opened here in 1888, the post office was not established until 1898. Subdivision of the land began early this century; the Green Point subdivision, for instance, was being sold in 1905.

Until the 1950s Newport was a peaceful beach suburb beloved of artists and writers seeking to escape from city living, and a holiday resort for visiting country dwellers. Improved bus services and cars have made it a near-Sydney suburb, and shops have changed from small family businesses to supermarkets. A large number of the residents are retired folk with bowling and boating interests, and Newport caters for both. The district retains a quiet atmosphere, however, and many houses have spectacular views.

# NEWTOWN
*Municipality of Marrickville, City of Sydney*
Location: 4.5 kilometres south-west of Sydney on the Main Suburban Line

In the 1840s Newtown was described like this: "a beautiful village of New South Wales, situated on the road to Cook's River, about three miles from the city of Sydney; it contains 323 houses and 1,215 inhabitants, of whom 631 are males and 584 females".

It is hard to believe that this inner-city suburb began its life as a farming area. Settlements sprang up along the Parramatta Road after officers of the New South Wales Corps were granted land in the areas now known as Camperdown and Stanmore. In 1794 Nicholas Devine received a grant of 120 acres (to which 90 acres were added in 1799), which ran from later Station Street south to the area of St Peters station. He called his property Burren Farm and today's Burren Street commemorates this early property. Thomas Rowley's grant, near the present Australia Street, was called Kingston Farm, and a street and lane in Newtown still carry this name. Eventually two settlements grew up here: O'Connell Town at the end of Missenden Road, and one near the present railway bridge. When John and Eliza Webster opened a store here in a weatherboard building, they called it the New Town Store. By 1832 the small settlement was referred to as New Town, and by 1838 Newtown was the form used. It was an unpopular title, and as late as 1893, demands of the suburb to be called South Sydney were still being made.

By 1838 the population had increased to "877 Protestants, 364 Roman Catholics, one Pagan and one Jew". The area, always a mixed one, with working-class homes and large estates standing side by side, began to evolve as a busy workers' suburb, until, in 1923, it was described as a "thickly populated suburb adjoining the city, with numerous works and factories, and a splendid tram service every two or three minutes down King Street; fare 3d; also all night trams". The main street — King Street — was "wood-blocked for one and three quarter miles in length lined on both sides with shops, one of the busiest suburban thoroughfares, and at the bridge is situated the station tramway depot". The municipality of Newtown was incorporated on 12 December 1862.

Some small shops of Newtown's early years were the birthplaces of larger stores in the city proper in the later years. Members of the families of Hordern and Marcus Clark (from 1883) at one time operated stores there.

St Stephen's Church of England in Church Street, off King Street, replaced a smaller St Stephen's on 13 acres of land in Stephen Street given by the O'Connell family. The new church was shared by Camperdown and Newtown. It was designed by Edmund Blacket (1817–83), and is regarded as one of his best designs. The foundation stone was laid in 1871 and when the church was consecrated in 1874 it opened free of debt. Its adjacent graveyard, on land purchased from the O'Connells' Camperdown estate, holds the remains of hundreds of early residents of Sydney. The first burial was of Sir Maurice O'Connell, whose remains were transferred from the Devonshire Street Cemetery in 1849. One mass grave is given to those drowned in the wreck of the *Dunbar*. The captain mistook The Gap at Watsons Bay for the opening to Sydney Harbour and the ship was wrecked on 15 August 1857. Only one man survived, 23-year-old James Johnson; 122 others perished.

A character in Charles Dickens's famous novel *Great Expectations* is said to have been inspired by the fate of a Newtown resident, the daughter of Judge Donnithorne, who was jilted on her wedding day, a few years after her father's death in 1852. She became a recluse, locking her door against her friends and neighbours. The breakfast was never disturbed and remained set out until her death. Miss Donnithorne never left the house until carried to her resting place in the old cemetery of St Stephen's. It is believed that Dickens based the character of Miss Havisham on the legend of the judge's daughter.

When the Sydney to Parramatta Junction (now called Granville) railway line came through this suburb in the 1850s, a railway station opened opposite Station Street, on 26 September 1855. Originally it was named New Town, recognising the Websters' general store, but later the site was moved to the Burren Farm land, and the station's name became Newtown.

The official post office opened in 1854, and the first public school opened in Newtown in 1863.

Today Newtown is a busy inner-city suburb that has been favoured by immigrant families, and the interesting shops, cafes and restaurants of King Street reflect the suburb's mixed population. It also provides a home for some of those at the nearby University of Sydney and workers at Camperdown's Royal Prince Alfred Hospital. Newtown remains a densely populated residential suburb with some industry.

# NORMANHURST

*Shire of Hornsby*
Location: 23 kilometres north-west of Sydney on Pennant Hills Road and the Main Northern Line

This northern suburb began its life with the name of Hornsby, and today's Hornsby, a village that grew up at Pearce's Corner (see Waitara), was known as Hornsby Junction. So much confusion arose that a complete name change was suggested, and the new name honoured a brilliant civil engineer, Norman Selfe (1839–1911), who had property where the Normanhurst Boys High School now stands. When the railway station had to be renamed in 1900, it was decided to honour this remarkable man. It became Normanhurst, "hurst" being the old English word for a wooded hill.

Selfe was involved in the design and installation of the plant at the Hartley shale mine, as well as engineering the first ice-making equipment and the first grain elevators in New South Wales. He also designed the scenic railway at Katoomba in the Blue Mountains,

St George's Hall, completed in 1887, was a theatre in the 1920s, dance hall in the 1930s, printery in the 1950s and bindery in the late 1970s. Now owned by the Department of Education it will form part of the Newtown School of the Performing Arts

one of the engineering wonders of its day. Sclfc also agitated for a cross-harbour bridge and drew up a design for it. When he built his home in this district in 1894, it was a quiet country area and his property included an extensive orchard.

An early land grant in this area was of 320 acres to Constable Samuel Henry Horne in 1831. The grant, which lay between the present Thornleigh and Pearce's Corner, was made in recognition of his work in helping Chief Constable Thorn capture two bushrangers, one of whom was the notorious John Macnamara. Horne later became a gaol wardsman at Parramatta, before moving to Patrick Plains, where he became chief constable. He settled with his wife and eleven children at Singleton, where he died. His

property, known as Horne's Grant or Hornesby Place, eventually gave its name to the suburb of Hornsby. Adjoining his grant was the one given to Chief Constable John Thorn, who gave his name to Thornleigh. Thorn never lived on his property, and after his death it was subdivided into several small blocks, which were sold for farming.

The first post office in this suburb opened as Hornsby in August 1864, but another change of name took place before the final choice. It changed to South Hornsby in May 1900, and finally to Normanhurst on 15 September 1905.

Normanhurst today, like its neighbour Wahroonga, is noted for its purity of air and freedom from pollution. It is a residential area, but it retains its bushland setting.

## NORTHBRIDGE
*Municipality of Willoughby*
Location: 7 kilometres north of Sydney on the western side of Middle Harbour

This suburb takes its name from a suspension bridge known as North Bridge. It was constructed at a cost of £100,000 by a firm of land developers, the North Sydney Investment and Tramway Company, who expected that a bridge crossing the gorge between North Sydney and a large area of land around Middle Harbour would attract some buyers to the area. The bridge was completed, but not the tramlines, when economic recession forced the company into liquidation as the

Aerial photograph of the majestic North Bridge taken in 1966

land boom also collapsed.

The stone bridge, the first of its kind in Australia, was opened in the early 1890s and quickly became one of Sydney's most interesting sights. It was 180 feet above water, with a main span of 500 feet. There was a wonderful view from its turret lookouts, and people came by the tram from Milsons Point to marvel at this modern and unusual structure. Originally known as North Sydney Bridge, it soon became North Bridge and as such gave its name to the suburb.

In 1912 the suspension bridge was taken over by the state government and used for trams from 1912 to 1936, when it was condemned. It reopened in 1939 with a concrete arch for safety, although its castle-like appearance remained unchanged.

The land where the bridge was built was owned by a Sydney jeweller, Arthur Twemlow. He built a two-storey house on Fig Tree Point of sandstone quarried on the estate. The house, called The Hermitage, was ready for family occupation in 1870. The area from The Spit through to Seaforth and Balgowlah was still natural bushland, but Twemlow created a beautiful garden around his home and planted a Moreton Bay Fig tree which flourished and was still alive in 1965. The area at that time could have been considered lonely, but gradually other houses were built, and telephone and electricity services were added. Transport was quite a problem: Twemlow had to sail through The Spit and around Middle Head to the Quay, from where he walked to his shop in Sydney Arcade. On one occasion the boat was caught in a violent storm on the journey home; the servant who handled the sailing was drowned, while Twemlow was fortunate to escape.

The suburb has some splendid homes still nestling among natural bushland, yet it is now considered a convenient distance from Sydney.

# NORTHMEAD

*City of Parramatta, Shire of Baulkham Hills*
Location: 26 kilometres west of Sydney on Windsor Road

The name of this suburb to the north of Parramatta describes its situation. It was the north "mead", or meadow, of the governor's domain, or park. It is a hilly area, rising from the Darling Mills Creek, north towards Winston Hills, with Darling Mills Creek and Toongabbie Creek as its other boundaries.

A station for a light railway opened here in January 1923 and was known as Woollen Mills, because of the Darling Mills nearby. The line, which carried goods and passengers, opened in 1902 and ran from Parramatta Station to Baulkham Hills. A new line to Castle Hill from Northmead and Westmead opened in 1923. Seven months later the name was changed to Northmead, which has remained as the suburb's name, although both lines had closed by 1927.

The official post office opened in June 1916, and the first school was established in January 1924.

The residents here are home-lovers, as their houses and gardens show. Nearby are the shopping centres and sports facilities of Blacktown and Parramatta.

The area was originally one of orchard and poultry farms, and retains something of the tranquillity of its farming days.

# NORTH ROCKS

*Shire of Baulkham Hills, City of Parramatta*
Location: 26 kilometres north-west of Sydney on Pennant Hills Road

Part of the Hills District, this suburb began its life in the 1880s as a farming and fruit growing area. It lies north of Parramatta and is semi-rural.

In the early 1960s the Royal New South Wales Institution for Deaf, Dumb and Blind Children (now the Institute for Deaf and Blind Children) bought land here on which it built spacious school buildings, leaving room for further expansion. The school opened on 5 June 1962, with thirty children. The Wahroonga School for the Blind and the Darlington School for the Deaf were also transferred to this pleasant, healthy area. The schools are today called the Central School for Deaf Children and School for Blind Children, and seventy-five children are enrolled.

North Rocks is a growing residential area. Improved bus services and subdivision of former rural land have opened up the district for housing, so the formerly quiet suburb is fast becoming a busy town.

# NORTH RYDE

*Municipality of Ryde*
Location: 15 kilometres north-west of Sydney at the junction of Epping Road and Lane Cove Road

On 1 September 1885, a post office was established at North Ryde — "not before it was wanted", to quote the official record. The area west of the Lane Cove River had developed as settlers, mostly farmers and orchardists, moved into the northern heights of Ryde. The flat area of Ryde village gave way to the ascending rough, hilly country we now call North Ryde, described then as "a verdant forest and a hazy mountain".

Today the area is notable for Macquarie University and the Macquarie Centre shopping complex. Many light industries, warehouses and large modern offices have been established in the area, and progress shows its relentless hand in the highway linking Epping and North Ryde with city-bound traffic. Older landmarks in the area are North Ryde Golf Links, North Ryde Psychiatric Centre, and the Northern Suburbs Cemetery. Channel 10 television studios are also here.

An interesting connection lies between Macquarie University and Governor Lachlan Macquarie (1762–1824), after whom this seat of learning was named. During Macquarie's term of office (1810–21), convicts carved a pair of chairs described as "State Chairs of Government House, Sydney". When the governor left for home in 1822, the people of New South Wales presented them to him, and the chairs were shipped to his home on the Isle of Mull in Scotland. In 1967 a descendant of Governor Macquarie returned one of the chairs to Australia as a memento of this great governor's contribution to the development of the colony. The chair duly arrived, rather shabby but authentic and, when refurbished, was given to Macquarie University, to be used as a chancellor's chair on special occasions.

## NORTH SYDNEY
*Municipality of North Sydney*
Location: 3 kilometres north of Sydney at the beginning of the Pacific Highway, on the North Shore Line

The Aborigines from the north side of the harbour called the Sydney Cove area *warung*, meaning "the other side", while the tribes on the Sydney Cove side called the north side by the same name — *warung*, "the other side". To further confuse matters the first name given by the English settlers to the land on the north side of Sydney Harbour was Huntershill. Today's North Sydney was

originally part of the area known as St Leonards. The township was laid out as St Leonards in 1836 in the area surrounded by the present Miller, Walker, Lavender and Berry Streets. By 1846 there were 106 houses in the area. By 1859, when the foundation stone of the School of Arts was laid on the site of the present courthouse, the commercial centre had extended from Milsons Point to Miller and Mount streets, but the businesses were still small. A bus run by Jeremiah Wall joined Milsons Point

A posed photo of Bernard Holtermann with the Beyers and Holtermann specimen, reputedly the largest single mass of gold, quartz and slate ever mined

Weight : 630 lbs
Height : 4ft.9m.
Width : 2ft.2 in
Average Thickness 4 inches
Value £1000..

Looking from Arthur Street, North Sydney, in 1963 just before the area was levelled to make way for the Warringah Expressway

to the "North Sydney shops". As time passed houses were built or bought, and North Sydney began to develop an identity of its own. In the 1880s the courthouse and the town hall, in Alfred Street, were built.

One of the oldest houses in North Sydney is believed to have been an early farmhouse, built perhaps as early as the 1820s. Don Bank, at 6 Napier Street, North Sydney, is a timber house, once called St Leonards Cottage, part of which is believed to be a house built on Edward Wollstonecraft's land. The North Sydney municipality acquired it in 1979, and it was opened in 1981 as a local history museum and as the home of the North Shore Historical Society.

One of the largest houses in the area was occupied by

parliamentarian Francis Lord, three times member of the legislative council in the 1840s, 1850s and 1860s. He was the second son of Simeon Lord (1771–1840), one of Sydney's most successful emancipist merchants. The house was called Ma-sa-lou and is now the Convent of Monte Sant'Angelo, in Miller Street. On the corner of Berry Street and Lane Cove Road (now the Pacific Highway) Captain Robert Pockley (d.1892) built Pictonville, named after Picton where his wife lived before her marriage. Helena Antill, whom he married in 1854, was the daughter of Henry Colden Antill (1779–1852), a magistrate and former aide-de-camp to Governor Macquarie. Pockley later became portmaster of Sydney Harbour. The Priory was built by Colonel Barney, who designed Victoria Barracks, and was at different times colony commissioner for crown lands, and surveyor-general.

The house known as Holtermann's Tower was built by Bernard Otto Holtermann, who arrived in Sydney in 1858. The 23-year-old German later became wealthy from his gold finds, but he is perhaps best-known as a sponsor of early photography. The Mitchell Library holds several thousand wet-plate negatives in the Holtermann Collection. The work of photographers Beaufoy Merlin and Charles Bayliss at Hill End and Bayliss at Gulgong, they show scenes of the gold diggings. In 1875 Bayliss took panoramic photographs of Sydney Harbour from the 22.4 metre high tower of the house. Three of the negatives produced, each measuring $1 \times 1.6$ metres, are also in the Mitchell Library.

Rockleigh Grange was once the home of the artist Conrad Martens (1801–78), who arrived in Sydney in 1835 and whose paintings depict Sydney scenes with great accuracy. He was involved in designing and carving the font for the first St Thomas's Church, which is still in use in the present church.

St Thomas's Anglican Church stands in Berry Street, North Sydney. The first Anglican church erected on the site in 1843, and opened in 1846, became inadequate for the increasing congregation and in 1877 when it was decided to enlarge the church, a new chancel and transepts were erected around the old St Thomas's. In due course funds were provided for the completion of the new church, designed by Edmund Blacket (1817–83). It was dedicated in 1884. The largest parish church in Australia, it was built on the plan

of Goulburn Cathedral.

Well-known names are connected with the building of the first St Thomas's, contributing money or other assistance. Some of them are Alexander Berry, of Crow's Nest Cottage; Edward Wollstonecraft, an early office-bearer of the Chamber of Commerce and assistant commissary-general of New South Wales; William Miller, after whom Miller Street, North Sydney, was named; his deputy Thomas Walker, who is commemorated by Walker Street; William Gore, whose property, Artarmon House, is recalled in that suburb's name; and James Milson junior, whose father is remembered in the name Milsons Point.

St Thomas's cemetery in West

Street, north of the church itself, is now a rest park. It was established in 1845, the first burial being that of Elizabeth Berry, Edward Wollstonecraft's sister. Elizabeth's husband, Alexander Berry, gave the land for the burial ground. Judge-advocate Ellis Bent, remembered by Bent Street, Sydney; Captain Owen Stanley, after whom the Owen Stanley Range in New Guinea was named; and Lieutenant-Colonel George Barney, the engineer responsible for the construction of Fort Denison and Victoria Barracks, Paddington, were all interred there.

The first rector of the church of St Thomas's was the Reverend William Branwhite Clarke (1798–1878), a friend of Alexander

View from the post office tower down the Pacific Highway, North Sydney, 1932

Berry. A brilliant geologist as well as a clergyman, in 1841 he discovered gold particles near Hartley in New South Wales and predicted the area would be rich in gold. In 1847 he pressed for surveys of the state. He was proved correct when Hargraves announced the discovery of gold at Ophir in 1851. In 1877 the young midshipman who later became King George V of England visited St Thomas's and laid the foundation cornerstone of the new St Thomas's tower.

The North Sydney municipality was incorporated in 1890, when, after many disputes the name North Sydney was chosen. It included the Mosman area at that stage and the population numbered 18,000; 3,200 houses had been erected.

The post office opened in 1854 as St Leonards, but this title was changed to North Sydney on 1 November 1890. The first school also opened as St Leonards in 1874 and became North Sydney in July 1910. There are a number of schools in the area today: North Sydney Demonstration School, opened in 1932; North Sydney Boys High, opened on the present site in Falcon Street in 1915; and North Sydney Girls High, opened on the Pacific Highway in 1914. All of these schools, however, have much longer histories than their present buildings suggest. Private schools include Wenona Girls School, whose history goes back to 1886; Monte Sant'Angelo; and Shore, the Sydney Church of England Grammar School, on the site of the home of Bernard Holtermann, which was sold to the school by Sir Thomas Gibbs, who had acquired the property after Holtermann's death.

A hospital also stands in North Sydney on the site of an old house. This is the Graythwaite Nursing Home in Edward Street. Sir Thomas Dibbs, a banker and philanthropist, presented the house to the Red Cross during the First World War. The two-storey stone house had been built as Euroka by Edward Mawny Sayers in the 1850s; Dibbs changed the name to Graythwaite when he bought it from Sayers, and he added a lookout and attic. Despite extensions to the hospital, the original residence has been preserved.

Fortunately North Sydney has retained in good condition some of its older buildings and churches. The older cottages blend well with the progressive trend of high-rise units and office blocks in a suburb that has seen rapid commercial as well as residential development since the Second World War.

# NORTHWOOD
*Municipality of Lane Cove*
Location: 8 kilometres north-west of Sydney on the Lane Cove River

A place of views would be an appropriate name for this small residential suburb on a peninsula between Longueville and Greenwich. Descending to the Lane Cove River from a hilly area, it affords a wide vista of the water and bush-softened shores. It was known as Penry, or Pendray, Point in the 1850s, after a military pensioner who owned land there. Later the land came into the possession of the Davey family.

A spacious home, Northwood House, was designed by Edmund Blacket (1817–83) and erected by Mrs Jane Davey in 1878. Mrs Davey also built a wharf at her own expense so that her family could travel to the city by ferry. The suburb took its name from this house, which is descriptive of its location in the north of a woodland area.

Another early name in the district was Reid. James Reid and his wife lived in these parts before moving on to Milsons Point at the end of the 1850s.

Gore Bay on the east of the peninsula is named after William Gore (1765–1845), provost-marshal in Bligh's governorship (1806–08), who bought up some older grants in the district (see Artarmon). Gore Hill also commemorates him.

# OATLEY
*Municipalities of Hurstville and Kogarah*
Location: 21 kilometres south-west of Sydney on the northern side of the Georges River and on the Illawarra Line

This picturesque suburb was named after a man who never lived in the area. He was James Oatley (1770–1839), a convict clockmaker who arrived in the colony on 27 January 1815 to serve a life sentence.

The Hyde Park convict barracks, built between 1817 and 1819, was designed to include a clock, which was made by Oatley. He was paid £75 and later, when he was pardoned, he received several land grants. One of these, granted in 1833, was 300 acres near the Georges River. He called his property Needwood Forest, after woodlands in his native Warwickshire in England. Oatley never built on the land, but lived on a farm called Snugsborough near Beverly Hills. It stood on a 175 acre grant received in 1831. He had a watchmaker's shop in George Street opposite the present

Section of a panoramic view of Oatley Bay, 1922

Sydney Town Hall and, when he retired, his third son, Frederick, took over the work. He died in 1839, and was buried at Snugsborough, where his grave was found in 1921. Needwood Forest passed to Frederick, who sold it to Charles Cecil Griffiths in 1881. The property extended from Gungal Bay, on the suburb's western edge, to the later Boundary and Hurstville Roads. Oatley's second son, James (1817–78), became a member of the old City Council and later the Municipal Council and in 1862, Mayor of Sydney.

When the Hurstville to Sutherland railway line passed through Oatley's old property in the 1880s, the station, opened in 1886, took the clockmaker's name. Oatley Bay and Oatley Park were also named after him, the latter being a favourite picnic spot for local residents.

The post office opened in 1903. The St George Institute of Education, formerly the Alexander Mackie Teachers College and now part of Sydney College of Advanced Education, stands in this suburb.

## OXFORD FALLS

*Shire of Warringah*

Location: 20 kilometres north of Sydney on the Wakehurst Parkway

In 1878, Alexander Bowman was granted 200 acres of land in this area, north-east of Frenchs Forest, which was then named Bloodwood Gully. Bowman is believed to have been a timber-cutter, culling wood from this forest area to sell to builders. The suburb's new name, Oxford Falls, was chosen and gazetted in 1902.

The Oxford Falls are on Middle Creek, which flows north to meet Oxford Creek. The Falls and Middle Creek are surrounded by a large recreation reserve adjoining Narrabeen Lakes to the east. The suburb remains one of sparse settlement in an area of natural bushland.

The Wakehurst Parkway, a main thoroughfare named after John de Vere, Baron Wakehurst, governor of New South Wales from 1937 to 1946, cuts through this small suburb, and runs north-east to the National Fitness Camp and Narrabeen Lakes, an area of unspoiled natural beauty.

The first Church of England church service was held at Oxford Falls in 1917, when thirty-seven residents attended. A tree was marked to commemorate the spot, and a church was erected there in 1926. The church, built in one day by voluntary local labour, is known as St Andrew's. It opened on 29 May 1926. In 1928 the church hall was used for the first school, to be later replaced by the school building erected by the Department of Education, in Dreadnought Road, named after a famous British battleship launched in 1906. A one-teacher school, it was closed in 1986.

## OXLEY PARK

*City of Penrith*

Location: 44 kilometres west of Sydney on the Great Western Highway

Explorer John Oxley (1785?–1828) received a grant of 600 acres near St Marys, in 1823, on the site of the present suburb.

The suburb of Oxley Park has been named in honour of this former notable surveyor-general, who discovered the Lachlan River, Liverpool Plains and Port Macquarie, named in honour of the governor of the time, Lachlan Macquarie. He also explored

Moreton Bay and the Brisbane River in 1823, and his favourable report on the area led to the formation of the penal settlement there. In his capacity as surveyor-general he also drew up regulations on land grants and sales. He died at Kirkham, a fine country estate he established at Camden.

The suburb named after him is a small residential area south-east of St Marys railway station, its main streets named after state capitals such as Brisbane and Canberra. The main thoroughfares of Hobart and Melbourne Streets hem in this neighbourhood, with the Great Western Highway forming the southern boundary. Oxley Park Public School stands in Adelaide Street.

# OYSTER BAY

*Shire of Sutherland*
Location: 26 kilometres south of Sydney on the southern bank of the Georges River

Situated on a peninsula on the southern bank of the Georges River between Carina, Coronation and Double Bays on the west and Oyster Bay on the east, the suburb takes its name from the area's abundant oyster harvests. Maps prepared by Surveyor Wells in 1840 show the bay already named Oyster Bay, indicating that the farming of this delicious delicacy was well established by that date. It is now a charming residential suburb with access to Sydney from Como or Jannali on the Illawarra Line.

# PADDINGTON

*City of Sydney, Municipality of Woollahra*
Location: 3 kilometres south-east of Sydney on Oxford Street

This suburb, which took its name from the London borough of Paddington, lies in what were once paddocks adjacent to Victoria Barracks. It was the first of the early suburbs that was not self-sufficient — its inhabitants, unlike those of Balmain or Newtown, where work was available in local industries, had to go away each day to their places of employment. Development of the Eastern Suburbs (Edgecliff, Double Bay, Point Piper and Woollahra) surrounded this area with wealthy people's homes so this small hilly suburb lost all hope of harbour views.

The central part of Paddington is a steep valley, Lecrosia Valley, which was granted to W. Thomas; the other early land-holder was Thomas West, whose grant adjoined Thomas's.

The area developed after a road was constructed to link up with a pilot station that was to be built at Watsons Bay. John Palmer, the settlement's commissary, refused to allow people to cross his land grant, so the road had to follow a roundabout way through Paddington to bypass his 100 acres. In addition, in 1818 a distillery had been built, and the carters travelled to the city by a long winding route, trodden out by bullocks as a rough track, along the route of the present Glenmore Road.

For all this, only a handful of workers lived in the area, and it was not until 1838, when it was decided to build a new military barracks in Paddington, that life came to the area. From 1848, when the Victoria Barracks were opened

and homes for the soldiers and their families had been erected, Paddington began to assume a real identity.

The first houses in the suburb were built in 1840 on the Elfred Estate to house workmen on the barracks. Some of these simple cottages still stand in Gipps and Shadforth Streets. In 1842 the Paddington Estate, on the original 100 acre grant in the area, was on the market and the name soon became attached to the whole suburb. Once the soldiers and their families moved here, shopkeepers followed. Builders moved into the area and put up 3,800 houses between 1860 and 1890. These terraces give today's Paddington its air of individuality. The builders mostly sought land that would accommodate four or six houses then built on the first and last blocks of the land. The builder and his family usually occupied the first house and the chief worker or foreman, or perhaps another member of the family, lived in the last. Then the houses in between were built, in the same style, with an unbroken pattern of wrought-iron "lacework" decoration on the balconies and similar colour schemes. The terrace design was brought from London, where the close building pattern gives warmth and protection against the colder climate. Residents soon realised that group housing could be hot in summer, but today many of these terraces have added a roof-room or opened up the basement to catch breezes. The first school in the area was opened in the Presbyterian manse in Oxford Street, built in 1845.

Victoria Barracks, designed by Lieutenant-Colonel George Barney (1792–1862), are one of the highlights of Paddington. Originally the soldiery were housed in the George Street

Re-laying tram tracks at Five Ways, Paddington, 1926. The Royal Hotel is still a landmark at the well-known intersection

Barracks in the city, defined by George, Barrack, Clarence and Jamison Streets. As these quarters became old and inadequate it was decided to build better quarters, and in 1838 Barney, an engineer, advised selling the old barracks and building at Paddington. Construction began in 1841 but the barracks did not open until 1848 because of the many problems encountered. The land was sandy — in fact a huge sandhill was located on the western side in the Greens Road area, and the foundation trenches had to be dug very deep, to locate firm stone for the foundations. Stone was mostly quarried in the area: the stonemasons were free settlers who

had worked on the erection of the Customs House at what was then Semi-Circular Quay.

When the barracks, sited on 29 acres of land, were eventually completed in 1848, the houses for workmen and incoming military families were also completed, and the 11th Regiment had a new home in an area the soldiers grew to hate because of its desolate, sandy atmosphere and its distance from the delights of the city. But their children loved it — playing in sand became their chief joy.

From 1848 the barracks were occupied by 800 British troops, who left New South Wales in 1870. Today Victoria Barracks serve as a focal point for army activities in New South Wales and as the headquarters of the Eastern Command. The barracks are also

tangible evidence of the military history of New South Wales, and a steadily developing museum is housed there. They remain the largest and best preserved complex of colonial Georgian buildings in Australia. Visitors can see a ceremonial changing of the guard here and tour the barracks afterwards.

In today's busy Paddington it is hard to imagine that in 1822 the mansion Juniper Hall stood alone, without the many neighbours it has today. Set in a flagged garden, it had attic windows that gave panoramic views to Rushcutters Bay and Botany Bay. The first house in Paddington, it was built for Robert Cooper (1776–1857), an emancipist merchant and distiller, who in 1822 was marrying for the third time. His wife was to be 20-year-old Sarah May from Windsor. Cooper, with partners James Underwood and Francis Ewen Forbes, had received 100 acres from the governor, Sir Thomas Brisbane in about 1818, covering the whole of north Paddington, and they agreed to erect three mansions and a distillery there. The Glenmore Distillery was built at the foot of Cascade Street near Taylor Square, but Cooper bought out his partners, and only Juniper Hall was erected, and named in honour of the gin that contributed to Cooper's fortune. The Coopers occupied the house from 1824, had eight daughters and six sons, which, added to the children from his other two marriages, made Robert Cooper the father of twenty-eight children. The Coopers were part of the social scene of their day and entertained many notables of that time. After they left it, the house was renamed Ormond House, to disassociate it from the gin image, and it passed through many hands, gradually becoming smothered by the building of small shops in front of the house. Today its historical significance as one of Sydney's oldest houses is recognised and it is being restored to its former glory by the National Trust.

Paddington is an ideal suburb in which to stroll on a sunny winter's day. Its streets are rich in colonial buildings and the decorative iron lace, which is a particular attraction of Paddington. It exhibits not only geometric and classical patterns but also Australian motifs of ferns, waratahs and wattles.

Today few of the area's original working-class residents remain, as the suburb's proximity to the city has made it popular with business and professional people who prefer inner-city living in this historic area. The suburb's shopping centre, concentrated on the northern side of Oxford Street, has also changed from one serving local needs to one of cafes, specialty shops and boutiques filled with expensive and often extreme fashions. Much of this is related to the changing population and the Village Bazaar, or Paddington Markets, held at a church in Oxford Street every Saturday. The bazaar, which has operated since the mid-1970s, draws visitors from all over the city and has contributed to Paddington's development as one of Sydney's favourite tourist spots, along with Bondi Beach and The Rocks.

## PADSTOW

*City of Bankstown*
Location: 22 kilometres south-west of Sydney between Riverwood and Revesby on the East Hills Line

This suburb was named after Padstow Park Estate, itself named after a town in Cornwall, England. The estate was made up of grants to three settlers: Simon McGuigan had received 130 acres; Joseph Cunningham, 50 acres; and Michael Conroy, 40 acres. The estate, bounded by the present Cahors, Lester, Doyle, River, Uranus and Faraday Roads, would have taken in the area situated around the railway station, which opened on 21 December 1931. Like many suburbs, Padstow developed from the time the railway came through.

In January 1927, a post office known as Padstow Park opened, but its name was changed to Padstow in 1939. The first school opened in January 1929.

Today, like its neighbour Revesby, Padstow is a busy residential area with modern shopping facilities, a far cry from the early days of the Padstow Park Estate, when timber-getting and small farming were the main activities. The neighbourhood known as Padstow Heights extends south to the northern bank of the Georges River, with Georges River Parklands and Beauty Point Reserve on its southern boundary. Salt Pan Creek forms the western boundary of both Padstow and Padstow Heights.

## PAGEWOOD

*Municipality of Botany*
Location: 8 kilometres south of Sydney, just west of Maroubra

Originally planned as a garden suburb, after the pattern of neighbouring Daceyville, this area was developed to provide housing in a period of shortage in Botany municipality after the First World War.

The new suburb was created in 1919, in the area between Birdwood Avenue and the present Heffron Road. A ballot for lots was held that year, deposits paid by future residents, and houses built to plans provided by the housing board. The first houses completed were in Monash Gardens. A second subdivision was made later. Most of the street names honour Victoria Cross winners and generals. Heffron Road, formerly Maroubra Bay Road, was named after R. J. Heffron, member for the area in parliament and premier of New South Wales in 1952–59. The suburb was named Pagewood in 1929, in honour of Alderman F. J. Page of Botany Council.

Thirty years later, this accepted name was threatened. In August 1960 the residents of this pleasant suburb near Botany woke to hear the unpleasant news that the name of their suburb might be changed to East Botany. Needless to say they began to do battle to preserve the established name. The most important reason for retaining the old name, they claimed, was that Botany proper was fast becoming a centre of industries, while Pagewood was known as a residential suburb. Finally it was decided that Pagewood would retain its name and identity.

In the early days of the colony, Pagewood like many suburbs in this area, was part of the Church and School Lands set aside to support clergy and teachers. Today it is a pleasant, convenient suburb for home-lovers and families.

The National Film Studios at Pagewood, c. 1935

## PALM BEACH
*Shire of Warringah*
Location: 41 kilometres north of Sydney at the tip of Barrenjoey Peninsula

This peninsula jutting into Broken Bay between Pittwater and the ocean was visited by Governor Phillip in an early exploration of the Pittwater area on 2 March 1788. By 1797 boats were plying between Sydney and the Hawkesbury River, transporting fine timber and grain past the sheltered beach with its proliferation of cabbage palms that gave the beach its name. An earlier title was Cranky Alice Beach, so obviously one early resident lacked the courtesies found in today's residents. The suburb today has two sides to its character: an almost Riviera gaiety on the ocean side, especially at holiday time, and a quieter residential life on the Pittwater side.

Palm Beach was isolated until the Barrenjoey Road came through the suburb and the government bus service offered access to day-trippers. In the 1920s the road from Newport to Palm Beach was completed and the cart track that had been Old Barrenjoey Road was upgraded and bitumenised.

One of the first settlers was Pat Flynn, who in 1808 was growing vegetables in the area. The Palm Beach Estate, originally a grant of 400 acres made to James Napper in 1816, stretched from Whale Beach to Newport. Napper named it Larkfield. Between the 1830s and 1850s fishermen lived in the area in caves and huts. Smuggling was rife at this time, with cargoes being landed in the Hawkesbury instead of Sydney. In 1843, however, a customs post was established at Broken Bay — on Barrenjoey, below the present lighthouse — and operated until 1870. A Chinese fish-drying business was operated

James Barnet

on the beach beside Palm Beach jetty.

Changes came to this northern beach suburbs when the land on the peninsula and at Palm Beach was subdivided and sold by Raine and Horne. By the time the second lots of land were ready for sale roads were being built and named. In 1914 Miss Haynet, who ran a guest-house, became the district's first post-mistress.

Barrenjoey Head at the northern end of the suburb, was named by Governor Phillip, although the spelling varied considerably in the early days. Barrenjoey Lighthouse at the entrance to Broken Bay was designed by James Barnet, the colonial architect, and it began operation on 1 August 1881. During the construction of the freestanding tower two men lost their lives on this dangerous site. Before the erection of the lighthouse, two wooden buildings, known as the Stewart Towers, stood on the site. They were built in 1868 and showed light from suspended lanterns. Broken Bay was a thriving port by the 1850s and the first lights were needed to guide shipping safely to port. Today the Barrenjoey Light is

visible for 40 kilometres on a clear day, the same distance as Macquarie Light on South Head. The lighthouse has views to Lion Island and across the bay to Umina and Brisbane Water.

The Aboriginal name Barrenjoey means "a young kangaroo", and Pittwater was named in honour of William Pitt the younger, English prime minister from 1783–1901 and 1801–06.

In 1906 a challenge race between two locally built sailing skiffs marked the beginning of the Pittwater Regatta. The following year the Pittwater Regatta was so successful that the residents decided to make it a permanent annual event.

## PANANIA

*City of Bankstown*
Location: 25 kilometres south-west of Sydney between Revesby and East Hills on the East Hills Line

This Aboriginal word has the inspiring meaning of "sun rising in the east and shining on the hills". The area, south of Bankstown and on the north bank of the Georges River, was originally part of the district known as East Hills, and most of the early land grants there extended into Panania (see East Hills).

In the early 1800s, as in neighbouring suburbs, timber-cutting was the main livelihood, but it was not until the 1890s that the first settlement began, on small orchards, farms and poultry farms. With the coming of the railway from Tempe in 1931 a new name was needed for this portion of East Hills, which was to be regarded as a new suburb. (At that time it was the

terminus of the line, which was later extended to East Hills.) Various names were suggested and rejected in quick succession — Linden Park, Nioka and Emswood among them. The final choice was Panania, today a well-settled area in the municipality of Bankstown. The remainder of East Hills retains its original name. These suburbs are on the branch line of the main Illawarra railway, which will be linked to the main Southern Line at Glenfield by 1988.

Picnic Point, a popular area for recreation since early this century, is in the south-eastern part of the suburb and is now part of the Georges River State Recreation Area.

## PARKLEA

*City of Blacktown*
Location: 39 kilometres north-west of Sydney, west of Old Windsor Road

This suburb has been part of Blacktown's history from the early 1890s, when the area known as Parklea was subdivided and received its name, the origin of which is unknown.

By 1920 a village had been established, and the Anglican church of St Aidan's had been built, although it is no longer standing.

The atmosphere remained distinctly rural, however, and the area was known for its numerous poultry farms. But its pride was in its orchards and vineyards, which stood on a stretch of land extending to Baulkham Hills. In that area in 1887, E. H. Pearce was recorded as selling his orchard crop while on the trees for £4,000 to a buyer in Victoria. Like its neighbours Kings Langley and

Lalor Park, Parklea is one of the areas developed in recent years as residential suburbs of Blacktown.

In recent times the state government used some of the housing commission land in the areas for a new prison. Parklea Maximum Security Prison, on the Quakers Hill side of Parklea, is an enormous complex and its construction within the residential area of Parklea raised many protests from residents. Another controversial project nearby, a large market in the style of the city's Paddy's Markets and the Weekend Markets at Flemington, was opened in 1987.

# PARRAMATTA

*City of Parramatta, Shire of Baulkham Hills*

Location: 23 kilometres west of Sydney on the Parramatta River and the Main Western Line

The Parramatta area was first seen by Europeans on 23 April 1788, when Governor Phillip's party reached the land at the head of the Parramatta River. They were impressed by the good soil, and the following spring Phillip established a government farm there on 2 November 1788. He called the area Rose Hill after George Rose, one of the secretaries to the treasury and Phillip's patron.

The colony's first privately owned farm was established here when James Ruse (1760–1837), an ex-convict, was granted 30 acres in 1789. He named his property Experiment Farm, because Phillip had granted the land as an experiment to see how quickly a farmer could become self-sufficient. His farming ventures were successful, but he sold in 1793 to Surgeon John Harris, who owned the adjoining

land (see Harris Park). The house built on the property by Harris, at some time between 1798 and the 1830s, is still standing in Ruse Street.

Other early grants in the area were made in 1791 and 1792 to Charles Williams, James Stuart and William Cummings (who received 20 or 30 acres each). All of these were later acquired by John Macarthur, who in 1793 received 100 acres, which became Elizabeth Farm, and in 1794 another 100 acres (Edward Farm). He gradually bought up other grants and eventually owned 850 acres extending into Camellia and the present Rosehill areas. His wife, Elizabeth (1767?–1850), conducted the first merino-breeding experiments here while John was in England in the aftermath of the overthrow of Governor Bligh in 1808. Elizabeth Farm House, built in 1793, with some later additions, still stands in Alice Street. The Macarthur family sold Elizabeth Farm in 1881 and it was subdivided from 1883. Mr Swann, a Parramatta pioneer, purchased the house in 1904, as a home for his growing family. Another house with Macarthur associations still standing in Parramatta is Hambledon Cottage, which was built in the 1820s for the Macarthur children's governess, Penelope Lucas, who came from England in 1805.

The town was laid out in June 1790 and named Parramatta on 4 June 1791. In the 1790s it was the main settlement of New South Wales and Sydney was only its harbour town. The earliest town lease was made in 1796 to Macarthur; others followed, but most residents had only permissive occupancies until Governor Brisbane regularised the situation in 1823. The present settlement, declared a city in 1938, is built

partly on land reserved for town purposes and partly on the early grants.

Other grants now in the town area include those made to D'Arcy Wentworth, James Meehan and Samuel Marsden. Over 6 acres were held by D'Arcy Wentworth (1762?–1827), medical practitioner, in the area of Darcy and Fitzwilliam Streets. His residence was named Wentworth Wood House after a family property in England. The area was leased in 1799, and granted in 1810. In 1873 it was subdivided. One hundred acres were granted to surveyor James Meehan (1774–1826) in 1816, and his property was later increased to 165 acres. His land was south of the Great Western Highway and west of Charles Street, where the first racecourse in Parramatta was built. This property was subdivided in 1842. North of the river, properties included the Reverend Samuel Marsden's (1764–1838) 18 acre grant given in 1822. Newlands House was built on the land in 1835, but the property was subdivided from 1841.

Governor Macquarie played an important part in the development of Parramatta. He laid out new streets in 1811 and initiated the construction of many buildings, such as the enlarged Government House, first built in 1799 and extended in 1815, barracks for troops (the Lancer Barracks) built in 1820, convict barracks (1820), and the Female Orphanage in 1818 (see Rydalmere). Old Government House, the oldest public building on the Australian mainland, and the Lancer Barracks, the oldest military barracks on the mainland, both designed by John Watts, Macquarie's aide-de-camp, are both still standing.

Phillip had built the original,

single storey, lath and plaster Government House at Parramatta and reserved a large area for its domain. Governor John Hunter built a new house in 1799 (the front part of an existing two-storey, brick building). Macquarie enlarged the house and formalised the area of domain. Government House was used as the country residence for the governors until the 1840s. It was renovated by The King's School in 1909 and handed to the National Trust in 1967. Governor Brisbane added an observatory in 1822 and a bath-house in 1823 in the domain; the former was demolished in the 1860s, and the latter was converted to a pavilion in 1886. In 1858 the domain area was broken up, but over 200 acres were reserved as Parramatta Park. The rest was subdivided from 1859 (see especially Northmead and Westmead).

Section of a panoramic view of Parramatta, 1922, taken by photographer R. P. Moore

St John's church was another early building in Parramatta. A temporary wooden building was put up in 1796 and by 1808 the first permanent building was completed. Twin towers (modelled on those of the church at Reculver in Kent) were added in 1820. These towers are still standing, but the rest of the church was rebuilt in 1852–55. The first incumbent was the Reverend Samuel Marsden, who was assigned here on his arrival in the colony in 1794. The church's name was originally given by Governor King in 1802 to honour Governor John Hunter (St Phillip's in Sydney honours the colony's first governor), but when the foundation of the new church was laid it was rededicated in 1852 to St John the Evangelist. The church is now St John's Cathedral.

Australia's textile industry began in Parramatta when Governor King organised the production of linens and woollens in the gaol by the female convicts held there. The woollen cloth made here was called

Parramatta, but in the early days the wool clip was so coarse that only a poor quality cloth, considered suitable only for convict work clothes, was produced. When Macquarie built the Female Factory (see Rydalmere) in 1818–21, the factory moved there. It closed in 1847.

The King's School opened in 1832 in George Street, Parramatta, and operated in the suburb until 1864. It was re-established in 1868 at Macquarie Fields but moved back to Parramatta in 1869. Between 1955 and 1962 it was moved to Gowan Brae at North Parramatta.

Some splendid modern buildings have been erected in Parramatta during the past ten years. Services for health, rehabilitation and retailing are among the most up-to-date in New South Wales. Several industries are also located in the district and Parramatta is a centre for transport services to outlying areas. An annual

Eisteddfod attracts hundreds of entries in all the arts, from both children and adults. Foundation Day, on 2 November, is marked each year by a parade and special bus tours around the city. The city football team is noted for its success, and facilities for swimming, athletics and related sports are also available in the district. Parramatta now has a large migrant population, hundreds of whom have become naturalised and are proud of this city and its surrounding area which they have adopted as their own.

## PEAKHURST

*Municipality of Hurstville*
Location: 21 kilometres south-west of Sydney north of the Georges River

As early resident of this suburb east of Salt Pan Creek and extending south to Lime Kiln Bay in the Georges River is remembered by its name. He was John Peake, who bought 10 acres near the junction of the present Forest Road and Henry Lawson Drive in 1838. He gave a block of land on which was built in 1855 the first church in this suburb, the Wesleyan church. This building was later used for a private school as well as for Sunday worship until the department of education took . on the responsibility of schooling in the area in 1871. The name of the school was suggested by a government school inspector in recognition of the interest shown in the district by this outstanding man, and the name was later adopted for the suburb.

Robert Townson's grant of 1808 (see Penshurst) covered the area east of Bonds Road and Boundary

Road. Most of the land to the west, however, was not granted until the 1830s to 1850s. The land was then granted in lots of 50 to 200 acres, the largest grant being made to William Hebblewhite in 1838, when he received 200 acres.

As in nearby suburbs the first industry here was timber-cutting, the surrounding natural forests being thick with a variety of woods. Peakhurst was rich in turpentine, a durable wood much in demand for wharf piles and paving blocks. The timber was carted to Sydney by bullock teams.

As the land was cleared orchardists followed the timber-cutters. The land was rich and suitable for fruit growing, but road conditions at this time made the settlers' life hard. In wet weather the unsealed roads became seas of glutinous mud, into which waggons sank axle-deep.

The railway line to Wollongong came through the area in 1884 and brought increased development for Peakhurst as new roads were built to connect it to Mortdale or Penshurst railway stations. In 1885 a post office called Peakhurst was opened, and as the forests were cleared, more settlers came to live in the area.

In the 1920s this suburb was described as "a settlement" west of Mortdale station, with a bus service from Hurstville and Penshurst stations. At that time it was still a country-style village and indeed it owed its further development to the increased use of the railway, which lessened its isolation. Today it is a busy middle-class suburb with the accent on family life. Peake Parade remembers its early notable settler.

## PEARCES CORNER

*Shire of Hornsby*
Location: A locality 22 kilometres north-west of Sydney at the junction of Pennant Hills Road and the Pacific Highway

Pearces Corner took its name from Aaron Pierce (see Waitara) who was transported to the colony with a life sentence in 1810. His wife, Ellen Holland, was also a convict. Pierce, a timber-getter, built a slab hut near the corner where a sawyers' track branched north off the Lane Cove Road (now the Pacific Highway). Pearces Corner was the original name of Wahroonga railway station (see Wahroonga).

## PENDLE HILL

*City of Parramatta, Municipality of Holroyd*
Location: 30 kilometres west of Sydney north of the Great Western Highway, on the Main Western Line

Pendle Hill, west of Parramatta, began to come to life when the railway came through the area in the 1880s, although the station did not open until 12 April 1924.

In 1923 George Bond (1876–1950) established a cotton spinning mill in the district, in the first attempt to spin and weave cotton in Australia, using cotton from two farms his company owned in Queensland. He requested that the area be named after Pendleton, in Lancashire, the centre of England's cotton industry, and Pendle Hill was the result. An American, Bond, came to Australia in 1906 and was naturalised in 1922. He began a business in Sydney, importing hosiery and underwear, but during the First World War he began manufacturing hosiery in Redfern. By 1925 he was producing one-quarter of Australia's output in hosiery and knitted goods. In 1927, after rapid expansion, the company was forced into liquidation and a new group established. Bonds Industries Limited became a flourishing public company, but Bond was no longer associated with it. Bonds Spinning Mills are still located nearby in Wentworthville.

The early settlers were poultry farmers, but today Pendle Hill is a residential suburb with attractive homes and gardens. The neat shopping centre, sporting facilities and modern schools have taken away something of the country atmosphere, but the people of this suburb still maintain the friendliness of an earlier age.

By the 1920s the suburb had a School of Arts and a local band. The first government school opened in August 1955 and the post office followed a year later, on 2 October 1956.

## PENNANT HILLS

*Shire of Hornsby*
Location: 25 kilometres north-west of Sydney off Pennant Hills Road, on the Main Northern Line

The name Pennant Hills, originally applied to all of the northern area between Ryde and Parramatta and Pearces Corner, was in use at the time of the governorship of Philip Gidley King (1800–06). Two schools of thought exist about the origin of the name. One is that its name honours Thomas Pennant (1726–98), a botanist colleague of Sir Joseph Banks. The second opinion concerns the district's connection with the series of signal stations from which semaphore messages were passed to Sydney. The first flag signal station was on Taverner's Hill, Petersham, then the route followed the ridges to one on high land near Thompsons Corner, West Pennant Hills, to be received in Parramatta at the signal point established by Governor Brisbane in Parramatta Park.

As the settlement at Parramatta expanded and free settlers began to arrive in the colony, the area known as the Hills District was established. The conditions in this newly opened area proved ideal for orchards, and the forest land was so thick with trees of a superior quality that timber getters moved there and saw pits were soon established. A sawmill had been established in what is now Oxford Street, Epping, during Governor Macquarie's time, and as road-making started in the Colony the Pennant Hills blue metal quarry (see Dundas) became important.

The problem for the suburb's early development was transport. In 1886 the Main Northern Line was extended from Strathfield to Hornsby, and Pennant Hills station opened in 1887. As a result, its land-use of small farms, orchards and timber-cutting changed. Eventually subdivisions were made in the area around the railway station and home-sites sold. By the 1920s good building prospects became available on elevated sites. Some early developments in the area can be attributed to the area's elevation. The principal wireless station had also been erected in the district, bringing Pennant Hills into great prominence. Red Hill Observatory, in use from 1899 to 1930, was built alongside the main road, and a rifle range is only ten minutes walk from the station.

By the 1950s a large area of land within walking distance of Pennant Hills Station had been developed by the Housing Commission. New subdivisions, improved roads and altered traffic routes all combined to change the bushland atmosphere of this suburb.

The story of Pennant Hills would not be complete without mention of its part in the history of early radio. Australia's first radio station was built there in 1912. The station had a daylight range of 1,250 miles, and its call sign was POS. Later it became VLS. The success of this station at Pennant Hills, together with another built in Western Australia, contributed to the development of radio in Australia. Experiments were carried out and the increasing number of amateur radio broadcasters led, in 1910, to the birth of the Wireless Institute of Australia. Founded by the notable aviation and radio pioneer, George A. Taylor (1872–1928), it was the first organisation for amateur radio experimenters in the British Empire.

Koala Park Sanctuary, where visitors can see kangaroos, koalas and other native animals and birds close up, attracts thousands of Australian and overseas tourists each year.

See also the entry on West Pennant Hills.

## PENRITH

*City of Penrith*
Location: 54 kilometres west of Sydney facing the Nepean River, on the Main Western Line

Once regarded as a country town, located at the foot of Governor Macquarie's Carmarthen Hills, now known as the Blue

Old Penrith Court House, High Street, Penrith, was constructed in 1880 by government architect James Barnet. It was the third court house constructed on the site and was used until 1964. After a long fight it was finally demolished in 1979. This photo, c. 1915, shows the local mounted police

Mountains, Penrith is another satellite city that developed rapidly during the 1970s. Before this, the biggest yearly event in the area could have been the GPS Regatta, held on the Nepean River. On regatta day the banks of the river are still alive with shouting teenagers, barracking for their school or their favourite team.

So what has happened to change this historic place? Its rapidly changing image can be attributed to two factors. First, people looking for a pleasant suburb within reach of Sydney are buying homes in the newly opened suburbs of Penrith, where shopping facilities, restaurants, hotels and entertainment are growing. Once there were 14,500 people living in the area; today there are over 140,000. Tourism

has also taken a leap ahead. No longer does Penrith seeming to be asleep in the warmth of a hot summer afternoon, or closed down against a cold westerly wind in winter. Instead the Nepean River has become an attraction for the growing population in Sydney's Western Suburbs, with water sports and boating, or just a comfortable relaxation spot on the grassy river bank, available. *Nepean Belle*, an old time paddle-wheel steamer cruises along the river. Penrith is also developing a series of lakes in the Castlereagh area which will be another tourist attraction, and some of the area's original abundant bird-life will also be encouraged here. These should be completed by 1988.

What a splendid development for an area that was discovered by Europeans in 1789, when the Nepean River was explored and named after Lord Evan Nepean, under-secretary to the home department. The area was first named Evan by Governor Phillip at the time of naming the Nepean

River, but Governor Macquarie, who made several trips to the area, renamed it Penrith in 1818, honouring the English Penrith, in Cumberland. It is said that the situation of the settlement near the river banks recalled the other Penrith to Macquarie. Macquarie later ordered a new road to be built to the Hawkesbury with whatever bridges were necessary, and the road opened in April 1811. In 1817, when the way over the mountains had been found and William Cox was constructing a road in the area, the road from Parramatta to the Nepean River at Penrith was built, linking up with the road across the mountains. Later Penrith became important as a stopping place when the coaches began their run from Sydney to Bathurst. Penrith became a municipality in 1871 and was declared a city in 1959.

Captain Daniel Woodriffe was the first settler in Penrith. In 1804 he received a grant of 1,000 acres here, along the Nepean River. The Reverends Henry Fulton

(1761–1840) and Robert Cartwright (1771–1856) feature in the religious life of Penrith's early history. The Reverend Mr Fulton, transported as an Irish political prisoner, was given Castlereagh (which included Penrith) and Richmond in 1814, where he remained active until his death in 1840.

Some of the early grants of land and the properties established there have provided names for the new suburbs of Penrith, which are still in the early days of making their history.

For the suburbs of Penrith see the separate entries on Badgerys Creek, Cambridge Park, Colyton, Cranebrook, Erskine Park, Jamisontown, Kingswood, Kingswood Park, Lemongrove, Mount Pleasant, Oxley Park, St Clair and Werrington.

## PENSHURST

*Municipalities of Hurstville and Kogarah*
Location: 19 kilometres south-west of Sydney at the junction of King Georges Road and Forest Road, on the Illawarra Line

Robert Townson (1763–1827) received one of the first land grants in this area. The 1,605 acres he was granted in 1808, were west of the present King Georges Road, extending to today's Boundary Road. In 1809 he received another 480 acres north of his original grant. His property passed to John Connell in 1830, whose name was taken for a subdivision of the land in 1869. J. C. and E. P. Laycock acquired the land and carried out the subdivision, which they called Connell's Bush, the western part of which was bought by Thomas

Mort (see Mortdale). Located on the Illawarra railway line between Hurstville and Mortdale, Penshurst received its present name in honour of Penshurst in Kent, England. Many Sydney suburbs are named after places in England, apparently given by homesick settlers.

The early work in this area was timber-cutting and small farming. The railway came through in 1886 and opened up the suburb as a residential area; the platform was established in 1890. A former governor-general of Australia, Lord de L'Isle, whose family seat in England is Penshurst Place, visited this suburb in 1961 during his term of office from 1961 to 1965. Penshurst in Kent has the same misty quality our Penshurst had in earlier times, when southerly winds blew a sea mist across from Oatley Bay on the Georges River. Today the larger number of buildings in the area make this quality less evident.

## PETERSHAM

*Municipality of Marrickville*
Location: 7 kilometres south-west of Sydney between Stanmore and Lewisham on the Main Suburban Line

In October 1793, the lieutenant-governor, Major Grose, sent a number of workmen to clear virgin bush and plant corn and wheat in this area south-west of the town to ease the food shortage in the colony. He gave the district the name of Peters-Ham in memory of his native village near Richmond, in Surrey, England. That Peters-Ham is an ancient village with records dating from the ninth century.

Petersham remained an

agricultural area for a long time. In 1803 Governor King gave prizes for the best crops and stock produced on farms in the colony, and Petersham was one of the areas in which prizes were awarded. Kangaroo hunting became a popular sport in the area. Toothill Street, now in neighbouring Lewisham, on a hill sloping down to New Canterbury Road, was a rallying point for the hunts. The street name, originally Toot-hill, recalls the rallying cry to the huntsmen.

Originally the name Petersham covered a much wider area than today. An early Sydney barrister, Dr Robert Wardell (1793–1834), purchased land from many grantees in the district in 1831, extending from Petersham to Cooks River. Eventually he held 2,000 acres, and his home was built on the site later occupied by the Petersham Public School. Shortly after his murder by escaped convicts in 1834, the first subdivision of his estate took place. One of the buyers was Thomas Weedon, who built the Cherry Tree, the first inn in Petersham, on Parramatta Road.

Stanmore Road, a mere bush track in those days, was opened in 1835, although by 1841 it had not been much improved. New Canterbury Road was laid out in 1859. Petersham was the first resting place for the bullock teams going from Sydney to Parramatta and Liverpool, and beyond. It took the bullocks a day to come from Sydney to Petersham, and this first stop was a blessing for man and beast.

In 1842 a race track was opened at Petersham, near today's Railway and Croydon Streets, but as few people patronised it, it was closed in 1849.

The railway line from Sydney to Parramatta opened in 1855, and the trains stopped at Petersham by 1857, to pick up and set down. But no platform was provided, so the travellers had to climb up or down from the line. Complaints were numerous, and a makeshift structure was provided, although the official platform did not appear until 1863. Further improvements were made in 1883. In 1866 a description in the *New South Wales Gazetteer* said that early Petersham was a quiet hamlet, but after the railway station was established the change was great. The area gradually began to house people who worked in the city, but the population was still small and scattered at this stage.

The first official post office opened as Norwood in May 1860, but in 1870 it was moved to Petersham railway station and the name changed to Petersham in July 1872, when the former "Petersham" post office, established in 1855, became Annandale post office. The first public school opened in December 1878.

Today it is hard to believe that the stretch of Parramatta Road running through Petersham was once a favourite pitch of the bushranger Bold Jack Donohue (1806?–1830). Donohue, who arrived in Sydney as a convict in 1825, and his gang terrorised settlers and travellers in the area in the late 1820s. In 1828 he was sentenced twice to death, but he escaped and continued bushranging until he was killed in 1830.

Petersham originally had its own council, but amalgamated with Marrickville in 1948. The municipality was incorporated in 1871.

## PLUMPTON
*City of Blacktown*
Location: 46 kilometres north-west of Sydney north of Mount Druitt

In the early nineteenth century the site of Black's Town was where the suburb of Plumpton is now located. By the 1860s, the name had been transferred to the village at the railway station, now 8 kilometres from its present site. A new settlement was made in 1887 when Walter Lamb (1825–1906), who had extensive orchards of stone fruits, established a cannery and fruit preserving factory on his estate in the area. As a hobby, Lamb set out a greyhound course, modelled on the Plumpton system. The grounds were later acquired by the New South Wales government, which established the suburb and named it Plumpton in honour of the efforts of Walter Lamb. There was a small village here by the beginning of the twentieth century, with several stores, a post office and a public school, established in 1875, but its population remained small. The suburb continues to grow, now backed by the facilities and local government plans of its neighbour Blacktown.

## POINT PIPER
*Municipality of Woollahra*
Location: 6 kilometres east of Sydney off New South Head Road on Port Jackson

Maritime Services Board records tell us that Point Piper, the peninsula between Rose Bay and Double Bay, was once known as Elizabeth Point. The name changed when Captain John Piper (1773–1851), a Scottish-born military officer who arrived in the colony in 1792, built his mansion there. Piper received this choice piece of land in a grant of 190 acres from Governor Macquarie in 1816. The governor agreed to renaming it Point Piper, which is probably the reason for Captain Piper's honouring his elegant home with the name Henrietta Villa, after the governor's wife, Elizabeth Henrietta Macquarie. Piper also bought up earlier small grants in the area extending around to Rose Bay and Double Bay, and he had earlier bought the property on which Vaucluse House now stands.

As a government official in the colony in charge of customs and tariffs, Captain Piper held magnificent parties in his home. Completed in 1822, it cost £10,000 and was said to be the most expensive house built in Australia up to that time. The views down the harbour were beautiful, and all shipping entering or leaving Port Jackson could be seen from the rooms. The house was surrounded by a magnificent garden, with trees producing choice fruit. Piper had a carriageway built through the bush to Sydney to make a comfortable route for the many friends and notables who came to Henrietta Villa. He also had a special wharf built for those coming by water.

An inquiry into the running of the Bank of New South Wales, of which Piper was chairman from 1825, and shortly after of his administration as Naval Officer, showed his affairs to be in a sorry state. He resigned from the chairmanship in 1827 and was suspended from his naval office, for mismanagement rather than dishonesty. He tried to drown himself, but was rescued. He moved his family to his country estate at Bathurst, known as Alloway Bank, but the property

Above: Etching of Point Piper, 1853

Left: Oil painting of Mrs Piper and her family by Augustus Earle, c. 1826

was not successful and he lost it in the depression of the 1840s. The house on the point was sold in 1826, to Solomon Levey and Daniel Cooper. Cooper later bought out Levey's share (see Woollahra). Henrietta Villa was demolished and in 1883 Woollahra House was built in its place, shortly after subdivision of the land which began in about 1880.

A nearby sandy beach is known as Lady Martin's Beach, which honours Lady Martin, wife of Sir James Martin, three times premier of New South Wales (1863–65, 1866–68, 1870–72), after whom Martin Plaza (formerly Martin Place) was named.

Today the harbourside homes of Point Piper continue the tradition of John Piper's Henrietta Villa for extravagance and elegance, and the area houses many wealthy people. Lady Martin's Beach, or Lady Beach, is one of Sydney's two official nudist beaches.

# PORT HACKING
*Shire of Sutherland*
Location: 26 kilometres south of
Sydney on the northern side of
Port Hacking

An extensive waterway south of
Sydney, Port Hacking has become
an aquatic playground for
Sydneysiders. It was named after a
First Fleeter, Henry Hacking
(1750?–1831), the quartermaster
on Governor Phillip's flagship,
HMS *Sirius*. Hacking became a
skilled and adventurous bushman,
and led many hunting expeditions
to supplement the small meat
ration available for Australia's first
settlers. In 1795, he was among the
party that found the lost
government cattle at Cowpastures.
During one of his hunts he
discovered Port Hacking, which
was named after him by George
Bass and Matthew Flinders when
they explored the area in 1796. The
northern headland is known as
Bass and Flinders Point.

The small suburb known as Port
Hacking is on a northern peninsula
of Port Hacking, between Dolan's
Bay and Little Turriell Bay. Lilli
Pilli is an adjacent suburb on the
peninsula. Port Hacking High
School is situated on the corner of
Kingsway and Wandilla Road,
Miranda, and Port Hacking rugby
field is a reserve in Sylvania
Waters, between Belgrave
Esplanade and Gwawley Parade.

# POTTS POINT
*City of Sydney*
Location: 3 kilometres east of
Sydney on Woolloomooloo
Bay

The name of this suburb honours a
self-made man, Joseph Hyde Potts.
When the Bank of New South
Wales opened for business in 1817,
Potts was employed as a "porter
and servant" of the bank, and he
slept on the premises, guarding the
strong-box. He received rations
from the King's store and a salary
of £25 a year. The bank's officers,
however, decreed that Potts was
not to marry. When he met and
courted a young woman and
wanted to marry and bring his
wife to live at the bank, the board
refused his request. Poor Potts,
deciding that his future lay with
the bank, called off the marriage.
Fifteen years later, Potts was
granted leave of absence for ten
days, and during this holiday
(possibly his first) he met and
married Emma Bates, who had
arrived in Australia the previous
year.

Life and work at the bank was
not without excitement. In 1821
Potts faced an intruder who
climbed down the chimney and
landed in the grate. Potts tried to
persuade the intruder to have
something to eat and talk over the
reason for the break-in, but the
would-be thief, who proved to be
a former servant, ran off.

Potts was a bright young man.
In his free time he designed the
Wales's bank notes, and within
twelve years of his employment,
he had advanced to the position of
bank accountant. He then
purchased 6½ acres of harbourside
land from Judge Wylde and called
his property Potts Point.

An early land grant in the area
was made to Judge-Advocate John

Wylde in 1822 (after whom
Wylde Street is named). He
received 11 acres at the end of the
point. To the south of his property
was an 1831 grant made to H. C.
Douglas, then the grants, also
made in 1831, held by John Bushy,
A. B. Spark, Justice John Stephens,
Alexander Baxter and Edward
Hallen.

The local sandstone has been
used extensively in foundations
and fences in the early homes in
the area. Among the area's historic
buildings are Tusculum, a house
designed by John Verge and built
between 1831 and 1835 at 3
Manning Street; the Minerva, a
theatre built in 1938–39 at 28
Orwell Street, but now operated as
a cinema; and Tarana, built in
about 1889 in Wylde Street. A
house with a history was
Rockwall, at 7 Rockwall Crescent,
which gave its name to that street.
This house, now restored as part of
the Chevron Hotel complex, was
designed by John Verge
(1772–1861), and was built on a
grant made to John Busby
(1765–1857) in 1831. Busby was
the engineer responsible for the
scheme that pumped water from
Centennial Park to Hyde Park (see
Busby).

Before the arrival of the settlers,
the point was known by a variety
of names, among them Paddy's
Point, Kurrajeen (or Currageen),
and Yarrandabbi. The last two are
certainly Aboriginal names, and
"Paddy" may have been Patrick
Walsh, who received a grant of 30
acres here in 1809. Colonel
Paterson made the grant in the
period between Governor Bligh's
departure and Macquarie's arrival,
but, as Macquarie did not confirm
the grant, the land reverted to the
Crown.

Potts Point is no longer a point,
as the peninsula was joined to
Garden Island in 1942 by the

Looking across the houses of Potts Point toward Fort Denison

construction of the Captain Cook Dock. Since 1866 Garden Island has been used as a naval depot with control passing from Imperial authorities to the Commonwealth government in 1913. The island can be visited by tour groups.

## PRAIRIEWOOD

*City of Fairfield*
Location: 34 kilometres west of Sydney off The Horsley Drive

Prairiewood is a neighbourhood of Fairfield, situated between Smithfield and Fairfield. The name was given to the area when Prairiewood Estate was subdivided and developed. When the neighbourhood was recognised as an independent area, the council decided to use the subdivision name for the suburb.

Today Prairiewood is a residential area and a public school is situated in Prairie Vale Road.

## PRESTONS

*City of Liverpool*
Location: 37 kilometres south-west of Sydney off Camden Valley Way

A suburb of the city of Campbelltown, Prestons is named after a local family. At the turn of the century the family managed the post office on the corner of Bringelly and Ash Roads, which was commonly referred to as Preston's.

A gracious Georgian mansion, Horningsea Park House, on the Hume Highway next to Greenlands Golf Course, was built between 1830 and 1839 by Joshua John Moore (d.1864), who had received a grant of land there in 1819. He called his 500 acres after his birthplace, Horningsea in Cambridgeshire, England. At that time, Moore was the clerk to the colony's judge-advocate. Moore had accompanied his brother-in-law, John Wylde, who had been appointed deputy-judge-advocate,

to the colony in 1816. He lived at Horningsea until the death of his first wife in 1839. The Polish explorer Paul Strzelecki (1797–1873), who discovered and named Mount Kosciusko, lived here in the early 1840s.

Prestons stands on the south-west side of Liverpool Showground. A public school is in Kurrajong Road, and neighbouring Lurnea's high school is not too far away. Although quite a distance from Sydney, Prestons is showing steady development, with a fresh climate and still natural environment in its favour.

# PROSPECT

*City of Blacktown*
Location: 32 kilometres west of Sydney south of the Great Western Highway

In 1788 Governor Arthur Phillip stood on a hill in this area south-east of later Blacktown and looked over the country toward the mountains in the west; he named the eastern side of the hill Bellevue. In 1789 Captain Watkin Tench (1758?–1833), an officer of marines, climbed to the top of the hill and saw the distant Blue Mountains. He was so enraptured by their rugged beauty that the rise was given the name of Tench's Prospect Hill; the title was later shortened to Prospect.

Governor Phillip formed a farming settlement of at least twelve families at Prospect in 1791, granting land to convicts. When Governor Macquarie paid a visit to the area in 1810, he was favourably impressed by the comfortable conditions that had been created.

The dominant feature of the suburb today is the Prospect Reservoir. Part of the Upper Nepean water scheme completed in 1888, it conserves water for Sydney and suburbs. It is on the western boundary of the Holroyd municipality (formerly known as Prospect and Sherwood) and is mostly on the land of the Lawson estate.

William Lawson (1774–1850), who crossed the Blue Mountains with Gregory Blaxland and W. C. Wentworth in 1813, lived in a house in Prospect called Veteran Hall. Built in 1810 as a small cottage, it was extended to a forty-room mansion in 1822 by Lawson. His descendants continued to improve the house until the 1880s. It was used by the military in the First World War and it was later

William Lawson

offered to the Commonwealth government as a convalescent home. The offer was refused, however, and the house was demolished in 1926. Its site is in the Prospect Reservoir grounds.

When he arrived in Sydney in 1800, Lawson was an ensign in the 102nd Regiment. He received a grant at Prospect of 500 acres in the period after the overthrow of Governor Bligh, and the grant was confirmed by Governor Lachlan Macquarie. He was a lieutenant in the New South Wales Veterans Company, which gave the name for his home, Veteran Hall. He had married Sarah Leadbeater on Norfolk Island while serving there between 1800 and 1806, and they had eleven children, born between 1803 and 1826. One of the daughters, Sophia, was born at Prospect, and, when she died in 1906, she was the last surviving child of this large family. The family vault at St Bartholomew's in Prospect shelters the remains of several members of the family.

Lawson served as a magistrate and his influence in New South Wales was evident in exploration, farming and road-building, a record of service that would be hard to better. In 1970 a

monument was erected in the main street of Mudgee in his honour, using stone from the foundations of Veteran Hall.

The historic St Bartholomew's Church of England was built by the pioneers of Prospect with funds collected from 1837. The Friends of St Bartholomew's today give the church where Lawson was buried, on 16 June 1850, constant care. The church was consecrated in April or May 1841. The first minutes of the vestry meeting are dated 1842, and refer to the opening of the parish registers by the Reverend H. H. Bobart, who was the rector of St John's, Parramatta.

The nearest railway station is Toongabbie, but Guildford, Merrylands and Wentworthville all give access to Prospect. The climate is bracing, and originally the area was used by orchardists and poultry farmers. Gradually extensive manufacturing establishments moved into the area, and by 1923 brickworks, tile works, and a hat-making factory were located there.

# PUNCHBOWL

*Municipality of Canterbury, City of Bankstown*
Location: 17 kilometres south-west of Sydney between Canterbury Road and King Georges Road, on the Bankstown Line

This suburb took its name from Punchbowl Road, and two different reasons for the name have been suggested. The name Punchbowl was originally applied to an area north of the present suburb (the area that is now Belfield), where John Stephen had a property from the 1830s. His land was opposite the present Coronation Parade in Enfield. Stephen is said to have given the name Punch Bowl to a natural basin in a bend of the Cooks River on his property. Wells Gazetteer of 1848 states that "Clairville or Punchbowl, in the Parishes of St George and Bankstown, is the property of Sir Alfred Stephen [the son of John Stephen]. It is situated in a sort of basin, surrounded by gently rising ground, hence the name Punchbowl." The road running through this area from Liverpool Road was called Punchbowl Road. In the 1830s an inn built by George Faulkener, almost on the corner of Liverpool Road was called the Punch and Bowl. The Inn was near the corner of a road later named Punchbowl Road, and when the railway station opened in April 1909, it adopted the same name.

One of the earliest grants in the area was made to James Ruse (see Parramatta) in 1809. He received 100 acres in the area of the present Punchbowl Park, but he soon moved on. In 1810 grants were made to Thomas Moxon, Frederick Meredith, Richard Calcutt and William Bond in the area south of the later Canterbury Road and west of Belmore Road. In the 1830s James Wilshire bought up most of the western part of the suburb, but after his death in 1840, his property was broken up.

The soil in the area was poor, but agriculture was carried on, with some market gardening. The chief industry, however, was timber-cutting, and the district's forested land provided a livelihood for industrious bark-strippers and timber-cutters.

By 1923 the scene had changed completely. A suburban directory of that year said that "there are some fine residential sites in this locality, and dwellings are being erected in all directions. It may be here mentioned that the Electrification Scheme for the suburban railways shall be first installed on the train services passing through Canterbury, Belmore and Punchbowl."

An official post office began business in 1913. A primary school opened in 1922 and a boys high school in 1955. In the south-western part of the suburb are reserves around the headwaters of Salt Pan Creek.

## PUTNEY
*Municipality of Ryde*
Location: 16 kilometres west of Sydney on the northern bank of the Parramatta River

Late last century, many areas on the Parramatta River received the names of places on the banks of the Thames, and this small residential suburb was named Putney after the London suburb. The suburb is south of Ryde and extends to the Parramatta River between Kissing Point Bay and Morrison's Bay. The area was granted to Nicholas Bayly, who received 116 acres in 1799. Bayly's property was later held by Eugene Delange, who in 1856 subdivided his estate, calling it the Village of Eugenie. Many of the street names, such as Pelissier, recall the Crimean War period. The remaining lots from the subdivision were sold in 1859.

Kissing Point Bay's name has a nautical origin. On certain tides boats touch or "kiss" the seabed in this bay. In the 1920s a punt operated between Mortlake and Putney Point. It gave picnickers access to the parks on the northern side of the Parramatta River, which at that time was a waterway of great beauty, with clean bathing areas and few factories. The area was also the venue for yachting and sculling races. Lovers of the river hope that those times may return and the pollution of the waterway will be strictly controlled.

## PYMBLE
*Municipality of Ku-ring-gai*
Location; 18 kilometres north-east of Sydney on the Pacific Highway and the North Shore Line

Pymble is an attractive suburb, 119 metres above sea level, with an invigorating climate. On the North Shore line between Gordon and Turramurra, the suburb increased in popularity in the 1920s, when young couples wishing to put the grimness of the First World War behind them bought home-sites in the area and built attractive homes. The area offered the tranquillity of a bushland setting with easy access to Bobbin Head, while only a short distance by train to Sydney.

This suburb takes its name from a free settler, Robert Pymble (1788–1861) a former silk-weaver,

Robert Pymble

Above: View of Pymble from the site of the present train station, 1887

Left: The Presbyterian Ladies College at Pymble, c. 1930. After the formation of the Uniting Church it was renamed Pymble Ladies College

Pymble is high enough to give views of the city skyline and the Harbour Bridge to the south-east and to the south-west, across the Lane Cove River valley, Macquarie University at North Ryde.

When Robert Pymble established himself in this area, the only way to reach his land was along a muddy, pot-holed track, known as Lane Cove Road. Today we know it as the Pacific Highway, its traffic a far cry from the bullock drays and horse traffic of Robert Pymble's time. In 1843 the New Inn was established by Daniel Bullock on what is now the Pacific Highway, just north of Mona Vale Road. In 1854 it was bought by Owen McMahon, who changed the name to Travellers' Home.

The first public transport on the North Shore began in 1879 at Pymble when Richard Harnett initiated the Stoney Creek Bus. Six

who arrived in the colony from England in 1821. In 1823 he captured a bushranger, and as a reward was given a grant of 600 acres in what is now Pymble. He built a house just south of the present Pymble station and soon had a timber business established. He also established the first orchard in the area, to the east of the station. Pymble's wife died in 1823, shortly before they came to the district from Parramatta, and he was left to raise their six children alone. The youngest, Robert, was eight months old when they arrived in the colony, and he lived until 1910. Direct descendants of Robert Pymble (the elder and younger) still live in the district.

The area was gradually opened up by other orchardists, who provided much of the city's early fruit supplies. Among them was Joseph Sainty, who established an orchard in Merrivale Road in 1870. His property later extended into Turramura.

The Presbyterian Ladies College (now called Pymble Ladies College), at Pymble, opened in 1916, is a complex of impressive buildings near the shopping centre and, like much of the suburb, has extensive views of Sydney.

lively horses were handled by Tom Watson, one of the favourite drivers, and the forty passengers clung to their seats and enjoyed the thrill of the ride through the area's beautiful bushland. Later a thirty-passenger coach ran from Milsons Point to Pymble.

When the North Shore railway line was put through the suburb in 1890, it crossed Robert Pymble's property. The kitchen of his home became the station's booking office and the dining-room became the waiting-room. The station was appropriately named after this district pioneer.

A post office opened in August 1890, and a public school in January 1952. Today the area is one of beautiful homes with lavish gardens that seem to retain the area's original bushland setting.

## PYRMONT

*City of Sydney*
Location: 2 kilometres west of Sydney on the western side of Darling Harbour

This busy inner-city suburb received its name because of a bush picnic held there in 1806. The picnic was being held at Captain John Macarthur's estate at Cockle Bay (now Darling Harbour), and when a comfortable spot was sought for the festivity, one of the party came upon a spring of cold water bubbling out of a rock. Greatly excited, she described a similar natural mineral spring she had seen in Germany and suggested the place should be called Pyrmont, after that popular German spa near Hanover. Macarthur had bought the land in 1799 from Obadiah Ikin, who had bought it in 1796 from the grantee, soldier Thomas Jones. Jones had been granted 55 acres on the

The Sydney approach to Pyrmont Bridge under construction, 1900

The Pyrmont approach to the new Pyrmont Bridge, 1934. The dome of the Queen Victoria Building can be seen in the background

northern part of the peninsula between today's Darling Harbour and Johnston's Bay in 1795. The western and southern parts of Pyrmont were part of the Ultimo estate.

For many of us the name Pyrmont suggests not picnics, but rather the bridge that bears the suburb's name. The first Pyrmont Bridge spanned Darling Harbour over 120 years ago, opening in 1858. At that time there were no motor cars in Sydney, and the vehicles crossing the bridge were all horse-drawn — carts, wagons, saddle horses, landaus, phaetons, broughams and victorias, as well as hundreds of cabs, gigs and sulkies and horse-drawn buses. Many of these vehicles came from the elite suburbs of The Glebe and

Annandale; others brought goods and produce to Sydney for sale at the Queen Victoria Markets. This first bridge was a toll bridge operated by a private company as a very lucrative business.

In 1884 the state government took on the responsibility of building a new bridge for the ever-increasing volume of traffic. This larger bridge was completed in 1902 at the cost of £112,000. It had a swinging span so it could be opened for large ships passing up Darling Harbour. As the volume of traffic increased with passing time, the bridge opening caused delays and irritations, and the bridge was considered inadequate. A semi-freeway was built across Darling Harbour (completed in 1981), and the facelift continued to the adjacent area, resulting in a chain of elevated roads that today carry traffic in all directions in and out of the city. This huge

development meant destroying many of the old landmarks, including terrace houses and free-standing homes that had been part of Pyrmont since 1856 when development proceeded after subdivision of the Pyrmont estate. Evidence of some of the earliest industries, including flour milling and shipbuilding, was also destroyed. Since 1985 the freeway system has been further enhanced as a result of the 54 hectare redevelopment of Darling Harbour which includes exhibition and conference centres.

Some historic landmarks do survive in Pyrmont, including a memorial to men of the First World War in Pyrmont Square; the houses of Ways Terrace, designed by Professor L. Wilkinson and built in 1893; and near Pyrmont Bridge in Pyrmont Street, the Sam Hordern Fountain, built in 1896. The fire station, designed by government architect W. L. Vernon and built in 1907, and the Catholic church of St Bede's, built in 1867, are also in Pyrmont Street. These venerable buildings make W. Burley Griffin's incinerator in Saunders Street, built in 1935, seem almost a new building, but terraces, cottages, warehouses and other old churches survive to remind you of Pyrmont's history.

An interesting children's nursery school in Harris Street was named Maybanke Nursery, after the wife of Professor Francis Anderson, one-time professor of philosophy at the University of Sydney. Mrs Anderson had a great interest in pre-schools education, and the Pyrmont school to which she gave her name was a great success.

Pyrmont today is an industrial suburb, centred on shipping

The Pyrmont approach to the old Pyrmont Bridge, c. 1890

activities and overlooked by a huge powerhouse that is now disused. Talk in the town pubs is naturally about ships and shipping.

## QUAKERS HILL
*City of Blacktown*
Location: 41 kilometres north-west of Sydney just north-west of Blacktown, on the Richmond Line

The earliest land grant in this suburb, now on the Blacktown–Richmond railway line, was of 2,000 acres to Major West in 1814. The property later passed through several hands, and an early free settler Thomas Harvey, who arrived in the colony in about 1852, leased 100 acres for thirty years. He is thought to have been a

Quaker — certainly several Quakers did receive grants and settle here — and to have been the reason for the suburb's name.

The small suburb existed by farming and retained its peaceful existence until the coming of the branch railway line from Blacktown, when residential development increased. The stop was known as Douglas Siding, and Quakers Hill became the suburb's name after a big subdivision of land in the early 1900s, the first in the area. Arthur Ricard and Company, which handled the subdivision, advertised it as The Quakers Hill Estate.

In the early part of this century, the area was mostly devoted to poultry farms, but after the construction of Schofields Aerodrome, the noise put the hens off laying. The aerodrome was built on land, north of the Quakers

Hill property, which had been granted to Joseph Pye in 1813. The land was resumed in 1941 for the navy's aerodrome. The navy also has an apprentices school at the aerodrome site, called HMAS *Nirimba*.

East of the railway line merchant Robert Campbell held 1,500 acres, which were later bought by John Pearce, the grandson of Matthew Pearce of Kings Langley. The property was used for orange groves and vineyards.

## QUEENSCLIFF
*Shire of Warringah*
Location: 16 kilometres north of Sydney between Manly and Harbord

The history of Queenscliff, situated between Manly Lagoon and Freshwater, is closely bound up with that of Harbord, Freshwater and South Curl Curl. It became popular in the early 1900s and until the First World War, was a favoured holiday centre. Named in honour of Queen Victoria, its first residents were holiday-makers who had vacation shacks on the rocky headlands, descending to the ocean beach sheltered by Curl Curl Head. A general store was eventually built near Queenscliff Lagoon, and tents for camping could be hired, to enable people to enjoy a back-to-nature weekend. Small houses, or weekenders, appeared during this time, built along the beachfront from Curl Curl.

In 1885 a wooden bridge was constructed at Queenscliff over the Manly Lagoon. This, with the Queenscliff Steps, which gave access up and down the rocky coastline, greatly improved access to Harbord. By 1890 sealed roads

were being planned and subdivisions and land sales were taking place. Permanent residents built homes with foundations and piers of stone quarried locally. Jock Hardie brought a local bus service to the area, which was used until 1934 when better roads saw government buses in the area.

Today, Queenscliff is a residential area with government bus services from Brookvale to Manly. It still has a good surfing beach (the northern end of Manly Beach), although the early peace has been lost with the enthusiastic crowds visiting the area during summer weekends.

## RABY
*City of Campbelltown*
Location: 46 kilometres south-west of Sydney west of the Hume Highway

A suburb of the city of Campbelltown, Raby took its name from a property granted to free settler Alexander Riley (1778?–1833) in about 1809. He called his estate Raby in honour of his mother, who was Miss Margaret Raby before she married.

Riley used his farm for sheep breeding, and he introduced the first cashmere goats into the colony. He built a handsome home on the land, but in 1817 he decided to return to England, perhaps because of the difficulties of trading. He left his affairs in the hands of his brother Edward Riley. In England he developed the commercial interests he had in New South Wales, but he soon realised the value of his land and he planned, with Edward, to improve wool production by importing Saxon merino sheep. By the time the sheep arrived in the colony in

1825, Edward (1784–1825) had died, and his son, also named Edward (b.1806), had to take over. Alexander Riley directed the venture from London, providing detailed instructions on the management of the flock, and by 1830 it had become extremely profitable. Riley received a grant of 10,000 acres near Yass in 1831 as a reward for his contribution to the development of the wool industry, but he never returned to the colony.

Raby, which lies south of Liverpool, was a peaceful hamlet in the early days, set in undulating country with small farms in the surrounding valleys. The area's first school opened in March 1895, but closed in December that year. Today, like its neighbours, St Andrews and Eagle Vale, it has become a suburb of Campbelltown, a satellite city on Sydney's southern outskirts.

## RAMSGATE
*Municipalities of Rockdale and Kogarah*
Location: 16 kilometres south of Sydney on the western shore of Botany Bay just north of Sans Souci

This is another suburb that had several name changes. The first name of this suburb just north of the mouth of the Georges River was Seven Mile Beach, after the splendid stretch of beach on Botany Bay. Later it was renamed Lady Robinson's Beach in honour of the wife of Governor Sir Hercules Robinson, who held office from 1872 to 1879. Finally Ramsgate was made the official title for this seaside suburb, after a famous English seaside town. The beach retained its name in honour of Lady Robinson.

When this suburb was being planned, a model village at the northern end of the beach was suggested, but the idea was soon abandoned. The large park in the north of the suburb, Scarborough Park, commemorates the First Fleet convict transport *Scarborough*, which anchored briefly in Botany Bay in 1788. The park was created in the 1830s from a soggy piece of land known as Patmore Swamp. Perhaps Governor Phillip, who came ashore in the area, had seen this piece of land when he complained of "rotten spongy bogs into which we crashed knee deep at every step".

Today the suburb is a pleasant residential settlement, with the advantages of beach and parks. The entire foreshore of Lady Robinson's Beach, from Dolls Point in the south to the mouth of Cooks River in the north, is called Cook Park. Unexpectedly, this

park, a favourite spot with locals and visitors during the summer, was not named in honour of Captain James Cook. Instead it remembers Samuel Cook, who advocated its dedication as a pleasure area for the public.

## RANDWICK
*Municipality of Randwick*
Location: 6 kilometres south-east of Sydney east of Anzac Parade

A once fashionable suburb containing many mansions and attractive villas, this suburb lies south-east of Centennial Park.

One of the earliest land grants was made in 1824 to Captain Francis Marsh, who received 12 acres bounded by the present Botany and High Streets, and Alison and Belmore Roads. In 1839 William Newcombe acquired

the land north-west of the present town hall in Avoca Street.

Randwick takes its name from the town of Randwick in Gloucestershire, England. The name was suggested by Simeon Henry Pearce (1821–86) and his brother, James. Simeon was born in the English Randwick, and the brothers were responsible for the early development of both Randwick and its neighbour, Coogee. Simeon had come to the colony in 1841 as a 21-year-old surveyor. He bought 4 acres of market gardens, from Marsh's original grant, in 1847 and built Blenheim House on the property, which he called Randwick. Blenheim House is still standing in Blenheim Street, in rather poor condition and hemmed in by blocks of home units, so that it no longer enjoys panoramic views of

Blenheim House, the first home built in Randwick. This shot, taken in 1885, shows Simeon Pearce and family gathered outside

Above: Old St Jude's Church of England, Randwick

Above right: Simeon Henry Pearce

the city and the beach. The brothers bought and sold land profitably in this area and elsewhere. Simeon also campaigned for the construction of a road from the city to Coogee (achieved in 1853), petitioned Sir Thomas Mitchell to preserve the vegetation on the area's sandhills, warned of the danger of draining sewage into the harbour, and promoted the incorporation of the suburb. Once the municipality was gazetted, Simeon became the first mayor and was later twice re-elected to the same position. He later became a magistrate and held a number of official posts.

The first Church of England services in the area were held in Blenheim House, but Pearce sought the construction of a church modelled on the church of St John in his birthplace. In 1857 the first St Jude's stood on the site of the present post office, at the corner of the present Alison Road and Avoca Street. In 1861 the foundation stone for the present church was laid on the new site, not far to the north in Avoca Street. The church, completed in 1865, was

designed by Edmund Blacket (1817–83), who may also have designed the nearby rectory, built in 1870. The construction of the church was initially made possible by the bequest of £3,000 by Frederick Jones, a member of the congregation. In 1889 the west windows of the church were erected as a memorial to Simeon Pearce, and the church hall was built in 1899. There is a chapel to honour the First World War dead in the church building, known as the Warriors Chapel. St Jude's also has a peal of eight steel bells, cast in Sheffield, England, in 1864. First rung in 1865, by Simeon Pearce, they are still in use today.

Adjoining the church is a cemetery, which is older than the present church building. The earliest date discernible on the tombstones is 1843, but it is believed that some of the graves could be much older. Many well-known early settlers are buried in this graveyard, including Simeon Pearce.

One of the early worshippers at St Jude's was Isaac Nathan, former music master to George IV's daughter, Princess Charlotte. He built a house at Randwick and named it Byron Lodge, after the

poet Lord Byron, his friend and patron. Nathan Street commemorates this early resident. A second Byron Lodge, originally called Ocean Spray, was built at 25 Byron Street in about 1866 for Alfred Cook.

Another historic house still standing in Randwick is Nugal Hall, in Milford Street. Designed by the colonial architect Mortimer Lewis (1796–1879), this stone house was built in 1853 for the politician and businessman Alexander McArthur. The style is reminiscent of Gothic Revival, with elegantly shaped windows, a splendid staircase, and fireplaces and interior columns of marble.

In 1856 the Destitute Children's Asylum was built in Avoca Street, Randwick, to a design by Edmund Blacket. Simeon Pearce, as commissioner of crown lands, had negotiated the long-term lease of the site for the relocation of the asylum that had been established in Paddington by a society headed by Dr Henry Grattan. The new asylum provided accommodation for children aged between 4 and 10 years whose parents were unable or unwilling to look after them. Older children were taught skills that would enable them to earn a living. If the children were found employment, they could remain at the institution until they were 19, providing a cheap labour force and helping to support the asylum. The Catherine Hayes Hospital was built as part of the complex in 1870. Designed by J. Horbury Hunt, it was named after an Irish singer who gave the proceeds of a concert for its construction. In 1915 the asylum became a hospital for soldiers. It later became part of the Prince of Wales Hospital, which extends west along High Street and was initially used for nursing training.

Randwick was, nonetheless, slow to progress. The village was isolated from Sydney by swamps and sandhills, and although a horse-bus was operated by a man named Grice from the late 1850s, the journey was more a test of nerves than a pleasure jaunt. Wind blew sand across the track, and the bus sometimes became bogged, so that passengers had to get out and push it free.

From its early days, Randwick had a divided society. The wealthy lived elegantly in large houses built when Pearce promoted Randwick and Coogee as a fashionable area. But the market gardens, orchards and piggeries that continued alongside the large estates were the lot of the working class. Even on the later estates that became racing empires, many jockeys and stablehands lived in huts or even under canvas. An even poorer group were the immigrants who existed on the periphery of Randwick in a place called Irishtown, in the area now known as The Spot, around the junction of St Paul's Street and Perouse Road. Here families lived in makeshift houses, taking on the most menial tasks in their struggle to survive.

In 1858, when the New South

Wales government passed the Municipalities Act, enabling the formation of municipal districts empowered to collect rates and borrow money to improve their suburb, Randwick was the first suburb to apply for the status of a municipality. It was approved in February 1859, and its first council was elected in March 1859.

Randwick had been the venue for sporting events, as well as duels and illegal sports, from the early days in the colony's history. Its first racecourse, the Sandy Racecourse or Old Sand Track, had been a hazardous track over hills and gullies since 1860 — punters often wondered whether their fancies would even complete the race. When a move was made in 1863 by John Tait, later described as the Father of the Australian Turf, to establish Randwick Racecourse, Simeon Pearce was furious, especially when he heard that Tait also intended to move into Byron Lodge. Tait's venture prospered, however, and he became the first person in Australia to organise racing as a commercial sport. The racecourse made a big difference to the progress of Randwick. The horse-bus gave way to trams that linked the suburb with Sydney and civilisation. Randwick soon became a prosperous and lively place, and it still retains a busy residential, professional and commercial life.

Today, some of the houses have been replaced by home units. Many European migrants have made their homes in the area, along with students and workers at the nearby University of New South Wales and the suburb's Prince of Wales Hospital. Traces of the suburb's history can still be seen, and the thrill of the turf at Royal Randwick Racecourse has never been lost.

## REDFERN
*City of Sydney*
Location: 3 kilometres south of Sydney, on the Main Suburban Line and a junction station for the Illawarra, Bankstown and East Hills Lines

This inner-city suburb commemorates a pioneering doctor who came to the country as a convict in 1801. William Redfern (1774?–1833) was a surgeon's mate in the Royal Navy, and he was aboard HMS *Standard* when its crew took part in the revolt in 1797 known as the Mutiny of the Nore. Because Redfern had advised the men to be more united, he was included among the leaders who were court-martialled. Although sentenced to death, he was reprieved because of his youth, and in 1801 he arrived in Sydney as a convict. He served on Norfolk Island as an assistant surgeon. In 1803 he was pardoned, but he remained on the island until 1808, when he returned to Sydney, where he was appointed assistant surgeon after being examined in medicine and surgery by Surgeons Jamison, Harris and Bohan. In 1816 he took charge of the new Sydney Hospital, but maintained a private practice as well. In 1814 he reported on the conditions on convict transport ships, and his recommendation that all such ships should have a surgeon aboard whose duties were to superintend the health of the convicts was put into practice. He resigned from government service in 1819 when he was not appointed to succeed D'Arcy Wentworth as principal surgeon. Despite his valuable service, many were contemptuous of him as he was an emancipist, although he had the friendship of Governor Macquarie.

In 1818 Redfern received a grant

Redfern Railway Station at the turn of the century. It was the focal point for the Sydney tramway network and was located midway between the present Central and Redfern Stations

of 1,300 acres at Airds, now a suburb of Campbelltown. He named the property Campbell Fields, in honour of Mrs Macquarie (neé Campbell) and lived on this property. He later received more land in the area, and at the time of his death in 1833 in Edinburgh he owned, through grant and purchase, over 23,000 acres in New South Wales. In 1817 he had been granted 100 acres in the area of the present suburb of Redfern. The boundaries of the property were approximately the present-day Cleveland, Regent, Redfern and Elizabeth Streets. The commodious home Redfern built on his land was considered to be a country house, surrounded by flower and kitchen gardens. His neighbours were John Baptist and Captain Cleveland, an officer of the 73rd regiment, remembered by

Cleveland Street and, before its demolition, by his home, Cleveland House. John Baptist had bought land here in 1832. He eventually owned or leased 40 acres where he ran a nursery and seed business. On the subdivision of his property, the streets were given plant names, such as Telopea, Boronia and Zamia, and Baptist Street also commemorates him.

When Sydney's original railway terminus was built in the Cleveland Paddocks, which extended from Devonshire and Cleveland Streets to Chippendale, the station's name was chosen to honour William Redfern. The station was built of iron and the first stationmaster was a Mr Fielding. In 1874, the station was replaced by a brick and stone structure, covering two platforms. At that time the present Redfern station was known as Eveleigh, after a lovely old home standing on the western side of the railway

line. When Central Station was built, on the site of the Devonshire Street cemetery, the name of Eveleigh Station was changed to Redfern. The name Eveleigh was retained for the huge railway workshops, just beyond the station, on the site of the original Hutcheson Estate.

All that remains of Cleveland Paddocks is Prince Alfred Park, where the exhibition building was erected in 1870 for an inter-colonial exhibition. It was opened by Governor Belmore, after whom Belmore Park was named, on 30 August 1870. Today the park boasts a splendid swimming pool and ice-skating rink.

Redfern was the scene of the maiden trip of the first double-decker tram in 1879. The tram travelled between the old Redfern station to the corner of Hunter and Elizabeth Streets in the city. Four steam engines and six tramcars were imported from the United States to start the service, which was originally planned to convey passengers to the Botanic Gardens, where special displays were being held in the exhibition building there.

Rachel Forster Hospital is an important institution in Redfern today. Lady Rachel Forster, the only daughter of the first Lord Montague of Beaulieu, was very interested, like her friend Emily Pankhurst, in the cause of the needy. When the hospital was founded in Lansdowne Street, Surry Hills, in 1922, it was decided to name the hospital after Rachel Forster. Some time later the hospital moved to larger premises in George Street, Redfern. In 1941, when it was well known as a teaching hospital, it reopened in the present building at 150 Pitt Street, Redfern. Today it specialises in treatment for arthritis, and in orthopaedic treatment and surgery.

Redfern Mail Exchange has also achieved a kind of fame throughout Sydney. It was built in 1965 after 300 people had been evicted from their homes on the 2.15 hectare site. An automated mail-sorting centre, it was the scene of many industrial disputes, and because the mail-sorting machinery destroyed many of the letters it was supposed to sort efficiently, it became unpopularly known as the Redfern Mangler. In 1984 mail-sorting was decentralised, the exchange became redundant and its role in serving the public was considerably reduced.

Redfern at the end of last century was characterised by its many gardens, but at the turn of the century industry was taking over the area. At that time, many of the businessmen in the area were from Syria, such as George Dan, who established his business in 1890; Stanton and Aziz Melick, in

1888; and Anthony and Simon Coorey, in the 1890s. Like other inner-city suburbs, the area still has a high migrant population, including many now from Lebanon, as well as a large Aboriginal population. There is still industry in the area among the high density residential occupation.

# REGENTS PARK
*Municipality of Auburn, City of Bankstown*
Location: 22 kilometres south-west of Sydney south of Auburn, a junction station for the Bankstown — Cabramatta Line

A near neighbour of Auburn and Sefton, this suburb was named after a local property, built by a Mr Peck and a Mr Jackson in 1879. They had named it after Regent's Park in the north-west of London, which had once been a favourite spot of the Prince Regent, who later became George IV, and is today the site of the famous London Zoo.

The first subdivision of land was made in the suburb in 1880 by Hardie and Gorman. As early as July 1899 a school had been established. It was known as Potts Hill School, but in October 1907, the name was changed to Sefton Park School, as at this time the whole area was known as Sefton Park. Finally, in June 1929, it became Regents Park School.

In 1914, the suburb celebrated the opening of a railway station, known as Regents Park. The site of the station was changed in October 1924, when the present station commenced operation on the line connecting Lidcombe to Bankstown. Industry began to move into the area in 1913, in anticipation of the opening of the

railway, when rolling stock and carriage workshops were set up by Messrs Kilborn and Willick. Shops, a hotel and a local bus service were all established in the following years.

Like the school, the first post office changed its name several times. In September 1901, it opened under the name of North Bankstown, in 1906 it became Sefton Park, and fourteen years later it was called Sefton. Finally, in May 1929, Regents Park became its permanent title.

Today this suburb is a busy area, the home of many immigrants from European countries.

# REVESBY
*City of Bankstown*
Location: 22 kilometres south-west of Sydney between Padstow and Panania on the East Hills Line

A suburb south of Bankstown, Revesby was named in 1913 in honour of the home of Sir Joseph Banks (1743–1820), the famous botanist who sailed with Captain James Cook in the *Endeavour* when he discovered the east coast of Australia in 1770. Banks had inherited his father's estates of Revesby Abbey, in Lincolnshire, and was known as the Squire of Revesby. He retained a special interest in this country and greatly influenced the British government in colonising New South Wales. Sir Joseph is also commemorated by the Sir Joseph Banks High School in Turvey Street.

An 1804 land grant to George Johnston (1764–1823), officer of marines who had arrived in the First Fleet, covered the southern part of the present suburb (see East Hills). In 1813 his wife, Esther

Julian, who had come to the colony as a convict on the same ship in 1788, was granted 570 acres to the north, extending to the present Milperra Road. The earliest large land-owners did not reside in the area, and the only mansion built in the early days was The Pah, in Tompson Road. It was built in 1896–97 by Samuel John Hales on the 14 acres he had bought from the Weston estate. Although the property was subdivided in 1926, the house has survived.

The railway station, on the Tempe to East Hills Line, opened on 21 December 1931. The first school, known as Bankstown South Public School, opened in April 1896. In 1910 the name was changed to East Hills, and finally in March 1930, a third change settled on the name Revesby Public School. An official post office for this suburb opened in June 1955.

Revesby today is a busy place between Padstow and Panania, connected by a regular bus service to Bankstown. Revesby's street names show a variety of sources. Some are named after famous generals, such as Brett, Blamey, Montgomery and Macarthur; a group in the centre of the suburb are Arab, Sphinx, Cairo and Pyramid, recalling the land of Egypt, and finally there is a group of astronomical names — including Mars, Uranus, Neptune, Centaur and Vega — in the south.

Revesby Heights is a neighbourhood in the south-eastern part of the suburb, alongside Little Salt Pan Creek. The parklands of Picnic Point separate Revesby and Revesby Heights from the Georges River.

# RHODES
*Municipality of Concord*
Location: 16 kilometres west of Sydney on the southern side of the Parramatta River, on the Main Northern Line

On a southern peninsula of the Parramatta River between Homebush Bay and Bray's Bay, Rhodes was named after the home of an early resident, Thomas Walker (1791–1861). He built his house on the north-eastern side of the peninsula, on Uhr's Point, which remembers George Uhr, one-time sheriff of New South Wales. Walker named his property Rhodes after his grandmother's home, Rhodes Hall, near Leeds, in England. In 1819 Thomas Walker married Anna Blaxland, daughter of John Blaxland of Newington (see Silverwater). A later resident of the house Walker had built was Henry Allport (1890–1965), whose delicate pencil drawings and sketches of buildings in Sydney show the early character of this city. Thomas Walker is not to be confused with Thomas Walker of Yaralla (see Concord).

The beautiful setting of the house, with the tranquil river passing the door, contrasts sharply with today's Rhodes, where factories and industrial works predominate. Walker's property was one of the victims of this change. The house was demolished in 1919, when the land was purchased by the John Darling flour mills; it was later owned by Allied Feeds Limited. In 1919 the estates of Rhodes and Bay Grove were subdivided and the village began to take shape.

Rhodes is on the main Northern railway line running from Strathfield to Hornsby. Rhodes station opened in 1886.

# RIVERWOOD
*Municipalities of Canterbury and Hurstville*
Location: A neighbourhood 18 kilometres south-west of Sydney on a tributary of the Georges River, on the East Hills Line

Designated by the Geographical Names Board as a neighbourhood, Riverwood was formerly known as Herne Bay, from the small cove on the eastern bank of Salt Pan Creek, itself named after a popular watering place on the Kentish coast in England.

This area north of Peakhurst originally comprised small land grants of 30 to 80 acres. Herne Bay Estate was subdivided in 1919, but during the Second World War it became a United States Army base. After the war it was used for emergency housing.

With the extension of the East Hills line through the area in 1931, local development increased. The station was called Herne Bay, but local business people and residents decided to seek a change of name to avoid the stigma associated with the emergency housing project. In 1957 a group known as A Change of Name Association came up with the new and attractive name of Riverwood, and, with government and council agreement, the new name was adopted in November 1957, and gazetted in 1958.

Since then, Riverwood has achieved a complete change of character, with a modern post office in Belmore Road and a local park, bounded by Coleridge and Hunter Streets, and Salt Pan Creek. Some of the street names, however, recall the American presence in the suburb, such as Wyoming Place, Idaho Place, Roosevelt and Truman Avenues and Montana Crescent; the school in Union Street is called Pennsylvania Public School.

# ROCKDALE
*Municipality of Rockdale*
Location: 12 kilometres south of Sydney on the Princes Highway and the Illawarra Line

This suburb began its life as the heart of a farming area known as West Bexley, although sometimes it was disparagingly referred to as Frog Hollow or White Gum Flat. Eventually the population increased sufficiently to support a local post office, and the postmistress and tollgate-keeper, Mary Ann Geeves, suggested the name Rockdale, which described its situation in a hollow surrounded by rocky outcrops. This new name became official in 1887.

Yeoman Geeves, Mary Ann's husband, farmed land here that later became the site of Rockdale railway station. Yeoman Geeves and his young wife had met on a migrant ship in 1860. Yeoman and his brother Alfred were coming to

the colony to seek gold. Mary Ann Jordan was travelling with her parents, who established a farm in Kogarah on their arrival. Yeoman went to the goldfields at Lambing Flat, now the township of Young, but he returned to Sydney, married Mary Ann Jordan and settled in Rockdale.

The area was hilly and heavily wooded in those days, but farming was becoming established. Gangers, including Yeoman Geeves, worked on a construction project to remake a hazardous road. The new road is now Rocky Point Road, running from Cooks River Dam to Sans Souci (formerly known as Rocky Point). The small shop and post office opened by Yeoman and Mary Ann was on the site now occupied by Woolworths store, on the corner of Bay Street and the Princes Highway, Rockdale.

Two other names from the suburb's early history are Pearce and Beehag. Simeon Pearce (see

Randwick) and his brother, James, in 1852 acquired land adjacent to that of the Beehag brothers, James and William, which had boundaries to Bay Street and Rocky Point Road (now the Princes Highway). The Beehags, devout Wesleyans, built the first Methodist church in the St George area, made from saplings, tea-tree and calico. Simeon Pearce's land was later sold and the present shopping centre erected.

With the decline of the timber-cutting industry, the quarrying industry developed. A quarry was established between Rockdale and Carss Park, where a solid cliff of sandstone provided material used in construction of many homes in the area. One of the largest quarries was operated by William Blake, whose name is remembered by the suburb Blakehurst (see Blakehurst).

Rosevale Villa was built in 1873 by William John Ilisse alongside his nursery at Rockdale. The house was demolished in the early 1960s and replaced by a petrol station

The area became noted for its stone cottages, now sadly demolished and replaced by high-rise blocks of units. One of the stone mansions to survive was Lydham Hill, in Lydham Avenue, Rockdale, an elegant stone building dating from 1855. It was built by Joseph Davis, a successful master butcher, who used the surrounding area as grazing paddocks for his cattle.

Rockdale was slow to get two suburban essentials — a hotel and a fire station. The first hotel in the municipality was built at Arncliffe, and was called the Yorkshire Man's Arms. When the municipality of Rockdale was established in 1871, there were two inns in the area, and the first council meetings were held in one of these. But when the owner of the other inn objected to their preference, the council decided the time had come to erect their own council chambers. Some years later the first hotel was built in Rockdale. The suburb waited a long time, however, for its first fire station. In 1897 it was built in Rocky Point Road and equipped with a Merryweather manual horse-drawn fire engine. In 1938 a modern fire station was built in Bay Street.

Rockdale went ahead with the coming of the railway to Sutherland in 1884. By the 1920s it had become a pleasant residential suburb and an important township on the Illawarra line. Today it is a bustling commercial centre as well as a large residential area with a large migrant population, its cheerful noisiness a far cry from its original peaceful farmlands.

In 1971, to mark its centenary year, the council applied for, and was granted, a coat-of-arms by the Royal College of Arms. The arms, designed by H. Ellis Tomlinson, showed Captain Cook and an Aboriginal warrior supporting a shield featuring the *Endeavour* in full sail. The former motto of the municipality — It thrives by progress — was retained.

## THE ROCKS (SEE MILLERS POINT)

## ROOTY HILL
*City of Blacktown*
Location: 40 kilometres west of Sydney just east of Mount Druitt, on the Main Western Line

There are at least three versions of the origin of the name of this suburb west of Blacktown. According to one theory the name is Indian, derived from the Hindustani word "ruti", meaning wheat. This story says that in 1799 a William Dean owned a large grant in this area, where he proposed to grow wheat for India; the bags of grain for export were marked "ruti". The Bishop of Australia, at that time also the Bishop of India, is said to have referred to the area as Ruti Hill, and this name, adopted by local residents, became the districts's official title. In 1799, however, the new colony was barely able to produce enough food for its own survival, and it certainly could not have exported grain.

A second theory says the name goes back to the last century, when most of the horses used by the Indian army came from Australia. A camp for the horses was established in the suburb now known as Rooty Hill, where the Indian grooms came to collect their horses. Because the Indians held frequent parties they called the place Rooti, which is also the Indian expression for a "bread feast". The third suggestion is that Governor King is said to have named an area on Norfolk Island Rooty Hill, in 1802, and he later saw a resemblance to the area of Rooty Hill in New South Wales. Whatever its origin, the name is an old one that appeared on maps as early as 1803.

Rooty Hill was the site of Minchinbury House, a mansion of twenty-five rooms with sandstock brick walls 1 metre thick. Built in the 1890s, this house was associated with the site of an early venture in the Australian wine industry. Some of the outbuildings on the site dated back to 1821, when a Mrs Minchin began growing grape vines from cuttings. The estate was a grant of 1,000 acres given in 1819 by Governor Macquarie to Captain William Minchin (1774?–1821), who had been involved in the rebellion against Governor Bligh in 1808.

Later Dr Mackay acquired the property, built a winery in 1870 and grew grapes as a commercial venture. The property then passed to James Angus, a rail builder, who built the house, calling it a Cornish House. He was killed at Rooty Hill rail crossing in 1918. By 1912 the winery had been purchased by Penfolds, and the huge old cellars of the mansion, renamed Minchinbury House, were holding hundreds of gallons of maturing wines.

In March 1978, the Commonwealth Bank acquired the site, and the house, which had become an historical curiosity in the district, was demolished to make way for new bank premises. Although the house has gone, the association with the wine industry is commemorated by streets named

Minchinbury, Reynell, Penfold, Cawarra, and Seppelt.

Rooty Hill High School and the suburb's public school stand north of the railway station, which is on the main Western line from Blacktown.

## ROSE BAY
*Municipalities of Woollahra and Waverley*
Location: 7 kilometres east of Sydney on New South Head Road overlooking Port Jackson

Rose Bay was named by Governor Arthur Phillip to honour his friend and mentor, George (later Sir George) Rose.

Aborigines once camped on the site of the present Rose Bay Park and fished from Lady Martin's beach on Point Piper. In 1919 local workmen dug up a box containing newspaper cuttings from the *Sydney Gazette* of 27 November 1830, which referred to the death of "Bungaree, King of Broeken Bay tribe", who had died at Garden Island and been buried "at Rose Bay, beside the remains of his late Queen". Bungaree had sailed with Matthew Flinders around Australia in 1801–02. Like many Aborigines, he was an outstanding humorist and a clever mimic — he was especially good at imitating the peculiar mannerisms of the colonial governors. Bungaree wore pieces of cast-off uniforms, as well as a brass breast-plate engraved with the New South Wales colonial arms, and the words "Bungaree — King of the Blacks".

During its history, a number of mansions have been built at Rose Bay, which encircles the bay of that name between Point Piper and the Nielsen Park peninsula. In the 1830s wealthy businessmen already realised the desirability of living in the area, and the establishment of a tram service also encouraged settlement.

One of the loveliest buildings in Rose Bay is now a school for girls — Kambala. Originally known as Tivoli, the house was built on a land grant of 1812 to Samuel Breakwell. The grant, covering 60 acres, extended from the foreshores of Rose Bay to the Old South Head Road. Breakwell came from County Cork, in Ireland, where there is a small village named Tivoli, which may be the reason for his choice of name. In 1831 Breakwell, who had returned to Ireland, sold the property to Thomas James, a Sydney merchant, who also sold it.

Eventually part of the property was acquired by Captain William Dumaresq (1793–1868), brother-in-law to Governor

As tranquil a setting then as it is now, Rose Bay, 1918

Lithograph of Bungaree by Augustus Earle

Darling. A veteran of the Peninsular War and the Battle of Waterloo, Dumaresq became a civil engineer and an inspector of roads and bridges in the colony. He also supported John Busby's scheme to pipe water from Centennial Park to Hyde Park (see Busby). In 1830 Dumaresq married Christina Susan, second daughter of Alexander Macleay. In 1841–42 he built a stone cottage, which he called Tivoli, and the house became the scene of social and

family life for more than thirty years. In 1881 it was purchased by Maurice Black, who engaged the services of a well-known architect of the day, John Horbury Hunt, to redesign and rebuild it. Many of the earlier colonial features were preserved, with additions in the Italian style. In 1912, when it became a private school its name was changed to Kambala by Miss Gurney and her colleague, Mademoiselle Soubbeiran. These two ladies had already been conducting teaching establishments, the most recent in

a house known as Kambala, so they brought the school's name to their new premises.

The Scots College, a well-known Presbyterian boys school, occupies an 8 hectare site in Victoria Road overlooking the harbour. It was founded in 1893.

The Rose Bay Convent Kincoppal began in 1882 when Claremont, with 17 acres of land, was leased for an order of French nuns, Sisters of the Sacred Heart, who came to Sydney to open a school for girls. Over the years this school has flourished, and its premises have been extended on land that enjoys a commanding view of the harbour. The fine chapel of the convent was built in 1896 to a design by Horbury Hunt.

John Horbury Hunt (1838–1904), who trained as an architect in the United States, arrived in Sydney in 1863 on his way to India, but he was persuaded to settle in New South Wales by James Barnet, the acting colonial architect. At first he worked in the office of Edmund Blacket, but in 1869 he established his own practice. He designed several churches, including the Anglican cathedrals at Grafton and Armidale, as well as houses for wealthy clients. One of those houses was Booloominbah in Armidale, built in 1888 and later the centre where the University of New England was established. Horbury Hunt lived in Cranbrook Cottage in Rose Bay, which he was forced to sell in 1897 after his business collapsed in the depression of the 1890s and his health deteriorated.

Rose Bay today still has a small base for flying boats, although it was until 1975 the base for commercial flying-boat services. Its use was largely discontinued because an airfield had been constructed at Lord Howe Island, which had previously relied on the service.

Apart from the large estates established last century, much of the present suburb was devoted to market gardens, which could still be found in the area in 1923. In the first twenty years of this century, however, the area's swampy land was being drained and gradually residential development took over much of the suburb. The Royal Sydney Golf Club and the Woollahra Municipal Golf Links occupy a large area here.

Today Rose Bay has lost a little of its former elegance, becoming busier and the site of blocks of home units. There are still many large houses set in fine gardens, however, and the suburb is still attractive and home for many wealthy people.

Undated painting of Claremont by Conrad Martens, probably c. 1860

## ROSEBERY

*City of Sydney, Municipality of Botany*
Location: 6 kilometres south of Sydney between Southern Cross Drive and Botany Road

This inner southern suburb, situated between Kensington and Mascot, was named in honour of Archibald Phillip Primrose, the fifth Earl of Rosebery, prime minister of England in 1894–95, who visited Australia with his wife for two months in 1883–84. The suburb was named in honour of this visit.

Rosebery was once the site of an early racecourse, which opened in 1906 as a pony track. Meetings at Rosebery Racecourse were conducted under the auspices of the Associated Racing Clubs, and its midweek meetings became as popular as those at Randwick, particularly during the 1920s.

In 1940–41 soldiers of the 8th Division (later to become prisoners of war at Changi) were camped at the course. The track remained an army camp until 1946, when it was used by the Sydney Turf Club as a training track. The club purchased the track in 1948, and during the 1950s over 200 horses were trained every week at Rosebery.

In 1961 the Rosebery Town Planning Company bought land in the South Sydney area, adjacent to Kensington and including Rosebery, for £450,000. The new suburb soon became a busy industrial area, and the housing commission purchased the remaining acres for high-density housing.

Reflecting on the origin of this suburb's name, it is easy to understand why many of its streets carry the names of men associated with the parliaments of Britain. While Primrose Avenue

commemorates the Earl Rosebery, Morley Avenue (Viscount Morley of Blackburn), Crewe Place (Marquess of Crewe) and Asquith Avenue all honour other famous English parliamentarians.

# ROSEHILL

*City of Parramatta*

Location: 23 kilometres west of Sydney north of the Western Freeway, on the Carlingford Line

In 1883, 850 acres of John Macarthur's Elizabeth Farm (see Parramatta) were subdivided for industrial purposes and the land was sold in three sales, in the months of February, May and October. Part of the estate, 140 acres in all, was made into a recreation area, which in 1885 became a rececourse called

Rosehill. The suburb's name derives from this subdivision, rather than from the hill behind Old Government House which had been named Rose Hill nearly a hundred years earlier by Governor Phillip, before the suburb had been named Parramatta.

Rosehill lies east of Parramatta and has the Parramatta River on its northern boundary and Duck Creek on the east and south. It is close enough to the city of Parramatta to enjoy its benefits, while retaining an identity of its own. Australians first saw an aeroplane in the air here on 19 April 1910. It flew only a short distance over the racecourse, while its occupant, Houdini, the handcuff king, made yet another successful stunt escape, this time from the air. More conventionally, many famous horses have raced at Rosehill, including the legendary Phar Lap, who had his first win

there, and race days are still enjoyed by crowds of locals and visitors alike.

The first school opened on 14 September 1886, and sixty-one pupils were enrolled. A new two-storey building was erected in 1918, and a large infants department was added in 1929. The railway station, on the Carlingford line, opened in 1888 when this was a private railway. It was taken over by the government in 1904.

The brightly coloured parrot known as the rosella was first named in this area as these noisy birds frequented the district. In the early days of the settlement the Parramatta area was known as Rose Hill, so locals called the birds rose hillers, the words eventually sliding together to become rosellas.

Rosehill Racecourse, 1 May 1910. Escapologist Harry Houdini is at the controls of his Voison plane

Today Rosehill has some older-style houses and some light industry. Shell's Clyde Oil Refinery was the first in Australia and is one of the ten now operating. Part of the site was on Macarthur's land.

## ROSEVILLE

*Municipalities of Ku-ring-gai and Willoughby*

Location: 12 kilometres north-west of Sydney on the Pacific Highway and the North Shore Line

A beautiful residential suburb on the North Shore, Roseville began its life as a grant of 160 acres made to Daniel Mathew, who arrived in the colony in 1812. By 1814 he had a farm and sawyer's operations on the land, which was known as Clanville. Mathews disputed boundaries with neighbour Richard Archbold, who had

arrived in the colony in 1814 and later opened a school. In 1825 he had been granted 600 acres adjoining Clanville, and later Archbold acquired Clanville. Archbold established an orchard on Clanville, which included Moore's Creek, which runs into Middle Harbour, and what is now East Roseville and East Lindfield. After Archbold's death in about 1837 his wife, Mary, continued to run the estate with the help of four assigned convicts and her eldest son. Properties adjoining Clanville were Isaac Nichol's 200 acres, and William Gore's 150 acres, which extended into Artarmon.

Another local orchardist, George Wilson, Richard Archbold's son-in-law, was indirectly responsible for making this suburb. His picturesque stone cottage, named Rose Villa, stood on the land resumed for the building of the North Shore railway line and station, which opened in 1890. His stone cottage was demolished, but the station

Although opened amidst much excitement in 1924, the old Roseville Bridge, seen in the foreground, had by the late 1950s become inadequate for the volume and type of traffic needing to use it. The new, Department of Main Roads designed Roseville Bridge, seen in the background, opened in 1966

and the suburb took the name Roseville.

A post office opened on 8 July 1901, and the first public school, still a busy place of learning, opened on 19 August 1913. There were two teachers and thirty pupils on that first day. Located in Archbold Road (named after the district's pioneer) it celebrated its seventieth anniversary in August 1983.

There are no orchards in today's Roseville, but the houses in the area are set in pleasant gardens.

East Roseville and Roseville Chase are residential suburbs with local shopping centres. They extend from the main suburb of Roseville to Middle Harbour, and the reserve of Roseville Chase extends to the harbour shores.

# ROUSE HILL

*Shire of Baulkham Hills, City of Blacktown*

Location: 42 kilometres north-west of Sydney on Windsor Road

This suburb, situated in the Hills District north-west of Castle Hill and Kellyville, was named after the estate of a free settler, Richard Rouse (1774–1852), who arrived in the colony in 1801. He was given his first grant in 1802, and in 1816 received a second grant of 450 acres, near Castle Hill. Macquarie suggested the estate be called Rouse Hill, and the peaceful hamlet was born.

Rouse was made superintendent of public works for Parramatta, Richmond and Windsor, and is best known for building the tollhouse and turnpike at Parramatta in 1811, the inn known as the Australian Arms in Parramatta, and supervising the construction of Parramatta Hospital, completed in 1818.

Richard Rouse had occupied his grant in at least 1813, before it was made official, and began to build a house there soon after. Rouse Hill House was built by convict labour from stone quarried at Parramatta. Memories of the convict uprising must still have been strong, as the house was built with double protective shutters both inside and outside its windows.

Rouse was a horse breeder of note, and Rouse Hill House included stables with named horse boxes for the string of horses he bred. Names such as Jorrocks and Reprieve stayed on the stalls long after the horses had gone, and Reprieve was immortalised in a poem written by A. B. Paterson, who had visited the house, inspired by the famous horses bred there. The breeding and training talent was apparently inherited by a descendant, Rodney Rouse Dangar, who bred Peter Pan, winner of the Melbourne Cup in 1932 and 1934.

Rouse Hill House is still standing on the main Windsor Road, 18 kilometres from Parramatta. Until 1966, it was the oldest home in Australia still occupied by members of the original family.

Possibly the most historic event in this area was the convict uprising in 1804, culminating in

"Major Johnston with Quartermaster Laycock, one serjeant and twenty five privates of ye New South Wales Corps defeats two hundred and sixty six armed rebels 5th March 1804" is the inscription beneath this well-known watercolour depicting the Castle Hill Rebellion

the Battle of Vinegar Hill. The exact location of Vinegar Hill, site of the first serious uprising on Australian soil, is still debated, but it is likely to be the site of the present trig station at Rouse Hill, between the Old Windsor Road and Schofields Road. The uprising known as the Castle Hill Rebellion occurred in March 1804 (see Castle Hill) when convicts, armed with stolen rifles and makeshift weapons, planned to march from Castle Hill to Parramatta, rallying convicts on the way. The plot was betrayed and the convicts were overpowered at the site that became known as Vinegar Hill. Many Irish political prisoners were involved in the revolt, so the place where the authorities regained control was named after Vinegar Hill in County Wexford, Ireland, where the Irish and English forces had clashed in 1798.

# ROZELLE

*Municipality of Leichhardt*
Location: 4 kilometres west of Sydney on Victoria Road between Iron Cove and Rozelle Bay

Here is a suburb unique in being named after birds. Before white settlers arrived, the Parramatta River was the breeding ground for flocks of wild birds. The brightly plumaged rosellas were named by early settlers of Parramatta, then called Rose Hill, who saw the birds there, and called them Rose Hillers, which soon became rozellas. The presence of these brilliant birds in a quiet bay near the present suburb initiated the name Rozella Bay, and later the suburb became Rozelle.

Rozelle, which lies south-west of Balmain between Rozelle Bay and

Male students appear to outnumber female students in this photograph of Rozelle Public School taken in 1885. The left-hand building, designed by J. Horbury Hunt, was completed in 1878, and the right-hand wing was designed five years later by William Edmund Kemp

Iron Cove, is rich in historical names. White Bay, with its busy rail sidings and shipping, was named after First Fleeter Surgeon White; Victoria Road, a main thoroughfare to the west, commemorates that great English queen; Darling Street, winding along the top of the hill through Balmain until it reaches Darling Harbour, honours Governor Ralph Darling. The area of the present suburb was originally part of the land grant made in 1800 to William Balmain (see Balmain). The land was subdivided between about 1860 and 1880.

In its earliest days, the iron bark trees were thick on the shores of this area, and it became known as Iron Bark Cove. With passing time and with the opening of a bridge in 1882, the reference to the iron bark trees was forgotten and the cove and the bridge became simply Iron Cove. Ferries were used for crossing the river until the Iron Cove Bridge was built.

Rozelle Hospital, a psychiatric centre, occupies a large site south of Iron Cove Bridge overlooking the water. John Brenan (1798–1868) was born in Ireland and received a colonial posting as solicitor with

the Bank of Australia in 1834. In 1839 he built Garry Owen House on the Fairlight estate in what is now Lilyfield. Brenan lost all his assets in land speculation and in 1864 the mansion was bought by John Gordon, who renamed it Callan Park.

In the late 1870s, Frederick Norton Manning, then "Inspector of the Insane", made moves to ease the overcrowding at the Gladesville asylum. Callan Park was purchased and a new complex designed by colonial architect James Barnet was completed in 1885. Most of the stone was quarried on the site and the main group of buildings was named after an American doctor, Thomas Kirkbride. The grounds were laid out by Charles Moore, then curator of the Botanic Gardens.

Broughton Hall, also built by John Brenan, was so named by John Keep, who purchased it in 1864. It was sold to William and Frederick Langdon in 1912 and during the First World War they turned it into a hospital for shell-shocked soldiers. It was acquired by the Commonwealth government in 1918 and became a psychiatric clinic in 1921. Now owned by the state government and part of Rozelle Hospital, Broughton Hall is unused and has been badly vandalised.

## RUSE

*City of Campbelltown*
Location: 52 kilometres south-west of Sydney just north-east of Campbelltown

A suburb of the city of Campbelltown, Ruse lies east of Leumeah and north of Airds.

The name Ruse is well known from the early history of New South Wales. James Ruse (1760–1837), formerly a convict, received the first land grant in the colony as an experiment in 1789, Governor Phillip being anxious to see how long it would take a settler to become self-sufficient. By 1791 he was able to support himself and his wife, and he received the title to his 30 acres of land, which were in the area of the present sports stadium in Parramatta Park. The house he built for himself and his wife, Elizabeth Perry, was known as Experiment Farm and was situated at Rose Hill. In October 1792 Surgeon John Harris bought the land from Ruse, rebuilt the house and added the property to his Harris Park holdings. Experiment Farm Cottage which remained in the Harris family until 1923, is now furnished as a gentleman's residence of the early 1800s and is open for inspection in Ruse Street, Parramatta.

In 1794 James Ruse was granted

land on the Hawkesbury River, near Windsor, and became one of the early farmers in that area. After floods spoilt his crops, he made a fresh start in the Bankstown district, where he was granted 100 acres of land in 1810. In 1828 he came to the Campbelltown area, where he bought a farm at Macquarie Fields, which had proved to be a valuable wheat-growing area. James Ruse died at Minto on 5 September 1837, and he is buried in St John's cemetery at Campbelltown.

Ruse is now one of the residential areas developed as a suburb of Campbelltown. Streets honour many of the names associated with New South Wales's early history, such as Solander, Greenway, Macarthur, Flinders and Bass, as well as explorers, such as Kennedy, Leichhardt, Burke and Lasseter, and ships such as *Endeavour, Supply,* and *Sirius.*

## RUSHCUTTERS BAY

*City of Sydney, Municipality of Woollahra*
Location: 3 kilometres east of Sydney on the southern side of Port Jackson

This suburb east of Kings Cross takes its name from the bay between Macleay Point and Darling Point. The area was first referred to as Rush Cutting Bay by the English settlers. The swampy land was covered with tall, strong rushes, which were suitable for thatching huts and for bedding in horse stables. In those days a stream of fresh water flowed from Lacrozia Valley, across what is now South Head Road, and into the bay. Stepping stones across the stream connected with a path that led to Darling Point at low tide.

The area was later used for market gardens. In 1878 an Act of Parliament reserved 6 acres here for recreation and to allow reclamation work. Today Rushcutters Bay Park, fringing the bay, fulfils that purpose, with a sports oval and tennis courts, as well as parkland. Nearby are marinas and the Cruising Yacht Club. In 1894 the powerhouse was built with tram sheds, which operated the cable trams to Edgecliff. It was later used as a garage for trolley buses. Rushcutters Bay Park, fringing the bay, fulfils that purpose, with a White City, home of the Lawn Tennis Association. White City was established just before the First World War on land resumed from Chinese market gardeners. On these tennis courts many famous players have made their debut. Next door is the Sydney Grammar School's Weigall Sports Ground, named in honour of A. B. Weigall, an early master of the school.

A former landmark was the old Stadium, scene of many fights and of exciting performances by local and overseas entertainers, but demolished when the Eastern Suburbs Railway came through the area. The Stadium, in New South Head Road, was built in 1908, and the first boxing contest held there coincided with the visit of the American fleet. Some of the famous names in the pugilistic world appeared at the Stadium in its heyday, such as bantam-weight Jimmy Carruthers, heavyweights, Jack Johnson and Tommy Burns and flyweight Joe Symonds.

In the 1920s pulling boats could be hired from Rushcutters Bay, at a rate of 2 shillings an hour, by day-trippers who rowed out to Clarke and Shark Islands for a day's picnic, or a first class view of a harbour regatta. Steamers also called at these islands on Saturdays

Unique in its time, White City open-air amusement park at Rushcutters Bay was almost a miniature city with lakes, canals, fountains and pleasure palaces. The Lawn Tennis Association acquired the eleven acres in 1921 and converted the area into one of the best tennis grounds in the world

and holidays. "Every convenience for visitors" was the motto of the area around Rushcutters Bay.

# RYDALMERE

*City of Parramatta*

Location: 21 kilometres west of Sydney on Victoria Road facing the Parramatta River, on the Carlingford Line

Rydalmere is a small suburb lying just north of the upper reaches of the Parramatta River, with a railway station on the Carlingford line. The first free settler in the district, Phillip Schaffer (d.1828?), who arrived in the *Lady Juliana* in 1790, was granted 140 acres there in 1791. Schaffer, of German birth,

came from England to be a superintendent of convicts, although he remained in the position for only a short time as his English was poor. Instead he took up farming on his land grant. He built a house he called the Vineyard and in 1811 married a First Fleet convict, Margaret Mackinnon. He planted grape vines, as well as grain, on his property.

In 1797, Schaffer sold the property to Captain Henry Waterhouse (1770−1812) for £140. In 1796 Waterhouse had bought a flock of Spanish merino sheep at the Cape of Good Hope, and when he landed them in Sydney in 1797, they were the colony's first merinos. When Waterhouse left the colony in 1800, he sold most of the flock to William Cox (1764−1837). Both Cox and Gregory Blaxland lived at the farm.

In 1813 John Macarthur's nephew Hannibal Hawkins Macarthur (1788−1861) bought the Vineyard. He came to the colony in 1805, returned to England in

1808, and came back to the colony in 1812. That year he also married Anna Maria, eldest daughter of Philip Gidley King, the colony's third governor. Their large, happy family of six daughters and five sons gradually outgrew the original Vineyard house, and in 1835 Hannibal built an elegant stone mansion on the site. When the Bank of Australia failed in 1843, he lost much of his property and the family fortunes never recovered. He later sold the house to Thomas Icely who soon afterwards sold it to Bishop Polding of the Catholic Church. It was renamed Subiaco, after the town in Italy where St Benedict is reputed to have lived, and was opened as a convent and school by Benedictine nuns. In 1961 the property was sold and the house demolished, the graceful verandah columns being given to the University of New South Wales. The house is commemorated by Vineyard Street and Vineyard Creek in the west of the suburb.

Subiaco or Bishop Creek, which also runs through the suburb, recalls the later days of the property.

By the 1830s all the land in the area had been alienated, and it remained rural, until 1866 when land speculator Thomas O'Neill, who owned part of the old Vineyard estate, began subdividing land. He named the estate after Rydal in the lake district of England, where he was born, adding "mere" (used in the lake district to indicate "lake") to give Rydalmere. Wealthy settlers bought land, roads were put through, and the area moved ahead.

One of the earlier roads marked out from Parramatta to North Brush, the wooded area on the high ridge between Eastwood and Parramatta, was surveyed in December 1806. Kissing Point Road, at first named High Road, was marked out in 1813 and served as a main road to Ryde from Parramatta until the present Victoria Road was laid out in 1887. When the railway line between Clyde and Carlingford opened, the station at Rydalmere opened as Victoria Road on 20 April 1896. The line was a private one, but later it was taken over by the government, and the station was renamed Rydalmere on 1 August 1901.

The first official post office opened in January 1888, and the public school in January 1891. The suburb was included in the municipality of Dundas when that was established in 1889, but in 1891 it broke away to form the municipality of Rydalmere and Ermington. In 1948 Rydalmere was incorporated in the city of Parramatta.

Rydalmere remained a rural settlement for many years, rich in orchards, and not until the 1900s

did industry begin to establish itself in the district.

An interesting building in the suburb is the Rydalmere Psychiatric and Rehabilitation Hospital. It is built on a grant of 60 acres made in 1792 to Thomas Arndell (1753–1821), who was the first doctor in Parramatta. His grant was taken over by Governor King as the site of a female orphanage. This building, erected in 1818, is part of the hospital.

Many ex-servicemen from the Second World War bought land and built in Rydalmere in the 1950s. The Housing Commission also resumed large tracts of land, and with the development of larger industries, the area flourished to become the busy suburb it is today.

# RYDE
*Municipality of Ryde*
Location: 13 kilometres north-west of Sydney at the junction of Victoria, Concord and Lane Cove Roads, on the Main Northern Line (West Ryde)

The Ryde area has the distinction of being the third oldest settlement in Australia, after Sydney and Parramatta. First known by the Aboriginal name of Wallumetta, the area was named the Field of Mars by the early settlers. This name covered the whole area between the Parramatta and Lane Cove Rivers. By 1792 the eastern part was called Eastern Farms and by 1800 that name was being replaced by Kissing Point, which probably refers to the furthest point up the Parramatta River that sea-going vessels could go before their keels "kissed" the bottom. From the 1840s the name Ryde was used and was adopted in 1870

as the name of the municipality. It was called after the town of Ryde on the Isle of Wight. This may have come about when Mr G. M. Pope, who lived in the Isle of Wight's Ryde, came to the colony and settled in the area, opening the Ryde Store. The wife of the Reverend George Turner, St Anne's first vicar, also came from that town and saw a strong resemblance in the two places.

Ryde in the early days was a beautiful area, with hills sloping down to fertile valleys. The first hops in the colony were grown there in about 1802 by James Squire (1755?–1822), a former convict and one of the most notable residents of the area. He brewed for Lieutenant-Governors Grose and Paterson and also sold his beer in a tavern alongside his brewery. Both stood on his 30 acre grant in Ryde, where he was also a successful farmer. By 1822 he owned about 1,000 acres in the district and Bennelong, the Aborigine befriended by Governor Phillip, was buried here after his death in 1813.

The area was highly suitable for farming and orchards, and early grants to marines were given to encourage agriculture. In 1792 land in the area was granted to eight marines; two of the grants were in the area of modern Ryde. Isaac Archer and John Colethread each received 80 acres of land on the site of the present Ryde–Parramatta Golf Links, now in West Ryde. Later in 1792, in the Eastern Farms area, twelve grants, most of them of about 30 acres, were made to convicts. Much later these farms were bought by John Macarthur, Gregory Blaxland and the Reverend Samuel Marsden. The district remained an important orchard area throughout the nineteenth century.

Probably the most well-known

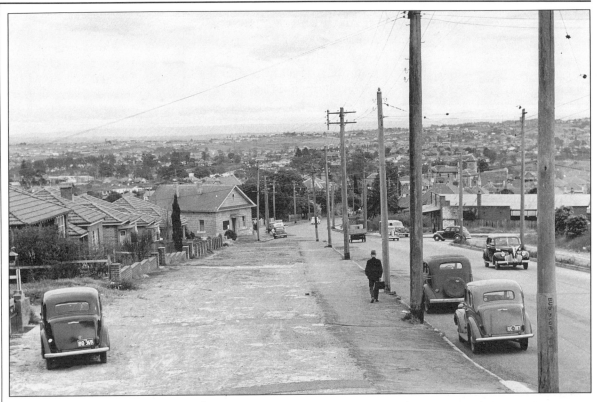

Looking west from Devlin Street down Victoria Road, Ryde, 1949, before the road was widened. The stone building, now a police station, was built in 1837

historic building in Ryde is St Anne's Church of England, perched high on one of the hills, in Church Street. It is the third oldest church in Australia. It was opened in 1829, but it was enlarged and the tower added in 1861.

Subdivision of the area began in 1841, and in the same year a post office, called Kissing Point, opened. This marked the beginning of the village of Ryde, which formed around the church.

Fortunately the Ryde district has preserved some of its oldest historic buildings, which remind us of the early settlement and its people. One example is Ryde House, built in 1845 by James Devlin (after whom Devlin's Creek and Devlin Street are named). It is still standing, renamed Willandra, on the corner of Victoria Road and Devlin Street.

By 1866 Ryde had achieved a Court of Petty Sessions, and the 1872 directories show that a Thomas Kendall Bowden was a practising solicitor there. In 1875 George White came from the Liverpool–Campbelltown area to also take up the position of district solicitor, encouraged by Alfred (later Mr Justice) Cheeke.

In 1886 the railway line from Strathfield to Hornsby came through the area, and a station opened as Ryde on 17 September 1886. The new station was located about a mile west of the main Ryde area. Until the Gladesville and Iron Cove Bridges were built in 1881–82, the area had been connected to Sydney by a ferry service, running since 1832, across the Parramatta River from Bedlam Point and one from Ryde to Rhodes, which began operation in 1896. Ryde Bridge opened in 1935.

The business area and housing gradually developed around the new station and it soon became

necessary to define two areas within the suburb. This was done in October 1945, when the railway station became officially known as West Ryde and the older portion of the suburb remained as Ryde or colloquially, Top Ryde.

There were denominational schools in the area until 1868 when the first public school opened. A second public school opened near the railway station in 1917. Meadowbank Public School opened in February 1917, and became Ryde West Public School in July 1930.

Ryde's character is constantly changing as industry and increased housing bring people into the district, but the Ryde Police Station on the corner of Belmore Street and Victoria Road, built as a watch-house in 1837, and a stone section of the Ryde Public School, built in 1878, on the corner of Tucker Street and Pope Street, still remind us of those early days.

See also North Ryde.

# SADLEIR

*City of Liverpool*
Location: 37 kilometres
south-west of Sydney just west of
Liverpool

This suburb, just north of
Cabramatta Creek in the Liverpool
area, was named after Richard
Sadleir (1794–1889), who was
Liverpool's first mayor in 1872. He
was born in Ireland and became an
officer in the Royal Navy. He took
a great interest in the affairs of
early Liverpool, and was a master
of the male orphan school.

Sadleir is part of the Green
Valley housing estate, which was
subdivided in 1960. The name
Green Valley comes from the
Green Valley Creek, which flows
through several suburbs in this
large estate, once lush pastoral
land.

Richard Sadleir

# ST ANDREWS

*City of Campbelltown*
Location: 46 kilometres
south-west of Sydney between
Campbelltown Road and the
Hume Highway (South-western
Freeway)

A Scottish migrant, Andrew
Thompson, established a farm here
on Bunburry Curran Creek, north
of the present city of
Campbelltown. In 1810 Governor
Macquarie, who greatly favoured
the Campbelltown area, called on
Thompson, and was impressed by
the farm. It consisted then of a slab
hut beside the creek, and the
beginnings of a sheep and cattle
property. At that time the property
covered 1,240 acres. Later
Thompson demolished the house
and rebuilt it in a better situation
on the top of a nearby hill.
Unfortunately it was destroyed by
fire. When Thompson died his
widow inherited the property,
which by that time included a total
of 90 cattle and 1,400 sheep. To his
friend and adviser Governor
Macquarie, Andrew Thompson
left the large sum of £6,000.

Street names in the area continue
the Scottish theme of the suburb's
name, with Caithness, Galashiels
and Bannockburn Avenues, and
Paisley, Oban and Skye Places, for
example. The modern St Andrews
Public School is in Ballantrae
Drive.

# ST CLAIR

*City of Penrith*
Location: 49 kilometres west of
Sydney south of the Western
Freeway

St Clair, a suburb of the city of
Penrith was once known as South
St Marys. St Clair was the name
given to a private housing
development created in the area in
the 1970s. When the scheme failed,
the Land Commission of New
South Wales (known as Landcom)
took over the development in
1977. Originally only 2,000 homes
were to be built, but the
government extended the plan so
that today St Clair is an
independent community with
shopping, educational and church
facilities and a branch library. The
modern St Clair Public School is in
Endeavour Avenue. Its name has
no historical connections.

# ST HELENS PARK

*City of Campbelltown*
Location: 56 kilometres
south-west of Sydney between
Appin Road and the Georges River

St Helen's Park lies south-east of
Ambarvale, south of Bradbury on
the Appin Road and with
Rosemeadow to the south, much
as three early properties in the
area were situated. In October
1816 Governor Lachlan Macquarie
made two grants of land that
covered the area of this
neighbourhood, one to Samuel
Larken, the other to John Wild.
Larken, an artist, called his
property Ambarvale, and John
Wild gave his land the name of
Egypt Farm. Later other grants
were made in the area, and the
names Harding, Nowland and
Paton came into the district.

In 1886 the original grantees
appeared to have disposed of land
to George Westgarth, a name still
known in the business world of
Sydney, and at that time a
homestead known as St Helen's
was erected on the property. In
1970 the property, bounded by

Appin and Woodlands Roads was still in operation, being used for grazing. St Helen's was a two-storey building, the design following the pattern of late Victorian architecture. It was built of smooth sandstone from Minto and the stone used in the foundations was quarried on the property.

## ST IVES
*Municipality of Ku-ring-gai*
Location: 20 kilometres north of Sydney on Mona Vale Road

The North Shore suburbs of St Ives, St Ives Chase and North St Ives lie north-east of Pymble, extending east to Davidson Park around Harbour Creek. In 1885 local residents petitioned for a post office to be established in the area. The name of Rosedale was suggested, as early settler Daniel Mathew's property in the Pymble area had been given this name, and most of the later residents here used Rosedale in addressing letters. The postmaster general's department rejected this name, so Philip Richardson, an important land-owner in the area, suggested St Ives, probably after the town of St Ives in Cornwall, England. The first postmaster was Sydney Smith, and the suburb took its name from that first office.

The earliest land-use here was timber-getting. Daniel Dering Mathew, who arrived in the colony in 1812 and held a grant in the Roseville area, applied for a lease to 800 acres in the Pymble—St Ives area, where he established the first timber mill in the district. He imported special equipment for the mill, which he called Cowan. It stood at the corner of present Cowan and

Mona Vale Roads. Mathew's second land grant was made in this area. He called this property Rosedale and built a house on it, which is still standing in Mona Vale Road. This land covered the area from Rosedale Road to Station Street, Pymble.

Once timber-cutters had cleared this whole area it was occupied by orchardists, and even until the Second World War it remained a fruit-growing district. Italian prisoners of war held in a camp near Richmond Avenue worked in the orchards during the war. Most of the residential development of the suburb occurred in the 1960s and 1970s.

Today's homes have embraced the natural surroundings, and those on the periphery and adjacent to the parks look into the surrounding untouched bushland. Sydney Grammar Preparatory School stands in Ayres Road. This gracious suburb has its village shopping centre and Avondale Pony Club among its several attractions.

## ST LEONARDS
*Municipalities of Lane Cove and North Sydney*
Location: 6 kilometres north-west of Sydney on the Pacific Highway and the North Shore Line

The oldest railway station on the North Shore line, St Leonards opened in 1890. The line originally ran only from St Leonards to Hornsby, so passengers travelled from St Leonards to the Milsons Point ferry terminal by horse-bus. The suburb was named to honour English statesman, Thomas Townshend, Viscount Sydney of St Leonards. The name St Leonards originally applied to the area from

the present suburbs of North Sydney north to Gore Hill. The township of St Leonards, laid out in 1838, is now North Sydney. The present St Leonards lies to the north-west of the original township, and north of Wollstonecraft. Subdivision took place in 1871.

In 1877 a young Australian acrobat, Harry L'Estrange, calling himself the Australian Blondin, advertised that he would walk across Middle Harbour. L'Estrange chartered every ferry available, to bring spectators from Sydney, and organised special food stalls at strategic points for watching patrons. On the great day — 14 April 1877 — 8,000 people crammed the area from St Leonards to Middle Harbour, and at 4 pm Australia's Blondin, made his dramatic tightrope walk across Middle Harbour, carrying an 18 metre balancing pole. The long rope, spliced in the centre, swayed as the young acrobat walked quickly and confidently forward, waving to the crowds below. Women closed their eyes, some fainted, but L'Estrange reached the other side safely. For his day's work, he made £10,000, and became a celebrity. The governor of New South Wales at that time, Sir Hercules Robinson, had missed the exhibition and made it known that he would like to have seen it. Harry L'Estrange offered to do it again, under vice-regal patronage. But the second time only 2,000 people turned out. L'Estrange had made it all seem too easy, and the thrill of a chance fall or of him breaking his neck was now remote.

St Leonards today is known for its large, modern hospital, the Royal North Shore, the title Royal being granted in 1902 to commemorate the coronation of King Edward VII. It began as a

The Royal North Shore Hospital, St Leonards, is now one of the state's leading teaching hospitals. One hundred years ago it began as a small cottage hospital at Crows Nest with a capacity for fourteen patients

cottage hospital at Crows Nest. The foundation stone was laid in 1887 by Sir Henry Parkes, and the hospital opened the following year with fourteen beds. After the move to the site behind Gore Hill Cemetery, North Shore became a teaching hospital in 1948.

## ST MARYS

*Cities of Penrith and Blacktown*
Location: 45 kilometres west of Sydney on the Great Western Highway and the Main Western Line

This suburb, between the now major centres of Blacktown and Penrith, was originally known as South Creek. It was part of a 1,000 acre grant made to Major George

Druitt (1775?–1842). Macquarie appointed Druitt acting-chief engineer and inspector of public works in 1817, and he held these two positions continuously for four years (see Mount Druitt).

The suburb takes its name from the railway station, which was named after St Mary Magdalene's Church on the Great Western Highway. It stands on land given for the purpose of building a parish church by the family of Governor King, who had received large grants in the area in 1806. The foundation stone was laid in November 1837 and the church was consecrated in 1840. The adjoining graveyard shelters the remains of many members of the King and Lethbridge families, who were important settlers in the district. A splendid stained-glass window on the north side of the church remembers John King Lethbridge.

The Reverend Samuel Marsden (1764–1838), first Anglican chaplain in Parramatta, owned a

Reverend Samuel Marsden

farm at St Marys. This 1,030 acre grant of 1804 was known as Mamre, which has a biblical connotation. Fine fruit and vegetables were grown there, the wool of his merino sheep rivalled that of the wool king John

Macarthur. Mamre Road commemorates this old farm.

The railway station was opened in 1862 as South Creek, but the name was changed to St Marys in 1885. South Creek passes under the line about 1 kilometre west of the station. St Marys was proclaimed a municipality in 1890.

In the early part of this century, St Marys became an industrial town, with wagon-builders and tanneries. During the Second World War a large munition works was located in this suburb, which like its neighbours, Werrington, Kingswood and Penrith, is fast becoming an outer suburb of Sydney.

South Creek, St Marys, in flood, 1912. Flooding of the creek was and is a regular occurrence, but in the early days it meant isolation for the township. In 1937 a flood free roadway and bridge were built to alleviate the problem

# ST PETERS
*Municipality of Marrickville*
Location: 7 kilometres south of Sydney on the Princes Highway and the Illawarra Line

Both St Peters, south of Newtown, and Tempe were named by Alexander Brodie Spark (1792–1856), a merchant who arrived in the colony in 1823. He named Tempe after the mansion he built on his farm on the southern bank of Cooks River, and named St Peters after the church around which the suburb was developed. In 1838 he called for tenders to replace a temporary church built on the site in 1835. The church of St Peter's, on Cook's River Road (now the Princes Highway), was to become the mainstay of all other Anglican churches in the surrounding districts. When this church was finished, it was very impressive, with a tall steeple. Alterations were made in 1875 by Edmund Blacket and in 1963 the handsome steeple and tower were demolished, because the

deterioration of the hand-made bricks and ironbark used in the construction made them unsafe. It is now the third oldest Anglican church in the suburbs of Sydney, and its adjoining graveyard, consecrated in 1840, holds the remains of many early and notable residents of the district.

At first the church stood alone, but Spark laid out a village around it, naming it after the church. Among the many large residences built here in the early nineteenth century was Barwon Park House, erected in 1815 by Spark on land leased from Robert Campbell. It was demolished in 1953. Alexander Brodie Spark, who had given the land, was married in the completed church, and, on his death some years later, was buried in its precincts.

The first large land grant in the district had been made as far back as 1799, to Provost-Marshal Thomas Smyth. His 470 acre grant extended from the present Campbell Street to the Cooks River. He died in 1804 and in 1805

the property was acquired by Robert Campbell (1769–1846), Sydney's first merchant, who built the row of early warehouses along the Sydney Cove waterfront, and became known as Campbell of the Wharf. He sold the property in 1830, but reserved land for the church.

Vast deposits of clay were discovered in St Peters changing the whole character of the suburb. It became the chief brickmaking centre of the city, and many of the bricks and tiles used in houses in the expanding Sydney suburbs came from these brickworks. This period marked the change of St Peters from the woodlands with scattered houses of its early days to increasing industrialisation, although the site of the former brickworks is now being converted to a recreation and sports park, to be known as Sydney Park. The park may in time surpass in fame the suburb's well-known garbage dump, Tempe Tip, where thousands of people have mulled over other people's throwaways in the hope of a great find.

Princes Highway, St Peters, 1925

The railway station opened on 15 October 1884, accounting for an increase in residents and workers in this suburb. A post office had opened in October 1851, and pupils attended a school that began lessons in November 1881. The borough of St Peters had been incorporated in 1871.

## SANDRINGHAM
*Municipality of Rockdale*
Location: 18 kilometres south of Sydney at the tip of the Sans Souci Peninsula

Sandringham, south of Dolls Point on Botany Bay, began its life as Strippers Point in the 1830s. Situated near the mouth of the Georges River, its early name identified the local occupation of tree-felling and bark-stripping. Later the suburb was renamed by an early hotel-keeper, William Edward Rust. He had first bought a house from Thomas Holt (see Sutherland) at Sans Souci, which he turned into a luxurious hotel. Parting with this business, he

moved on to Strippers Point, renaming it Sandringham, and built the Prince of Wales Hotel there. He was an ardent royalist, and it is thought he chose the new name to honour Edward VII, who was then Prince of Wales and was at that time (1872) building a royal residence at Sandringham, in Norfolk, England. In 1876 Rust gathered together some of his neighbours and built a road, now known as Sandringham Street, running from the present Rocky Point Road to Dolls Point, to connect with a quarry he opened on Thomas Holt's property on Kogarah Bay.

Sandringham became well known and patronised for its delightful picnic grounds, and visitors could enjoy good fishing and boating offshore. In the 1920s steamers took visitors from Sandringham to Brighton-le-Sands and Kurnell on Sundays and holidays. The trip to Sandringham on Saywell's steam tram cost the princely sum of threepence.

## SANS SOUCI
*Municipalities of Rockdale and Kogarah*
Location: 17 kilometres south of Sydney on the northern side of the Georges River where it runs into Botany Bay

Thomas Holt (1811–88), wood merchant and politician, owned large areas of land in this district on the tip of the peninsula between Kogarah Bay and Botany Bay. He acquired land in Rocky Point Road in 1853 where he built a grand home for his German wife, calling it Sans Souci, a French phrase meaning "without care", after the palace of Prussian Frederick the Great at Potsdam. But Mrs Holt found it too isolated and refused to live in it. Holt built her another house at Marrickville overlooking Cooks River, which he called The Warren. Here he bred rabbits for hunting, kept exotic animals such as alpaca, and entertained lavishly. In the 1860s Holt turned his attention to the Sutherland area and William Rust acquired Sans Souci, and opened it as a hotel, which became popular despite the area's isolation (see also Sandringham). The suburb then adopted the name of the house.

The area of the present suburb was given as a 100 acre grant to Catherine Cooper in 1830. She and her husband, Robert Cooper junior, built a home on the land, which was known as Charlotte Point or Rocky Point. Cooper later operated a distillery there.

A steam tram ran to Kogarah in the 1890s and people began to come to Sans Souci to enjoy the good boating, fishing and bathing. In 1937 a silent electric trolley-bus service was introduced, running to Rockdale, Kogarah, Sans Souci and Dolls Point, but in 1959, despite local protests, diesel buses replaced the service.

Thomas Holt

# SCOTLAND ISLAND
*Shire of Warringah*
Location: 33 kilometres north of Sydney at the head of Pittwater opposite Church Point

Andrew Thompson (1773?–1810) operated saltworks on this island in Pittwater opposite Church Point in the early 1800s. In 1810 he received a grant of the island as a reward for courageous rescue work during floods, and he named it for his native land. In 1812, after his death, it was advertised for sale, the property consisting of 120 acres, the saltworks, a house, workmen's rooms, and a partly built 90 ton boat. Thompson Street, which encircles the island today, commemorates this pioneer.

Thompson, sentenced to fourteen years transportation for the theft of cloth, arrived in the colony in 1792. In 1793 he joined the police force and in 1796 was appointed to Green Hills (now Windsor), where he remained for the rest of his life. In 1798 he was pardoned and he soon became a chief constable, although he was dismissed from this post during the Rum Rebellion government in 1808. As well as his distinguished efforts in the police force, Thompson soon became both respected in the community and a wealthy man, acquiring land by both grant and purchase. He also built ships, ran a general store, a brewery and an inn, and established model farms for Governor Bligh. In 1810, when he was appointed magistrate at Windsor, he was the first emancipist to hold that position.

Various claims to the island were made in the ensuing years, but Charles Jenkins and Joseph Ben were finally recognised as tenants in common in the 1870s. The island was subdivided on 25 November 1911, and it has since proved a popular place for people seeking an away-from-it-all life-style close to the city.

# SEAFORTH
*Municipality of Manly*
Location: 13 kilometres north of Sydney overlooking Middle Harbour

Situated west of The Spit Bridge, Seaforth has splendid views over The Spit and Middle Harbour. It was once owned by Henry Halloran, who subdivided it and held the first auction in November 1906. The houses that were built on the land boast some of the finest harbour views in Sydney. Seaforth was named after Loch Seaforth and Seaforth Island in Scotland.

Seaforth Crescent gives a scenic drive from the main road around Bluff Head to Powder Hulk Bay, so named because hulks (ships that are no longer seaworthy) storing gunpowder were moored there from 1878 to 1919. The area behind the bay was originally a 30 acre grant made to James William Bligh in 1857.

Dalwood Home in Seaforth was once owned by Theodore Gurney (1849–1918), second professor of mathematics and natural philosophy at the University of Sydney from 1877. He was a fine teacher but it was said of him that "Mentally equipped with every gift except ambition he has as you know never published a line." Gurney Crescent and Dalwood Avenue commemorate his residence in the district, and there is also a Gurney Way named after him in Cambridge, England.

Spit Road, Seaforth, in the early 1900s.
This road is now known as Avona Crescent

## SEFTON

*City of Bankstown*

Location: 23 kilometres south-
west of Sydney north of the Hume
Highway, on the Regents Park –
Cabramatta Line

This suburb on the Regents Park
railway was first settled in 1839,
when James Wood received a grant
of 340 acres between the present
Wellington and Auburn Roads and
Brodie and Rose Streets. He called
it Sefton Park, after a place in
London, England. To the west of
his land was the 614 acre property
of T. L. Spencer, between Orchard
and Rose Streets, and when the
railway station was built in 1924, it
was sited on this property.

Like its near neighbour Chester
Hill, Sefton in its early days was an
area of orchards, market gardens,
and some poultry farms. The 1920s
brought subdivisions to the area;
shops soon followed, and when the
railway came through houses took
the place of the farms. But the
greatest increase in population was
in the years after the Second World
War.

Today Sefton is a busy suburb
of Sydney, with a majority of
hard-working family home-
owners as its residents.

## SEVEN HILLS

*City of Blacktown*

Location: 34 kilometres
north-west of Sydney east of
Blacktown Road, on the Main
Western Line

Located on the Western railway
line between Parramatta and
Blacktown, a siding opened here in
December 1863, and in 1869 the
station was built.

This area was first settled when
Matthew Pearce, a free settler who
arrived on board the *Surprise* in
1794, was granted 160 acres in
1795. He named it King's Langley
after an English village of that
name, about 30 kilometres south of
London; it is believed that Pearce
was born in the manor house in
that village (see also Kings
Langley). The grant was bounded
by the present Old Windsor Road,
Seven Hills Road, Chapel Lane
(Baulkham Hills) and Toongabbie
Creek. Because his family could
see seven hills from their home,
the area became known as Seven
Hills, a title it has borne since
1800.

Pearce was interred in St John's
Cemetery, Parramatta but later his
remains were removed. Today
Matthew Pearce and his family lie
peacefully in a private cemetery
which his descendants set up at the
corner of Seven Hills Road and
Old Windsor Road.

In the early years of this century,
there was a small village in the

area. A tileworks was established in about 1900 and continued to operate for about sixty years. Today Seven Hills has a Department of Agriculture poultry research station, established in 1939 on the site that had been Grantham poultry farm before the First World War. Nearby Grantham High School is on land that was also part of the Pearce estate.

# SHALVEY
*City of Blacktown*
Location: 34 kilometres north-west of Sydney north-west of Mount Druitt

Shalvey is another suburb developed during the housing boom of the 1960s and 1970s. The Blacktown City Council, keen to retain names of historical significance in the areas under its care, chose the name Shalvey for this neighbourhood near Blackett and Lethbridge Park. Shalvey Road was a thoroughfare through crown land in the early days of Blacktown's settlement.

Today Shalvey is a developing housing area in the municipality. By 1981 the population was 4,563. Its streets, in common with those of other new communities, follow the contours of the land rather than a grid pattern. Streets have been named after great Australian tennis-players, such as Laver, Stolle, Smith and Roche, along with a place named Margaret Court, and cricketers, such as Bradman, Kippax and Lindwall.

# SILVERWATER
*Municipality of Auburn*
Location: 20 kilometres west of Sydney between the Parramatta River and the Great Western Highway

There is no reliable record to tell us how this suburb came by such a beautiful name. It faces both Duck River and the upper reaches of the Parramatta River, both of which, in early days, could hold "silver" in reflections of sunlight or moonlight.

Today Silverwater is a busy, rather noisy area. The Silverwater Bridge, opened in 1962, carries heavy traffic across the Parramatta River, and south to Auburn and Clyde, and the industrial suburbs beyond. The Mulawa Training and Detention Centre for Women (a maximum security prison), and the Silverwater Work Release Complex (for men) are also in the area. Industrialisation of the area began as early as 1816–17, when a factory for producing blankets and tweed was opened here, to be followed in 1819 by a mill and later by a bone-crushing mill and lime-works.

In 1797 Governor John Hunter and his party explored this area between the Duck and Georges Rivers. Shortly after, two officers, formerly of the *Sirius*, Lieutenant John Shortland and Captain Henry Waterhouse, each received a grant of 25 acres, which they stocked with animals especially brought from the Cape. A First Fleet marine, Isaac Archer, was the next lessee, receiving his grant of 80 acres, next to Shortland Farm, on 26 August 1800. The Waterhouse grant was known as Waterhouse Farm and later formed part of the grounds of Newington. These earliest grants were made north of Parramatta Road, because the sole

John Blaxland

means of transport was the adjacent Parramatta River.

In 1800 Richard Atkins took out a lease on land east of Duck River and north of the Sydney–Parramatta Road, but it was soon cancelled. The area was included in the grant of 1,290 acres made in 1807 to John Blaxland (1769–1845), who arrived in the colony in 1807, as a wealthy free settler. The grant covered all the land between the Parramatta River and Parramatta Road, and Duck River and Haslam's Creek, except for land held by Waterhouse, Shortland, Archer and Haslam. Blaxland called his house there Newington, after the family property in Kent.

Blaxland and his younger brother Gregory (the explorer) began to develop a cattle industry. They bred fat cattle, and slaughtered and salted them. They were the first to produce usable salt, made from the brine gathered from the marshes on the river near the house. The site of the Queen Victoria Building in George Street, Sydney, was used by the Blaxland family to graze some of their herds of cattle. Blaxland had been promised 8,000 acres before he left for New South Wales, but it was not until 1831 that he was finally given the full quota of his land, when he received 10,240 acres in different areas. He finally held 29,000 acres in the colony.

The present Newington House was built in about 1832 in the style of an English mansion, with disciplined English gardens, and a private chapel (St Augustine's), built in 1838. In 1845, John Blaxland died and the family moved away, leasing the property to owners of a slaughtering industry. In 1863 John Manton, a Methodist clergyman, who had been engaged to undertake missionary pastoral work in the newly developed city of Parramatta, acquired Newington on behalf of the Methodist Church to start a boys school. By 16 July 1863, his objective had been achieved, and nineteen boys

formed the nucleus of what was to become the third of the GPS schools, Newington College. The old bell, which had summoned Blaxland's convict servants, now called the boys to lessons, and free hours could be spent roaming the surrounding gardens and parklands. In 1880 the school was moved to its present site at Stanmore. The nineteen original pupils had by then swelled to several hundred, but the first headmaster, John Manton, did not live to see the changeover. He had died in September 1864 and was buried at Parramatta, the pupils of the first Newington forming a marching guard of honour along the whole route. Newington House is now part of the prison complex.

# SMITHFIELD

*City of Fairfield, Municipality of Holroyd*

Location: 34 kilometres west of Sydney on the Horsley Drive

This suburb north-west of Fairfield began its life as a village known as Chisholm's Bush. It was a semi-rural settlement populated in 1867 by vine-growers, gardeners and wood-cutters, but not without its inn, smithy, shoemaker and schoolteacher.

John Ryan Brenan (1798–1868), in 1836 was granted 1,650 acres here, part of 12,300 acres Governor

The intersection of Albert Street (now The Horsley Drive) and Liverpool Road (now Smithfield Road), c. 1904

King originally allotted for the Orphan Institution in 1803 (see Cabramatta). He decided to subdivide the estate and call it Donnybrook, but changed the name to Smithfield, as it was hoped to build cattle saleyards in the area and the name Smithfield commemorated the big meat markets in London. Saleyards opened in 1841 and, although the project to establish a village around the yards failed, the name remained.

In the subdivision Brenan offered an extra adjoining allotment to any buyer who built a cottage with a brick chimney and enclosed the property with a fence. Some of the early names known in the district were Elijah Brown, James Mansfield, Samuel Crook, James Coleman, Thomas Betts, S. Critchley and Thomas Downey. The public school opened in 1850 and by the 1880s Smithfield was well provided with churches, three denominations adding a burial ground adjacent to the church buildings.

Today the suburb retains the air of an old-fashioned township, and although its nearest railway station is Fairfield, it keeps in touch by an excellent and regular bus service to surrounding areas.

## SPIT JUNCTION AND THE SPIT

*Municipality of Mosman*
Location: 9 kilometres north-east of Sydney on Spit Road reaching down to Middle Harbour

Spit Junction stands north of Mosman shopping centre and west of Balmoral. The Spit is to the north on the tip of the peninsula jutting into Middle Harbour.

E. and W. E. Brady bought 9 acres in the area of the present Spit Junction in 1855. In those days it

Looking from Seaforth, a view overlooking the Spit Bridge and Middle Harbour, c. 1949. The wooden bridge seen here was built in 1924 and was replaced by the present bridge in 1959

was the site of a bush racetrack, which lasted until the area was subdivided in 1902. At first the area was known as Trafalgar Square, the name given to a block of shops built at the junction of what is now Spit Road and Military Road.

The Spit Bridge is one of two bridges crossing Middle Harbour, the other being Roseville Bridge some kilometres upstream. Once a punt ferried vehicles and people across the stretch of water. Today's bridge is a concrete and steel structure with an impressive span which opens at set times to allow high-masted yachts a safe passage.

Nearby Chinaman's Beach is so named because some Chinese residents had market gardens and salt pans there.

# STANMORE

*Municipality of Marrickville*
Location: 6 kilometres south-west
of Sydney south of Parramatta
Road, on the Main Suburban Line

The southern part of this suburb,
which stands between Annandale
and Marrickville, was once part of
an estate owned by John Jones
who gave it the name Stanmore
after his birthplace in England.
This early settler willed 20 acres of
the estate to the Methodist
Church, and in 1880, Newington
College was built on this site, after
the school was transferred from
Silverwater, near Parramatta.

At first a building was rented by
the school in Stanmore at £250 a
year, as the owner did not wish to
sell, but after seven years, when
the school had raised enough
money to buy the acres adjoining
the land given by John Jones, a
new school building was erected.

One of the earliest land grants in
the area was made in 1793, when
Thomas Rowley was granted 100
acres. The property, which he
called Kingston Farm, extended
from the present Australia Street to
Stanmore station, and was later
enlarged to cover 240 acres. Major
Johnston's Annandale estate (see
Annandale), granted in 1793, also
extended into the area, and
Annandale House, built in 1799,
was on the south side of
Parramatta Road.

Stanmore Road, once a dirt
track, runs through the suburb, and
before they were banished from
the Sydney transport scene, trams
provided a reliable service along
this road. The opening of the
railway line from Sydney to
Parramatta Junction (today's
Granville) made a big difference to
the residential potential of this
suburb, and a railway station
opened in 1878. The station was
later known as "one of the best

kept on the line" and Harry
Dutton was one of the youngest
stationmasters.

Stanmore today lies on both
sides of the railway line, extending
as far as Parramatta Road. Many
post-war immigrants have made
their homes in this suburb and
opened shops that follow the style
in their home countries. Alongside
the area's old cottages, there is also
some industry in this inner-city
suburb, although some of the older
landmarks in the area have in
recent years been relocated in the
newer industrial suburbs.

Stanmore Public School,
established in 1884, is a reminder
of a typical Victorian public
school. The original main building
still stands, with its curved
entrances, set back from the road,
and with the heavy trees typical of
the period. The added buildings
and modern facilities give this
school, which celebrated its
centenary in 1984, the facilities to
cater for its present multilingual
population.

# STRATHFIELD

*Municipalities of Strathfield, Burwood
and Concord*
Location: 14 kilometres west of
Sydney south of Concord, a
junction station for the Main
Northern Line

This suburb, extending from
Concord to the Cooks River, was
part of the area known as Liberty
Plains, so called because the first
free settlers received grants there.
James Wilshire received his grant
of 570 acres in 1808 and called it
Wilshire Farm. The grant lay
between the present streets The
Boulevarde, Chalmers Street and
Liverpool Road. To the west of
this grant were Church Lands,
declared in 1823 to support clergy
in the colony, which extended into
present Flemington. In 1841 this
land was sold and the part south of

The front garden of Agincourt, Albert
Road, Strathfield. The estate included
stables, a tennis court, an orchard, poultry
houses and two paddocks, one with a tame
emu

Barker Road was acquired by Joseph Newton. The grant was sold to Samuel Terry (1776?–1838) in September 1824, and he renamed it Redmire Estate. He paid £600 for the property, and the name Redmire (changed in about 1865 to Redmyre) honoured a village in North Yorkshire, England, which was near the birthplace of the Terry family.

In 1877 when a railway platform was erected it was named Redmyre, but was renamed Strathfield in 1885. A station was built on a new site in 1900, and yet again in 1922. In 1885 the area was incorporated as Strathfield. This new title came from the name of a mansion built in the district by John Hardie, a wealthy early settler, who chose the name to honour the English estate given in 1817 by a grateful nation to the Duke of Wellington.

Other magnificent homes were built in the area last century. Albert House in Albert Road was erected by the Hordern family in 1885; Mount Royal, now known as Mount St Mary's was built by John Hinchcliffe and later acquired by Sir George Reid, one-time premier of New South Wales and prime minister in 1904–05; and Washington H. Soul occupied a house called Agincourt, now called Jesmond, in Homebush Road. The Boulevarde, Strathfield, became a thoroughfare associated with elegance and fine living. Remnants of those days still remain, although the residents and their lives have changed.

Santa Maria del Monte Convent is one of the area's pleasing reminders of times past, as is Santa Sabina Convent with its beautiful chapel. Santa Maria del Monte was built in 1885 by William Spence Brunton, a colonel in the Light Horse. It passed through several hands and it was a Mrs Bailey who changed its name to Del

Monte. In the 1950s she left the house to the Sisters from the Dominican convent of Santa Sabina, opposite her house, as they had nursed her through a severe illness. Today the house is used as the junior school for Santa Sabina College. Santa Sabina Convent, now Santa Sabina College, was, in 1870, the home of Charles Pilcher, who took a major part in the anti-Federation debate. In 1890 a group of Dominican nuns, who had been requested by Cardinal Moran to come to Sydney and open a school,

A number of the Strathfield mansions of yesteryear have been maintained in all their splendour—seen here are 1 Florence Street (top) and 78 Abbotsford Road

came to live at Santa Sabina, where a number of additions have since been made to house the girls school. Another well-known property, originally named Illyria and owned in 1890 by Charles Hoskins, changed hands in 1911 to become the property of George Adams, of the Adams Hotel in Sydney, famous for its Marble Bar. A former Cobb & Co. driver, he had a family of several daughters, all of whom attended Santa Sabina College. Illyria eventually became the property of the school and was renamed Holyrood House. For some time it was the living quarters of the Dominican sisters.

A public school opened in this suburb in February 1881, with the name of Druitt Town, the area on the Liverpool Road having been named after Major George Druitt, a friend of the owner, Judge Josephson. The name was changed to Strathfield South in January 1893. The official post office, which was known as Redmyre in 1881, became Strathfield in 1886. Strathfield's first mayor was George Hardie, who held that office for one year in 1885.

In North Strathfield land was purchased in Concord Road from the Yaralla Estate of Thomas Walker, and a public school, at first known as Yaralla School, was

built. It later changed its name to North Strathfield Public School. North Strathfield today contains a splendid golf links, a busy shopping centre, and a row of retirement houses built by Dame Eadith Walker for her staff. The Walker land stretched from this part of North Strathfield through to the Parramatta River (see Concord).

When the line from Strathfield to Hornsby was completed in the 1920s, Strathfield became the junction of all trains going north and west. Today Strathfield remains an attractive residential area, with many houses set in spacious gardens. It is home to a number of private and public schools, conveniently situated near this important railway junction. There is only a small shopping centre near the station, but the area is close to the major shopping centre of Burwood.

## SUMMER HILL

*Municipality of Ashfield*

Location: 8 kilometres west of Sydney at the junction of Parramatta Road and the Hume Highway, on the Main Suburban Line

The name of this suburb west of Lewisham was originally Sunning Hill, the name of Nicholas Bayly's property north of Parramatta Road, which he held from 1803 to 1826 (see Haberfield). The name was apparently applied loosely to the area south of the road too, and especially to a racecourse. There is, however, no indication of why the name changed to Summer Hill.

In 1794 and 1804 emancipist Henry Kable received grants south of Parramatta Road in the area of the present Summer Hill. To his grants, which totalled 75 acres, he added 100 acres bought from

The town centre at Summer Hill, c. 1915

grantees to the west. The property was sold in 1822 to James Underwood (1776?–1844), merchant, distiller and shipbuilder. It was leased to various people until it sold in 1878–79.

In 1832 an area south of the railway line was set aside as a Sheep Quarantine Ground to prevent sheep infected with scab travelling the roads. By 1882 an official post office had opened at Summer Hill, and a school followed a year later in April 1883. The railway station was already operating by 1879, and the suburb, with its neat Victorian homes, and spired churches grew. Rapid development followed the 1878–79 sale of the James Underwood estate, and in 1885 the Sheep Quarantine Ground was also subdivided and sold.

# SURRY HILLS
*City of Sydney*
Location: 2 kilometres south of Sydney

This inner-city suburb stretching from Central Station east to Dowling Street was probably named after the Surrey Hills in England, an area of great beauty. It is hard to imagine our Surry Hills either beautiful or as a farming area, but its first use was indeed as a farm, owned by Major Joseph Foveaux (1765–1846) in about 1811. His property was known as Surry Hills Farm, and Foveaux Street in Surry Hills today honours this soldier and administrator of the colony's early days.

In the first half of the nineteenth century John Terry Hughes built the Albion Brewery, a site now owned by Toohey's Brewery. Adjacent to the brewery was Albion House, where his nephew, J. T. Hughes, lived with his wife.

Surry Hills had an air of elegance in the 1800s, when buildings in the style of the Macquarie era were constructed. One of the most interesting was Durham Hall. George Hill bought the site from Thomas Broughton and the mansion was erected in 1835. The Hill family was descended from an early colonist, William Hill, who was associated with a timberyard in George Street, was the overseer of several slaughterhouses, and owned city inns. In the 1830s his several sons were all in business running inns — the Butchers Arms, the Carpenters Arms and the Wheelwrights Arms, all in Pitt Street, Sydney; his son, David, kept the William the Fourth Inn in Sussex Street. Durham Hall was still standing in its original state in 1946, but in 1957 the site and the house were purchased by the Commonwealth Trading Bank of Australia.

The Devonshire Street cemetery, where many early settlers were buried, was located in this area. When Central Station became the Sydney railway terminus, the cemetery was moved to various other locations, and Central Railway Station opened on the site on 4 August 1906. This altered the traffic plan, and the flow of trams and horse-drawn vehicles moved along George Street and past the new Anthony Hordern Palace Emporium, built after a disastrous fire in 1901, which had burned the previous Hordern store almost to the ground and caused the death of four employees. For many years this southern part of the city was the main shopping area because its nearness to Central Station made it accessible from all over Sydney and the state.

The area around Cleveland and Elizabeth Streets was known as Strawberry Hills, and the Strawberry Hills post office was

located for many years on the corner of these two streets, but is now at the corner of Chalmers and Cleveland Streets.

From the 1850s terrace houses and workers' cottages were being built in Surry Hills, which gradually became a working-class suburb. Work was available locally as light industry, particularly the clothing industry, became established in the area. The suburb was also favoured by families newly arrived in Australia in the years after the Second World War, when property values were low and the area provided inexpensive accommodation. Today the suburb has a multicultural aspect, with a large Lebanese population joining older immigrant families. Many of the area's old houses are also being restored as the middle class moves into the area to enjoy the benefits of inner-city living.

# SUTHERLAND
*Shire of Sutherland*
Location: 26 kilometres south of Sydney on the Princes Highway and the Illawarra Line and a junction station for the Cronulla Line

Historians are divided on just how Sutherland received its name, and three theories have been put forward. In May 1770 a member of the crew of Captain Cook's HMS *Endeavour* died of tuberculosis in New South Wales and was buried at Kurnell. His name was Forby Sutherland, and Cook named Point Sutherland in his memory. The second possibility involves the report made by Surveyor-General Thomas Mitchell. In 1828 he began a new survey of the southern portion of the County of Cumberland, and when this was

John Sutherland

presented to the governor in 1835, the area south of the Georges River was noted as Southerland. This spelling was used officially until 1881, when a change to the spelling Sutherland was adopted. During the 1870s another Sutherland came into the story of this shire. He was John Sutherland, a minister for works, who for twelve years argued in Parliament for the extension of the railway across Georges River, thus opening up the Port Hacking area. Sutherland station, opened in 1885, was named after him.

Timber-cutting was the first industry in the heavily forested Sutherland area. After the construction of the railway line, in the 1880s, the suburb rapidly developed, although by 1886 there were only four permanent buildings: the newly opened railway station, the station-master's residence, the railway-keeper's cottage and a general store run by a man named Bromley. For the rest, local residents lived in humpies and tents in the bush, and timber-cutting remained the chief occupation. Some residents were boring for coal, which was said to

run through the district, but no record of its successful mining is to be found today.

Once the land was cleared, farms were established, and by 1900 a small township was developing around Sutherland Railway Station. An official post office had opened on 1 September 1886, and a school had begun classes in March 1887. By 1910 a steam train was running between Sutherland and Cronulla. Once the original farming areas were subdivided, new settlers came to the Sutherland area, and the new suburbs of Sylvania, Miranda, Caringbah, Gymea and Cronulla developed.

One of the area's most important early settlers was Thomas Holt (1811–88), a free settler who arrived in Sydney in 1842, accompanied by his wife Sophie. He became a successful businessman and financier, and in the 1860s he purchased about 13,000 acres in the area stretching from Sutherland to

Cronulla. A man of great enterprise, Holt initiated many commercial projects, including sheep farming, timber-cutting, oyster farming and coal mining. In 1881 he built a forty room mansion, Sutherland House, on the shores of Sylvania, with a driveway along the edge of Gwawley Bay. He built swimming pools and luxurious dressing sheds, and the property had its own wharf and boatsheds. The mansion was destroyed by fire in 1918, which was thought to have been lit deliberately. Holt returned to England in 1881 and died in Bexley, Kent, in 1888. The Thomas Holt Memorial Village, a retirement village in Acacia Road, Kirrawee, opened in the 1950s. Built on land donated in memory of settler Thomas Holt, this project is a fitting memorial to the man whose influence was so important in the development of this suburb.

Sutherland Shire Council chambers, c. 1926. The building was demolished in 1965

In the earliest days of its history, the only communication between the small settlements in the Sutherland area was by river or bush tracks. The first public road was South Road, constructed in 1842 to a survey by Sir Thomas Mitchell. Later the Illawarra Road, which followed the ridges of high land into the valley of the Woronora River, was built, running to the present Woronora Road.

In 1906 the shire of Sutherland was proclaimed by the then state governor, Sir Harry H. Rawson, and the official name of Sutherland was declared. The first meetings of the council elected at the end of that year were held in the new shire clerk's home, located in the road now known as Princes Highway. Council Chambers were built in 1915.

An expectant crowd gathered for a subdivision land sale at Sydenham on 2 February 1884. It was described as a "clearance sale" offering "wonderfully easy terms"

## SYDENHAM
*Municipality of Marrickville*
Location: 8 kilometres south of Sydney on the Princes Highway, a junction station for the Illawarra, Bankstown and East Hills Lines

Named after a suburb of London, Sydenham has a location similar to its English counterpart, near the city and a railway junction. Like its neighbours, Marrickville and Tempe, Sydenham developed when the Illawarra railway line came through the area, from Sydney to Hurstville. While it was under construction, the station was known as Illawarra Road, but it opened on 15 October 1884 as Marrickville, and on 19 May 1895 its name was changed to Sydenham, because a new line was being built to Bankstown and the first station on the new line was to be called Marrickville. To add to the confusion, Sydenham post office was first known as Tempe Park when it opened in April 1899, but in 1964 it was renamed

Sydenham. The suburb today has a mixture of residential and industrial land-use.

## SYLVANIA
*Shire of Sutherland*
Location: 22 kilometres south of Sydney on the Princes Highway on the southern side of the Georges River

This suburb is situated in the area of Horse Rock Point, on the south side of the Georges River at a point where the Georges River Bridge crosses the water to Tom Ugly's Point. The naming of the suburb is somewhat obscure, but it is thought to have evolved from the beauty of its sylvan setting, and Sylvan Street, off Holt Street, seems to lend confirmation to the naming of this suburb as Sylvania.

A village grew up here following the formation of Sutherland Estate Company by

Above: Cars in seemingly endless line awaiting Tom Ugly's Punt at Sylvania, 1928

Left: Tom Ugly's punt, c. 1915. Looking toward Sylvania from Tom Ugly's Point

## TAREN POINT
*Shire of Sutherland*
Location: 20 kilometres south of Sydney on the Georges River

This small suburb stands on the peninsula where the Captain Cook Bridge crosses the Georges River to Sans Souci. First called Comyns Point, its name was then changed to Cummins Point and later Commins Point, apparently in honour of an early local resident. Later it became known by its present name of Taren Point, but there is no information about the origin of this name either — although both names were recorded on early maps.

The suburb is a pleasant residential area, with the accent on family life. Holt Road commemorates early land-owner Thomas Holt (see Sutherland). The local public school and post office are both in Taren Point Road, and

Thomas Holt in 1881. The area was part of Thomas Holt's estate (see Sutherland), and he had built Sutherland House on the foreshores north of Gwawley Bay, on the eastern side of the present Sylvania, in 1818. He is commemorated by Holt Street, which extends into Sylvania Waters, an area reclaimed from the shallow parts of Gwawley Bay. L. J. Hooker developed this area as Sylvania Waters Estate in the 1960s. Most of the blocks of land

had water frontages offering swimming or boating facilities. Streets in this area emphasise the water associations by being named after rivers, such as Shoalhaven, Snowy, Barwon and Tweed.

A post office opened in Sylvania in 1883 and a school opened in 1884. For the privilege of their education, the pupils paid "a penny a week", but the school closed in 1891 and was not reopened until 1925. Sylvania Heights Public School opened in 1955.

Aerial photograph looking toward Taren Point and Gwawley Bay, which can be seen at the top of the picture, c. 1935

transport is provided by a government bus service. Like other Georges River suburbs, Taren Point retains much of the area's natural beauty.

## TELOPEA
*City of Parramatta, Shire of Baulkham Hills*
Location: 21 kilometres north-west of Sydney between Pennant Hills Road and Kissing Point Road, on the Carlingford Line

The title of this suburb, situated south of Dundas, sounds like a foreign name, and it is. The word is made of two Greek works that mean "seen from a distance". A botanist, however, would tell you that *Telopea* is the botanical name for the waratah. When these large red flowers were seen against the green-grey colours of the Australian bush, they could be "seen from a distance", so they were given the name Telopea. In the days of its first settlement, waratahs grew here in abundance.

One of the area's earliest landowners was Thomas Arndell (1753–1821), the first doctor in Parramatta, who received a grant of 70 acres in 1794, extending south of the present Pennant Hills Road and cut by Bettington Road. Oatlands House, still standing in Bettington Road (now in Dundas) was built in the area in the 1830s, and extended in 1840, to the design of Ambrose Hallen (d.1845), who became colonial architect.

Telopea developed after the Second World War, when the Housing Commission opened up the Dundas Valley for the many young couples seeking homes. Oatlands Golf Links are adjacent to this suburb.

## TEMPE
*Municipality of Marrickville*
Location: 9 kilometres south of Sydney on the Princes Highway, a junction station for the Illawarra and the East Hills Lines

The first impression of Tempe is one of the old and quaint terrace houses, and the charm of the village corner shop, but it is a busy inner-city suburb, south-west of the city on the Cooks River. The name Tempe is Greek; the Vale of Tempe in Thessaly, Greece, was celebrated for its beauty. The name was given to the suburb by Alexander Brodie Spark (1792–1856), a businessman and trader in the colony's early days. He built a mansion on the southern bank of Cooks River which he named Tempe House (see Arncliffe). Erected in 1828, the design is thought to have been by John Verge (1772–1861), one of the finest architects of the day, and

253

the suburb takes its name from this house. The house still stands and is part of a training centre for socially maladjusted girls conducted by the Order of the Good Samaritan nuns.

Spark also gave money towards the purchase of land and the building of St Peter's Church of England, which gave its name to a suburb north of Tempe (see St Peters).

A high school and a public school are situated in Unwins Bridge Road, Tempe. Frederick Wright Unwin, who gave his name to this thoroughfare, was a clever man in the legal profession in its early days in Sydney. William Bede Dalley, one of the members of the first parliament under responsible government in 1856, after whom Dalley Street was named, studied under him.

Trams used to run to Cooks River from Circular Quay but with the coming of buses, the tram depot near the Cooks River between Sydenham and Tempe became the bus depot, and now buses terminate at Tempe. The railway station opened in 1884, but it was originally given the name of Cooks River.

# TENNYSON
*Municipality of Ryde*
Location: 13 kilometres west of Sydney on the Parramatta River just south of Gladesville

This neighbourhood on the north bank of Parramatta River was, in the early years of this century, a popular weekend pleasure place for picnicking. In the 1920s it was reached by steamer from Circular Quay. For many years the area was known as Farnell's Point, after James Squire Farnell, who had an estate here, which was subdivided

Hallam, Baron Tennyson

in the 1880s. The present name came from a later subdivision, called Tennyson, in 1905. It was not, however, named in honour of the poet Alfred, Lord Tennyson, poet laureate during the reign of Queen Victoria, but there is a family connection. Most of the Sydney streets named Tennyson, and indeed this neighbourhood, take their name from Hallam, Baron Tennyson, who came to Australia as governor of South Australia, and eventually became the second governor-general of the Commonwealth in 1902–04. He was the eldest son of the famous poet, and his Christian name, Hallam, was given to honour his father's greatest friend Arthur Hallam. This friend, who was engaged to the poet's sister, died before the marriage, and Tennyson's poem "In Memoriam" was written in his honour.

Tennyson Road leads to Raven Point, which separates Morrison's Bay from Glade's Bay. The point

was named after early settler Captain William Raven, who from 1795 held 100 acres purchased from the original grantee in the area of the Field of Mars known as Eastern Farms. Governor Hunter granted him a further 60 acres in 1795 and another 285 acres in 1799 in the same area. Morrison's Bay was named after Archibald Morrison, a private in the New South Wales Corps, who received 55 acres there in 1795.

# TERREY HILLS
*Shire of Warringah*
Location: 25 kilometres north of Sydney on Mona Vale Road

Like its neighbour Duffy's Forest, Terrey Hills is a suburb of the Warringah Shire that has developed in the bushland of Ku-ring-gai National Park. Land there was held by Obadiah Terrey, who acquired 640 acres in 1881 and built his home at the junction of Mona Vale Road and Forest Way. He used the land for sheep raising. A nearby property was the 100 acres held by Samuel Hills from 1881. Called Mount Pleasant, it stood on the site of the present council rubbish tip behind Mona Vale Road. The suburb takes its name from these two early settlers.

The suburb is a popular riding area, and several riding schools are located there. The New South Wales Gun Club, devoted to target shooting, also has its headquarters in Terrey Hills.

The Ku-ring-gai Chase area and Pittwater were explored by Governor Phillip as early as 1790. Official records and maps show that Surveyor William Govett, who explored Blackheath with Sir Thomas Mitchell, was also active in the Pittwater area. In May 1829 he was instructed to survey the land side of Ku-ring-gai Chase. In April 1832, Surveyor James Larmer was instructed to complete Govett's work, and for the first time the name of McCarr's Creek, which flows through Terrey Hills, was recorded. McCarr's Creek was again mentioned in the Lands Department records of 1879.

Almost a century ago a conservationist named Eccleston du Faur was responsible for the preservation for the future of the area we know as Ku-ring-gai Chase. He suggested to the minister for lands, Henry Copeland, in 1892 that it be dedicated as a national park. Copeland agreed and in 1894 gave the area of more than 20,000 acres the Aboriginal name it now bears. Du Faur and Copeland deserve our thanks for saving this beautiful area from development.

All the street names in Terrey Hills are Aboriginal, such as, Tooronga Road (leeches), Thuddungra Road (water rushing down), Coonawarra Road (honeysuckle rise) and Kallaroo Road (cold weather).

Tumble Down Dick Hill near Terrey Hills belonged to William Oliver (see Church Point), who used bullock drays to cart timber from the Church Point area. Tumble Down Dick was one of his leading bullocks, a temperamental beast, who would refuse to carry too heavy a load of felled timber up the steep rise towards Terrey Hills. This creature would fall to his knees and refuse to budge. It has been thought that the creature was named after Richard Cromwell, son of Oliver Cromwell, Lord Protector of England. The bullock, Dick, behaved like Richard Cromwell whom a biographer described as, "Gentle and virtuous in his nature, but a peasant who became not greatness".

## THORNLEIGH

*Shire of Hornsby*
Location: 25 kilometres north-west of Sydney on Pennant Hills Road and the Main Northern Line

In 1830, John Thorn, chief constable of Parramatta, was patrolling the Windsor Road with Constable Samuel Horne (see Normanhurst), keeping a look out for bushrangers. Nor was he disappointed! As he passed a clump of undergrowth two men leapt out and one fired at Thorn, who was fortunately uninjured. Raising his musket he shot the bandit dead. The dead man was John Macnamara, leader of the North Rocks Gang, with a price on his head. The second bushranger ran off, but was captured shortly afterwards. For the part he played in apprehending the two wanted men, John Thorn was rewarded by a fine land grant of 640 acres on Pennant Hills Road. After his death, George Henry Thorn, his beneficiary, opened the area for settlement in 1840 and named it Thornleigh.

When the railway line went through the northern area from Strathfield to Hornsby in 1886, the station took the name Thornleigh, after daring Chief Constable John Thorn.

The first official post office opened in March 1888, and the first public school in April 1891.

## TOONGABBIE

*Cities of Parramatta and Blacktown, Municipality of Holroyd*
Location: 30 kilometres west of Sydney north of the Great Western Highway, on the Main Western Line

Toongabbie, north of Wentworthville, is one of the oldest settled areas in the city of Parramatta. It was named by Governor Phillip. Toongabbie is an Aboriginal word meaning "a place near the water" or "meeting of the waters", and the area now called Old Toongabbie stands at the confluence of Toongabbee and Quarry Creeks. The old spelling of Toongabbee Creek, one variant of this name, is often still used.

A government farm was established in 1791 to produce food for the colony, but gradually the farm area was reduced as parts were given away as grants. By 1804 it was used only for cattle grazing and as a camp for convicts working in the area. Early grants included one to Thomas Daveney, superintendent of convicts at Toongabbie, who received 100 acres in 1794.

Major Joseph Foveaux (1765–1846) held 1,770 acres in the area. The property was acquired

Hamilton Hume

by John Macarthur (1767–1834) by 1801, but he returned it to the Crown in 1821 in exchange for his Camden property.

Many of the early settlers created orchards on the land, and more were established when the Western railway line came through in 1880, linking Toongabbie with the thriving town of Granville.

One of Australia's explorers was born at Toongabbie on 18 June 1797. He was Hamilton Hume (1797–1873), who, with W. H. Hovell, explored the route overland to Port Phillip in Victoria and back in 1824–25. His hot-headed Irish father, Andrew Hamilton Hume, came to the colony as a free settler, was employed as a superintendent of convicts and was given a grant in Toongabbie in 1794.

The original district cemetery, known as May's Hill Cemetery, is nearby (see Mays Hill).

The first official post office opened in August 1887 and had several name changes before a second post office opened in 1922, known as Toongabbie West. Finally, it became Toongabbie post office on 5 December 1960. In April 1886, the first public school began classes. Its name also underwent several changes before becoming Old Toongabbie School in 1960. The name Old Toongabbie for the suburb alongside the creeks, north-east of present Toongabbie, probably first came into use to distinguish the older part of the suburb from the railway station. The present primary schools are Toongabbie, Toongabbie East and Toongabbie West. The three post offices in the district today are Old Toongabbie, Toongabbie, and Toongabbie East.

The township here only came into being after the Second World War, when holdings were being broken up and shops began to appear. Toongabbie today has an improved transport service, and the new Westmead Hospital is not far away. It is developing into a busy, residential district.

# TREGEAR
*City of Blacktown*
Location: 46 kilometres west of Sydney just north-west of Mount Druitt

A new suburb, Tregear is part of the Mount Druitt housing development of the 1960s. Originally a land grant made to James Whalan in 1831, it was later purchased by the Lethbridge family, which was associated with the family of Governor King through marriage. They named Tregear after the Lethbridge family's property in Cornwall. The family held the property until 1942, when it was taken over by the Royal Australian Air Force, which sold it in 1951.

The street names in this suburb commemorate explorers of the Antarctic, such as Mawson Road, McMurdo Avenue and Amundsen Street. Other streets have been named Seal, Penguin, Polar, Erebus and Nella Dan, complementing the names of early explorers.

A pleasant park, known as Tregear Reserve, is located at the eastern end of Ropes Creek, off Wilkes Crescent. The suburb is a family residential area, and a modern primary school is in Wilkes Avenue.

# TURRAMURRA
*Municipality of Ku-ring-gai*
Location: 20 kilometres north-west of Sydney on the Pacific Highway and the North Shore Line

This suburb on the North Shore railway line has as its neighbours North Turramurra and South Turramurra, which extend north to Ku-ring-gai Chase and south to the Lane Cove River. Only a half hour drive to Cowan Creek, the district is a natural beauty spot close to the Hawkesbury River. Aboriginal tribes passing through from the Lane Cove River to Cowan Waters, by way of tracks through St Ives and Pymble, always rested near this high land, which they called "turramurra" or "turraburra", meaning "big hill". When early settlers moved into the area they referred to the place as Eastern Road, and when the railway station was built in 1890 it was given that name. Less than a year later, on 14 December 1890, the suburb was officially called by the Aboriginal name Turramurra. Many of the early streets also have Aboriginal names, such as Womerah Street, Warragal Road, Nulla Nulla Street and Warrangi Street, while Eastern Road, running from the railway station north to Boundary Road commemorates that early name of the suburb.

By the 1840s the best timber in this forested area had been taken and the timber-cutters had moved to areas further from Sydney. As in many of the northern suburbs, orchards were then established, the first in the area of the present suburb by John Brodie. Brodie and Sons were also the general carriers for the area.

An interesting old home in the area is Ingleholme, built in

Boomerang Street in about 1896 to a design by John Sulman (1849–1934).

The first post office opened for business in 1890. A public school began giving instruction in May 1921 and is still operating in Kissing Point Road. Since those early days, Turramurra High School has been built at South Turramurra, making this suburb educationally self-sufficient.

The Lady Davidson Home in Bobbin Head Road was established as a tuberculosis sanatorium shortly after the beginning of the Second World War, when it was found that some of the men and women in the forces were suffering from the disease. Soon after, it was taken over by the Department of Rehabilitation, as a hospital for military personnel. Now run wholly for treatment of former members of the forces, it is under the control of the Department of Veteran Affairs.

Many fine homes have been built in this area, which has tree-lined streets of great natural beauty.

## TURRELLA
*Municipality of Rockdale*
Location: 10 kilometres south-west of Sydney just north of Arncliffe, on the East Hills Line

The name of this suburb, which is situated in the parish of St George just south of the Cooks River is an Aboriginal word meaning "a reedy place" or "water weeds". The Wolli Creek, which runs through the original site of settlement, was first known as Woolly Creek, and it is quite likely that the weeds in the water gave it a thick appearance.

In about 1842 William Favell and his wife, Eleanor, farmed a property known as Hillside on the site of the present suburb. Their neighbours were the families of Thomas Curtis and Henry Blackwell, who were orchardists and gardeners.

Turrella is near Undercliffe and Arncliffe, and, like all the suburbs with railway stations, it developed when the railway came through the area and farm and orchard land was subdivided for home development. The railway station opened as Turrella on 21 September 1931. The first post office, however, was originally called West Arncliffe when it opened on 26 April 1933, but in January 1948 it became Arncliffe West. Finally, in August 1952, the name was changed to Turrella. The post office closed on 21 December 1970.

Those peaceful days of early Turrella have gone forever, and the suburb today is a mixture of industry and residential development. One of the biggest factories in the suburb is owned by Streets Ice Cream, which is near the railway station. Other light industries are located nearer the creek, while most of the residential development is on the south side of the railway line.

## ULTIMO
*City of Sydney*
Location: 2 kilometres south of Sydney

Pyrmont and Ultimo are near neighbours at the head of Darling Harbour (formerly called Cockle Bay). The owner of an estate here, who gave Ultimo its name, is also remembered by Harris Street, which runs from Broadway through Ultimo and Pyrmont to Johnston's Bay. Dr John Harris (1754–1838), of the New South Wales Corps, was a surgeon in the first days of the colony, who was to be court-martialled in 1803, charged with divulging confidential information about a trial. But Harris, clever and quick-witted, noticed a clerical error in his charge papers. The court official had mistakenly recorded the date of the offence as "ultimo" (meaning "of last month") instead of "instant" ("of this month"), so legally the trial had already taken place. The judge had no alternative but to withdraw the charge, and the jubilant Harris celebrated by calling his new estate Ultimo Farm, and the name eventually passed to the suburb.

Ultimo Farm was a grant of 34 acres that Harris received in 1803. Eventually the estate included earlier grants made in 1794 to John Malone and William Mitchell and three more grants made to Harris in 1806 (9¼ acres and 135 acres) and 1818 (12¾ acres); by then he held 233 acres, extending from Ultimo into nearby Pyrmont. Harris's famous brick and wattle-daub house, which was called Ultimo House, was on the site now occupied by the Sydney Technical College. It was completed in June 1804 and demolished in 1932. Descendants of Dr Harris still own a row of terrace cottages in Wattle Street.

Some of Sydney's notable buildings were constructed from sandstone quarried on Harris's land, and the main quarries were still visible in present-day Pyrmont as late as 1979.

The estate was subdivided in 1859 and became built up during the land boom of the 1880s. It became industrialised in the late nineteenth century and this development continued into the 1920s when Darling Harbour goods yards and a meat freezing works were built. The City Council's electrical powerhouse, which stood alongside, is at present being converted into the new home for the Museum of Applied Arts and Sciences, which for many years stood in Harris Street, Ultimo.

Today the area is still heavily industrialised. The technical college has been considerably extended, with new buildings constructed, or old buildings converted. Nearby, on Broadway, is the New South Wales Institute of Technology adding to the area's educational facilities. Many of the English terrace-style houses in the area have undergone renovation so that Ultimo's character is preserved, although it bears little resemblance to its farming days in the earliest years of the colony.

Ultimo Powerhouse under construction, 1899

## UNDERCLIFFE
*Municipality of Canterbury*
Location: 10 kilometres south-west of Sydney on the southern bank of the Cooks River

A heavy sandstone outcrop is evident in this neighbourhood, which was established under this natural "umbrella". The name of this suburb describes its unusual site. In the 1840s a grant, on which a house was constructed, was known as Undercliffe Estate, and the suburb took its name from this property.

The area, south of the Cooks River between the river and Wolli Creek, is rich in sandstone, and quarrying was an important local industry. Many homes in the district have stone foundations, and some were built throughout in sandstone.

A strong wooden bridge was built across the Cooks River in 1836 to carry the Illawarra Road across the river. It was known as Tompson's Bridge, after Mr P. A. Tompson's father, who purchased the Bexley Estate from James Chandler. This low-level bridge was, however, washed away several times by flood waters, and eventually Frederick Wright Unwin, a Sydney solicitor of some note, had a bridge built across the river to provide access to his property on the peninsula between Cooks River and Wolli Creek. His large home, which stood nearby, was known as Wanstead, after a village in Essex, England. Unwin had bought the property from Arthur Martin in 1840. Wanstead Avenue and Wanstead Avenue Reserve commemorate this estate, while Unwin's Bridge, Unwin Street and Unwin's Bridge Road

This almost eerie view of the hillside at Undercliffe, on the Cooks River, was probably taken around 1895

honour this pioneer attorney.

At the tip of the peninsula is Waterworth Park, set aside as a reserve in 1906 when the area was declared unhealthy and unsuitable for residences.

## VAUCLUSE
*Municipalities of Woollahra and Waverley*
Location: 8 kilometres north-east of Sydney on New South Head Road overlooking Port Jackson

This elegant suburb between Rose Bay and Watsons Bay takes its name from historic Vaucluse House, now open for public inspection, but once the home of William Charles Wentworth (1790–1872). Wandering along its peaceful paths set in the gracious grounds, one cannot imagine the colourful history surrounding the mansion.

The original Vaucluse House was built and named by a daring character, Sir Henry Brown Hayes, who was transported to New South Wales for kidnapping a wealthy Irish banker's daughter, whom he vowed he adored. A widower with two children, a large load of personal conceit and few funds, he felt sure his suit would not be rejected. When he reached the colony in 1802, he was allowed to buy land, which had been granted to Thomas Laycock, who received 80 acres in 1793, and Robert Cardell, who received 25 acres in 1795, around Parsley Bay. He built a home there, where he lived as a prisoner in great comfort. His influence must have been considerable, as he was given permission to import soil from Ireland, which was laid around the house to keep snakes away. Hayes returned to Ireland in 1812.

Captain John Piper acquired the house in 1822. It was then taken over by William Charles Wentworth, barrister and explorer, in 1827, and he lived there until 1853. Many structural changes and additions were made, and the building is now in 1830s Gothic style, with turrets and castellations. The fifteen rooms are decorated in a style appropriate to the period. The garden and parkland, which cover 27 acres, extend down to a harbourside beach. When responsible government was granted in 1856, the first cabinet meeting is said to have been held there. Wentworth began subdivision of the land in 1838, and by 1915 almost all of the estate had been sold off.

The suburb today is pleasant, with fine houses, beautiful gardens, and charming views toward the harbour. Nielsen Park, Parsley Bay and Vaucluse Bay are all within its boundaries.

One of the finest homes in the

suburb is Greycliffe House, which has been restored by the National Parks and Wildlife Service as their headquarters for the Sydney Harbour National Park. With an idyllic harbourside setting, it is Gothic in design, with typical nineteenth-century ornate gables. John Reeve, a Gippsland grazier, who married Fanny Catherine in February 1847, built this house. His father-in-law was William Charles Wentworth, who sold the land on which Greycliffe House was built to his future son-in-law, far too cheaply, according to a recorded comment by his sister-in-law, Sarah Wentworth. The young couple did not stay long in Greycliffe House. They leased it to a commercial leader of Sydney, Joseph Scarfe Willis, a founder of the Sydney Stock Exchange and one-time director of the Bank of New South Wales. Greycliffe Avenue honours this house, and a main road, Hopetoun Avenue, commemorates Australia's first governor-general, Lord Hopetoun (1901–03).

# VILLAWOOD

*Cities of Bankstown and Fairfield*
Location: 25 kilometres south-west of Sydney north of the Hume Highway, on the Regents Park–Cabramatta Line

Here is an interesting name which evolved from turning around the name of Woodville Road, which runs through the suburb south from Parramatta to join the Hume Highway at Lansdowne. The railway station was named Woodville Road when it opened in 1922, but because of confusion with another Woodville, near Newcastle, the name was transposed to create Villawood.

One of the earliest land-holders in the area, which is just east of Fairfield and south of Old Guildford, was John Thomas Campbell. His 1,000 acre grant of 1823, which was called Quid Pro Quo, was west of Woodville Road and covered part of the present suburb. The area was settled from the 1840s to the 1860s, when most of the properties were orchards in this isolated district overrun with wild dogs. Woodville Road, which passes through the suburbs of Villawood, Yennora, Guildford and Granville, was called Dog Trap Road by early settlers, because traps were set along the length of the road to control the packs of wild dogs that roamed the area. The Parramatta Hunt Club also hunted the dogs. William and John Lackey, who received land grants in this area in 1838, farmed their land, but in the 1840s William started a hotel on the Dog Trap Road.

During the Second World War the suburb supported a large munitions factory, and an extra railway station, Leightonfield, was added in 1942. A migrant hostel was established in the district after the war, and many immigrants have lived there on their way to establishing a new life in this country.

The first school was opened in October 1924, and was known as Mark Lodge; this name changed to Villawood in December 1924. The official post office opened for business on 1 January 1927, but its name was changed to Carramar, when that new suburb was developing in June 1927. Villawood's second post office opened in May 1950.

# WAHROONGA

*Municipality of Ku-ring-gai, Shire of Hornsby*
Location: 22 kilometres north-west of Sydney on the Pacific Highway and the North Shore Line

The meaning of this Aboriginal name is "our home" — highly appropriate for this suburb south-east of Hornsby, where many fine houses have been built in natural bushland settings.

George Caley (1770–1829), a botanist who had been sent to the colony in 1795 by Sir Joseph Banks to collect flora specimens for Kew Gardens, was one of the first to explore this bushland area. In 1805 he walked along a cattle path on the ridge towards Fox Valley, near the 640 acres that were later granted to Thomas Hyndes by Governor Darling (1825–31). The north-western part of the grant, later known as Pearce's Corner (see Waitara), extended past the present Sydney Adventist Hospital. On Hyndes's death the grant was bought by John Brown, and it became known as Brown's Paddock. When John Brown died in 1881, the grant was resurveyed, and the larger portion became Fox Ground Estate, which was purchased by a Francis Gerard.

The first church built in Wahroonga was the Anglican church of St Paul's at Pearces Corner, where Pennant Hills Road joins the Pacific Highway. Land was donated by two enthusiastic men, Herbert Cunningham Fowler and the Reverend Robert Taylor, and the parishioners cut the timber to build the small church, which was completed in 1861. The building was also used as a schoolhouse. Twenty years later the first church was replaced by a new building of locally quarried

The old Sanitarium Hospital, c. 1926. The hospital was badly damaged by fire the following year

stone. In 1881 the village around St Paul's became known as Normanhurst, although the church was still considered to be part of Wahroonga. In about 1894, another Anglican church, St Andrew's, was built in the newly recognised area of Wahroonga.

When the railway line came through the North Shore from Hornsby to St Leonards, a station in this area opened, on 1 January 1890, and was named Pearce's Corner. The construction name had been Noonan's Platform, because the property belonging to Patrick Noonan came within the new railway's boundary. The name was changed to Wahroonga on 30 August 1890.

The post office opened on 15 October 1896, and the first public school began instruction in January 1944. The public school in Burns Road has for years been called the

Bush School or the school in the trees, which describes its delightful setting most accurately. The infants school operated alone from 1944 to 1950, and in 1951 it became a public school with a primary department. The Wahroonga School for the Blind operated in the area from 1947 to 1962.

Two important institutions have become familiar names in this suburb. One is the Sydney Adventist Hospital (formerly known as the Sanitarium) and the other is Abbotsleigh, a large school for girls. Each tells a story of the inspiration and endurance of the pioneering spirit.

The Seventh-day Adventist Church had been established in Australia in 1885 when American evangelists arrived in the colony. In 1891 Ellen Gould White, a writer and spiritual leader, had offered to come "down under" to guide and support the early founders, who had set up a church and health

home at Ashfield. In 1897 they found larger premises in Summer Hill and commenced a nurse-training program. In 1899, when only three houses stood in Fox Valley Road, Wahroonga, the Adventists purchased land there by pledging everything they could afford. Paid and voluntary workers put willing hands to the task of erecting a large wooden building, completed in 1903. From that date a constant program of enlargement gave the opportunity to serve hundreds of people, and nurse them back to health by using methods unique to "the San", as it soon became known. The original hospital building was partially destroyed by fire and by 1933 had been extensively rebuilt and refurbished. The building was finally demolished in 1973 upon completion of today's splendid new complex.

The history of Abbotsleigh School, equally interesting, is a story of the dedication of three

261

women to the cause of education. Its founder was Miss Marian Clarke, who came to Sydney in 1884 with her sister Emily to help an elder sister, Ellen, with Normanhurst, a school she had founded at Ashfield. The three sisters had fine intellectual and organising abilities in an age when women were disregarded academically, and to leave Victorian England and face the unknown rigours of a strange country says much for their courage. In 1885 they moved to North Sydney (the area then being known as St Leonards), and opened a school. In 1888 the school moved to Parramatta, which was fast becoming busy and an elegant city, where an increasing population sought education. By 1840, there were thirteen private schools in Parramatta, so competition for prospective students was keen. Marian Clarke named her school after a friend of long standing — Miss Abbot of Abbots Leigh in England. She also chose the name because it placed her school first on an alphabetical list of places of instruction. In 1898 Abbotsleigh moved to Wahroonga, and to greater strength. The accent was on three-way development — intellectual, spiritual and physical. Many fine women were to guide the school in this direction — another early name that springs to mind is that of Miss Margaret Murray, who bought the school in 1913. Her valuable contribution as headmistress in those progressive days ended when ill-health forced her to sell the school in 1924 to the Church of England, under which the school has further developed.

# WAITARA
*Shire of Hornsby*
Location: 23 kilometres north-west of Sydney on the Pacific Highway and the North Shore Line

One of the last stations to open on the North Shore railway line, Waitara is a Maori word meaning "hail, pure water", or "hail, wide steps"; it is also the name of a small port in Taranaki province, New Zealand. The name was first used on a subdivision in Hurstville, when Miles McCrae sold his land there to a development company, whose manager gave it the name Waitara. McCrae later bought land near Hornsby, and, after the station was opened in 1895, he suggested the name Waitara, which was formally adopted.

Although close to Wahroonga, this suburb is entirely different. Whereas Wahroonga retains the natural bushland setting in its residential areas and is undisturbed by the commercial world, Waitara is the site of business developments, including several motels, car sales yards and some light industry. This area was noted in early times as an orchardist's and nurseryman's paradise, and these activities extended right into Hornsby. Despite development, Waitara still has a fresh atmosphere in its quieter side streets. Waitara Creek flows through this suburb. A fresh-water stream rising near Waitara railway station, it flows into Berowra Creek.

The name Pearce crops up frequently in the history of the upper North Shore, and Pearces Corner, where three suburbs meet — Normanhurst, Waitara and Wahroonga — honours an early settler whose name was actually spelled Pierce.

Aaron Pierce was an illiterate convict who arrived in the colony with his future wife on 1 August 1811. On receiving a conditional pardon, he worked as a timber-cutter along the ridge from Kissing Point to the present Pacific Highway (formerly Lane Cove Road). Three tracks converged at this point, and Pierce built a hut to house his family and set out an orchard. He was said to reside there by 1831, and the corner was then known as Pierce's Corner. A village developed on the opposite corner (see Normanhurst) around St Paul's Church (see Wahroonga). It became known as Pearce's Corner Township, the spelling probably changing in error. Descendants of this family are said to have lived at the corner until nearly 1900, when Miles McCrae bought land in the area.

The public school opened in 1927 and the post office in 1913. Barker College, a Church of England school for boys that is now co-educational in its final years, is on the Pacific Highway between Waitara and Hornsby.

# WAKELEY
*City of Fairfield*
Location: 35 kilometres west of Sydney west of Fairfield

This relatively new suburb in the Fairfield district is located near Canley Heights. Developed in 1980, its name honours Daniel Wakeley, a free settler who owned land suitable for poultry farming and crop raising. The headquarters of Fairfield Council are in this suburb.

# WARRAWEE

*Municipality of Ku-ring-gai*
Location: 21 kilometres
north-west of Sydney on the
Pacific Highway, and the North
Shore Line

Situated between Turramurra and
Wahroonga, this was the last
station to be opened (in 1900) on
the North Shore line before it was
extended to North Sydney.
Warrawee is an Aboriginal word
meaning "stop here", and it is said
this part of the North Shore was a
favourite resting place for the
Aborigines.

In 1805 George Caley
(1770–1829), the young botanist
sent to the colony by Sir Joseph
Banks to seek out Australian flora
for Kew Gardens, in England,
walked through the area of today's
Warrawee in his tramp across the
ridges and through the Fox Valley.

An early settler in the area was
George Wood, who was granted
60 acres in the area between the
present Pacific Highway, Finlay
Road, Monteith Street and Roland
Avenue in 1831. In 1882 the
property was formally acquired by
Owen McMahon, who had
occupied it for fifty years, as no
heirs for Wood had been found.
McMahon sold it to Reginald
Finlay, who built Blytheswood
there. After the property changed
hands again, the land was
gradually sold. Warrawee Public
School stands on part of the
property.

Sir Charles Mackellar lived in
Warrawee and his daughter poet
Dorothea Mackellar (1885–1965)
spent her early life there, a
contemporary and friend of Miles
Franklin, the writer of *My Brilliant
Career*. In those days — even as
late as 1923 — the district and its
surroundings were more rural than
suburban, and they appealed to a
number of successful businessmen
who decided to buy the Mackellar
home, Earlstone, and open a boys
school. This became Knox
Grammar School, on the Pacific
Highway, near Warrawee station.
The Presbyterian General
Assembly had planned such a
school since 1917. Neil Harcourt
MacNeil, son of a Presbyterian
clergyman and a man of wide
experience as a scholar and a
soldier, was the school's first
headmaster.

Today Warrawee is a wholly
residential suburb, and like its
neighbours has many attractive
houses, some in the Federation
style, set among tall trees and
large gardens.

# WARRIEWOOD

*Shire of Warringah*
Location: 26 kilometres north of
Sydney on Pittwater Road facing
the Pacific Ocean

The name of this suburb north of
Narrabeen came from a large
subdivision in 1906, when Henry
F. Halloran subdivided the
Warriewood Estate, purchased
from the McPherson family. The
romantic history of the area begins
as far back as the 1880s, when a
district character, Leon Houreux,
built the Rock Lily Hotel (see
Mona Vale). Before that he had
lived in a hut in 1886 in the
Warriewood scrub and worked as a
timber-cutter. At that time the area
was heavily forested, and timber
getting and sawing were the most
profitable industries. Leon
Houreux also conducted an illicit
still for brewing liquor and had
planted wine grapes in the area.

Like some of the other northern
suburbs, Warriewood at the end of
last century and early this century
was the destination of day-trippers
and picnickers. Today it is a
pleasant residential suburb behind
Warriewood Beach, which is just
north of Turimetta Head.

# WARWICK FARM

*City of Liverpool*
Location: 30 kilometres
south-west of Sydney on the
Hume Highway and the Main
Southern Line

This suburb just north of
Liverpool between the Georges
River and Cabramatta Creek was
first occupied by Irish political
prisoners transported after the Irish
Rebellion of 1798, who were
settled along the banks of
Cabramatta Creek. In 1809, 40 acre
grants were made in the same area
to a number of the transportees,
including Michael Dwyer, a
Wicklow chief constable. Many of
the convicts sent to New South
Wales, including these political
prisoners, were professional men,
and their abilities were recognised
and sometimes used after they had
served a small part of their
sentences. This was the case with
Michael Dwyer, who was
eventually appointed chief
constable at Liverpool.

The area was named by John
Hawley Stroud, the superintendent
of the Liverpool Orphans School.
He received a grant in 1804 that
covered the site of the present
Warwick Farm racecourse. Stroud
named his farm after the town of
Warwick in England.

In the 1880s a racing stable was
established here by William
Alexander Long, whose Chipping
Norton property extended into this
area (see Chipping Norton). In the
late 1880s Long's property was
sold to W. A. Forrester, who was
involved with the Warwick Farm

The official stand and scratching tower at Warwick Farm Race Course, early 1900s. The first race broadcast in Australia took place at Warwick Farm in August 1933

racing club. The first race meeting in the area was held in 1889, by the Warwick Farm Syndicate Race Club and organised by Forrester. In 1923 the Australian Jockey Club bought the racecourse area (the site of the original Stroud grant), remodelled it, and in 1925 conducted its first meeting. Eventually the course had its own railway station, and on race days special trains stopped at a platform inside the course. Later a road entrance was made on the Hume Highway via a bridge over the Georges River.

During the Second World War the British naval shore base HMS *Golden Hind* was situated in this area. After the end of the war, when housing was in short supply, the war-time buildings were used for an emergency settlement named Hargrave Park, which commemorated the aeronautics pioneer, Lawrence Hargrave

(1850–1915). Since then houses and shopping facilities have taken the place of the postwar housing, and a modern suburb has grown up here. Streets have been named after some of the heroes of the skies, including Hargrave and Bert Hinkler (1892–1933), a pioneer aviator who flew a single-seater plane from England to Australia. McGirr Parade honours a former premier of New South Wales, of the late 1940s and early 1950s and Gallop Street is named after a former chairman of the Housing Commission, which planned and carried out the rebuilding of the emergency settlement.

## WATERLOO
*City of Sydney*
Location: 4 kilometres south of Sydney

By the 1820s this inner-city suburb was already supporting a number of industrial operations, including

the Fisher and Duncan paper mill and the Waterloo Flour Mills owned by William Hutchinson, Daniel Cooper and others. The suburb took its name from the mill, which had been named after the Battle of Waterloo in 1815, when the English and Allied Forces under the Duke of Wellington defeated the French forces led by Napoleon. The area around the mill remained crown land until 1823, when 1,400 acres were granted to William Hutchinson, superintendent of convicts and public works, as Waterloo Farm. He held the land for two years before selling it for £2,700, which was paid in Spanish dollars by Daniel Cooper (1785–1853) and Solomon Levey (1794–1833). When Daniel Cooper died the Waterloo Estate, which included Levey's share as Cooper had bought him out, passed to his son, also named Daniel, who was the first speaker of the New South Wales Legislative Assembly, and later became Sir Daniel Cooper (1821–1902). On his death in 1902 the great estate passed to his son William. Because there were no land-size regulations during Sir Daniel's lifetime the Waterloo Estate was leased out in large blocks, which the lessees in turn subdivided into many small allotments for lease.

In the 1850s Waterloo became an industrialised suburb with factories such as Buckland and Waterloo Mills, Alderson's woolwash, Forsythe's ropeworks and a number of local dairies located there even though there were no made roads in Waterloo at this time. The suburb was bounded to the east by sandhills and scrub, which eventually became Moore Park, and was thought to be a long journey from Sydney.

Just before the First World War the Waterloo Estate was subdivided. By the 1920s a frequent tram service was operating from Circular Quay via Elizabeth Street and Redfern. It took twenty-six minutes to travel the distance of 2 to 3 miles and the fare was threepence. Factories had been modernised and fine cottages were erected alongside to house the works managers.

In 1861 a school was being held in St Silas Church of England, on Botany Road. By about 1906 St Silas had one of the largest young people's church groups in the suburbs of Sydney. The Reverend Fred Dillon was then the rector, an eager young man with a wife and baby son, Cecil, who grew up to follow in his father's footsteps and become a clergyman.

Today Waterloo is a densely built-up area, characterised by factories and some small dwellings with pocket-sized gardens. Waterloo Park and Oval stand in Elizabeth Street and Waterloo Public School is in Botany Road, one of the area's major thoroughfares.

## WATSONS BAY
*Municipality of Woollahra*
Location: 11 kilometres north-east of Sydney at the northernmost end of Old South Head Road

This historic suburb adjoining the military reserve on the tip of South Head has some of the most beautiful harbour views in Sydney. It bears the name of Robert Watson (1756–1819), formerly of HMS *Sirius*, who was appointed harbour pilot and harbourmaster of the port of Sydney in 1811 and first superintendent of the Macquarie Lighthouse on South Head in 1816.

The name of the suburb was in use by 1811. The area was settled early in the colony's history, with the first land grant being made in 1793, when Edward Laing received 20 acres in the Camp Cove area. In 1801 Robert Watson was given land, on which he built a stone house, although the land was not formally granted. For many years Watsons Bay had only an isolated village of fishermen and harbour pilots, and it was not until the 1860s that the suburb began to develop slowly, although land values did not begin to rise until after about 1900.

One of the most dramatic events in the history of this suburb occurred on 20 August 1857, when the sailing ship *Dunbar*, with 121 people aboard, was wrecked against the cliffs below The Gap. The people of Sydney only discovered the tragedy the next day, when debris was washed up onto harbour beaches. There was only one survivor and a memorial to the passengers and crew who died was set up in the cemetery of St Stephen's, Camperdown, where some were also buried. In fog, the captain of the *Dunbar* had mistaken the bay of The Gap for the harbour entrance, so as a result of the

disaster Hornby Light, on the tip of South Head, was built.

Perhaps the suburb's greatest importance throughout its history has been as the site of South Head Signal Station and Macquarie Light. The signal station, established in 1790, is one of Australia's oldest links with the past. Governor Phillip's orders had been to establish a settlement in Botany Bay, which on arrival he found unsuitable. Any ships sailing to the new colony from England would also be ordered to go to Botany Bay as there was no means of quick contact to indicate that anchorage had been made in Port Jackson. Ships coming from England with food supplies could have sailed away, not knowing the settlement was at Sydney, so Phillip had a flagstaff and a lookout erected on South Head, with some huts to shelter the men staffing the lookout, to indicate the location of the new settlement. Captain John Hunter and Surgeons White and Worgan (who brought the first piano to Australia) and a group of seamen erected the station. Lieutenant Daniel Southwell was then put in charge, and, with a gunner as an assistant, he remained at the South Head lookout from May 1790 until March 1791. During this time he planted a garden and wrote home to England describing it in what is probably the earliest recorded letter written from South Head.

At this time food was in seriously short supply in Sydney, as early food-raising efforts were often unsuccessful and the colony was still dependent on store ships from England. You can imagine how anxiously people watched for the raising of the South Head flag, indicating a ship was approaching. The first signal was made on 5 April 1790, but joy turned to sorrow when the arrival turned out to be HMS *Supply* reporting the loss of HMS *Sirius* at Norfolk Island.

In 1790 a column painted white, visible for many miles out to sea, was erected near the signal station, and in 1794 an iron basket on a tripod was set up, in which a fire was lit if a ship signalled at night. In 1818, the Macquarie Light, designed by the architect Francis Greenway (1777–1837), was completed. The column was demolished, the flagstaff moved, and the vigilant eye of the Macquarie Light began its long life on the eastern side of the headland.

In 1873 it was decided that the power of the light should be increased. James Barnet (1827–1904), designer of the present GPO in Martin Place, gave his opinion that "very considerable alterations" to Greenway's original design were needed, indeed some criticism was levelled at Greenway. Barnet estimated that it would cost £15,000 to bring the light up to date, and he also preferred to use electric light, which caused some opposition. The new lighthouse, completed in 1883, was completely electrified and gave a superior light under cloudy, stormy conditions.

Fishing boats landed their catch at Watsons Bay until about the 1950s and one of Sydney's best-known seafood restaurateurs, Peter Doyle, has two restaurants there. Waterfront land on South Head is now part of Sydney Harbour National Park.

# WAVERLEY

*Municipality of Waverley*
Location: 7 kilometres east of Sydney on Bronte Road

Waverley, south of Bondi, took its name from the title of a book written by the famous Scottish author and poet, Sir Walter Scott. Its connection with the suburb of Waverley comes through Barnett Levey (or Levy, 1798–1837), who came to Sydney in the 1820s to visit his brother. When he saw how prosperous the city of Sydney was becoming, he decided to settle here and set up a business. In 1831 he was granted 60 acres in the area bounded by the present Old South Head Road, Birrell Street, Paul Street and Hollywood Avenue. He must have occupied the land before the official grant because he had built himself a substantial two-storey home on Old South Head Road in 1827, naming it Waverley House after the title of the book by his favourite author, Sir Walter Scott. As time passed, the house became a distinctive landmark and gave its name to the surrounding district, which was simply called Waverley. In 1837 the house was taken over for a Catholic school or orphanage, but it was demolished early in this century.

Levey became a general merchant in George Street in the city, but he wanted to establish a permanent theatre in Sydney. He established a company in 1827 and six months later had built a temporary theatre at the back of his premises and later converted the front of the building to the Royal Hotel. After some success his licence for balls and concerts was revoked because the government considered them unsuitable for the city's prison population. In 1832 he received the first theatre licence in the colony, and in 1833 the Theatre Royal was built behind the hotel. But Levey's ambitious schemes did not pay. His projects finally consumed nearly all his money, and when he died in 1837 he left his wife and four young children in poverty. Nonetheless he had begun professional theatre in Australia, and his associates mourned him as "the Father of Waverley".

Waverley municipality was proclaimed in June 1859. By the 1880s trams were running to the beaches in the Eastern Suburbs and Waverley became a popular picnic spot. Waverley Park had a splendid oval, used by the established Waverley District Cricket Club.

Waverley Cemetery was established in 1877 on the site of the old tram terminus. It stands on a beautiful site near the ocean and is the resting place of many historically notable people, among them Walter Hall (1831–1901) and Eliza Hall (1847–1916), who donated an institute of medical research to the University of Sydney and a pair of polished granite water troughs near the entrance to the university as a memorial to Amelia Hall (1809–91). Walter Hall had worked on the goldfields in Victoria, driven a coach for Cobb & Co., and become part-owner of a mine at Mount Morgan in Queensland. Inside the cemetery's main gates is the grave of Reuben Uther, one time owner of the Imperial Arcade; to the east is the grave of Henry Lawson, beloved Australian writer and poet. The poet Roderick Quinn, his headstone inscribed with one of his own verses, lies in this graveyard, as does W. H. Paling, founder of Paling's music shops. Harry Rickards and his family, well-known in theatrical circles, Lieutenant-Colonel George

Johnston of Annandale, and Henry Kendall, the Australian poet who wrote "Bell Birds", all rest eternally in this historic place.

The 1866 New South Wales Gazetteer described Waverley as having Clough's Windmill, Allan's Soap Works, Dickson's Soap and Candle Works and Scott's Blacking and Fireworks Factory. There were also four quarries producing excellent freestone. Today, however, it is an attractive residential suburb, just west of Tamarama Beach.

# WAVERTON
*Municipality of North Sydney*
Location: 4 kilometres north of Sydney between the Pacific Highway and Balls Head Bay, on the North Shore Line

In 1893 the North Shore railway line was extended south from St Leonards to Milsons Point. One of the new stations on this line was known as Bay Road, taking its name from the thoroughfare that crosses the line near the station, and then runs from the Pacific Highway to Balls Head. The station, between North Sydney and Wollstonecraft, was known as Bay Road for nearly forty years before the local progress association recommended a change. The new name, chosen in 1929, was taken from the Waverton Estate of an early resident, Robert Old. The land and house had been the property of William Carr, who had named it after an English village connected with his family. The Waverton Estate was one of the oldest properties in the vicinity of the station. Later the house was demolished and modern housing has been built in its place.

This attractive residential suburb looks towards Berry Bay to the

North Shore Gas Company's works at Oyster Cove, Waverton, under construction, 1914. The white building in the background was retained from Robey's Sugar Works which was built on the site in 1857

south-east, and Balls Head Bay to the south-west where the naval shore base of HMAS *Waterhen* is situated on the waterfront.

At the southernmost point of the suburb is the peninsula between Balls Head Bay and Berry Bay known as Balls Head. The peninsula, road and the reserve there were named in honour of Henry Lidgbird Ball (d. 1818), lieutenant-commander of the HMS *Supply*, one of the ships of the First Fleet. Ball named Lord Howe Island, which he explored in 1788, in honour of Richard, Earl Howe, the British admiral who was First Lord of the Admiralty in 1783. Berry Bay was named in honour of merchant Alexander Berry (see Crows Nest, and Wollstonecraft).

# WENTWORTHVILLE

*City of Parramatta, Municipality of Holroyd*
Location: 27 kilometres west of Sydney on the Great Western Highway and the Main Western Line

This suburb west of Parramatta is not named after Australia's first home-grown patriot, William Charles Wentworth (1790–1872), but instead honours his father, D'Arcy Wentworth (1762?–1827), a colonial surgeon. In 1810 D'Arcy Wentworth, who had become a public figure of some importance in Parramatta, received a land grant, to which he added by purchase until he held 2,750 acres. He called the estate Fitzwilliam Place and the house, Wentworth Wood House, after an English property of that name owned by Thomas Wentworth, Earl of Strafford, who was executed on Tower Hill in 1641.

In the 1840s a highly respected citizen, William Fullagar, established the Star Inn near Ettalong and Western Road. This inn was the social centre of the day. Fullagar also opened, in 1845, what were for many years the principal cattle saleyards in the colony.

When the bushland was cleared and land sold, orchards, poultry farms and market gardens came to the area, becoming highly productive. The suburb's railway platform opened as T. R. Smith's Platform in 1883, but the name was changed to Wentworthville on 1 August 1885, and the suburb has borne that name ever since. The line cut through the Wentworth Estate, and in the 1880s subdivision of the land began; the Wentworth estate finally amounted to 600 lots. It was not until after the First World War, however,

that closer settlement development became a reality at Wentworthville. Darcy Road and Wentworth Avenue commemorate the suburb's early settler.

In October 1890, the first official post office opened for business, and three months later, in January 1891, the first public school began enrolling pupils.

Today Wentworthville is densely populated but well catered for by churches, schools, sporting facilities and clubs, and still with the bracing air that was offered as an attraction for buying land and building in the 1920s. Wentworthville South lies south of the Great Western Highway.

# WERRINGTON

*City of Penrith*
Location: 47 kilometres west of Sydney north of the Great Western Highway, on the Main Western Line

This suburb between St Marys and Kingswood, is a near neighbour of the satellite city of Penrith and benefits from the close proximity of its many modern facilities, although Werrington itself is developing rapidly.

The suburb is named after a house and property, Werrington House, the homestead built on a grant of land made in 1806 to Mary Putland, Governor Bligh's widowed daughter. After her marriage to Sir Maurice O'Connell, Mary acquired a further 1,055 acres nearby in 1810. Sir Henry Parkes rented Werrington House from 1860 to 1871, and during that time the railway platform was known as Parkes Platform, reverting to Werrington when he left. Parkes Avenue commemorates this great man.

Mary Putland's home still stands in its tree-studded parkland, and is listed on the National Trust register. Today the property is owned by the Department of Youth and Community Services, and cottages have been built in the grounds to house intellectually handicapped male wards of the

Werrington Park homestead was once the home of Sir Maurice O'Connell and his wife Mary, daughter of Governor Bligh. Since 1954 it has been a New South Wales government school for mentally handicapped boys and is now the proposed site for the new university of the west, Chifley University

state between the ages of 12 and 31 years. A sheltered workshop is included in the complex, and some of the boys work there, while others go out to another sheltered workshop each day.

Another Mary also owned land in Werrington. The youngest daughter of Governor King and his wife, Anna Josepha, Mary King was born on 1 February 1805, and at that time 790 acres in Werrington, part of land owned by her mother, were transferred to the baby's name. In 1806 Governor King's son Phillip Parker King and his three sisters also received transfers of land in the same area. The 1806 grant to Mary Putland was next to baby Mary King's. During one of his journeys in those areas Governor Lachlan Macquarie "called on Mrs King's farm for refreshment, on the right bank of South Creek", and it is most likely that this property belonged to a member of this family.

When she was 21 (in 1826), Mary King married Robert Lethbridge, and her brother Phillip King, who was educated in England and later served in the Royal Navy with distinction, further united the two families by marrying Robert's sister Harriet Lethbridge. The Lethbridge and King names appear on old maps of the South Creek, St Marys and Dunheved areas.

Werrington County is a residential estate north of Werrington Creek, extending towards an area of land owned by the Commonwealth. It was opened up as a housing area towards the end of 1970.

Werrington Downs is north-east of Cambridge Park and separated from Werrington County by a north to south line passing through the crossing of Dunheved Road with Francis Street. Named in 1976, it is a residential area.

# WESTLEIGH
*Shire of Hornsby*
Location: 27 kilometres north-west of Sydney just south-west of Hornsby

This pleasant residential suburb was subdivided and developed in the 1960s. Its location west of Thornleigh is the reason for the choice of the suburb's name.

The area was originally heavily timbered, but the clearing for home-sites has been carried out carefully to preserve bushland settings for the modern houses. Many of the streets also bear the names of Australian trees, such as Stringybark Close, Spotted Gum Road, Eucalyptus Drive, Peppermint Gum Place and Ironbark Close.

Max Ruddock, a well-remembered personality in the Hornsby shire, who died in 1976, is honoured by a park named after him in this area. A one-time member of the New South Wales parliament, he took an official interest in the Elouera Bushland Reserve and Ruddock Park acknowledges his efforts to preserve areas of natural bushland.

# WESTMEAD
*City of Parramatta*
Location: 26 kilometres west of Sydney north of the Great Western Highway, on the Main Western Line

The name of this suburb — located between Parramatta and Blacktown — combines the old English word "mead", meaning "meadow", and "west" indicating its location just west of Parramatta. The present suburb of Westmead was originally the western part of the former domain of Government House at Parramatta. The remains of the domain are now Parramatta Park.

The name Westmead was not used until 1859 when the first part of the domain was subdivided. (Subdivision of the domain was completed in 1889.) Following this subdivision, orchards were established by many new settlers, including some whose names were well-known in the Parramatta, area — George Oakes, Nat Payten and William Fullager among them.

Although the railway had gone through Westmead in 1861, the suburb did not have a railway station. Early in 1883 residents successfully petitioned the Railways Department for a station and by April of that year Westmead became the newest station on the Western line from Sydney.

The development of this suburb was slow. In 1883 the orchards began to disappear, and the land was sold to home-builders. The township with its shopping facilities was built on the land that had been George Oakes's orchard, subdivision of which began in 1883. Eventually the residential area became firmly established.

A landmark of modern-day Westmead is Westmead Hospital, now one of the Parramatta Hospitals group. Begun in 1974, it is the most up-to-date specialised general hospital in New South Wales. It has 925 beds and teaching departments providing medical, dental, paramedical and nursing courses. At present the hospital caters for approximately 250 patients a day, as well as 2,000 outpatients a week. The hospital serves the large and rapidly increasing population of Sydney's western suburbs.

# WEST PENNANT HILLS

*Shire of Baulkham Hills*
Location: 25 kilometres
north-west of Sydney west of the
junction of Castle Hill Road and
Pennant Hills Road

Situated west of Beecroft and
south-west of Pennant Hills station
on the northern railway line, West
Pennant Hills has become a suburb
in its own right. The area was
originally covered with thick
forest, and its houses today are still
set in natural bushland in an area
that retains a rural atmosphere.

West Pennant Hills includes
Thompson's Corner, named after
Andrew Thompson (1773–1810),
a convict (see Scotland Island),
who received a grant of 100 acres
in 1796 opposite the signal station
in Pennant Hills. Workmen on the
railway from Strathfield to
Hornsby established a camp and
stores depot there in about 1890.

During Lachlan Macquarie's
governorship (1810–21), a timber-
sawing establishment stood near
today's Thompson's Corner. In
those early days the pit-sawyers
roamed the countryside, and the
saw pits were set up at various
places close to forest areas. One of
the great stands of cedar grew in
the Pennant Hills area, and this
beautiful, glowing wood was
mostly cut by the pit-saw, a large
rip saw, about 2 metres long, with
a handle at either end. Tree trunks
were hauled or rolled into position
onto a platform built over a large
square-cut hole in the ground, and
an old colonial verse describes the
action that followed: "Top sawyer
above on a log, below / His mate
in the pit in the sawdust flow".

# WHALAN

*City of Blacktown*
Location: 44 kilometres west of
Sydney just north-west of Mount
Druitt

Whalan is a new suburb with an
old name. Its name commemorates
James Whalan, who received a 300
acre grant in the area in 1831.

The Whalan family were early
pioneers, James's father, Sergeant
Charles Whalan, having been
Governor Macquarie's confidential
orderly sergeant and in charge of
the Light Horse Guard. James
Whalan later explored areas around
the Jenolan Caves in the Blue
Mountains and discovered the
splendid natural rock formation
known as the Grand Arch. The
suburb of Whalan is sited on the
greater part of his 1831 grant.

Whalan, just north-west of
Mount Druitt railway station, is
one of the newer parts of the
Mount Druitt housing
development of the 1960s and
1970s. In 1981 Whalan's population
numbered 7,483.

# WHALE BEACH

*Shire of Warringah*
Location: 38 kilometres north of
Sydney on the Barrenjoey
Peninsula

This is a small neighbourhood just
south of Palm Beach, with the
beach itself on the east and Careel
Bay on the west facing Pittwater.
There are two schools of thought
about the naming of this area. One
claims it was so named because a
whale was washed ashore at the
turn of the century, creating great
excitement. The second theory
claims that the northern headland,
Little Head, has a whale-like shape
which gave the suburb its name.

The area of the present suburb
formed part of the land grant of
1833 to Father John Joseph Therry
(see Avalon). There was, however,
no occupation in the area until the
Palm Beach Land Company,
which owned all the land from
Avalon to Palm Beach, erected a
house there in 1927 for their road-
builder, Jack Webster. Subdivision,
however, had been carried out in
1919, and in the 1920s lots
gradually became popular as sites
for holiday homes. Now, with
improved transport services, many
residents live permanently in the
area, able to enjoy the magnificent
views along the northern coastline.

# WHEELER HEIGHTS

*Shire of Warringah*
Location: 22 kilometres north of
Sydney inland of Collaroy

This suburb, developed in the mid
1960s and situated west of
Collaroy Plateau, was named after
early pioneers in the area. The
Wheeler family purchased land in
1836 on the banks of Narrabeen
Lagoon in the vicinity of South
Creek. They built a house of
rough-hewn timber, which was
the home of James Wheeler from
1836 until his death in 1890. He
also owned 230 acres in different
parts of the south side of the
lagoon and made another purchase
in 1842, buying 86 acres, known
as Fox's Flat, on the northern side
facing Pittwater Road. When
James Wheeler died, he was buried
near his homestead, as was the
custom of those times. His death is
recorded in the burial register of St
Matthew's, Manly. Wheeler
Creek, named in 1885, is a
tributary of South Creek and it
also honours this pioneer and his
family.

A farm recorded by Surveyor William Govett (1807–48) as belonging to the Jenkins family was already in the area when the Wheelers arrived. Wheeler also established a farm and sent produce by boat to Sydney from North Harbour, Manly.

The War Veterans Home, reached by Veterans Parade, is adjacent to this small locality and is bounded on the north by parks alongside Narrabeen Lagoon.

# WILEY PARK

*Municipality of Canterbury*
Location: 17 kilometres south-west of Sydney east of Bankstown, on the Bankstown Line

This suburb between Punchbowl and Lakemba was named after a reserve given by Mr J. V. Wiley, who, in 1906, bequeathed 20 acres of his land for a park and recreation ground for local residents, laid out according to his plans. This caused some dissension in the local council, and a public meeting was arranged to discuss the idea. After much debate it was decided to accept Mr Wiley's bequest, and the park was created on the gift of land. The park, bounded by King Georges and Canterbury Roads, and by Edge and Clio Streets, remains as a memorial to this rather strong-willed personality, whose name gave the area a new identity.

Wiley Park Public School is in King Georges Road in neighbouring Lakemba, and Wiley Park Girls High School stands in The Boulevarde in Punchbowl.

# WILLMOT

*City of Blacktown*
Location: 49 kilometres north-west of Sydney north of St Marys

In 1971, as part of the Mount Druitt housing development, the new suburb of Willmot was established. The area was to be called St John, but because a St John's Park already existed in the western suburbs, Blacktown Council sought a different name, favouring one with local historical significance. The answer was Willmot, which honours Thomas Willmot, first shire president of Blacktown from 1906 to 1910 and again from 1911 to 1914. Thomas Willmot, who died in 1938, was well known for his interest and endeavours on behalf of Blacktown and its neighbours, so it is appropriate that a new neighbourhood should have been named in his honour.

Willmot is separated from its neighbour, Shalvey, by a large reserve. Its streets, like those of other new housing developments in the area, curve around the contours of the land. They have been named to honour mariners, map-makers and ships, and they include Hartog Avenue, Bass Place, Baudin Place, Mercator Crescent, Resolution Avenue and Reliance Crescent.

# WILLOUGHBY

*Municipality of Willoughby*
Location: 8 kilometres north of Sydney east of Chatswood

There is much conjecture as to how this suburb got its name. Some historians claim it was named after a parish of that title; others maintain that Surveyor-General Sir Thomas Mitchell decided to commemorate Sir James Willoughby Gordon, under whom he had served during the Peninsular War and who was the quartermaster-general in England when the First Fleet sailed for Botany Bay.

The municipality of Willoughby was incorporated in 1865, when the area was still rural. An early concern of the council's was the construction of roads and bridges. By the 1890s the population of the area had increased rapidly because of the improvement in public transport, particularly when the North Shore railway line opened in 1890. The suburb was soon outstripped by Chatswood, however, as it was nearer the line and other new facilities.

The first mayor of Willoughby was James Bligh, who is commemorated by Bligh Street, Northbridge. Other people who have contributed to the development of Willoughby are remembered in local park names: Beauchamp Park, after Earl Beauchamp, a governor of New South Wales (1899–1901), and Bales Park for Alderman Bales, several times mayor of Willoughby. A memorial to the suburb's Victoria Cross winner, Lieutenant Albert Chowne, is in Willoughby Park.

The Forsyth family is well remembered in Willoughby. James Forsyth was mayor in 1875 and is buried in the Methodist churchyard on the corner of the Pacific Highway and Mowbray Road. Thomas Todd Forsyth was an alderman for twenty-seven years and mayor in 1882–87 and 1888; Robert Todd Forsyth (1877–1939), the best-known of this remarkable family, served on Willoughby Council for twenty-eight years, a number of times as mayor, in 1911, 1915–18,

## WINSTON HILLS
*Shire of Baulkham Hills*
Location: 28 kilometres
north-west of Sydney on Windsor
Road

This suburb bordered to the south
and east by Toongabbie and
Quarry Creeks is north-west of
Parramatta. It was named after
Britain's wartime prime minister,
Winston Churchill (1874–1965). In
1972 the suburb, developed in the
late 1960s, was transferred from
Blacktown shire to Parramatta city
council.

A new residential area, it has a
modern shopping centre. Parks
were not overlooked when this
suburb was being planned, and
areas of cool greenness continue to
provide pleasure spots for
residents. Schoolchildren are also
well catered for, with several
schools located in the suburb.

Residential estates and
development of new roads are top
priority in this suburb. Some
streets have been named after great
writers and include Bronte Place,
Shelley Street, and Twain Street,
while Homer Street links to a
group of names from Greek
mythology, such as Troy Place,
Nestor Street and Ixion Street. To
the south, streets bear the names of
great scientists, such as Einstein,
Volta, Edison and Marconi, or
biblical names such as Goliath,
Gideon and Esther. Nearby
Johnston's Bridge crosses
Toongabbie Creek into the suburb
of Old Toongabbie and Pye's
Crossing leads across the same
creek to Seven Hills to the north-
west, both of them built well
above flood levels.

Above: Hannaford's Produce and Fuel store
stood on the corner of Oakville Road and
Penshurst Street, Willoughby, c. 1911. The
proud owners are assembled outside

Below: Willoughby Incinerator, opened in
1934, was one of twelve incinerator
buildings erected in various Australian cities
by Walter Burley Griffin's Reverberatory
Incinerator and Engineering Company

1919, 1920–21 and 1926–27.

Willoughby's greatest claim to
fame is perhaps its incinerator. The
brainchild of Walter Burley Griffin
(1876–1937), who designed
Canberra, and after whom Lake
Burley Griffin is named, this
sandstone structure in Willoughby
Road was the cause of heated
controversy in 1975 when the
health department ordered its
demolition. However, the
incinerator was classified as
historically valuable and unique,
and was restored by the Heritage
Council at a cost of $100,000. It
has been converted into a
restaurant.

Willoughby Road was first
called Flat Rock Road, because it
crossed Flat Rock Creek, which
was named in the early days of the
area's history when Governor
Phillip and his officers John Hunter
and William Bradley were
exploring the northern side of
Sydney Harbour. Flat Rock Creek
flows through Hallstrom Park and
Tunks Park to Middle Harbour.

# WOLLSTONECRAFT

*Municipalities of North Sydney and Lane Cove*

Location: 5 kilometres north of Sydney west of the Pacific Highway, on the North Shore Line

An early Sydney merchant is responsible for the naming of this lower North Shore suburb. He was Edward Wollstonecraft (1783–1832), the first settler to receive a land grant in the area when his tenure of 500 acres there was confirmed in 1825. He arrived in the colony in 1819, already established as partner of merchant Alexander Berry (see Crows Nest). Wollstonecraft was an important figure in Sydney's commercial world in the 1820s, and he combined his business enterprises with senior directorships of the Bank of New South Wales, the Bank of Australia and of the first Sydney Chamber of Commerce. The partners acquired 10,000 acres in the Shoalhaven area in the 1820s, while maintaining their merchandise warehouse in George Street in the city. In 1827 their association was strengthened when Berry married Wollstonecraft's sister Elizabeth. Both the Wollstonecraft and Berry families were related to the Wentworth family. Other members of this family were Mary Wollstonecraft (1759–97), who wrote *A Vindication of the Rights of Women*, and her daughter, Mary Wollstonecraft Shelley, (1797–1851), who married the poet Shelley and wrote the novel called *Frankenstein, or the Modern Prometheus*, one of the earliest horror stories.

Edward Wollstonecraft's land at Wollstonecraft was a grant to the partnership, so on his death in 1832 it passed to Alexander Berry (1781–1873), who in turn left the property to his brother, David Berry. The country town of Berry and Berry Island Reserve, on the tip of the peninsula between Gore Cove and Ball's Head Bay at the southernmost point of the suburb, were both named after Alexander Berry.

When the North Shore railway line was extended from St Leonards to Milsons Point, a railway station was opened in the suburb as Edward's Road on 1 May 1893, but its name was changed to Wollstonecraft on 1 September 1900. At the same time the thoroughfare Edwards Road became Shirley Road. The North Shore Gas Company Limited moved its main works to the suburb in 1917.

The suburb has developed into an elegant residential area, while retaining its natural bushland beauty, despite increasing numbers of high-rise home-unit blocks. It is a purely residential area, with neither schools nor a shopping centre.

# WOODBINE

*City of Campbelltown*

Location: 48 kilometres south-west of Sydney between Campbelltown Road and the South Western Freeway

The name given to this new neighbourhood of the city of Campbelltown is that of an early residence located on the western side of Campbelltown Road, near Leumeah Road, and adjacent to the overhead railway bridge of Leumeah station. The house was standing as early as 1837, set among a group of trees. It was demolished in the 1960s, but there is no information about its owners or history.

The present suburb is enclosed by the South Western Freeway, Campbelltown Road and Badgally Road, just south of the similarly new suburb of St Andrews. Streets in this far south-western suburb have been given the names of Sydney beaches, such as Maroubra, Long Reef, Whale and Clovelly.

# WOODPARK

*Municipality of Holroyd*

Location: 29 kilometres west of Sydney north of Fairfield

Main pipes of the Sydney water supply pass through this suburb between Greystanes and Smithfield. The main pipeline from Warragamba Dam runs parallel with Woodpark Road on its south side and with the Sydney water supply canal to the north, running from Prospect Reservoir.

This small suburb possibly received its name from Woodpark Road, called after an early estate. The streets have all been named after flowers, such as Hibiscus, Azalea, Dahlia, Viola, Nemesia, Carnation, Lupin, Oleander, Tulip, Poppy, Magnolia and Daffodil. There are three small reserves in the suburb, and Sherwood Grange Public School and Holroyd High School are nearby.

# WOOLLAHRA

*Municipality of Woollahra*

Location: 5 kilometres east of Sydney on Oxford Street

A name of Aboriginal origin, Woollahra means "camp", or "meeting ground" or "a sitting-down place". The name was adopted by Sir Daniel Cooper (1821–1902), a speaker of the New South Wales Legislative Assembly, when he laid the foundations of a mansion on the site of old Henrietta Villa (or Point Piper House) in 1856. He called it Woollahra House, and the suburb took its name from the house.

Woollahra's establishment and progress was mainly due to Daniel Cooper and his descendants. Cooper came to Australia as a child, returned to England to be educated, and came back to this country in 1843. Three years later he married Miss Elizabeth Hill. Already a successful merchant, he inherited much of the property of his emancipist uncle Daniel Cooper (1785–1853). His interests turned to politics and he was elected to the first Legislative Assembly in 1856.

View of Woollahra Heights, probably at the corner of Loftus and Annandale Streets, 1877

When the Cooper family returned to England in 1861 the house, which had an extensive water frontage and large grounds, was offered to the state government for £25,000 as a possible government house. Sir George Reid was premier at the time, and the offer was turned down, so the house was sold privately for £40,000. It was later resold at auction to Thomas Longworth, who paid £57,200 for the building and its 5 acres of gardens and grounds. Longworth Avenue, Point Piper, is named after him. The last sale of the property was on 8 March 1929, and the house came to a sad end when it was sold to demolishers for £979.

Another house of great beauty from the same elegant period is Rosemont, built in what became Rosemont Avenue in 1858–59 for Alexander Campbell. The former home of the Lloyd Jones family,

who bought it from Sir Samuel Cohen in 1930, it is one of the last survivors of the period when mansions in garden settings were the style in Woollahra. Another of the famous old houses of the area is Runnymede, built in about 1860. It was the residence of the Earl of Jersey, governor of New South Wales from 1891 to 1893.

The area was mostly residential, but a few industries were established there, including the Adelaide Brewery, now remembered by Adelaide Street, which was established in Edgecliff Road, Woollahra, in 1874, on a site chosen because it was near a natural spring of fresh water. When the brewery closed the land was subdivided and sold in 1901. Holy Cross Convent was erected on one of the subdivisions.

Trams to Bondi via Bellevue Hill began to travel through Woollahra in 1914, and the peace

of the suburb was disturbed. Trams were replaced by buses in 1960, and in 1979 the Eastern Suburbs Railway was added to the suburb's transport facilities. Away from the main thoroughfares, side streets retain their leafy peace and beauty, and many elegant houses remain undisturbed.

# WOOLLOOMOOLOO
*City of Sydney*
Location: 1.5 kilometres east of Sydney on Woolloomooloo Bay

This inner-city suburb stands at the head of Woolloomooloo Bay on the eastern side of the Domain. Very early records of the word Woolloomooloo refer to an area between South Head and Botany Bay that Governor Phillip had marked out as a reserve for Aborigines. It was known as Walla-Mulla, meaning "young male kangaroo", because it was the haunt of the rare black kangaroo. Many different spellings of the name were used until the present form became settled by the end of the 1830s.

In 1793, John Palmer (1760–1833), the colony commissary, was granted 100 acres at Garden Island Cove. He called it Woolamoola Farm, and the suburb's name derived from this early property. Palmer sold his land in 1822, and it passed through several hands before it was finally subdivided.

The Aboriginal reserve at Henrietta Town (see Darlinghurst), extended into the area of present Woolloomooloo. In the 1830s this land was given away as grants, and two of those who benefited were Judge James Dowling (afterwards Sir James Dowling) in 1831 and Edward Deas Thompson in 1835. Victoria, Brougham, Dowling, Judge, Forbes and Bourke Streets recall this period.

Some attractive terrace houses built in those early days still stand in this suburb. A group has been restored near Brougham Street and Butler Stairs, which were named after Edward Butler, a queen's counsellor, who had rooms nearby. The stairways of Woolloomooloo are another survival from those early days, when the streets running along the ridges in the area were accessible only by flights of stairs.

Macleay Regis, at 12 Macleay Street, represents a later era. Curved balconies and Art Deco details indicate how housing styles

Woolloomooloo Bay, c. 1895, looking from the Domain. The 110 metre-long wharf, called Admiralty Wharf, was built by the Imperial Government in the 1880s to provide deeper berths in the bay

changed, when the city became ringed with blocks of flats.

By the 1880s the suburb was firmly oriented towards wharves, fish markets and similar activities. Woolloomooloo Bay was the site of the old Domain Baths, established in 1908. Now rebuilt to olympic standard, the baths have been renamed after Andrew (Boy) Charlton (1907–75) in honour of one of our great Olympians.

The first vice-chancellor of the University of Sydney, Sir Charles Nicholson (1808–1903), whose name was given to the university's Nicholson Museum, is remembered in Woolloomooloo by Nicholson Street. By 1850 he had occupied Tarmons, in nearby Potts Point, which he bought from Sir Maurice O'Connell. A one time attorney-general and president of the Legislative Council, John Hubert Plunkett (1802–69), is commemorated by Plunkett Street. The street gave its name to the public school originally located there, which has now moved to Forbes Street, where it bears the name Plunkett Primary School. An earlier school had stood on the Plunkett Street site, built in 1866–67.

During the 1960s and 1970s the suburb underwent a decline as large areas were resumed for the construction of the Eastern Suburbs Railway and freeways. It is now becoming re-established as a residential area, with the state's Department of Housing and Construction building energetically to house low-income families.

# WOOLOOWARE
*Shire of Sutherland*
Location: 24 kilometres south of Sydney facing Woolooware Bay on the Georges River, on the Cronulla Line

A suburb on the southern bank of the Georges River, Woolooware has a name of Aboriginal origin: woolowa means "a muddy track", an apt description of the first Woolooware Road, now South Woolooware Road running north from Port Hacking to the main east–west road, Kingsway. The road existed before the suburb was established and in 1827 Surveyor Robert Dixon gave the road's name to the suburb, changing it slightly to Woolooware.

In the early part of last century it was a thickly forested area, and timber-getters were the first to move into the district. The land around Woolooware Bay was covered with mangrove swamps, which were later filled in to make parks and playing fields, such as Endeavour Field and Cronulla Golf Links. The area was subdivided following the building of the railway line from Sutherland to Cronulla in the 1930s. The first public school opened in January 1951, followed by the first post office in October 1954.

# WOOLWICH
*Municipality of Hunters Hill*
Location: 11 kilometres north-west of Sydney between the Parramatta and Lane Cove Rivers

A small residential suburb at the end of a long peninsula on the northern bank of the Parramatta River, Woolwich adjoins Hunters Hill. An early settler was John Clarke, who bought land on the peninsula in 1834. He was responsible for the naming of Clarke's Point. His third home there was Woodstock, which is still standing. Another land-owner, Samuel Onions, who had a large ironmongery business, gave the suburb its first name — Onions Point. He built in the area in 1835.

Sales of land in the "town of Woolwich" were being advertised in Sydney from 1841. The Rosemorrin Smelting Works were established in the area in 1849 by a Mr Ferris, and in 1888 the Atlas Engineering Company opened works in Woolwich on part of Clarke's property. This land was later sold for Mort's Dock, which opened in 1901. Thomas Sutcliffe Mort (1816–78, see Mortdale) had operated a dry-dock at Balmain since 1855, but by the end of the century the company required a larger site and the new dock was established in Woolwich. The army used the dock as Woolwich Barracks during the Second World War, but it was restored as a dockyard in the postwar years. After the enterprise was made bankrupt, it was taken over by the Department of Main Roads, which made the pylons for the Gladesville Bridge at the former dockyard. The site today is marked by Mort's Dock Reserve.

A public school is situated in Woolwich Road, and Woolwich Lookout is at the end of the same street. The suburb also has a pleasant local park, known as Weil Park, also in Woolwich Road.

# YAGOONA

*City of Bankstown*
Location: 20 kilometres
south-west of Sydney west of the
junction of Rookwood Road and
the Hume Highway, on the
Bankstown Line

This residential suburb just north
of Bankstown was known as
Irishtown, at least as early as 1833.
Two other suburbs in the area
(Bass Hill and North Bankstown)
were at one time also known by
that name. Like Bankstown,
Irishtown, or Yagoona as it
became known in 1927, was
classified as a rural area. The name
Yagoona is Aboriginal for "now"
or "to-day". The present suburb
was created by changing the
boundaries in the area, when
Bankstown began to expand.

In 1831 a number of grants of 30
to 50 acres were made north of
Liverpool Road. Early land-
owners included Thomas Walford,
Martin Short, Thomas Kennedy,
Samuel Terry, Patrick Whalan and
Joseph Eldridge (who received 100
acres in 1831). In 1839 Samuel
Thornton received a 100 acre grant
at Irishtown, east of the present
Saltash Street and south of
Liverpool Road. One of the earliest
churches in this suburb was the
Methodist church on Dutton's
Hill. A slab hut with a bark roof, it
was in use at the end of 1859.
Dutton Street, which connects
Yagoona and Bankstown, records
the name of that early locality.

The first police station was built
in Powell Street, Yagoona, in the
1950s when the suburb began to
develop and new houses were
being built. A post office had been
operating since June 1941, when
Alfred Victor Johnson was the first
postmaster. Today the RSPCA
Animal Shelter is located in the
suburb.

# YENNORA

*Municipality of Holroyd, City of
Fairfield*
Location: 29 kilometres west of
Sydney north of Fairfield, on the
Main Southern Line

This comparatively small suburb
between the municipalities of
Holroyd and Fairfield has an
Aboriginal name meaning "to
stroll". Its early history is meagre.
In 1927 when the railway line from
Granville to Liverpool was
constructed, the platform in this
area was given the name Yennora.
It eventually serviced the suburb's
wool stores, built by 1971.

In the early 1920s wool depots
were scattered throughout the
inner Sydney suburbs. Botany,
with a large woolwash centre, was
one of the most important and
possibly the largest. The
surrounding area, however, was
becoming increasingly congested,
as more factories were constructed,
so the Wool Board decided to
develop a single wool centre,
where all wool could be pressed,
packed and dispatched, as well as
providing a display centre. In the
1960s, the board looked at land in
the Bankstown area, which at that

time was reasonably priced. An
added attraction in the area was a
branch railway line, which had
been constructed at Yennora to
service proposed railway
workshops. In July 1971 the Wool
Centre was established. Today, the
Yennora Wool Centre receives
wool in its greasy state, prepares it
for sale, arranges inspection by
wool brokers, prepares the wool
that has been sold for export in
containers, and conducts wool
sales twice a year.

# YOWIE BAY

*Shire of Sutherland*
Location: 26 kilometres south of
Sydney on the northern shore of
Port Hacking

Yowie Bay is a beauty spot just
south of Miranda, at the head of
the bay of the same name on the
north side of Port Hacking.
Surveyor Robert Dixon (1800–58)
gave the name as Ewey when he
surveyed the area in 1827, and
some maps still refer to the water

Still a popular holiday retreat, Yowie Bay,
as it looked in 1962

by this name, although the surrounding land is generally called Yowie. The word yowie or ewie is Aboriginal for "echo".

In the 1920s Yowie Bay was a great holiday retreat, and some families maintained holiday houses in the area, but today it has a permanent residential population.

# ZETLAND

*City of Sydney*
Location: 5 kilometres south of Sydney between Dowling Street and Botany Road

The name of this inner-city suburb, just south of Waterloo, was chosen by Sir Hercules Robinson, governor of New South Wales between 1872 and 1879. During his term of office he leased the southern portion of Waterloo, sometimes referred to as Irishtown, where he established racing stables. He called his property Zetland, in honour of a relative in Britain, the Marquis of Zetland. He built a residence called Zetland Lodge and some of the finest racing quarters in the state, as well as a home for his trainer, Thomas Lamond, who later became mayor of the district. The Zetland stables became famous, and Elizabeth Street was extended from the city right through to Zetland Lodge. When Sir Hercules left New South Wales, his trainer, Lamond, took over the house and stables, which continued to produce some champions of the turf.

In the 1900s Victoria Park Racecourse opened in this suburb, continuing until the site was taken over by James Joynton Smith, who owned *Smith's Weekly* and gave his name to Joynton Avenue, Zetland. The buildings were later bought by British Leyland, the car manufacturers, which used the site in the 1960s; later it was acquired by the Department of Supply for naval stores.

The Royal South Sydney Hospital is in Joynton Avenue. In common with other inner-city suburbs, Zetland is conveniently located for access to beaches,

Hercules Robinson

Centennial Park, and the city itself. Many of its homes are free-standing and solidly built. Some industries are still located in Zetland, but the old days when it had the woolwash, the glue factories and the tanneries are no more. Instead, many tree-lined streets offer the peace and quiet of a bygone age.

# List of Sources

This book was originated by the late Gerald Healy of Holroyd Historical Society, who compiled a preliminary manuscript. Frances Pollon also had access to research material collected by Philip Geeves.

Definitions and some historical details were supplied by the Geographical Names Board's alphabetical index. Information regarding early land grants and subdivisions was taken from maps held by the Department of Lands and the Archives Office of New South Wales.

Local council organisations are increasingly publishing histories of their own areas and are excellent sources for further information.

The following reading list includes most of the main sources from which information for this book was gathered.

## Primary Sources

Collins, David, *An Account of the Australian Colony*. A. H. & A. W. Reed in association with the Royal Australian Historical Society, 1975

Draper, W. J. (ed.), *Who's Who in Australia, 1983*. The Herald and Weekly Times

Henning, Rachel, *The Letters of Rachel Henning*. David Adams (ed.), Penguin Books, 1969

*Historical Records of Australia*, Series I, Governors' Despatches to and from England, Vol. VII, January 1809—June 1813. The Library Committee of the Commonwealth Parliament, 1916

*Historical Records of New South Wales*, Vol. 1, Part 2, Phillip, 1783—1792. Charles Potter, Government Printer, 1892

Hunter, John, *An Historical Journal of Events at Sydney and at Sea 1787—1792*. John Bach (ed.), Angus & Robertson Publishers in association with the Royal Australian Historical Society, 1968

*Land Grants 1788—1809, New South Wales Norfolk Island — Van Diemens Land*. Indexed by K. A. Johnson and M. Sainty. Sydney Genealogical Publications, 1974

Learmouth, A. T. A. and A. M. (eds), *Encyclopaedia of Australia*. Frederick Warne and Co., 1968

Macquarie, Lachlan, *Journals of his tours in New South Wales and Van Diemens Land 1810—1822*. Trustees of the Public Library of New South Wales, 1956

Nairn, Bede (ed.), *Australian Dictionary of Biography*, Vol. 6, 1851—1890. Melbourne University Press, 1976

Pike, Douglas (ed.), *Australian Dictionary of Biography*, Vol. 2, 1788—1859, Vols 3, 4 and 5, 1851—1890. Melbourne University Press, 1967, 1969, 1972, 1974

## Secondary Sources

Ancher, Edward, *The Romance of an Old Whaling Station: The Story of the Pioneers of Mosman and Cremorne*. Mosman Historical Society, 1976

*The Australasian Sporting Magazine*, 1850

Bayley, William, *History of Campbelltown*. Campbelltown Municipal Council, 1965

Burnswoods, J. and J. Fletcher, *Government Schools of New South Wales 1848—1983*. Directorate of Planning Services, NSW Department of Education, 1983

Cambage, R. H., *Exploration Beyond the Upper Nepean in 1798*. Royal Australian Historical Society, 1919

Campbelltown City Council, *Suggested Names for Suburbs, Neighbourhoods, Localities*

Canterbury and District Historical Society, *Bi-centenary Publication — the History of Belmore, Campsie, Earlwood and Kingsgrove*. Canterbury Municipal Council

Carmichael, Dorothy, *Tales of Beecroft*. 1965

Charlton, Catherine, *A History of Kenthurst and Annangrove*. 1981

Cramp, K. R., *A Calendar of Events in Australian History*. Royal Australian Historical Society, 1933

Dowd, Barney, *The Centenary of the Municipality of Waverley 1859—1959*. Waverley Municipal Council, 1959

Ellis, Malcolm, *Lachlan Macquarie — His Life, Adventures and Times*. Angus & Robertson Publishers, 1947

Emanuel, Cedric and Philip Geeves, *Philip Geeves' Sydney*. Angus & Robertson Publishers, 1981

—— and Tess van Sommers, *Historic Parramatta*. Parramatta City Council, 1977

Geeves, Philip, *Places of Pioneers — The Centenary History of the Municipality of Ryde*. Ryde Municipal Council, 1970

George, Vance, *Fairfield — A History of the District*. Fairfield City Council, 1982

Granville Centenary Celebrations Committee, *Granville Centenary 1880—1980*.

*Grist Mills — Journal of the Campbelltown & Airds Historical Society*, June 1984, Vols 2 & 3. Campbelltown and Airds Historical Society

Halstead, Gay, *The History of St. Ives.* 1982

Henderson, C. W. T., "Pittwater — A Port from 1843–1900", *Port of Sydney.* Maritime Services Board

*Historical Australia*, January–February 1982. White House Publishing Group

*Historical Records of Australia*, Series I, Governors' Despatches to and from England, Vol. XX, February 1839–September 1840. The Library Committee of the Commonwealth Parliament, 1966

Hogan, Mark, *History Lives — Sydney's West from the Beginning.* West Sydney Radio Pty Ltd, 1981

Holt, Henry E., *An Energetic Colonist — Biographical Account of Hon. Thomas Holt*

Horsley, M. G., *Lilyfield — How was its name Derived?* Notes held in the local history archives at Leichhardt Council Library

Jervis, James, *Place Names in Ku-ring-gai Chase.* Notes dated 13 September, 1939, from private collection, Mitchell Library

Kelly, Max, *A Paddock Full of Houses (Paddington) 1840–1890.* Doak Press, 1978

Kennedy, Barbara and Brian Kennedy, *Sydney and Suburbs, A History and Description.* A. H. & A. W. Reed, 1982

Kohen, Jim L., *The Aborigines of Western Sydney.* Blacktown and District Historical Society, 1983

Larcombe, Frederick, *The History of Botany 1788–1970.* Botany Municipal Council, 1963

Leppington Public School, *Raby...Leppington, The Story of Leppington.* Written by pupils of class 6A under the guidance of Miss B. Allen from material held in the local history archives at Liverpool City Library, 1972

Liverpool City Council, *Liverpool Community Calendar.* 1983

——— *Liverpool Today.* 1972

Macquarie, Lachlan, *Journal of a Tour in NSW 16 November 1810–15 Jan 1811.* Trustees of the Public Library of New South Wales

Mann, G. V. F., *History of North Sydney.* North Sydney Municipal Council, 1938

Mansfield, Bruce and Fay, Richardson, *Knox — A History of Knox Grammar School 1924–1974.* 1974

Matthews, Michael R., *Pyrmont and Ultimo — A History.*

Moore, Kevin, *A Brief Outline of Blacktown.* Blacktown City Council, 1979

Moylan, Geraldine (comp.), *Return to Mount Druitt 1925–1985.* Compiled from information supplied by Mt Druitt Historical Society. Blacktown City Council

Ollif, Lorna, *There Must Be a River.* 1973

Parramatta Marist High, *The Parramatta Marist Story — The First Hundred Years.* 1975

Penrith City Council, *Place Names and Their Origins Within the City of Penrith.* 1985

Peters, Merle, *The Bankstown Story — A Comprehensive History of the District.* 3rd edition, 1980

Pollard, Jack, *The Pictorial History of Australian Horse Racing.* Paul Hamlyn Pty Ltd, 1971

Pollon, Frances (ed.), *The Best of Geeves.* Angus & Robertson Publishers, 1984

——— *Parramatta, the Cradle City, its History from 1788.* Parramatta City Council, 1983

Reed, A. W. (comp.), *Aboriginal Words and Place Names.* Rigby Press, 1977

Rockdale Public School and Centenary Committee, *Not a Step Backwards — A Centenary Commemoration of Rockdale Public School 1883–1983*

Russell, Eric, *Willoughby — A Centenary History of the Municipality from Earliest Times.* Willoughby Municipal Council, 1966

St George Historical Society, *Rockdale — A Century of Progress.* Rockdale Municipal Council, 1971

St Jude's Church, Dural, *The History of St. Jude's Church, Dural*

*Sands Directories 1887 and 1893.* Lilyfield entry.

State Rail Authority of New South Wales, *How and Why of Station Names — Meanings and Origins.* 1965

Stephensen, P. R. (comp.), *Sydney Sails — The Royal Sydney Yacht Squadron 1862–1962.* Angus & Robertson Publishers, 1962

Swancott, C., *Dee Why to Barrenjoey and Pittwater.*

——— *Manly — Its Story 1788–1968.* Manly-Warringah Historical Society

*Sydney Adventist Hospital, Wahroonga Annual 1973*

Tan, Linsie, *A Guide for Visitors.* Liverpool City Library, 1980

——— *History of Liverpool's Suburbs.* Liverpool City Council, 1985

——— *I Named It Liverpool.* Liverpool City Library, 1985

Tranter, Peter, "Last Tram to the Spit", *Sydney*, Feb. 1982. Murray Publications

Walker, Robert Cooper, *Sutherland Estate Report*, 1868

Wells, William Henry, *A Geographical Directory — A Gazetteer of the Australian Colonies, Sydney, 1848.* Council of the Library of New South Wales, 1970

Wickham, J. A. and P. J. Yeend (comps), *Origins of Names of Suburbs, Streets and Localities in and about the Parramatta Area.* The King's School, 1980

## NEWSPAPER ARTICLES

*Advance*, 25 November 1981, p. 14. Article on the history of Wakeley

*Australian*, 9 February 1836. Description of James Chandler's property, Bexley

*Campbelltown Ingleburn News*, 10 April 1970. Article on early settlements in Campbelltown

*Campbelltown News*, January 1920–January 1921. Various articles on Campbelltown

———— 22 October 1920. J. P. McGuanne, "Our Old Hotels"

*Daily Mirror*, 11 November 1985, p. 24. "The Great Suburban Name — A–Z of all the stories behind your addresses"

*Echo*, April 1890–February 1891. Boxall, "The Suburbs of Sydney". Sydney Morning Herald

*St George and Sutherland Shire Leader*, 23 February 1972. Article on Monterey

*Sydney Gazette*, 20 June 1833

*Sydney Mail*, 18 December 1886. Article on Thomas Saywell's enterprises at Brighton-le-Sands

*Sydney Morning Herald*, 1 June 1843 and 8 November 1856. Articles on early land sales at Arncliffe

———— 9 June 1870. Article on movement for the incorporation of Rockdale (then West Botany) Municipality

———— 8 July 1961. Article on A. B. Spark and his property, Tempe

———— 23 November 1985. "Mt Druitt Shakes Off Its Old Image"

———— 5 December 1985. "Western Adventures. A Guide to Tourist Attractions on Sydney's Western Fringes"

## JOURNALS OF THE ROYAL AUSTRALIAN HISTORICAL SOCIETY

Cambage, R. H., *Exploration Beyond the Upper Nepean in 1798*. Vol. VI, pp. 1–36

Deane, M. E., *Notes on "Sydney's Ferry Boats"*. Vol. XXIII, p. 160

———— *Reminiscences of Parramatta and Lane Cove Steamers*. Vol. XXIII, p. 161–6

Dowling, Arthur, *Some Recollections of the New South Head Road at Woollahra*. Vol. X, pp. 40–56; 119–20

Havard, Olive, *Mrs Felton Mathew's Journal*. Vol. XXIX, pp. 88–128

Jervis, James, *Beginnings of the Settlements in the Parish of Castle Hill*. Vol. XV, Parts 1 & 2

———— *The Origin of the name in Port Jackson*. Vol. XXXI, pp. 390–402

———— *Settlement in the Parish of Hunters Hill*. Vol. XLVI, pp. 187–205

———— *Settlements at Hunters Hill and District*. Vol. XLVI, pp. 289–306

———— *Illawarra: A Century of History 1788–1888*. Vol. XXVIII, Parts 1–5

Millin, B., *Origins of Names in Port Jackson*. Vol. XXXI, p. 319, Elizabeth Bay; p. 323, Drummoyne, Five Dock; p. 324, Cabarita, Chiswick; p. 332, Chowder Bay; p. 334, Clontarf

Rowland, E. C., *The Story of the New South Wales Railways*. Vol. XL, pp. 245–86

———— *The Story of the South Arm — Watsons Bay, Vaucluse and Rose Bay*. Vol. XXXVII, pp. 217–44

Watson, James H., *James Mario Matra — The Father of Australia*. Vol. X, pp. 152–68

———— *The North Shore of Port Jackson*. Vol. IV, pp. 15–24

———— *Notes on Some Suburbs of Sydney*. Vol. XIII, pp. 21–40

———— *Ultimo House: Its Origin and History*. Vol. IX, pp. 219–21

# PICTURE CREDITS

The publishers gratefully acknowledge the following people and organisations who gave permission to reproduce photographs and illustrations on the pages noted. Every effort has been made to trace copyright holders and apology is made for any unintended infringement.

AGL Historic Photograph Collection, 267
Arnott's Biscuits Limited, 124
Blacktown City Library (Local History Section) 31, 83, 84
Campbelltown City Library Collection, 46
Sheena Coupe, 43
Curzon Hall, Marsfield, 166
Fairfield City Library Collection, 49, 103, 244
Hills District Historical Society Collection, 56
Historic Houses Trust, 110
Historic Photographic Collection, Macleay Museum, University of Sydney, 9, 18, 41, 73, 87t, 149t
David Latta, 79
Liverpool City Library, Local History Collection, 57, 155, 161, 236, 264
Mitchell Library, State Library of New South Wales, 1, 4, 6, 7, 8, 13, 15, 16, 17, 19, 20, 21, 22, 25, 29, 32b, 33, 34, 36, 37, 38, 42, 45, 48, 50, 58, 63, 64, 65, 66, 67, 68, 71, 75, 77, 78, 80, 85, 88, 90, 92, 93, 94, 95, 96, 97, 99, 100, 101, 102, 104, 111, 112, 117, 120, 122, 128, 130, 137, 139, 141b, 142, 146−47, 148, 149b, 150, 153, 157, 164, 166, 168, 170, 172, 177, 178, 179, 180, 181, 187, 190, 194, 196, 199, 200, 207, 209, 210, 211, 212, 217, 218, 220, 223, 227, 228, 231, 242, 243, 248, 250t, 251, 252t, 254, 255, 258, 259, 274, 275, 278
National Film and Sound Archive, 198
National Library of Australia, 55 (photo Dr Jorna Pohjanpalo), 127t, 226, 230, 238b
New South Wales Department of Education, History Unit, 51, 87b
New South Wales Department of Environment and Planning, 134
New South Wales Department of Main Roads, 10, 11, 32t, 82, 106, 129, 131, 138, 141t, 143, 147t, 158, 160, 188, 191, 192, 213, 214, 215, 225, 229, 235, 240, 245
New South Wales Government Printing Office, 127b, 135 (Randwick Social History Photographic Collectors), 156
Penrith City Library Collection, 140, 204, 239, 268
Frances Pollon, 173
Stanton Library, North Sydney, 144, 174
Strathfield Central Library (Mr Pollock), 246
Sutherland Council, Local History Collection, 12, 53, 74, 121, 154, 159, 170, 176, 241, 250b, 252b, 253, 277
Sydney Adventist Hospital, 261
Waverley Municipal Library, 39, 86
Willoughby Municipal Library, 59, 113, 183, 238t, 272
Woollahra Municipal Library, 233

# INDEX OF PEOPLE

*Numbers in italics indicate pages with illustrations.*